**NETFLIX**

# STRANGER THINGS

## THE COMPLETE SCRIPTS
## SEASON 3

# NETFLIX

# STRANGER THINGS

## THE COMPLETE SCRIPTS
## SEASON 3

CREATED BY THE DUFFER BROTHERS

RANDOM HOUSE
WORLDS

NEW YORK

Random House Worlds
An imprint of Random House
A division of Penguin Random House LLC
1745 Broadway, New York, NY 10019
randomhousebooks.com
penguinrandomhouse.com

2025 Random House Worlds Trade Paperback Original

Lyrics from "The Never Ending Story," words and music by Giorgio Moroder and Keith Forsey, © 1984 WC Music Corp. All rights reserved. Used by permission of Alfred Music.

ISBN 978-0-593-98407-9
Ebook ISBN 978-0-593-98408-6

Printed in The United States of America

3rd Printing

BOOK TEAM: Editor: Jacinta O'Halloran • Production editor: Abby Duval • Managing editor: Susan Seeman • Production manager: Nathalie Mairena • Proofreaders: Alissa Fitzgerald, Jacob Reynold Jones, Taylor McGowan

Book design by Elizabeth A. D. Eno

The authorized representative in the EU for product safety and compliance is Penguin Random House Ireland, Morrison Chambers, 32 Nassau Street, Dublin D02 YH68, Ireland. https://eu-contact.penguin.ie

# CONTENTS

# INTRODUCTION

When season two of *Stranger Things* released in October 2017 to positive reviews and responses, we felt a huge relief. We had proven—to ourselves and our audience—that season one wasn't a fluke but was a story worth continuing. There was, of course, one confidence shaker—the much-debated episode "The Lost Sister"—which had landed with a deafening thud.

But we were determined to not let it throw us. In fact, heading into season three, the first thing we told our writers was "We can't be afraid to make more big swings. We'll make more mistakes, without question, but the biggest mistake we could make is playing it safe." The show needed to continue to change and evolve and surprise.

The question then became, Where should it go next?

The answer, it turned out, lay in our shooting schedule. Because of season two's fall release, we were set to shoot season three during the summer—the first time we'd filmed outside the usual fall and winter seasons, with leafless trees and overcast skies. Visually, the show was going to look very different. So rather than fight that shift, we leaned into it. This was our opportunity to show a different side of the eighties—neon lights, vibrant colors, poppy pop music, swimsuits, short shorts.

We started thinking about the summer movies we grew up loving: *Jurassic Park, Indiana Jones, Die Hard, Back to the Future,*

*Fast Times at Ridgemont High, Romancing the Stone*. What if we embraced that spirit—not just in look and tone, but in scope and scale? What if we pushed the show into full-blown blockbuster territory: big monsters, big villains, big laughs, big action? It would still be *Stranger Things,* but *Stranger Things* on neon-colored steroids.

As we left to do some press, we asked our writers to brainstorm some summer specific ideas. What new locations and characters might we explore? When we returned a week later, the whiteboard was smothered in ideas. There was, of course, the obvious slam dunks, like the Hawkins pool. But one idea stood out at the very top of the list: a mall.

Instantly, childhood memories came flooding back. Growing up in Durham, North Carolina, we'd spent countless hours at South Square Mall—slurping down Orange Juliuses in the food court, gawking at the games in Babbage's, flipping through CDs at Sam Goody. We knew right away: Hawkins was going to get a mall, and it would play a central role in the story.

With Starcourt as our anchor, the season rapidly began to take shape. We added some new characters, including the "evil Russians"—an idea we had seeded with Murray in season two—and, of course, Robin Buckley, Steve's sarcastic, whip-smart, and proudly uncool co-worker. She was initially inspired by a young Janeane Garofalo, but a long casting process eventually led us to the incomparable Maya Hawke. Her personality reshaped the character entirely. A suggestion by our writer Kate Trefry to make Robin gay transformed her from a conventional love interest into something far more complex and ultimately led to one of our favorite scenes in the entire series: her coming out to Steve in the Starcourt bathroom.

But beneath all the summer fun, we wanted the season to carry an undercurrent of sadness and pain. The kids in the show weren't quite kids anymore. They were in one of the most awkward stages of life—caught in the messy transition from childhood to young adulthood. It's a confusing time, and one we ourselves had struggled with. Your body is changing in uncomfortable ways, stuck awkwardly between two points, and the social pressure to "be cool" intensifies dramatically. In the search to find yourself, you sometimes have to lose yourself first.

That tension—the painful process of growing up and leaving childhood behind—became the emotional engine and heart of the season. Combined with our new aesthetic, season three started writing itself, faster than any season before. We'd never had so much fun writing the show—before or since.

While we know this season is often debated, and sometimes criticized, for its sharp tonal shift, that shift was a deliberate choice: to capture, one last time, a celebration of childhood before it ends—and a much darker journey begins.

For now, we hope you enjoy revisiting these scripts. We had a blast writing them, and we hope you have just as much fun reading them.

Over and out,
Matt and Ross Duffer

**NETFLIX**

# STRANGER
# THINGS

## THE COMPLETE SCRIPTS
## SEASON 3

# CHAPTER ONE:
## SUZIE, DO YOU COPY?

WRITTEN BY **THE DUFFER BROTHERS**

**INT. LARGE EXPERIMENT ROOM - DAY 1**

A GLOVED HARD curls around a metal lever.  Yanks it down.

CHOOM!  A LARGE GENERATOR rumbles to life.  A THICK CABLE leads us from this generator to...

AN ENORMOUS MACHINE.  It looks both impressive and bizarre, like a jet engine crossed with a cannon.  Strangely, this "cannon" is aimed directly at a blank cement wall.

AN ARMY OF WORKERS scurry around the machine, turning on more generators.  They all wear exotic-looking gas masks. *Where the hell are we?*  Wherever we are, it isn't Hawkins.

CHOOM.  Another generator is switched on.

CHOOM.  *Another.*  CHOOM.  *Another.*

**INT. CONTROL ROOM - DAY**

BEEP.  BEEP.  BEEP.  A PANEL OF LIGHTS BLINK GREEN.

We are now in a large control room which overlooks the experiment room.  A HALF-DOZEN SCIENTISTS tap away on a COMPUTER DASHBOARD; GOVERNMENT MEN silently observe.

We settle on two men who seem of particular importance:

-- MAJOR GENERAL STEPANOV, 40s.  Stoic, severe, clearly an authority.

-- GRIGORI, 40s, very tall and very strong, the kind of classic '80s villain Indiana Jones loved to punch.  Then --

THE SOUND OF A DOOR OPENING.  Heads turn to find --

THE LEAD SCIENTIST entering.  He is small, frail, nervous. He carries a SILVER CASE in his hands.  He takes a seat at the dashboard next to a younger scientist named DR. ALEXEI.

The Lead Scientist opens the box to reveal...

TWO TRIANGLE-SHAPED KEYS.

The Lead Scientist takes one key; Alexei takes the other.

They insert their keys into separate slots, *WarGames*-style.

Then, with a nod from the Lead Scientist --

They turn the keys.

**INT. LARGE EXPERIMENT ROOM - DAY**

VAROOO!!!  A FEROCIOUS SOUND AS THE MACHINE SURGES TO LIFE.

A series of large mechanical gears begin to churn, generating a POWERFUL ELECTRICAL CURRENT.  The current travels the length of the machine... gathers at the tip of the "cannon"... then --

SHOOOM!  A POWERFUL ENERGY STREAM fires into the wall. Colors swirl, alternating between blue, yellow, and orange. It's almost beautiful.  Only it seems... unstable. *Dangerous.*

**INT. CONTROL ROOM - DAY**

The Lead Scientist wipes sweat from his brow.

Major General Stepanov drags a cigarette.

Everyone on edge as...

**INT. LARGE EXPERIMENT ROOM - DAY**

The energy stream continues to pummel the wall.  At last...

We hear something.  A FAMILIAR GROANING SOUND.  And then...

A HOLE BEGINS TO SLOWLY FORM IN THE WALL.  The hole is very small at first, so small we can't see through to the other side.  But then *something* SLITHERS out of the hole:

A WET VINE.  Then ANOTHER VINE slithers out.  ANOTHER.

The vines spread out like roots.  Clinging to the wall.

And suddenly it hits us.  They are opening --

A GATE TO THE UPSIDE DOWN.

**INT. CONTROL ROOM - DAY**

Government Men exchange awed looks.  *It's working.*

The Lead Scientist exhales.  *Relieved.*  But then he notices something strange: A pen is bouncing on the table.

Alexei notices coffee rippling inside a mug.

The entire room is SHAKING.

**INT. LARGE EXPERIMENT ROOM - DAY**

The SHAKING is even more intense in the experiment room.

The Workers look around in growing concern.  Lights above them begin to flicker.  Generators crackle, spark.  Then --

BOOM!  A LOUD SOUND causes eyes to snap back to the hole as --

The energy stream is suddenly pushed *away* from the wall, as if it is being shoved by some powerful, invisible force.

The energy is pushed back further... further... until...

ZOOOOP!  It slurps back into the "cannon" and --

**INT. CONTROL ROOM - DAY**

The shaking stops.

A moment of silence.  Then --

**INT. LARGE EXPERIMENT ROOM - DAY**

KABOOM!  THE ENTIRE MACHINE EXPLODES!  A TIDAL WAVE OF ELECTRIC ENERGY RUSHES OUTWARD, ENVELOPING THE MEN AND --

TIME SLOWS AS THE ENERGY LIFTS THEM UP INTO THE AIR --

THEIR BODIES CONVULSE AND THEY SCREAM IN PAIN AND --

THEIR SUITS BEGIN TO *MELT AWAY*.

**INT. CONTROL ROOM - DAY**

The Lead Scientist looks away in horror.

Major General Stepanov tenses.  Disappointed.  *Angry*.

He snuffs out his cigarette and --

**INT. LARGE EXPERIMENT ROOM - DAY**

HISS!  Smoke rises from the MELTED REMAINS OF WORKERS as...

Stepanov and his men fan out across the experiment room. It's a horror show in here.  The Workers are *melted,* smoke *hissing* out of their twisted and rotting corpses, and --

The machine is dead.  Scarred, sparking, *smoking*.

**FURTHER AHEAD,**

Stepanov inspects the wall where the interdimensional Gate had opened.  Touches it with his gloved hand.  But...

The wall looks normal now.  The Gate has sealed.

<u>Like it was never there</u>.

Behind him, the Lead Scientist finally works up the courage to speak.  To our surprise, he <u>speaks in RUSSIAN</u>:

> LEAD SCIENTIST
> (Russian)
> <Comrade-Major General...>

Stepanov turns to face him.

> LEAD SCIENTIST (CONT'D)
> <We are close.  You can see.  You
> can see our progress.  We just need
> more ti-- >

His voice catches as a gloved hand SNAPS around his throat.

<u>It's Grigori</u>.  He lifts the Scientist up off his feet, strangling him.  As the Scientist struggles to free himself, gagging, eyes popping, legs helplessly waving in the air --

Stepanov steps up to Alexei.

> MAJOR GENERAL STEPANOV
> <You have one year.>

Alexei gathers his composure.  Nods.

> ALEXEI
> <Yes, Comrade-Major General.>

Grigori finally releases the Lead Scientist.

WHOOMP.  His body drops limply to the floor.  <u>Dead</u>.

**EXT. LAB - DAY**

Major General Stepanov strides out of the lab with Grigori at his side.  As they head off toward a helicopter, its blades slicing the air, we PULL AWAY TO REVEAL...

This mysterious, top-secret lab sits in a snowy landscape.  Soldiers in Afghanka uniforms patrol a concrete terrace.

We PULL BACK FURTHER AND RISE to reveal...

A BRIGHT RED FLAG.  Emblazoned with a hammer and sickle.

SUPERIMPOSE: KAMCHATKA, RUSSIA.  JUNE 28, 1984.

The wind picks up.  The flag blows faster.

And right here, we CRASH TO --

**INT. UNKNOWN BEDROOM - NIGHT 2**

A BOOMBOX plays "Never Surrender" by Corey Hart.

SUPERIMPOSE:   ONE YEAR LATER.  HAWKINS, INDIANA.

We PULL AWAY from the boombox and begin to PAN across a bedroom *BACK TO THE FUTURE*-style.  Drawings plaster the walls, a mess of wrinkled clothes litter the floor, and VARIOUS COMIC BOOKS clutter a desk.

It looks like we're in a typical teenage kid's room.

But then our CAMERA finds a very *atypical* kid:

ELEVEN.  This is --

**ELEVEN'S ROOM!**

Eleven is sitting on her bed with MIKE.  We haven't heard them speak yet because, well, they're not speaking.

They're kissing.  And unlike before, they don't kiss once.

They kiss again.  Then *again*.  Then --

Mike takes a break to sing along with Corey:

> MIKE
> "And nobody wants to know you now.
> And nobody wants to show you
> hoooooowwwww -- "

> ELEVEN
> (giggling)
> Stop -- !

> MIKE
> "So if you're lost and on your own,
> you can never surrender -- "

> ELEVEN
> NO -- !

Eleven shoves a hand over his mouth, shutting him up.

Mike pulls her hand away, playful.

> MIKE
> You don't like it?

Eleven shakes her head, No!  Smiles.  Their hands intertwine.

It's so innocent.  So perfect.  So... *disgusting*.

As they begin to kiss again, we HARD CUT TO:

**INT. CABIN - MAIN ROOM - NIGHT**

HOPPER.  Slumped on the sofa.  Absolutely *miserable*.

He's trying to watch TV.  *Trying*.  But he can't focus.  He keeps glancing back at Eleven's room.  The door is cracked, but not enough for him to see what's going on in there.

He grumbles to himself.  Tries to focus on the TV again.

But he can't.  He just can't.  *Screw it*.  He leans back and cranes his neck... further... a little further... until...

HOPPER'S POV: He sees Eleven and Mike kissing!

Eleven spots him, gasps, narrows her eyes, and --

KA-WHAM!  <u>The door slams shut.</u>

> HOPPER
> Hey -- hey!  Three-inch minimum!
> Three inches!

But the door remains shut.

> HOPPER (CONT'D)
> Sonofa-- !

Hopper leaps off the couch, charges over to her door, but --

It won't open.  *Locked*.

> HOPPER(CONT'D)
> Hey El?  Open up -- !

He tries the door again.  *Still locked*.

> HOPPER (CONT'D)
> El -- !

He throws more weight into the door --

> HOPPER (CONT'D)
> Open the door right n-- !

WHOOM!  The door suddenly *opens* and --

**INT. CABIN - ELEVEN'S ROOM - NIGHT**

Hopper stumbles into the room, nearly falling right over!

He looks up to find Mike and Eleven.  They're now positioned on either end of the bed, innocently reading magazines.

They look up at him, confused.  *Like nothing happened.*

>                    MIKE
>          What's wrong?

Off Hopper, breathing hard, face bright red --

**EXT. OUTSKIRTS OF HAWKINS - NIGHT**

WHOOSH!  Tires cut past CAMERA as --

Mike bikes down a country road, laughing.  He is talking on his walkie-talkie, strapped to his handlebar.

>                    MIKE
>          His face -- did you see his face??

**INT. CABIN - ELEVEN'S ROOM - INTERCUT**

Eleven is lying on her bed, now with her *OWN WALKIE*!

She's laughing too --

>                    ELEVEN
>          It was -- like a tomato --

>                    MIKE
>          A *fat* tomato --

>                    ELEVEN
>          A *fat* tomato --

Her smile fades as she rolls over onto her back.

>                    ELEVEN (CONT'D)
>          I wish... I was still with you.

**EXT. OUTSKIRTS OF HAWKINS - NIGHT**

>                    MIKE
>          ... Me too.  But I'll see you
>          tomorrow, first thing, okay?

>                    ELEVEN
>          *Tomorrow.*

**EXT. STARCOURT MALL - PARKING LOT - NIGHT**

Mike zooms toward an enormous new building. This is --

STARCOURT MALL!  HOLY SHIT -- HAWKINS HAS A MALL!!!

**MOMENTS LATER**

Mike pulls up outside the mall entrance, where --

LUCAS, MAX, and WILL are waiting.  (Dustin is absent.)

They look... *irritated*.

>                    LUCAS
>           You're *late* --

>                    MIKE
>           Sorry --

>                    LUCAS
>           *Again* --

>                    WILL
>           We're gonna miss the opening -- !

Mike slots his bike into a bike rack.

>                    MIKE
>           If you guys keep on whining, then
>           yeah.  Come on, let's go --

Mike heads into the mall at a fast clip.

The others share looks, then follow.

**INT. STARCOURT MALL - TOP LEVEL - NIGHT**

Our kids are now quickly walking through the mall.

>                    LUCAS
>               (to Mike)
>           Let me guess.  You were busy --

Lucas makes SLOBBERY KISSING SOUNDS.

Will laughs.  But Mike is not amused.

>                    MIKE
>           Oh yeah, that's real *mature*, Lucas.

But Lucas doesn't let up, continues to mock:

>                    LUCAS
>           "Oh, El, El, I wish we could make
>           out forever and never hang out with
>           my friends -- "

Lucas makes more kissing sounds, even more slobbery now --

                    MAX
          Lucas, *stop* --

                    MIKE
          Yeah, seriously, what are you, six
          years old???

                    LUCAS
          Will thinks it's funny --

                    WILL
          Because *it is* --

                    MIKE
          Yeah, it's sooo funny I like
          spending romantic time with my
          girlfriend.

                    LUCAS
          *I'm* spending romantic time with my
          girlfriend.

Lucas takes Max's hand, smiling wide.

                    MAX
          Oh yeah you're a real *Don Juan*...

                    LUCAS
          Who's Don Juan -- ?

As Max rolls her eyes, *boys...* we CRANE UP over our kids to
reveal the FULL SCOPE OF THIS MALL.  It's huge, impressive.
Fountains, carpet, stores, shoppers, cool teens, oh my!

This is clearly *the* place to be in Hawkins.

                    MIKE/LUCAS/WILL/MAX (PRE-LAP)
          -- Excuse us -- sorry --

**INT. MALL - ESCALATOR - LOWER LEVEL - MOMENTS LATER**

CLOSE ON: Legs skipping down metal steps as...

Our kids hurry down the CROWDED ESCALATOR, weaving and
squeezing their way past ANNOYED MALLGOERS.

                    MIKE/LUCAS/WILL/MAX
          Sorry -- sorry -- really sorry!

They bump past an ANNOYED TEEN GIRL as they bound off the
escalator to the LOWER LEVEL of the mall.

                    ANNOYED TEEN GIRL
          Watch it -- !

A familiar voice calls out:

                    ERICA (O.S.)
          Yeah, *WATCH IT*, NERDS!

Lucas's eyes swivel -- it's ERICA and FOUR GIRLFRIENDS.
They're on a bench, licking ICE CREAM from GIANT CONES.

                    ERICA (CONT'D)
          Why are you in such a rush, there a
          *NEW TOY* on sale or something -- ??

Erica's girlfriends laugh.  She's *hilarious*.

                    LUCAS
          Isn't it past your bedtime -- ?

                    ERICA
          Isn't it time *you die* -- ?

                    LUCAS
          *Psycho* --

                    ERICA
          *Butthead* --

                    LUCAS
          *Mall rat* --

                    ERICA
          *FART FACE*.

Lucas flips her off -- Erica flips him off right back, *with
both middle fingers*.  Max shoots him a look.

                    MAX
          Now *that* was mature.

The kids head into an ice cream shop called SCOOPS AHOY!!

**INT. MALL - SCOOPS AHOY! - NIGHT**

It's sailor-themed.  And *incredibly* dorky.

ROBIN, 18, works the counter.  She is sarcastic, hyper, and
dressed in a ridiculous sailor uniform.  Her short hair is
tucked under a WHITE SAILOR HAT.

As soon as she spot the kids, she calls into the back:

                         13

                    ROBIN
          Hey dingus!  Your children are
          here!

A beat, then a pass through window shoots open to reveal --

STEVE HARRINGTON!  He is also wearing an absurd sailor
outfit.  Holy shit, Steve slings ice cream at the mall???

Steve eyes his "children."  Sighs.

                    STEVE
          Again?  Seriously?

Off the kids, *very serious...*

**INT. STARCOURT MALL - DELIVERY CORRIDOR - NIGHT**

A back door swings open as...

Steve lets the kids out into a DELIVERY CORRIDOR.

                    STEVE
          I swear, if *anyone* finds out about
          this --

                    LUCAS/MIKE/MAX/WILL
          We're dead.

The kids hurry away down the corridor.

"Dad" Steve grumbles.  Shuts the delivery door.  And --

**INT. STARCOURT MOVIE THEATER - NIGHT**

CLOSE ON: A door inches open and...

Mike peers out into a mysterious room, then...

                    MIKE
          All clear.

Mike leads his friends out of the delivery corridor.

WIDEN OUT TO REVEAL WE'RE IN A MOVIE THEATER!  This is a
new fancy *MULTIPLEX inside* the mall!  The walls are
lined with movie posters.  *Back to the Future.  Black
Cauldron.  Teen Wolf.*  God, what a year this was!

The kids slip into a theater playing --

*DAY OF THE DEAD*.  *SNEAK PREVIEW!*

**INT. STARCOURT MOVIE THEATER - AUDITORIUM - NIGHT**

The kids squeeze past some teens, drop into cushioned seats.

On the movie screen, MUSIC blasts as colorful words fly at us:

*"AND NOW FOR YOUR FEATURE PRESENTATION!"*

> MIKE
> See -- made it.

> LUCAS
> Missed the previews --

> MAX
> Still made it. *Fart face.*

Will opens his backpack to reveal a TREASURE TROVE OF CANDY.
He passes the candy out to his friends. This is clearly
their routine. They settle in as the movie begins...

ON SCREEN: A WOMAN IS ALONE IN A STARK CELL. MUSIC DRONES.

Our kids lean forward. Already engrossed. When --

WHOOM! The PROJECTOR ZAPS OUT and THE SCREEN GOES DARK.

A chorus of BOOOOS erupt across the auditorium.

ANGRY TEENS throw popcorn at the screen.

> MIKE
> Oh come on -- !

> MAX
> *You've gotta be kidding --*

But it's not just the theater...

**INT. STARCOURT MALL - VARIOUS - NIGHT**

A SERIES OF SHOTS as the lights SHUT OFF in the mall.

-- The neon signs in the food court go out.

-- The escalators stop, jolting everyone on them.

-- A MECHANICAL HORSE stops rocking. The CHILD on it cries.

-- Erica looks around in the dark, baffled.

**INT. SCOOPS AHOY! - NIGHT**

Scoops goes dark.

> STEVE
> ... The hell?

Steve flips a light switch on and off.

> ROBIN
> That's not gonna work, dingus --

Steve keeps trying anyway, and...

**EXT. HAWKINS - NIGHT**

We're now SOARING HIGH ABOVE Hawkins as...

The power outage ripples from the mall outward, spreading out across the town. *Whump. Whump. Whump.* The dying lights lead our *SOARING CAMERA* to...

A LARGE ABANDONED FACTORY. Lit eerily in this moonlight.

A LOW RUMBLE emanates from within the factory. Almost like a growl. What <u>is</u> that? *Is something... in there?* The sound becomes louder as we fly even closer to this factory...

We DRIFT THROUGH its broken roof...

MOVE DOWN into the large warehouse below...

SLIP THROUGH a metal grate in the floor and INTO...

**INT. ABANDONED FACTORY - BASEMENT - NIGHT**

An eerie, wet, moonlit basement.

The RUMBLE is much louder now. Almost too loud to bear.

Our CAMERA DROPS level with the ground. It looks like the dirt on the ground is moving. Shifting. Alive. Then...

A FEW DARK PARTICLES LIFT UP INTO THE AIR. THEN MORE. MORE.

WIDEN OUT: The particles hover six feet in the air. Then they begin to swirl, gather, coalesce, like some kind of DARK CLOUD. This isn't dirt. These are...

<u>MIND FLAYER PARTICLES</u>.

RATS scatter. Shrieking. As --

THE PARTICLE CLOUD GROWS -- ENVELOPING CAMERA -- AND --

**EXT. HAWKINS - OVERHEAD - NIGHT**

*Whump.  Whump.  Whump.*  Power returns to the town.

**EXT. STARCOURT MALL - NIGHT**

The Starcourt town mall sign lights back up.

**INT. STARCOURT MALL - VARIOUS - NIGHT**

The food court neon lights kick back on -- the fountain
starts spitting water -- the horse starts rocking again.

**INT. SCOOPS AHOY! - NIGHT**

Steve flips the light switch and --

The lights inside Scoops kick on.  He shoots Robin a look.

> STEVE
> And let there be light!

Robin rolls her eyes.  *What a dingus.*

**INT. STARCOURT MOVIE THEATER - PROJECTOR BOOTH - NIGHT**

FWOOM!  Celluloid shoots back through the projector as --

**INT. STARCOURT MOVIE THEATER - AUDITORIUM - NIGHT**

*DAY OF THE DEAD* returns to the movie screen!  A burst of
APPLAUSE and CHEERS.  Everyone is elated.  That is, everyone
but Will.  He reaches out and touches the back of his neck.

There are goosebumps.  Just like last year.

**A RAPID BARRAGE OF FLASHBACKS FROM LAST YEAR:**

*THE MIND FLAYER ROARS -- GOING INTO WILL --*

*THEN SUDDENLY WILL'S STRAPPED ON A BED --*

*THE PARTICLES ERUPT FROM HIS MOUTH --*

*EXPLODE OUT THE CABIN DOOR -- AND --*

> MIKE
> You okay?

Will snaps out of the dark memory, looks to Mike.

                              WILL
          ... Yeah.  Yeah.

                              MIKE
          You sure?

                              WILL
          Totally.

Will removes his hand from his neck, returns his gaze to the
movie.  ON SCREEN, the woman is standing by the wall when --

RARRRR!  ZOMBIE HANDS EXPLODE OUT FROM THE WALL --

THE CROWD SCREAMS -- AND --

**INT. UNKNOWN BEDROOM - MORNING 3**

WHOOM!  NANCY bolts up into CLOSE-UP.  Panicked.

A RAY OF MORNING LIGHT cuts across her face.

                              NANCY
          Shit --

She grabs her wristwatch off a nightstand.  Her panic grows.

                              NANCY (CONT'D)
          Shitshitshit!

WHOOM!  A groggy JONATHAN suddenly pops up beside her.

                              JONATHAN
          Wha-- what's wrong?

WIDEN OUT TO REVEAL we're in JONATHAN'S ROOM.  The teens are
in bed together, wearing T-shirts and not much else.  They
clearly had a fun night.  But right now, it's sheer panic as --

Nancy throws off the covers, leaps out of bed.

                              NANCY
          -- It's almost nine --

                              JONATHAN
          Wha -- ??

                              NANCY
          We forgot to reset the clock -- the
          power went out, remember -- ?

Jonathan grabs a DIGITAL CLOCK off his nightstand.

It blinks 12:00.  And suddenly it hits him too.

                    JONATHAN
          Oh -- *shit*!

He throws back the sheets and leaps out of bed and now --

<u>Both teens</u> are throwing on clothes as fast as they can.  As
Jonathan frantically pulls on his jeans, he trips and *crashes*
*to the floor* and --

**EXT. BYERS HOUSE - A LITTLE LATER - DAY**

WHOOM!  The bedroom window shoots open and --

Nancy leaps outside.  She then hurries around the house,
hopping a bit as she pulls on a shoe, as --

**INT. BYERS HOUSE - KITCHEN - DAY**

Jonathan races out of his room, buttoning his shirt.

                         JOYCE (O.S.)
               Jonathan, sweetie -- !

He swivels to find JOYCE, who is passing WILL freshly made
pancakes at the kitchen table.

                         JONATHAN
               -- I'll eat at work, Mom -- I --
               I'm late --

                         JOYCE
               Your cheek.

                         JONATHAN
               Huh?

                         JOYCE
               *Your cheek.*

Joyce motions to a spot on her left cheek.  Jonathan reaches
up and touches his matching cheek.  He comes away with...

A SMEAR OF RED LIPSTICK.

                         JOYCE (CONT'D)
                    (smiles)
               Got it.

Jonathan mutters an embarrassed thanks, then hurries out.

Will watches in disgust.

                         WILL
               *Gross.*

                    JOYCE
          You won't think it's gross when you
          fall in love --

                    WILL
          I'm *not* gonna fall in love --

Joyce starts to sit down at the table, when --

Her eyes narrow.  Noticing something odd.

She walks over to the refrigerator and kneels down.  A FEW
MAGNETS have fallen to the floor, along with a piece of
paper.  She picks up the paper.  It's --

THE DRAWING OF "BOB NEWBY, SUPERHERO."

A moment of remembrance here, sadness.

Joyce shakes it off, grabs a fallen magnet, and --

SNAP!  Pins the drawing back in place.

**EXT. COUNTRY ROAD - DAY**

VROOM!  Jonathan's car putters down the road.

                    NANCY (O.S.)
          Can you drive faster -- ?

**INT. JONATHAN'S CAR - DAY**

Nancy frantically puts on makeup, looking in the car mirror.

                    JONATHAN
          You wanna break down?  We're lucky
          this thing still drives at all --

                    NANCY
          I'm serious, Jonathan, I can't be
          late --

                    JONATHAN
          You mean *we* can't be late --

                    NANCY
          No, I mean *I* can't be late.  They
          like you no matter what you do --

                    JONATHAN
          They like you too --

                    NANCY
          They like that I'm a coffee
          delivery machine.  They don't
          actually like me -- or respect me --
          as, you know, a living breathing
          human being with a brain --

                    JONATHAN
          You just... have to be patient,
          Nance.  They're set in their ways,
          you know?  But when they realize
          what a gifted writer you are --

                    NANCY
               (interrupting)
          I *really* don't need another
          Jonathan Byers pep talk right now,
          okay?

                    JONATHAN
               (yeesh)
          Okay --

                    NANCY
          Can you please just -- drive
          faster?

Jonathan sighs.  Punches the accelerator.  And --

**EXT. COUNTRY ROAD - DAY**

VROOM!  Jonathan's car coughs and chugs its way past...

A YELLOW VOLVO, driving in the opposite direction.

Our CAMERA leaves Jonathan's car and PANS with this Volvo
instead.  Because this is no ordinary Volvo.  This is
Dustin's car!

                    DUSTIN (PRE-LAP)
          -- This is Gold Leader, returning
          to base.  Do you copy?  Over.

**INT./EXT. DUSTIN'S CAR - DAY**

CLAUDIA drives.  Dustin rides shotgun.

He wears a "CAMP KNOW-WHERE" science-camp T-shirt and a "CAMP
KNOW-WHERE" HAT.  The backseat is piled high with luggage.

He speaks urgently into his walkie headset:

                    DUSTIN
        I *repeat*: this is Gold Leader,
        returning to base.  Do you copy?
        Over.

There is no response.

                    DUSTIN (CONT'D)
        I *repeat*, this is *Gold Leader*,
        returning to base, do you copy?

Nothing.

                    DUSTIN (CONT'D)
        I repeat -- this is the GODDAMN
        GOLD LEADER --

                    CLAUDIA
        Dusty!

                    DUSTIN
        What -- ?!

                    CLAUDIA
        Relax!  For *goodness sake*.

Dustin rips off his headset.

                    DUSTIN
        I'm in range, they should be
        answering -- !!

                    CLAUDIA
        You've been away a whole month,
        honeybun.  Maybe they just forgot.

Dustin looks hurt.  Is it really possible... *they forgot?*

**EXT. HENDERSON HOUSE - DAY**

The Volvo rumbles up the driveway.

**INT. HENDERSON HOUSE - DUSTIN'S ROOM - DAY**

KA-WHOOMP!  Dustin drops his heavy luggage into his room.

He slumps onto his bed.  Feeling depressed.  *Forgotten.*

He looks at his terrarium.  *At YURTLE THE TURTLE.*

                    DUSTIN
        At least *someone's* happy I'm home.

Yurtle stares at him.  Emotionless.  And then --

                    LOUD VOICE
           I AM THE ATOMIC-POWERED ROBOT!

Dustin whirls with a start to find --

His MAGIC MIKE TOY ROBOT marching across the floor!  Then --

BAM!  A TOY TANK slams into Dustin's foot.  And then
CHOOCHOO!  A TRAIN zips through his legs.  And then VROOM!  A
RACE CAR.  Dustin looks around in shock to discover that --

ALL OF HIS TOYS ARE ALIVE.  He watches slack-jawed as --

The Robot leads this "toy army" out of the room.

**MOMENTS LATER**

Dustin grabs the FARRAH FAWCETT HAIRSPRAY off his shelf.

**INT. HENDERSON HOUSE - HALLWAY - DAY**

Dustin peeks out from his room.  Hairspray aimed like a gun.

The toys are making their way down the hallway.

                    DUSTIN
           This is just a dream... a dream...
           you're dreaming --

As Dustin follows the toys out, we MOVE into...

**INT. HENDERSON HOUSE - TV ROOM - DAY - CONTINUOUS**

Where we find Mike, Eleven, Will, Lucas, and Max -- *hiding!*

Eleven's nose drips blood.  She's using her powers!

Mike looks at her.  Nods.  *Now.*  And --

**INT. HENDERSON HOUSE - LIVING ROOM - CONTINUOUS**

WHUMP!  The toys crash to a halt.  *What in the hell?*

Dustin gathers his courage, walks over to the toys, and picks
up the robot.  As he stares at it, we RACK FOCUS TO REVEAL:

His friends sneaking up behind him.  They unfurl a "WELCOME
HOME" SIGN... slip noisemakers in their mouths... and...

WEEEEEEEEE!!!!!  THE KIDS BLOW THEIR NOISEMAKERS!!!

DUSTIN WHIRLS WITH A SCREAM:

                         DUSTIN
              AAAAAHHH!!!!!

HE INSTINCTIVELY FIRES HIS HAIRSPRAY.

IT SPRAYS LUCAS RIGHT IN THE FACE!

LUCAS DROPS, SCREAMING NOW TOO!

                         LUCAS
              AHHHHHHH!!!!!

                         DUSTIN
              AHHH!!!!

                         LUCAS
              AHHHH!!

AS HIGH-PITCHED SCREAMS FILL THE HOUSE, WE CRASH TO --

**EXT. HAWKINS POOL - DAY**

Another SCREAM pierces the air as --

                    OVERWEIGHT BOY
              AHHHHHHHHWOOOOO!!!!

AN OVERWEIGHT BOY runs and jumps off a diving board and --

SPLASH!!  He cannonballs into HAWKINS POOL.  It's peak pool
time, jam-packed with kids of all ages.

Our CAMERA SWINGS over to the shallow end, where we find --

HOLLY WHEELER playing Marco Polo with other YOUNG KIDS.

                         HOLLY
              MARCO -- !

                         KIDS
              POLO -- !

                         HOLLY
              MARCO --

                         KIDS
              POLO -- !

Our CAMERA CONTINUES PAST the children to find...

KAREN!  She's sunbathing in a lounge chair alongside a GAGGLE
OF MOTHERS.  She wears big sunglasses and a vibrant bathing
suit.  We must say... she's looking *pretty goddamn sexy*.

MOM #1 suddenly sits up, lowers her sunglasses.

                    MOM #1
          She's coming down, ladies...

Karen and the other mothers follow her gaze to the lifeguard
stand.  A pretty lifeguard, HEATHER, 18, is climbing down
from her perch.  Her shift is clearly coming to an end.

The mothers all perk up.  This clearly... means *something*.

We begin a POP SONG as they ruffle their hair, adjust their
bathing suits, change up their positions... *getting ready*.

Their eyes then move to the MEN'S LOCKER ROOM.

We PUSH IN on the waiting mothers, all in position now ...

                    MOM #1 (CONT'D)
          And... *SHOWTIME* --

The door swings open just as our POP SONG CRESCENDOS AND...

HE emerges.  BILLY.  FUCKING.  HARGROVE.  He's a lifeguard!!!

WE MOVE INTO SLOW MOTION as Billy strips off his shirt,
revealing a perfect bod.  He's the hottest man in Hawkins
and by God he *knows it*.  As he struts in their direction...

The mothers ogle him like teen girls.

PUSH IN ON Karen.  Her cheeks are flushed.  Clearly *turned
on*.

But this sexy slow-motion moment is interrupted when --

EEEE!!!!  Billy blows his whistle and screams:

                    BILLY
          HEY LARD-ASS!!

OUR CAMERA SUDDENLY WHIPS OVER TO FIND --

The Overweight Boy, who is running on the opposite side of
the pool.  He slides to a stop.  In fact, everyone in the
pool crashes to a stop -- all play temporarily freezing.

Everyone is terrified of this... *pool Nazi*.

                    BILLY (CONT'D)
          NO RUNNING ON MY WATCH!  I GOTTA
          WARN YOU AGAIN YOU'RE BANNED FOR
          LIFE!!!  YOU WANNA BE BANNED FOR
          LIFE, LARD-ASS???


                       25

The Overweight Boy shakes his head, terrified.

                    BILLY (CONT'D)
          Didn't *think so*.

Billy blows his whistle again and --

Everyone resumes playing.  *Like it never happened.*

The mothers share looks.

                    MOM #1
          So... *rough*.

                    MOM #2
          I can work with that.

                    MOM #3
          Mmmm-hmmm...

They quiet as Billy nears.

                    BILLY
          Afternoon, ladies.

                    MOTHERS
          Afternoon, Billy.

Billy clocks Karen, lowers his sunglasses.

                    BILLY
          Dig the new suit, Missus Wheeler.

Karen turns a brighter shade of red as Billy continues past.

The other mothers shoot looks at Karen, jealous.  But Karen's
not paying attention to them.  She's too busy watching --

Billy.  He climbs up into the lifeguard stand, settles into
his chair.  He leans back, looking like a *GOLDEN GOD*.

We PUSH IN on Karen, barely able to breathe, and --

**EXT. DOWNTOWN HAWKINS - VARIOUS - DAY**

Silence.  We're on Main Street.  It's quiet.  Empty.  We do a
quick survey.  It's changed since last year.  It's... *dying*.

-- The movie theater is now closed, the building FOR LEASE.

-- Another "FOR LEASE" sign hangs over a retail store.

-- A handwritten sign flutters on a pole, reads:

SAVE DOWNTOWN!  TOWN HALL -- TUESDAY -- 6 PM!!

-- And last but not least, a JULY 4TH-THEMED BANNER unfurls in the Melvald's General Store display window, reading:

BLOWOUT SALE!!  MASSIVE DISCOUNTS!!

**INT. MELVALD'S GENERAL STORE - DAY**

Joyce hangs the banner.  Just as she secures it --

DING!  The door chimes.  She turns, hoping for a customer.

But it's just <u>Hopper</u>.

> HOPPER
> You busy?

> JOYCE
> You're our first customer, so...

Joyce smiles.  Hopper doesn't return it.

> JOYCE (CONT'D)
> ... What now?

Off Hopper, about to explode, we SMASH TO --

**INT. MELVALD'S GENERAL STORE - DAY - MOMENTS LATER**

WHOOM!  A DESK DRAWER flies open as --

Joyce removes a STICKER GUN.  She begins to slap items with RED SALE STICKERS while an angry Hopper trails her, ranting:

> HOPPER
> -- Then El -- she just -- she slams
> the door, right in my face -- !

> JOYCE
> Uh huh --

> HOPPER
> It's that *smug little shit Mike*,
> I'm telling you -- he's corrupting
> her and -- and I'm gonna lose it,
> Joyce, I *swear to God* --

> JOYCE
> Hopper, take it down --

> HOPPER
> I just -- I need them to <u>break up</u>.

                    JOYCE
          That's not your decision --

                    HOPPER
          They're spending *way* too much time
          together, you do agree with me,
          right -- ??

                    JOYCE
          Well, they're just *kissing* right?

                    HOPPER
          You don't understand -- it's
          CONSTANT. *CONNNNSTANT*. It's *not*
          normal and it's NOT healthy --

                    JOYCE
          Okay, okay, but -- you can't
          just... force them apart --

Joyce carries her sales tags down --

**ANOTHER AISLE**

Hopper follows her like a lost puppy.

                    JOYCE (CONT'D)
          They're not kids anymore.  They're
          *teenagers*.  You order them around
          like a cop, they're gonna rebel.
          It's just what they do --

                    HOPPER
          So what?  I'm supposed to just --
          let them do whatever they want -- ?

                    JOYCE
          No, I didn't say that.  I think
          you should talk to them --

                    HOPPER
          Yeah see -- talking doesn't work --

Joyce shoots him a look.

                    JOYCE
          Not yelling, not ordering -- I mean
          a real talk.  A *heart to heart*.

Joyce turns, walks down...

**ANOTHER AISLE**

Hopper follows.  He's skeptical -- but curious.

                    HOPPER
          What do you mean exactly -- "heart
          to heart" -- ?

                    JOYCE
          I mean -- sit them down and *talk*.
          Like you're *their friend*.  Come to
          *their level*.  I've found, if you do
          that, they really do start to
          listen.  Then you can start to
          create some boundaries --

                    HOPPER
          Boundaries, right, okay --

                    JOYCE
          But no matter how they respond, you
          *have* to stay calm.  You can't <u>lose</u>
          <u>your temper</u>.

Hopper hesitates.  *That's... gonna be tough.*

                    HOPPER
          Maybe... you could do it for me?

                    JOYCE
          <u>No</u> --

                    HOPPER
          You could swing by after work and --

                    JOYCE
          <u>No</u>.  If this is going to work, it
          has to come from you...
               (beat, idea forming)
          But...

                    HOPPER
          *But...?*

Joyce strides away and...

**INT. MELVALD'S GENERAL STORE - DAY - MOMENTS LATER**

She sits at the front desk, grabs a pen.

                    JOYCE
          ... *Maybe* I can help you find the
          words.

She starts to scrawl words down on a notepad.  As Hopper
leans over her shoulder, trying to discern what the hell it
is that she's writing down, we PUSH PAST them to...

The front window.  A FAMILIAR FACE races past.  It's --

**EXT. HAWKINS MAIN STREET - SIDEWALK - DAY**

Nancy.  She is moving *fast* down the sidewalk.  Almost
running.  She's carrying a large brown bag.  *Stressed.*

**EXT. HAWKINS MAIN STREET - HAWKINS POST BUILDING - DAY**

Nancy hurries up some steps and into a BRICK BUILDING.

We PUSH into the sign above the door.  It reads:

THE HAWKINS POST: *COURAGE IN JOURNALISM SINCE 1931!*

**INT. HAWKINS POST - BULLPEN - DAY**

Nancy races through the newspaper bullpen.

She passes out more sandwiches as she goes.  There are only
FEMALE SECRETARIES out here -- men nowhere to be seen.

> SECRETARY #1
> Thanks hon --

> SECRETARY #2
> Thanks --

Nancy throws open a door and bursts into --

**INT. HAWKINS POST - PHOTOGRAPHY ROOM - DAY**

Jonathan looks up from a bath of developing film -- film
which, thanks to Nancy, has now been COMPLETELY OBLITERATED!

> JONATHAN
> Nancy -- !

> NANCY
> (grimaces)
> Sorry -- !

She flings him a sandwich and --

**INT. HAWKINS POST - SIDE ROOM - DAY**

Nancy races toward a closed door.  She flings it open and --

**INT. HAWKINS POST - CONFERENCE ROOM - DAY**

Here they are: A GANG OF NEWSPAPER MEN!

They're crammed around a large conference table.  Nancy
quickly moves around the table, passing them sandwiches as
they pitch stories to a grizzled Editor in Chief, TOM.

                    NEWSMAN #1
          -- how 'bout a piece on Iran --

                    TOM
          I want something local --

BRUCE, a sleazy-looking newsman, now speaks:

                    BRUCE
          I hear they're doing a beauty
          pageant at the fair this year --

                    TOM
          Yeah I'm looking for "above the
          fold" here, Bruce --

                    BRUCE
          You clearly haven't seen Lucy
          LeBrock then --

Bruce makes a motion with his hands, signaling big boobs.

                    BRUCE (CONT'D)
          Don't know if they'd fit above the
          fold, but --

The room bursts out laughing.

                    TOM
          Fellas, we've got six hours till
          print, I need something real --

                    BRUCE
          Oh, I think they're real.

More laughter.  Nancy heads for the door, when --

She stops.  Mind racing.  Then... *screw it.*

She turns back, spits out:

                    NANCY
          What about Starcourt?

The laughter abruptly dies as all heads swivel to --

Nancy.  She gathers her composure.  Steps forward.

                    NANCY (CONT'D)
          I was just thinking -- I know
          everyone loves the mall, but... how
          many small businesses have closed
          since it opened?  Five on Main at
          least.  I mean, it's -- changing
          the fabric of our town and --

                    BRUCE
          "The death of small-town America."
          I like it, yeah, I like it.
               (beat)
          But I *think* I've got something even
          *spicier*.  It's about the missing...

Bruce pulls back his hamburger bun.

                    BRUCE (CONT'D)
          ... *mustard* on my burger.

The room bursts out laughing again.

Bruce holds up his wrapped hamburger.  Waves it at Nancy.

                    BRUCE (CONT'D)
          Think you could follow the clues
          and solve the case of the missing
          condiment, Nancy Drew?

More LAUGHTER.  Nancy forces a smile.  *Ha ha.*  Then --

She takes Bruce's burger and heads out.  As soon as her back
turns to the men, her smile fades -- replaced with *anger*.

The laughter behind her grows as --

She explodes out of the room and --

**INT. HENDERSON HOUSE - KITCHEN - DAY**

WHOOSH!  A STREAM OF WATER *gushes* out of a faucet and --

                    LUCAS
          Ow ow ow ow -- !

Max helps flush out Lucas's eyes under the kitchen faucet.
He rips out his head, looks at Max, blinking --

                              32

                    MAX
          Better?

                    LUCAS
          Still stings --

His eyes narrow.

                    LUCAS (CONT'D)
          Is that a *new zit?*

                    MAX
          What is wrong with you?

                    LUCAS
          Just asking --

Max shoves his head back under the water and --

**INT. HENDERSON HOUSE - DUSTIN'S ROOM - DAY**

ZZZZZIPP!  Dustin unzips a duffel bag.

He removes a CLOCK and hands it to Mike, who passes it around
to the other kids.  Only this is no *ordinary clock*.  It's
handmade -- and its roof is a tin windmill.  Ummm...

                    DUSTIN
          -- I call it the Forever Clock.
          It's *powered by wind* -- very useful
          in the apocalypse --

As the kids inspect it, Dustin reaches into a bag, pulls out
another invention: AN ELECTRIC HAMMER called --

                    DUSTIN (CONT'D)
          The Slammer.

He hits a button and it jerks to life.

                    DUSTIN (CONT'D)
          Pretty awesome, right?

The "Slammer" starts to jerk out of control.  Dangerous.

Eleven backs up as it starts to hammer toward her and --

ZOOP.  Dustin quickly turns it off.  Tosses it.

                    DUSTIN (CONT'D)
          But this -- *this* is my masterpiece.

He grabs up a GIANT RUCKSACK.  Drops it onto the floor.

                    DUSTIN (CONT'D)
          Meet... Cerebro.

He kneels down and unzips the rucksack to reveal a MESSY
TANGLE OF EQUIPMENT.  Wires.  Motherboards.  A tripod.  And
lots of... metal poles?

The kids drop down to the floor to examine.  Uhhh --

                    MIKE
          What exactly are we looking at
          here -- ?

                    DUSTIN
          An unassembled one-of-a-kind
          battery-powered RADIO TOWER.

The kids remain unimpressed.

                    WILL
          So it's a... ham radio?

                    DUSTIN
          The *Cadillac* of ham radios.  This
          baby carries a crystal-clear
          connection over vast distances --
          I'm talking *north pole to south*.  I
          can talk to my girlfriend whenever
          and *wherever* I choose.

The kids exchange looks.  Did he just say --

                    MIKE/WILL
          Girlfriend?

Off Dustin, grinning ear-to-ear, we CRASH TO --

**INT. HENDERSON HOUSE - LIVING ROOM - DAY**

Dustin struts into the living room.  He's got a real swagger
about him now, the Cerebro rucksack slung over his shoulders.

Mike, Eleven, and Will chase behind him.

                    MIKE
          -- Her name is -- *Suzie* -- ?

                    DUSTIN
          With a Z.  Suzie with a Z.  She's
          from Utah --

                    WILL
          Girls go to science camp -- ?

                         DUSTIN
          Suzie does.  She's a genius --

                         MIKE
          Is she cute -- ?

                         DUSTIN
          Think Phoebe Cates -- only hotter --

The kids share skeptical looks as they stride past --

Lucas and Max, still in the kitchen.

                         MAX
          -- What's going on?

                         WILL
          We're going to talk to Dustin's
          girlfriend.

Lucas rips his head out of the faucet.

                         LUCAS
          Girlfriend??

But the kids are already gone, out the front door.

Lucas and Max share stunned looks, then --

Hurry after them and --

**INT. SCOOPS AHOY! - DAY**

SPLAT!  Ice cream slops into a waffle cone.

Steve is now working behind the counter at Scoops Ahoy.  He
passes the cone to a CUTE GIRL, 18, and HER FRIEND.

                         STEVE
          That'll be a buck fifty.

As the Cute Girl gathers money, Steve clocks her T-shirt:

                         STEVE (CONT'D)
          Purdue.  Fancy.

                         CUTE GIRL
          Yeah, I'm excited.

She passes him a five.  As Steve grabs her change:

                         STEVE
          You know, I considered it.  Purdue.
          But then I was like, "Know what?
                         (MORE)

                              35

                    STEVE (CONT'D)
I should get some real *life*
experience before I hit college --
see what it's like to earn a
working man's wage."  Know what I
mean?

                    CUTE GIRL
          (no)
Yeah -- totally.

Steve passes her the change.

                    STEVE
Anyway -- we should, like, hang out
again, you know, before you leave.
This weekend maybe -- ?

                    CUTE GIRL
Oh.  I'm busy this weekend...

                    STEVE
... That's cool, that's cool.
Honestly next weekend's better for
me anyway --

                    CUTE GIRL
I really... can't -- *sorry* --

The Cute Girl hurries away with her friends, giggling.

                    ROBIN (O.S.)
And... *another one* bites the dust!

Steve looks behind him to find Robin.  She's sitting on a
desk in the back room, cradling a WHITE BOARD.  She holds the
board up for Steve to see.  She's drawn up two columns.

Column One: "YOU RULE."  Column Two: "YOU SUCK."

"YOU SUCK" has six tally marks.  "YOU RULE": *zero*.

                    ROBIN (CONT'D)
You're oh for six, Popeye --

                    STEVE
Yeah yeah I can count --

A defeated Steve heads for the back room.

                    ROBIN
That means *you suck* --

                    STEVE
I can read too --

                    ROBIN
          *Since when*??

**INT. SCOOPS AHOY! - BACK ROOM - DAY - CONTINUOUS**

Steve slumps into a chair, defeated.

                    STEVE
          It's this hat, I'm telling you --
          it's *blowing* my best feature --

                    ROBIN
          Company policy is a real drag --

Robin puts down her white board, scooches closer to Steve.

                    ROBIN (CONT'D)
          I know this is, like, *totally out
          there*, but have you ever considered
          maybe... telling the truth for
          once?

                    STEVE
          Oh, you mean -- that I couldn't
          even get into Tech and my douchebag
          dad wants to teach me a lesson and
          now I'm making three bucks an hour
          and I have no future -- *that* truth?

                    ROBIN
          No, I mean -- *your secret truth*.

                    STEVE
          My secret truth?

Robin leans in.  Deadly serious.

                    ROBIN
          That you just really really love...
                (beat)
          Neckerchiefs.

She flicks his red neckerchief.  Smiles.

Steve stares.  Not amused.  When --

                    ROBIN (CONT'D)
          Twelve o'clock -- !

Steve whirls.  TWO NEW CUTE GIRLS have entered Scoops!

                    STEVE
          Shit.  Oh shit.  Okay, *okay* -- I'm
          going in --

Steve stands, starts to go, when --

                    STEVE (CONT'D)
          You know what -- ?

He swivels back to Robin --

                    STEVE (CONT'D)
          *Screw company policy.*

He tosses her his hat, freeing up those beautiful locks!

                    ROBIN
               (sarcastic)
          Wow.  You're like a new man!

                    STEVE
          Right???

Steve heads out.  Salutes the cute girls.

                    STEVE (CONT'D)
          Ahoy ladies!  Welcome to Scoops --

The girls *GIGGLE* as soon as they see him.

Robin rolls her eyes.  *Another one bites the dust.*  She grabs
her marker, SLASHES another "YOU SUCK" tally mark, and --

**EXT. MELVALD'S GENERAL STORE - DAY - ESTABLISHING**

We PUSH IN on Melvald's General Store.

                    HOPPER (PRE-LAP)
          ... I know this is a difficult
          conversation...

**INT. MELVALD'S GENERAL STORE - DAY**

Hopper is pacing.  Practicing his "lines."  While...

Joyce sits on her desk, listening.  *His audience.*

                    HOPPER
          "... But I care about you both,
          very much -- "

                    JOYCE
          Eye contact --

Hopper makes eye contact with Joyce.

                    HOPPER
          "And I know you care about each
          other very much..."

Hopper shakes his head.  He can't do this.

                    HOPPER (CONT'D)
          It just -- it doesn't sound like me
          at all --

                    JOYCE
          Just keep going --

Hopper grumbles, continues:

                    HOPPER
          "And that's why it's important that
          we set these..." uh...

He looks down at the notepad, but --

                    JOYCE
          No looking!

He sighs, looks back up at Joyce --

                    HOPPER
          "Why it's important we set these --
          *these boundaries* moving forward.
          So we can build an environment
          where we all feel comfortable,
          trusted, and, uh, open to... to..."

                    JOYCE
          "Sharing our feelings" --

                    HOPPER
          *"Sharing our feelings."*

Joyce applauds.  But Hopper just shakes his head.

                    HOPPER (CONT'D)
          This won't work --

                    JOYCE
          *It will.*  I promise.

Hopper slumps down next to Joyce on the desk.  He grabs a
cigarette from his pocket, slips it into his mouth.

                    HOPPER
          You're sure I can't just... strangle
          Mike?  I am the chief of police, you
          know -- I could cover it up, *easy* --

Joyce touches his arm, comforting.

                    JOYCE
          Hey.  You can do this.  I promise.

Hopper clocks her hand on top of his arm.  *And it brings all
the feelings.*  He looks back up, making that eye contact with
Joyce once again.  Then, screw it -- he goes for it:

                    HOPPER
          You want to... maybe, grab dinner
          tonight?  Gimme some more pointers?

Joyce looks... surprised.  She removes her hand.

                    JOYCE
          I... I can't.  I... have plans.

                    HOPPER
          Oh -- sure.  Yeah.

An awkward beat between them.  Then --

DING!!!  The door chime rings.  *Saving the day.*

Joyce turns to find a CUSTOMER.  She can hardly believe it!

                    JOYCE
               (to Hop, excited)
          A *customer*...

She leaps off the desk and races to greet the Customer.

                    JOYCE (CONT'D)
          Carol -- so *great* to see you again!

                    CUSTOMER
          Hey Joyce!  So... Georgie has his
          thirteenth birthday coming up and
          I'm a little lost...

Hopper watches from afar as Joyce helps the Customer.

Joyce is smiling.  Happy.  And Jesus -- *beautiful.*

Off Hop, falling for her, CUT TO:

**EXT. FIELD - DAY**

The sun glows HOT in the sky.  We TILT DOWN to find:

The kids all marching up a steep hill.  Dustin leads the way.

The excitement has died down.  They're tired and sweating
bullets.  Lucas wipes his brow, sweeping away the sweat.

                    LUCAS
          Aren't we high enough -- ?

                    DUSTIN
          Cerebro works best at a hundred
          meters --

                    MAX
          You know, I'm pretty sure people in
          Utah have telephones --

                    DUSTIN
          Yeah, but Suzie's Mormon --

                    LUCAS
          Oh shit, she doesn't have
          electricity -- ?

                    MAX
          That's the *Amish* --

                    LUCAS
          Oh --

                    WILL
          What *are* Mormons -- ?

                    DUSTIN
          Super-religious white people.  They
          have electricity and cars and
          everything, but they're real strict
          and since I'm not Mormon her
          parents would never approve.  It's
          all a bit... Shakespearean --

                    MAX
          *"Shakespearean"* -- ??

                    DUSTIN
          You know, Romeo and Juliet --

                    MAX
          Right --

                    DUSTIN
          Star-crossed lovers --

                    MAX
          I got it --

                    MIKE (O.S.)
          Hey guys?

The kids stops, turn to find --

Mike and Eleven.  Hanging back.  Mike taps his watch.

                    MIKE (CONT'D)
          This was fun, but --

                    ELEVEN
          I have to go home.

                    DUSTIN
          We're almost there -- !

                    MIKE
          Sorry, man.  Curfew.

                    ELEVEN
          Good -- luck.

On that note, the lovebirds turn and hustle back down the
hill, holding hands.  They don't seem upset to be leaving
their friends at all.  In fact, they seem... *excited*.

Dustin watches them go.  Flabbergasted.

                    DUSTIN
          Curfew at *four*?

                    LUCAS
          They're lying --

                    WILL
          It's been like this all summer --

                    MAX
          It's romantic --

                    WILL
          It's gross --

                    DUSTIN
          It's *bullshit*.  I just got home.

Dustin is clearly hurt by their abandonment.  But --

                    DUSTIN (CONT'D)
          Their loss.  Onwards and upwards!
          Suzie awaits!

Dustin turns and resumes his march up the hill.  Lucas and
Max share looks, then follow.  But Will stays behind.

Something feels... *weird*.  He touches his neck.

*The goosebumps are back.*

                    DUSTIN (CONT'D)
          Will, come on!

Will startles out of it, then hurries after the group.

As they march on, the CAMERA DROPS TO GROUND LEVEL and...

WHOOSH!  A RAT SCURRIES PAST.  Then another.  *Another.*

**EXT. ABANDONED FACTORY - DAY**

The rats make their way toward the abandoned factory.

**INT. ABANDONED FACTORY - MAIN FLOOR - DAY**

They scurry across the main floor... through a door...

**INT. ABANDONED FACTORY - BASEMENT - DAY**

... And down a flight of rusty stairs.  We're now in...

The bowels of this nasty place.  It's dark and dank down
here, scary.  For a moment we think the floor is moving until
we realize it is in fact covered in --

RATS.  *LOTS AND LOTS OF RATS*.  MUST BE HUNDREDS.  Only
something is not right with these rats.  Their bodies are
shaking, throbbing, and they are making high-pitched
CHATTERING NOISES.  They seem to be in... severe pain.

The terrible SHRIEKS grow louder, and louder, then --

SPLAT!  A RAT SUDDENLY IMPLODES.  BLOOD AND MUCUS SPRAYS.

THEN ANOTHER RAT IMPLODES.  SPLAT!  THEN ANOTHER.  SPLAT!
ANOTHER.  SPLAT!  ANOTHER!  AND ANOTHER!  AND --

**EXT. HAWKINS POOL - DAY**

SPLOOSH!  Water *SPLASHES* as --

Karen swims the backstroke in the pool.  *Adult swim.*

Billy watches Karen from atop his lifeguard perch.  TIME
SEEMS TO SLOW as he admires her body, scanning her up and
down, taking in all of her curves.  She's looking... *good.*

Without taking his eyes off her, he slips his whistle in his mouth. *Seductively*. Then -- he blows it. Long-short-long.

Adult swim is over. Kids squeal with excitement and --

Leap back into pool. SPLASH-SPLASH-SPLASH!

**EXT. HAWKINS POOL - DAY - MOMENTS LATER**

Karen climbs out of the pool. Dripping wet.

> BILLY (O.S.)
> Looking good out there, Missus
> Wheeler.

She turns to find Billy. He holds out a towel.

> BILLY (CONT'D)
> *Perfect form.*

Karen blushes, accepts the towel.

> KAREN
> Well, your form is -- amazing.

Karen can't believe she just said that. She grows flustered.

> KAREN (CONT'D)
> I mean... I've just... seen -- seen
> you teaching lessons -- swimming
> lessons -- and --

> BILLY
> You've been watching me, huh?

Karen turns bright red.

> BILLY (CONT'D)
> You know -- I could teach you if
> you want. I know all the styles.
> Freestyle... butterfly...
> *breaststroke* --

Karen drops her towel, quickly picks it back up.

> KAREN
> I -- I didn't think you taught...
> adults --

> BILLY
> Well... I offer more advanced
> lessons to... *select* clients.

He steps closer to Karen. Lowers his voice.

                    BILLY (CONT'D)
          There's a good pool at the Motel
          Six, out on Cornwallis.  Very
          quiet.  Very... *private*.

Karen flushes.  *Holy shit* -- is this actually *happening???*
She looks back over at her friends, suddenly paranoid, but --

They're reading magazines.  Not looking over here.

                    BILLY (CONT'D)
          Shall we say tonight?  Eight
          o'clock?

Karen snaps back to Billy.  She can barely breathe.  She
starts to say yes, but then regains her senses.

                    KAREN
          I'm sorry -- I -- I can't --

                    BILLY
          Can't what?  Have fun?

                    KAREN
          No, no -- I just -- I... don't
          think I need.... any lessons --

                    BILLY
          Oh I think you do.  I think you
          just haven't had the right...
          *teacher*.

Karen's breath catches --

                    KAREN
          I -- uh --

                    BILLY
          It'll be the workout of your life.
          *Promise*.

Billy takes a step closer.

                    BILLY (CONT'D)
          Come on.  What do you say?  Eight
          o'clock?

Off Karen, *wavering*, we SMASH TO:

**EXT. TOP OF THE HILL - DAY**

WHAM!  THE CEREBRO RUCKSACK slams onto grass.

                         DUSTIN
               Made it!!!

WIDEN TO REVEAL: The kids have reached the top of the hill!

Dustin looks around.  Hands on hips.  Very pleased.

But the other kids don't share his enthusiasm.  They're
exhausted, sweaty, *miserable*.  Will doubles over.

                         WILL
               Why couldn't we just play D&D...?

Lucas grabs a thermos from his backpack.  He chugs and chugs
and chugs until it's all gone.  Then -- his eyes shoot wide.

REVERSE ANGLE TO REVEAL: Max staring in disbelief.

                         MAX
               Did you seriously just drink the
               rest of our water?

Lucas spits some water back into the thermos.  Holds it out.

As Max stares at him, appalled --

**WE MOVE INTO A MONTAGE AS...**

Our kids work together to build "Cerebro."

-- WHUMP!  Dustin dumps out the rucksack, sending the mess of
metal and electronic parts scattering out onto the grass.

-- Rods are screwed together, creating a mast.

-- Batteries are plugged into a transceiver.

-- The mast is raised up like a flag pole.

-- The transceiver is switched on --

-- Lights blink green and --

**OUR MONTAGE ENDS AS...**

Our kids step back into frame.  Their eyes gaze skyward.

                         DUSTIN
               Impressive, right?

REVERSE ANGLE TO REVEAL: CEREBRO.  FULLY BUILT.  It's a giant
homemade radar tower, something like twenty feet tall.  It *is*
actually... rather impressive (in a haphazard sort of way).

Dustin looks back at his friends.

                    DUSTIN (CONT'D)
          Ready to meet my love?

The kids grumble.

                    LUCAS/DUSTIN/WILL
          Yeah, okay, sure...

Dustin's pulls the receiver up to his mouth.  He waits a beat
for dramatic effect.  Then... CLICK.  Hits the button.

                    DUSTIN
          Suzie?  This is Dustin.  Do you
          copy?

He releases the button.  Waits.  And...

No response.  That was... *anticlimactic.*

Dustin tries again:

                    DUSTIN (CONT'D)
          Suzie?  This is Dustin.  Do.  You.
          Copy?

He releases the button.  Waits.  And... still nothing.

The kids share looks, cross their arms.  This... *could be a
bit of a wait.*  As Dustin continues to call for his love...

**EXT. BYERS HOUSE - NIGHT 3**

Joyce's Gremlin pulls up to the house.  The sun is setting.

**INT. BYERS HOUSE - NIGHT**

Joyce enters.  She hangs her purse on the coat rack.

                    JOYCE
          Hey guys -- I'm home!

There is no answer.  WIDEN OUT: The house is empty.

**INT. BYERS HOUSE - KITCHEN - NIGHT**

A SERIES OF QUICK SHOTS show Joyce's evening "plans":

She grabs leftover lasagna from the fridge -- scoops the
lasagna onto a plate -- heats it up in the microwave --
uncorks some cheap wine -- pours herself a big glass -- and
then --

**INT. BYERS HOUSE - LIVING ROOM - NIGHT**

Joyce sits on the couch with her depressing dinner and wine.

She watches *Cheers* on the television.  Sam cracks a joke to an irritated Diane.  The studio audience laughs.

We PUSH IN on Joyce.  Remembering back.

A FAMILIAR LAUGH now transports us...

**INT. BYERS HOUSE - LIVING ROOM - NIGHT (FLASHBACK 1984)**

*BOB NEWBY sits next to Joyce on the couch.  LAUGHING.*

*They're watching Cheers together.*

> BOB
> *They're so funny, donchya think?*

> JOYCE
> *Yeah --*

> BOB
> *I just wish they'd get back together already!*

> JOYCE
> *Me too.*

*Joyce smiles.  Bob smiles back.  He takes her hand. Squeezes.  Then they turn back, return to watching their show.  Happier times.  And right here we make a SHARP CUT:*

**INT. BYERS HOUSE - LIVING ROOM - NIGHT (BACK TO REALITY)**

Joyce is all alone on the couch in her empty house.

As she cuts into the lasagna and begins to eat...

WE PULL AWAY, DRIFTING SLOWLY BACK INTO...

**THE KITCHEN - CONTINUOUS**

We turn our focus to the drawing of Bob Newby, superhero.

We HOLD on the drawing for a beat.  And then *something* begins to happen: All of the magnets on the fridge begin to shudder. As if being pulled by some powerful force... then:

WHOOM!  The magnets suddenly drop, *CRASHING* to the floor *and --*

**INT. HAWKINS POST - CONFERENCE ROOM - NIGHT**

WHOOM!  A PILE OF GARBAGE *DROPS* into a garbage bag.

WIDEN OUT: Nancy is cleaning up a very messy conference room, wearing rubber gloves.  She's all alone and looking quite miserable.  Suddenly: a phone begins to RING off-screen.

Nancy looks out the conference room door.  Sees --

The phone ringing on an unoccupied desk.

**INT. HAWKINS POST - SIDE ROOM - SECRETARY'S DESK**

Nancy, still wearing her rubber gloves, answers the phone.

> NANCY
> ... Hawkins Post?

She listens for a beat.  Her eyes narrow, her curiosity piqued by whatever is being said on the other end.  She holds the phone with her shoulder, grabs a scrap of paper, a pen --

> NANCY (CONT'D)
> I'm sorry -- can you... repeat
> that...?

Nancy begins to scribble down words:

*CLOSE ON:* "*DRISCOLL.*" "*DISEASE.*" And... "*RATS.*"

As Nancy underlines "*RATS*" a few times, PRELAP: POP MUSIC.

**INT. CABIN - ELEVEN'S ROOM - NIGHT**

POP MUSIC BLASTS from the boombox!  We're back in Eleven's room.

PULL BACK TO REVEAL: She is on the bed with Mike.  And yes --

They're kissing.  *Again.*

**INT. CABIN - MAIN ROOM - NIGHT**

Hopper paces in the main room, Joyce's script in his hand.

> HOPPER
> -- "Why it's important we set these
> -- *these boundaries* moving forward.
> So we can build an environment
> where we all feel comfortable,
> trusted, and, uh, open to... to..."
>     (can't remember)
> -- Goddammit!

He looks down at his cheat sheet.

> HOPPER (CONT'D)
> *"Sharing our feelings."*

Hopper takes a deep breath. *Okay... he can do this.*

Hopper folds up the script and slips it in his pocket.

He then walks up to her door. Gathers his composure. And...

Knocks. No answer. Knocks louder.

> ELEVEN (O.S.)
> ... Yes?

> HOPPER
> Can I... uh...
> (winces)
> Speak to you both for a moment?

A beat. Then *eeee*. The door opens up on its own to reveal...

**INT. CABIN - *ELEVEN'S* ROOM - NIGHT**

Eleven and Mike staring up at him from the bed.

Hopper stands in the open doorway. Vulnerable.

He smiles awkwardly. He actually seems... *nervous.*

> HOPPER
> Can, I, uh...?

He crosses to the boombox and hits off the music. He searches for a place to sit, but there's nowhere, *shit!* He grabs a stool, slides it in front of the bed, plops down.

He shifts uncomfortably. The stool is way too small for him.

The kids share looks. This is... *weird.*

> HOPPER (CONT'D)
> Listen. There's -- something I've
> been needing -- wanting to talk to
> you... about --

> MIKE
> Uh-oh I think we're in trouble --

Mike laughs. Eleven giggles. Gosh Mike is SOOO funny!

Hopper looks at Mike. He's triggered now.

He tries to follow Joyce's advice. Keep calm. *Keep. Calm.*

                    HOPPER
          No.  No one's in trouble.  Okay.
          It's... um... it's just...

Mike whispers something in Eleven's ear.  She giggles again.

Hopper can't rein in his anger anymore.  Ya know what...?

                    HOPPER (CONT'D)
               (to Mike)
          Your *mother called.*

Mike looks up at Hopper, surprised.  His smile fades.

                    MIKE
          What -- ?

                    HOPPER
          She wants you home right away.

                    MIKE
          Is everything okay?

                    HOPPER
          I'm afraid not.  No.  It's...

Where is he going with this...?

                    HOPPER (CONT'D)
          Your grandma.

Mike's face drops.  *What?!*

**EXT. CABIN - WOODS - NIGHT**

Hopper stomps through the woods, headed to his Blazer, fuming.

Mike trails, trying to keep up, freaked out.

                    MIKE
          Is she dead -- ??!

                    HOPPER
          No --

                    MIKE
          Does she have cancer -- ??!

                    HOPPER
          No --

                    MIKE
          Did she fall again -- ?

                    HOPPER
          NO --

Hopper throws open the car door and --

**INT. HOPPER'S BLAZER - NIGHT**

Hopper gets in the front seat, Mike passenger.

                    MIKE
          Then I don't understand -- what's
          wrong with Nana --

                    HOPPER
          NOTHING.  NOTHING IS WRONG WITH
          NANA.

                    MIKE
          *What* -- ?

                    HOPPER
          But there is something wrong --
          *very wrong* -- with this --

Hopper waves his arms in Mike's direction --

                    HOPPER (CONT'D)
          -- This *thing* between you and El --

Mike suddenly understands.  He can't believe it!

                    MIKE
          You lying PIECE OF SHIT --

Mike tries to get out of the car but --

CA-CHUNK!  Hopper locks the doors.  Trapping Mike in here.

                    MIKE (CONT'D)
          You're crazy -- !

                    HOPPER
          You wanna see real crazy?
          Disrespect me again.

Mike wilts.  This is a side of Hopper he doesn't know --

And it scares the *shit* out of him.

                    HOPPER (CONT'D)
          *Now.*  This is what's going to
          happen.  I'm going to give you a
          ride back home.  And during this
          ride, I'm going to speak.  And
          you're going to listen.  And maybe,
          *maybe*, if you're lucky, by the end
          of it, I'll allow you to continue
          to date my daughter.

Mike stares.  Stunned.  Speechless.

                    HOPPER (CONT'D)
          ... Nod if you understand.

A hard beat.  Mike swallows.  Takes a breath.  Then *nods*.

Hopper turns away, satisfied.

He hammers the accelerator and --

**EXT. CABIN - NIGHT**

VROOM!  The Blazer ROARS away, tires kicking dirt, and --

**EXT. TOP OF THE HILL - NIGHT**

Stars twinkle in the sky.  We HEAR a familiar call:

                    DUSTIN (O.S.)
          ... Suzie, do you copy?  This is
          your Dustin.  I repeat, Suzie, do
          you copy??

We DROP DOWN the length of the Cerebro antenna mast, until at
last we find Dustin, sitting cross-legged on the grass.  He
sounds... tired.  He's clearly been at this a while.

                    DUSTIN (CONT'D)
          ... Suzie, *do you copy*?

As Dustin continues to call for her, our CAMERA DRIFTS and...

We find the rest of our kids.  They're scattered all across
the hill, sprawled out on their backs, bored out of their
minds.

                    DUSTIN (CONT'D)
          Suzie... do you copy?  Suzie --

Max finally can't take it anymore --

53

                    MAX
          -- Dustin... come on -- she's
          obviously not there --

                    DUSTIN
          She's *there*, okay, she'll pick up --

                    WILL
          Maybe Cerebro doesn't work --

                    LUCAS
          Or maybe *SUZIE* doesn't exist --

Now this really offends Dustin:

                    DUSTIN
          She EXISTS -- !!

                    LUCAS
          Oh yeah?  She's a genius *and* she's
          hotter than Phoebe Cates??  No girl
          is *that* perfect --

                    MAX
          Is that so?

Lucas looks at Max.  Gulps.  He just STEPPED IN IT.

                    LUCAS
          I mean... you're... perfect...  In
          your own... special way...?

                    MAX
          Relax.  I was *teasing*.
               (beat)
          I'm obviously perfect.  And
          Dustin's *obviously* lying.

Max hops up, yanks on her backpack --

                    DUSTIN
          Where are you going -- ??

                    MAX
          -- Home.

She holds out a hand for Lucas.

                    MAX (CONT'D)
          ... Come on, Don Juan.

Lucas smiles and takes her hand, then the couple heads off
together down the hill.  Dustin watches them go.  Sighs.

                    DUSTIN
          ... Well, I guess it's just me and
          you now Byers...

He turns to Will.  His face drops.

Will is pulling on his backpack.  *Leaving too.*

                    WILL
          It's late -- sorry.  Maybe tomorrow
          we  can  play  D&D  or  something...
          fun.  Like we used to.
               (sad smile)
          Welcome home.

On that note, Will walks away, and before we know it --

Dustin is all alone.  Abandoned on this hill.  *Sad.*

                    DUSTIN
          Yeah.  *Welcome home...*

And that's when he hears it: A STATICKY VOICE.

He turns.  It's coming from Cerebro -- holy shit!!

He races over, grabs the receiver!

                    DUSTIN (CONT'D)
          Suzie??!  Is that you??!  Suzie??!

A VOICE breaks through the static again.  Clearer now.

But wait... it's *not Suzie*.  It's not even English.

It's... <u>A RUSSIAN VOICE</u>.

                    RUSSIAN TECH (O.S.)
          <The week is long -- the silver cat
          feeds -- when blue and yellow meet
          in the west -- a trip to China
          sounds nice -- if you tread
          lightly -->

As we PUSH IN on Dustin, his eyes widening, we CRASH TO:

**INT. MYSTERIOUS LOCATION - COMMS ROOM - NIGHT**

A RUSSIAN TECH on the other side.  He's speaking into a
DESKTOP MIC, repeating the same words over and over.  It
sounds like some kind of code:

                    RUSSIAN TECH
          <The week is long -- the silver cat
          feeds -- when blue and yellow meet
          in the west -- a trip to China
          sounds nice -- if you tread
          lightly -->

As this Comm Operator continues to read the code...

Our camera picks up ALEXEI as he walks past the tech and
heads up a flight of steps...

**INT. ANTE ROOM - CONTINUOUS**

He crosses the ante room and enters...

**INT. OBSERVATION ROOM - NIGHT**

A NEW OBSERVATION ROOM. (NOTE: We do not show the machine this time.) He walks up toward the glass windows, where several other scientists have gathered, looking out at something off-camera. Whatever it is, it's...

> SCIENTIST #1
> (to Alexei)
> <... Beautiful, isn't it?>

Alexei nods... But then, as Alexei continues to look out, his expression darkens a bit, *showing some concern*, and right here we CUT TO...

**TO OTHER SIDE OF A GLASS BARRIER.**

Our CAMERA remains angled on Alexei. In the face of the glass, we see the reflection of an INTENSE BLUE ELECTRICAL CURRENT. *The machine is going again.*

And we also hear something. A familiar ROAR.

<u>A NEW GATE IS OPENING</u>.

The ROAR grows louder. And louder. And...

**INT. WHEELER HOUSE - MASTER BATHROOM - NIGHT**

WHOOSH! A hair dryer blows as...

Karen, freshly showered, dries off her hair.

**INT. WHEELER HOUSE - MASTER BATHROOM - NIGHT**

Karen gets ready for a *wild night* in front of a mirror.

-- She runs a hand through her hair.

-- Adjusts a sexy dress.

-- Puts on makeup.

-- Sprays on perfume.

**INT. WHEELER HOUSE - STAIRS - NIGHT**

Karen hurries downstairs, nervous but excited.

She is almost to the front door when she pauses.  She hears
something... familiar.  It's the sound of... SNORING.

**INT. WHEELER HOUSE - TV ROOM - NIGHT**

Karen steps into the living room.  She looks over at --

TED.  He is fast asleep on his La-Z-Boy.  We TILT DOWN to
reveal that HOLLY is lying on his stomach, sleeping too.  Her
tiny body rises and falls with each snore.  *Rises and
falls...*

Off Karen, now *wavering*, we CRASH TO:

**EXT. COUNTRY ROAD - NIGHT**

VROOOOM!  Billy's Camaro ROARS past camera.

**INT. BILLY'S CAMARO - NIGHT**

Billy rocks out to MUSIC.  He bops his head, taps the wheel,
excited.  He checks himself out in the rearview mirror --

>               BILLY
>     "Hey Karen -- you don't mind if I
>     call you Karen now, do you?  Good,
>     cause --

BOOM!  SOMETHING LARGE AND DARK SUDDENLY STRIKES THE
WINDSHIELD OF HIS CAR WITH A SHRIEK -- SOME KIND OF
"CREATURE" -- THE GLASS SPLINTERS --

Billy startles, swerves the wheel, and --

**EXT. OVERGROWN FIELD - NIGHT**

WHOOM!  His car flies off the road and onto a field --

Blows through a line of tall weeds and --

BAM!  Smashes into a *POWER LINE*!

**INT. BILLY'S CAMARO - NIGHT**

Billy's head strikes the window and --

**EXT. OVERGROWN FIELD - NIGHT**

The car skids to a stop.  The RADIO STUTTERS, cuts out.

Looming behind the car, a familiar location:

THE ABANDONED FACTORY.

**INT. BILLY'S CAMARO - NIGHT**

Billy blinks, disoriented.  He touches the side of his head.

He finds a deep cut, spilling blood.

> BILLY
> Ah, shit...

He unbuckles his seatbelt and --

**EXT. OVERGROWN FIELD - NIGHT**

Billy stumbles out of the car.  Groggy.  His face drops.

The side of his beautiful car is crumpled.  *Ruined.*

> BILLY
> *ShitshitshitSHIT!*

*How the hell did this happen?*  His gaze shifts to the broken
windshield.  His eyes narrow.  There is *something* on the
broken glass.  Some kind of a... DARK SUBSTANCE.

He reaches out, touches it.  The dark substance is --

Wet and sticky.  Whatever it is... it's not blood.

CHCHCHCCKCKCK!  *SOMETHING* SKITTERS BEHIND BILLY!

He whirls around.  Freaked.  Sees only darkness.

> BILLY (CONT'D)
> Who's there???  Who's there??

No answer.  It's deathly silent out here.

CHCHCHCCKCKCK!  It's behind him now.

Billy whirls again.

> BILLY (CONT'D)
> I SAID WHO'S -- ??!

WHOOM!  A FLESHY TENTACLE WRAPS AROUND BILLY'S ANKLE AND --

HE'S YANKED!  HE FLIPS ONTO THE GROUND FACE FIRST AND --

WHOOSH!  HE'S SUCKED BACKWARDS AT A HIGH VELOCITY -- FLYING
BACKWARDS -- WHIPPING THROUGH BRUSH AND OVER DIRT --

HE FLAILS AND SCREAMS AS --

**INT. ABANDONED FACTORY - NIGHT**

He's dragged into the factory over to A BASEMENT DOOR.

He grabs onto the sides of the door.  Trying to hold on.

But whatever is pulling him is too strong and --

HE'S VIOLENTLY SUCKED BACK DOWN THE STEPS.

As he vanishes into the darkness, we --

<u>END EPISODE</u>

# CHAPTER TWO:
## THE MALL RATS

WRITTEN BY **THE DUFFER BROTHERS**

**EXT. ABANDONED FACTORY - NIGHT 3 CONT'D**

Stars wink in the sky.  We HEAR the FAINT DRONE OF MUSIC.

We TILT DOWN to find Billy's wrecked car.  It is still where
we last saw it, windshield smashed, the RADIO still playing,
skipping a bit.  We DRIFT PAST the car TOWARD the factory.

We hear a STRANGE SHRIEKING SOUND.  Then a POUNDING NOISE.
Like a METALLIC HEARTBEAT.  It grows louder and LOUDER and --

BOOM!  The factory door suddenly EXPLODES open and --

BILLY STUMBLES OUT!  STILL ALIVE.

He's pale and covered in sweat and gunk.  He trips, stumbles
to the ground, then looks back in horror at the door to this
place.  Nothing comes out.  Just darkness and silence.

He scrambles back to his feet and --

**INT./EXT. BILLY'S CAMARO - NIGHT**

WHOOM!  Billy leaps into his crashed Camaro.

Dirt flies as the car escapes the factory and --

**EXT. COUNTRY ROAD - PHONE BOOTH - LATER - NIGHT**

Billy's busted Camaro SCREECHES to a halt beside --

A RURAL PHONE BOOTH.

Billy staggers into the phone booth, grabs coins from his
pocket.  His hands are shaking so bad he drops the coins.

He finally gets them in, dials 911.

BRRRING BRRRING --

                    911 OPERATOR VOICE (OVER PHONE)
          911, what's your emergency -- ?

Billy is about to speak.  Then his voice catches as --

**WE CUT TO QUICK FLASHES OF NIGHTMARISH IMAGERY**

-- *BILLY IS YANKED BACKWARDS INTO THE FACTORY* --

-- *HE'S DRAGGED INTO THE MURKY BASEMENT* --

-- *RATS SHRIEK AND SCURRY AROUND HIM* --

-- *A FLESH-LIKE ORGANISM DARTS TOWARD HIM* --

*-- BILLY SCREAMS IN HORROR AND --*

**BACK TO THE PRESENT**

> 911 OPERATOR VOICE (OVER PHONE)
> Hello?  Is anyone there?  Hello?

Billy hesitates when --

The light in the phone booth begins to STUTTER.

He looks up at the light... then notices something else --

Something through the door of the phone booth.

He drops the phone.  It dangles, swinging.

> 911 OPERATOR VOICE (OVER PHONE)(CONT'D)
> *Hello??  Is someone there?  Hello?*

**EXT. COUNTRY ROAD - PHONE BOOTH (THE UPSIDE DOWN) - MOMENTS LATER**

EEEEE.  The phone booth door creaks open and...

Billy steps outside.  Wind blows, spores drift, fog lilts. He's in THE UPSIDE DOWN.  Before him, through a dense curtain of fog, he can make out...

A DOZEN SHADOWS.  *HUMAN* SHADOWS.  STANDING ON THE OTHER SIDE OF THE ROAD.  NOT MOVING.  JUST... STARING UNNERVINGLY AT BILLY.

Billy shouts at them.  Scared.  Crying:

> BILLY
> What do you want -- ??!  What do you
> want?!??!  WHAT DO YOU WANT??

The shadows begin to walk toward Billy...

Moving at the same speed...

And right here we --

SMASH TO:

**MAIN TITLES**

**EXT. HOPPER'S CABIN - DAY 4**

The morning sun peeks out from behind trees.  We TILT DOWN to find...

ELEVEN, pacing on the porch.  She appears a little distressed.  Her eyes look out toward the woods but --

There's no one there.

**INT. CABIN - DAY**

Eleven bursts back inside the cabin.

HOPPER looks up from a BOWL OF CEREAL.  Feigns concern.

> HOPPER
> Everything okay?

> ELEVEN
> (no)
> Yes.

Eleven grabs a CORDED PHONE off the wall.

**INT. WHEELER HOUSE - KITCHEN - DAY**

An anxious KAREN packs up a TOTE BAG with pool items when --

BRRRING!  The phone rings.  Karen answers, puts on a smile.

> KAREN
> Hello, this is the Wheelers!

She listens, then cups the receiver to her shoulder, shouts:

> KAREN (CONT'D)
> MICHAEL!  PHONE!

**INT. WHEELER HOUSE - BASEMENT - DAY**

Mike paces in the basement, anxious.

> MIKE
> OKAY!!!!

His eyes go to the BASEMENT PHONE.  Wide with terror.  But he gathers his composure.  Walks up to the phone.  And...

Answers.

> MIKE (CONT'D)
> ... Hello?

**INT. CABIN - INTERCUT**

Eleven is surprised to hear his voice.

She carries the phone into --

**INT. CABIN - ELEVEN'S ROOM - INTERCUT**

> ELEVEN
> It's nine thirty-two -- where are
> you?

**INT. WHEELER HOUSE - BASEMENT - INTERCUT**

Mike twists the phone cord, fidgeting nervously.

> MIKE
> Yeah -- sorry.  I was just about to
> call -- I uh...
> (winces)
> Can't see you today.

**INT. CABIN - ELEVEN'S ROOM - INTERCUT**

Eleven goes white with shock.  *WHAT?*

> ELEVEN
> Why... not?

> MIKE
> Oh, uh -- it's uh -- see -- my Nana --
> she's, uh, very sick --

Eleven narrows her eyes, confused.

> ELEVEN
> Hop... he said your Nana was okay.
> That it was... "false alarm."

**INT. WHEELER HOUSE - BASEMENT - INTERCUT**

Mike turns pale -- he wasn't expecting this!

> MIKE
> Oh, I mean, we thought it was, yeah,
> a false alarm -- but then, uh, she
> took like a real *turn for the worse.*

> ELEVEN
> Oh...

> MIKE
> Yeah, I mean, I think she might...
> *die.*

> KAREN VOICE (OVER PHONE)
> -- *WHAT* -- ?

Mike gasps.  He cups the receiver to his shoulder and shouts:

                    MIKE
          MOM GET OFF THE PHONE!!!  HOW MANY
          TIMES!!!

**INT. WHEELER HOUSE - KITCHEN - INTERCUT**

Karen is still on the other end.

                    KAREN
              *DID NANA CALL?!!*

                    MIKE
          NO MOM!  JUST -- GET OFF THE PHONE!!!

Karen hangs up the phone, totally confused, and --

**INT. WHEELER HOUSE - BASEMENT - INTERCUT**

Mike uncups the receiver, forces a laugh.

                    MIKE
          Sorry about that --

                    ELEVEN
          Was that -- your mom?

                    MIKE
          Yeah -- she's so upset she's making
          no sense.  Because, see, we have to
          go the nursing home now -- to see
          Nana --

**INT. CABIN - ELEVEN'S ROOM - INTERCUT**

Eleven narrows her eyes, skeptical.

                    ELEVEN
          You can come over... after?

                    MIKE
          No!  I mean -- I just -- I think I
          need to be alone today... with my
          feelings?

Eleven is *very* skeptical now.  *Something's* going on.

                    ELEVEN
          Do you... lie?

**INT. WHEELER HOUSE - BASEMENT - INTERCUT**

                    MIKE
          What??  No!  Friends -- don't lie.
               (pretends to hear something)
               (MORE)

MIKE (CONT'D)
What MOM?!
(back to phone)
My mom's calling for me -- better go,
talk tomorrow miss you already bye!

WHAM!  Mike quickly hangs up the phone and --

**INT. CABIN - ELEVEN'S ROOM - DAY**

EEEEEE.  DIAL TONE.  Eleven stares at the dead phone in
shock.

**INT. WHEELER HOUSE - BASEMENT - DAY**

Mike slams his head into the wall with a GROAN as --

**INT. CABIN - DAY**

Eleven hangs the phone back up.  Stunned.

Hopper looks over at her.  Feigns more concern.

HOPPER
What's going on?  El?

Eleven doesn't answer.  She just strides back into her room
and --

WHOOM!  She slams the door behind her with her powers.

Hopper's "concern" promptly drops, morphing into excitement!
As he munches cereal, *victorious*, Jim Croce begins to BLAST
and...

**INT./EXT. HOPPER'S BLAZER - ROAD - DAY**

Hopper drives, pounding the steering wheel, singing loudly:

HOPPER
"... *You don't tug on Superman's cape*
*You don't spit into the wind*
*You don't pull the mask off that old*
*lone ranger and YOU DON'T MESS AROUND*
*WITH JIM!!!*"

**EXT. MELVALD'S GENERAL STORE - DAY**

Hopper's Blazer swerves up to the general store and --

**INT. MELVALD'S GENERAL STORE - DAY**

DING!  Hopper strides into Melvald's, in the best mood *ever*.

He twirls, shouts dramatically as he enters:

                    HOPPER
          EMOTIONS HAVE BEEN SHARED.
          BOUNDARIES HAVE BEEN SET.  *ORDER.*
          *HAS.  BEEN.  RESTORED.*

JOYCE stands up, excited in spite of herself.

                    JOYCE
          It worked??

                    HOPPER
          Today will be the *first day* they
          won't see each other in six long,
          *excruciating* months.  So yeah, oh
          yeah -- I'd say it worked.

Joyce applauds.  Hopper applauds right back at Joyce.

                    HOPPER (CONT'D)
          No no, it's all you, *all you*.  I'm
          just a -- a puppet.  You're the
          master.

Hopper drops beside Joyce at her counter.  He lights up a
cigarette.

                    JOYCE
          So you remembered everything?

                    HOPPER
          Yeah, yeah.  I mean I had to
          improvise a little.  Turns out it was
          *Mike* -- getting to Mike was the key.

                    JOYCE
          You didn't yell at him did you -- ?

                    HOPPER
               (ducking question)
          I'll tell you all about it tonight --
          I was thinking Enzo's, seven o'clock?

Joyce is about to respond, but Hopper holds up a hand --

                    HOPPER (CONT'D)
          Before you say no, just hear me out,
          okay?  Because I feel I need to make
          something clear: This isn't a date.

Joyce's eyes shoot wide with shock --

                    JOYCE
          Date?!  I -- I never said anything
          about a date --

                    HOPPER
          Neither did I!  I'm just *clarifying*
          in case there was any confusion on
          your part --

                    JOYCE
          There's not -- !

                    HOPPER
          Then *come on* -- let's have a
          scrumptious dinner.  We've earned it,
          haven't we?

Joyce sighs.  *Is she breaking?*

                    JOYCE
          I -- I just -- I really can't be out
          late --

                    HOPPER
          You'll be home by nine.

                    JOYCE
          *Eight* --

                    HOPPER
          Eight-thirty.  I'll pick you up --

                    JOYCE
          I'll meet you there.

                    HOPPER
          <u>Deal</u>.  Seven.  Enzo's.  Meeting
          there.

Hopper's radio SQUAWKS.

                    POWELL'S VOICE (OVER RADIO)
          Hey Chief, you copy?  Chief?

Hopper answers.

                    HOPPER
          Yeah I'm a little busy here --

**EXT. HAWKINS TOWN HALL - DAY**

OFFICER POWELL is standing outside TOWN HALL.  A CROWD OF
ANGRY PROTESTORS shout behind him, waving HAND-DRAWN SIGNS.

*What in God's name is going on?*

                              69

                        POWELL
                     (into radio)
            Yeah well I'm *busier here* -- you
            still want your job tomorrow, I think
            you better get your ass to town hall.

**INT. MELVALD'S GENERAL STORE - DAY**

Hopper looks at Joyce with a shrug.

                              HOPPER
                    Duty calls.

Hopper leaps off the counter and heads for the door.  But
then -- he suddenly slides on something, almost tripping!

                         HOPPER (CONT'D)
                    Uh-oh -- clean up on aisle five!

And with that, Hopper heads out, still beaming.

Joyce can't help but smile a little, but then --

Her smiles fades.  Her eyes narrow.

**MOMENTS LATER**

Joyce kneels down.  Hopper nearly tripped on:

A PILE OF FALLEN MAGNETS.   ON THE FLOOR BY A DISPLAY STAND.

She picks them up, rolls them around in her hand, suddenly
concerned.  She places one back up on the freezer, but --

It drops right off.  She tries another one.  Same thing.

*They're de-magnetized...*

We PUSH IN on Joyce, mind now racing...

**INT. HAWKINS POST - KITCHEN - DAY**

WHOOSH!  Coffee pours into a MUG.

WIDEN: NANCY is making coffee at the Hawkins Post.

As she pours she looks over her notebook.  The words:
"DRISCOLL."  "4819 CORNWALLIS ROAD."  "RATS."  Suddenly --

The coffee begins to spill over the mug --

                              NANCY
                    Shit shit -- !

BRUCE watches with a pleased grin.

                              BRUCE
                    Careful there, Nancy Drew, *careful.*

Nancy forces a smile.  Then --

**INT. HAWKINS POST - TOM'S OFFICE - DAY**

Nancy strides into Tom's Office, places down the coffee.

> NANCY
> And *here you are* -- two creams, two
> sugars --

Tom looks up from a newspaper, flashes a smile.

> TOM
> Thanks, sweetheart.

> NANCY
> Of course.

Nancy starts to head out, then turns back.

> NANCY (CONT'D)
> Tom?

Tom looks up from his paper --

> NANCY (CONT'D)
> I... really hate to ask this, but...
> do you think maybe one of the other
> girls could grab lunch today?

Tom hesitates.

> TOM
> -- We need them at their desks --

> NANCY
> I know, I know.  It's just -- I
> really need to see the doctor.  I'm
> having some...

She steps forward.  Lowers her voice.

> NANCY (CONT'D)
> ... *Girl problems.*

Tom swallows his coffee down the wrong pipe and --

**INT. HAWKINS POST - PHOTOGRAPHY ROOM - DAY**

WHOOM!  Nancy bursts into Jonathan's dark room, once again
*obliterating* his developing photo with light.  Jonathan
groans --

But Nancy doesn't even notice -- she's in mission mode now.

                    NANCY
          Let's go.

**EXT. HAWKINS MAIN STREET - "POST" OFFICES - DAY**

WHOOM!  A door flies open to Hawkins and Nancy and Jonathan
hustle out.  Jonathan's FILM CAMERA now hangs from his neck.

He struggles to keep up as Nancy hurries down the sidewalk.

                    JONATHAN
          I just -- I don't know if this is
          such a good idea anymore --

                    NANCY
          Really?  Because I think it's the
          best idea I've had all summer --

                    JONATHAN
          All I'm saying is -- what harm is
          there in asking -- ?

                    NANCY
          The harm is Tom will say *no*.  We ask
          for forgiveness -- not permission.
          And if this story is as good as I
          think it is -- Tom won't care.  In
          fact, he'll *thank* us --

                    JONATHAN
          Yeah.  *Or* this old lady is nuts and
          the story blows up in our face and
          Tom *fires us* --

                    NANCY
          -- and then we never have to work at
          this shithole again --

Nancy flashes a smile, then climbs into his car.

Jonathan sighs, climbs in after her and --

**INT. STARCOURT MALL - DAY - ESTABLISHING**

SHOPPERS hustle through the mall.

**INT. SCOOPS AHOY! - DAY**

DING!  ROBIN passes a cone to a HAPPY CUSTOMER.

                    ROBIN
          Have a nice day!

The Customer walks away to REVEAL --

DUSTIN!  The next in line!  He flashes his patented smile.

                    DUSTIN
          Hi!

                    ROBIN
          Hi?

                    DUSTIN
          I'm Dustin!

                    ROBIN
          I'm... Robin?

                    DUSTIN
          Pleasure to meet you.  Is he... here?

                    ROBIN
          Is... *who* here?

                    STEVE (O.S.)
          -- Henderson???

STEVE suddenly pops out from the back.  He can't believe it!!

He races around the counter and performs a SECRET HANDSHAKE!

                    STEVE (CONT'D)
          You're back!!!

                    DUSTIN
          I'm back!!!  You got the job!!

                    STEVE
          I got the job!!

Robin stares at Steve.

                    ROBIN
          How many children are you friends
          with??

**INT. SCOOPS AHOY! - DAY - LATER**

THUNK!  A spoon plunges into an *ICE COLD* BANANA SPLIT.

WIDEN TO REVEAL: Steve and Dustin catching up in Scoops!
They're seated in the "boat" booth at the front of the store.

                    STEVE
          -- Hotter than *Phoebe Cates* -- ????

                    DUSTIN
          Brilliant too -- and she doesn't even
          care that my real pearls are still
          coming in.  She says my kissing is
          even *better* without teeth --

Dustin smiles wide.  Steve winces -- he didn't need to hear
that, but --

> STEVE
> I'm proud of you, dude, really proud.
> That's just, like -- *wow*.

Dustin nods, devours a giant spoonful of ice cream.  Then, through a full mouth:

> DUSTIN
> -- Can you really eat as much of this
> as you want???

> STEVE
> I mean, sure -- it's just not, like,
> a good idea.  Gotta stay in shape for
> the ladies --

Robin calls out from behind the counter:

> ROBIN
> Yeah, and how's that working out for
> you??

> STEVE
> Ignore her.

> DUSTIN
> She seems cool.

> STEVE
> She's not.
>      (quickly changes subjects)
> Where are the knuckleheads?

Dustin darkens at the mention of his friends.

> DUSTIN
> They ditched me yesterday.  My *first
> day back* -- you believe that -- ?

> STEVE
> Seriously -- ?

Dustin nods, devours another giant spoonful.

> DUSTIN
> But they're gonna *regret it* -- *gonna
> regret it* <u>*BIG TIME*</u> when they don't
> get to share in my glory.

> STEVE
> Glory?  What glory?

Dustin looks around, suddenly paranoid.  It's actually a little bit crowded in here.  He turns back to Steve.

                    DUSTIN
          Last night, I was trying to contact
          Suzie, when...

Dustin leans forward, whispers very low:

                    DUSTIN (CONT'D)
          *I intercepted a secret Russian*
          *communication.*

                    STEVE
          What?

                    DUSTIN
          *I intercepted a secret Russian*
          *communication.*

                    STEVE
          Dude, just speak louder --

                    DUSTIN
          I INTERCEPTED A SECRET RUSSIAN
          COMMUNICATION.

                    STEVE
          Yeah, okay, that's what I thought you
          said -- I still don't understand what
          it means.

                    DUSTIN
          It means, Steve, we could be heroes --
          *true American heroes.*

                    STEVE
          "American heroes" -- ?

                    DUSTIN
          *Yup.  Just think.*  You'll get all the
          ladies you want -- and more.

Steve considers.  He likes the sound of this.  But --

                    STEVE
          What's the catch?

                    DUSTIN
          No catch.  I just need your help --

                    STEVE
          With *what*?

Dustin digs into backpack again, pulls out --

A RUSSIAN-TO-ENGLISH DICTIONARY.


                             77

                              DUSTIN
                    Translation.

He slams the dictionary down onto the table and --

**EXT. MAX'S HOUSE - DAY**

WHOOSH!  Rubber wheels fly across cement as --

MAX skateboards outside her house.  She practices an ollie.
Misses.  Tries again when -- ZOOP!  The board suddenly *sucks
away* from her.  Max whirls around, stunned, watching as --

The skateboard shoots down the street and --

CRASHES INTO A PAIR OF FAMILIAR SNEAKERS.

The sneakers kick the board, popping it into the hands of --

ELEVEN!  Max stares.  Shocked to see her here.

                              ELEVEN
                    ... Hi.

                              MAX
                    ... Hi?

Eleven walks up to Max.  Hands her skateboard back.  Then...

                              ELEVEN
                    Can we... talk?

Off Max, SMASH TO:

**INT. MAX'S HOUSE - MAX'S ROOM - DAY**

Max pacing in her room.  Listening as --

Eleven recounts her story from this morning.

                              ELEVEN
                    And then -- he said he misses me --
                    and... hung up --

                              MAX
                    Well... he's a piece of shit.

                              ELEVEN
                    What -- ?

                              78

                    MAX
          Mike doesn't have jack shit to do
          today and his Nana obviously isn't
          sick.  I *guarantee you* he's playing
          Nintendo with Lucas right now.

                    ELEVEN
          But... friends don't lie.

                    MAX
          Yeah well -- *boyfriends* lie.  All.
          The.  Time.

**INT. WHEELER HOUSE - BASEMENT - DAY**

                    MIKE
          -- She knows I'm lying.  SHE KNOWS
          I'M LYING!

Mike paces in the basement. *Stressed.* LUCAS is listening to
him, concerned for his friend.  WILL, meanwhile, is setting
up a D&D game at the table, not interested *in the least*.

                    LUCAS
          I don't even understand -- *why lie*??

                    MIKE
          Hopper, he -- he *threatened* me --

                    LUCAS
          Did he say he'd kill you -- ?

                    MIKE
          What?!  No -- !

                    LUCAS
          So then what's the big deal -- ?

                    MIKE
          The *big deal* is if I don't do what he
          says, he'll stop me from seeing El!
          Like -- *permanently*.  I mean you
          don't understand, Lucas -- he's crazy
          -- he's LOST HIS MIND --

Will looks up from the game.

                    WILL
          Hey guys, I'm almost set up here --

Mike ignores Will, keeps talking to Lucas.

                    MIKE
          I had no choice, Lucas, I mean -- I
          really had <u>no choice</u> -- !

                    LUCAS
          I just wish you had consulted me.
          Because the way you handled this --
          you're in <u>DEEP SHIT</u>.

**INT. MAX'S HOUSE - MAX'S ROOM - DAY**

Max marches in front of Eleven like a drill sergeant.

                    MAX
          -- You're going to stop calling him.
          You're going to ignore *his* calls.  As
          far as you're concerned, he <u>doesn't</u>
          <u>exist</u> --

                    ELEVEN
          Doesn't... *exist* --

                    MAX
          -- He treated you like garbage,
          you're going to treat *him* like
          garbage.  Give him a taste of his own
          medicine --

Eleven is getting into this now.

                    ELEVEN
          Give him... *the medicine.*

                    MAX
          And if he doesn't fix this -- if he
          doesn't *explain himself* -- <u>DUMP HIS</u>
          <u>ASS</u>.

**INT. WHEELER HOUSE - BASEMENT - DAY**

Mike puts his head in his hands.

                    MIKE
          Ahggggh --

                    LUCAS
          It's gonna be bad -- I'm not gonna
          lie --

                    MIKE
          Ahghghgh --

                    LUCAS
          -- But you can *fix it*.  It's one
          little mistake -- I've made *hundreds*.
          Thousands!  Max has dumped me five
          times!

Lucas holds up five fingers.

                    LUCAS (CONT'D)
          But what have I done?  Huh?  Have I
          despaired?  No.  I've marched back
          into battle and I've won her back.
          Every.  Single.  Time.

Lucas curls his five fingers into a POWER FIST.

Mike feels a burst of hope.

                    MIKE
          ... How?

Lucas grins.

                    LUCAS
          I'll show you.  Come on --

Lucas grabs Mike and hauls him off the couch as --

**INT. MAX'S HOUSE - MAX'S ROOM - DAY**

Max lifts Eleven up off the bed --

                    ELEVEN
          Where -- where are we going?

                    MAX
          -- To *have* some *fun*.  There's more to
          life than stupid boys, you know!

As Max pulls Eleven out of the room --

**INT. WHEELER HOUSE - BASEMENT - DAY**

Mike and Lucas race up the basement steps, leaving --

Will alone with his game.  They forgot him!

                    WILL
          Hey guys -- I'm still here!  Guys?!

No answer.  Will sighs.  He hurries after his friends and --

**EXT. HAWKINS POOL - DAY**

EEEEE!!!  A WHISTLE BLOWS loudly as --

HEATHER (the lifeguard) yells at some ROWDY BOYS:

> HEATHER
> HEY!  NO DUNKING, CURTIS!!

**ON THE OTHER SIDE OF THE POOL,**

THE GAGGLE OF MOTHERS shoot daggers at Heather.

> MOM #2
> God, even her *voice* annoys me --

> MOM #3
> Nails on a chalkboard --

> MOM #1
> Don't worry, ladies -- just ten
> minutes till showtime.  Would you
> get my back, Liz?

As Mom #2 helps Mom #1 put on suntan lotion, we find...

Karen.  She looks distracted.  *Nervous.*  Suddenly -- her eyes
narrow.  She sees Billy walking through the pool house
breezeway.  He's headed into some kind of a supply room.

She looks at Mom #3.

> KAREN
> Jill, I -- I have to run to the
> restroom -- would you keep an eye on
> Holly for me?

> MOM #3
> Sure thing, hon.

**INT. HAWKINS POOL - POOL HOUSE - DAY - A MINUTE LATER**

We PULL AWAY from a POOL CHEMICALS SIGN to find...

Karen entering the supply room.  A LARGE POOL PUMP *CHURNS* AND
*GROANS*.  She doesn't see Billy.

> KAREN
> ... *Billy?*

She enters an open door, and...

**INT. HAWKINS POOL - STORAGE ROOM - DAY**

... Finds Billy. He's standing on the far end of this
storage room with his back turned toward us.

>                    KAREN
>      ... Billy...? What are you doing?

We now cut to Billy's face in EXTREME CLOSE-UP. He seems to
be in some kind of trance-like daze. We remain in this
unnerving CLOSE-UP of Billy as --

Karen walks toward him. Her voice sounds DISTANT, hollow.

>                KAREN (CONT'D)
>      I... understand if you're angry at
>      me. I just -- I wanted to explain...

Another step. Closer.

>                KAREN (CONT'D)
>      ... Why I didn't come last night...

Another step. *Closer.*

>                KAREN (CONT'D)
>      It's not you, it's just... I have a
>      family...

Another step. Closer still.

>                KAREN (CONT'D)
>      And... I can't do anything that will
>      hurt them. You understand that,
>      right? But... I shouldn't have said
>      I would. Yesterday. It -- it was a
>      mistake, and... I'm sorry. I'm so
>      sorry.

Another step. She's right behind him now.

>                KAREN (CONT'D)
>      Billy, please -- will you talk to me?

Billy suddenly turns around. Looks at Karen.

His eyes are bloodshot. Scary. Then, in a flash --

HE GRABS KAREN AND SLAMS HER HEAD INTO A SHELF AND --

WE JUMP BACK OUT INTO A WIDE SHOT TO REVEAL:

It was a vision. Karen is fine. Standing in front of Billy.

Billy fights back his desire to enact this vision.

Then, through gritted teeth:

> BILLY
> Stay away from me.

> KAREN
> Billy --

> BILLY
> Stay away.

He strides forward, shoving past Karen, and --

**EXT. HAWKINS POOL - BREEZEWAY - DAY**

Billy pushes through the crowd and...

Steps outside. He winces. Looks up. The sun burns bright in the cloudless sky. Sweat percolates on his skin.

Heather approaches him and speaks, but her voice is DISTANT, barely there. Billy forces a nod, continues his walk.

The Gaggle of Moms wave excitedly at him --

> MOMS
> Afternoon Billy -- !

But their VOICES SOUND DISTORTED too. Nightmarish.

**MOMENTS LATER**

Billy sinks into the empty lifeguard chair.

Sweat pours down his face as above him...

THE SUN GROWS HOTTER AND HOTTER AND --

**INT. SCOOPS AHOY! - FRONT COUNTER - DAY**

THUNK! A plastic spoon dives into ICE CREAM.

Robin passes the spoon to ERICA. She tastes it. Considers.

> ERICA
> Hmmm. Can I try the peppermint
> stick?

> ROBIN
> You've already tried the peppermint
> stick --

                    ERICA
          Yes and I'd like to try it *again*.

Robin sighs, looks over at the back room.  Door shut.

                    ROBIN
               STEVE!!!

**INT. SCOOPS AHOY! - BACK ROOM - DAY**

Steve hears Robin, ignores her.  He's pacing, listening to --

Dustin's TAPE RECORDER.  He's playing the RECORDING from last
night.  The RUSSIAN VOICE goes on for an additional five
seconds, then there is a strange burst of TINNY MUSIC...

Dustin hits STOP.  Looks at Steve expectantly.

                    DUSTIN
          So, what do you think -- ?

                    STEVE
          Sounded familiar --

                    DUSTIN
          What -- ?

                    STEVE
          The music -- there was some music
          there, right at the end --

                    DUSTIN
          Why are you listening to the music??
          Listen to the *Russian* -- THE RUSSIAN
          -- !

WHOOM!  Robin suddenly flings open the door, *not happy.*

                    ROBIN
               (to Steve)
          Alright, babysitting time's over --
          you need to get out there --

Robin suddenly gasps.

                    ROBIN (CONT'D)
          My board!

She races over to her WHITE BOARD.  The "You Suck" tally has
been totally erased, replaced with the RUSSIAN ALPHABET.

She whips back to Dustin and Steve.

                    ROBIN (CONT'D)
          That was *important* data, shitbirds --

                    DUSTIN
          I *guarantee* you what we're doing is
          more important --

                    ROBIN
          Yeah?  And how do you know these
          Russians are up to no good anyway?

The boys share looks.  Dustin whispers to Steve:

                    DUSTIN
          How does she know about the Russians?

                    STEVE
          I don't know --

                    ROBIN
          Hello??!  I can hear you!!

The boys snap back to Robin.

                    ROBIN (CONT'D)
          In fact, I can hear *everything* --
          you're both extremely loud.  You
          think you've got evil Russians
          plotting against our country on tape
          and you're trying to translate but
          you don't have a single word figured
          out because you didn't realize
          Russians have a different alphabet
          than we do.  Does that sound about
          right?

The boys are speechless.  *Were they really that loud??*

Robin walks over and reaches out for the tape recorder but --

Steve yanks it away --

                    STEVE
          What are you doing -- ?

                    ROBIN
          I want to hear it --

                    STEVE/DUSTIN
          Why -- ?

                    ROBIN
          Because maybe I can help. I'm fluent
          in four languages you know --

                    DUSTIN
          Russian??

                    ROBIN
          *Ouyay areyay umbday.*

Dustin and Steve share amazed looks.

                    DUSTIN
          *Holy shit.*

Robin rolls her eyes.

                    ROBIN
          That was *pig latin,* dingus.  But I
          can speak Spanish and French and
          Italian and I was in band for twelve
          years.  My ears are *little geniuses,*
          trust me.

She holds out a hand for the tape.  Steve hesitates.

                    ROBIN (CONT'D)
          Come on -- your turn to sling ice
          cream, my turn to translate.  I don't
          even want credit -- I'm just bored.

Steve looks at Dustin.  Dustin hesitates.  *Why not?*

Steve sighs, tosses Robin the cassette.

As her hand SNATCHES it --

**EXT. DRISCOLL FARMHOUSE - DAY**

Beautiful, rolling farmland.  Jonathan's car pulls up a
driveway, headed toward...

A DECREPIT AND SOMEWHAT CREEPY FARMHOUSE.

**EXT. DRISCOLL FARMHOUSE - FRONT PORCH - DAY**

Nancy KNOCKS on the wooden door.

The door CREAKS open.  A small old lady pokes out.  This
is...

                    NANCY
          Missus Driscoll?

MRS. DRISCOLL, 80s, blinks, confused.

                    MRS. DRISCOLL
          Yes...?

                    NANCY
          I'm Nancy -- Nancy Wheeler.  We spoke
          briefly on the phone last night --

                    JONATHAN
          We're from the Hawkins Post --

                    MRS. DRISCOLL
          Oh -- oh!  My goodness, yes.  My --
          you two look young for reporters.

                    JONATHAN
          We get that a lot.

The teens smile.  And then --

**INT. DRISCOLL FARMHOUSE - DAY**

Mrs. Driscoll leads the teens through her house.  Hobbling.
It's dark in here, dusty, *old*.  The floorboards MOAN.

                    NANCY
          ... Do you live here all alone?

Mrs. Driscoll nods.

                    MRS. DRISCOLL
          Jack -- my husband -- he passed away,
          my, what's it been now?  Ten years.

                    NANCY
          Oh -- I'm sorry --

                    MRS. DRISCOLL
          Don't be.  In truth, I don't mind the
          quiet.  I find it calming.

Mrs. Driscoll stops by a basement door.

                    MRS. DRISCOLL (CONT'D)
          At least... I *did*.

She opens the door.  It CREAKS.

                    MRS. DRISCOLL (CONT'D)
          ... This way.

Mrs. Driscoll ambles down into a creepy-looking basement.

Nancy and Jonathan share looks.  Then follow.

**INT. DRISCOLL FARMHOUSE - BASEMENT - DAY**

Jonathan and Nancy step down into the dark basement.

Mrs. Driscoll yanks a chain, lights the space.

                    MRS. DRISCOLL
          It's right over there...

Nancy and Jonathan follow her gaze, stepping toward...

A PILE OF SHREDDED PLASTIC BAGS SHOVED INTO THE CORNER.

Nancy kneels down.  Lifts up a bag.  It's... *FERTILIZER*.

The bag has been torn open.  *Shredded*.  The fertilizer gone.

                    MRS. DRISCOLL (CONT'D)
          You see their little teeth marks
          there, don't you?

Nancy inspects the bag.  Sure enough, looks like teeth marks.

CHOOM!  Jonathan snaps a photo, startling Nancy.

Nancy turns back to Mrs. Driscoll.

                    NANCY
          And these bags -- you're *sure* they
          were full before?

                    MRS. DRISCOLL
          I'm old, honey, not senile.  Bought
          'em at Blackburn's Supply, not last
          Tuesday.

Nancy jots this down.  *Blackburn's Supply.*

                    MRS. DRISCOLL (CONT'D)
          Now you tell me -- why would rats eat
          a poor old woman's fertilizer?

                    NANCY
          Are you sure they did?  Maybe they
          just... gnawed on the bag.  Eating
          fertilizer seems --

                    MRS. DRISCOLL
          *Crazy*.  Believe me -- I know, honey.
          And a normal rat, I'd agree.  But
          something's not right with *these*
          *rats*.

                    NANCY
          What does that mean, exactly?  "Not
          right"?

                    MRS. DRISCOLL
          Rabies, my guess.  That's why I
          thought, "Now Doris, you better call
          the paper -- if there are diseased
          rats on the loose, the people, they
          oughta know" -- wouldn't you agree?

Nancy starts to respond when --

A SHRIEKING SOUND interrupts.  Her eyes dart to --

A SMALL CAGE.  DRAPED IN A SHEET.  CAN'T SEE WHAT'S IN IT.

The cage shakes slightly.  *Something is clearly in there.*

                    MRS. DRISCOLL (CONT'D)
          Oh.  Yes.  I forgot to mention.
                    (beat)
          I caught one of the bastards.

WE PUSH IN ON THE CAGE AS IT SHAKES MORE -- AND MORE --

THE SOUND OF RAT SHRIEKING MORPHS INTO...

**EXT. HAWKINS TOWN HALL - DAY**

PROTESTORS chant in anger:

                    ANGRY PROTESTOR
          KLINE IS SWINE!!  KLINE IS SWINE!!!

THE PROTESTORS shake hand-made signs in the air: "DOWN WITH
STARCOURT!" "SAVE DOWNTOWN!!!" "MAYOR KLINE SOLD US OUT"!

**INT. HAWKINS TOWN HALL - HALLWAY - DAY**

The PROTESTORS' SHOUTING echoes inside, where...

We're suddenly following behind a TALL MAN.  His gloved hand
clutches A MOTORCYCLE HELMET.  There's something about his
gait that is oddly... familiar to us.  He walks through...

**INT. HAWKINS TOWN HALL - LOBBY - DAY**

... Where he passes by Hopper, sitting in a chair, waiting.

Hopper's eyes start to follow this TALL MAN, when --

                    MAYOR'S SECRETARY (O.S.)
          Jim -- ?

Hop turns to find a SECRETARY approaching.  She smiles.

MAYOR'S SECRETARY (CONT'D)
Mayor Kline is ready for you.

**INT. HAWKINS TOWN HALL - MAYOR'S OFFICE - DAY**

Hopper enters the Mayor's office to find --

MAYOR LARRY KLINE, 40s, a dangerous cocktail of ego and
neurosis. He strides over to Hop with a big smile and an
outstretched hand.

                    MAYOR KLINE
          Jim!  Thanks for coming by!

Hopper shakes his hand, but --

                    HOPPER
          I'm not doing it, Larry.

The Mayor smiles.

                    MAYOR KLINE
          Calm down, now, you don't even know
          what I want -- !

                    HOPPER
          You don't like your fan club out
          there, want me to shut them down --
          that sound about right?

Mayor Kline GUFFAWS, trying to laugh it off.

                    MAYOR KLINE
          When did you get so serious, Jim!
          Take a seat -- take a seat -- come on
          now --

The Mayor sits in his cushioned chair; Hopper sits opposite.

The Mayor opens up a box of cigars.

                    MAYOR KLINE (CONT'D)
          My "fan club" -- as you call them --
          now you know why they're out there
          don't you -- ?

                    HOPPER
          They're... not actually fans -- ?

The Mayor flashes a smile --

                    MAYOR KLINE
          They lost their jobs to the mall,
          blame me for helping make that
          happen.  Now -- you go ask anyone
          else in this town -- they all LOVE
          the mall.

The Mayor places his cigar in a cigar cutter.

                    MAYOR KLINE (CONT'D)
          It's helped our economy grow, it's
          brought in new jobs and just some
          *incredible* new stores, which is why
          they all stopped shopping at --
                    (motions to window)
          -- *their* mom-and-pops.  That's not
          me.  No, no.  That's just good old-
          fashioned American *capitalism*.

CHOOM!  The Mayor cuts his cigar.

                    HOPPER
          Well, seems to me they're just
          expressing their "good old-fashioned
          American" right to protest --

                    MAYOR KLINE
          Yes I agree if -- IF -- they have a
          permit.  Now -- correct me if I'm
          wrong here, Jim -- but I don't
          believe they secured a permit from
          your office, did they?

Hopper shifts in his chair.

                    HOPPER
          Not that I'm aware of --

                    MAYOR KLINE
          Then I do believe it's within *my*
          *right* to get rid of them.

                    HOPPER
          I'm not a politics guy, Larry, but if
          I force them out, without any sorta
          provocation -- that might not be a
          good look for your re-election
          campaign --

                    MAYOR KLINE
          Three days, Jim.  You know what's in
          three days?

                    HOPPER
          ... July fourth -- ?

                    MAYOR KLINE
          That's right.  And I'm gonna throw
          this town the biggest bash it's ever
          seen.  Fireworks.  Music.
          *Activities*.  And at the end of the
          day, that's all our voters will
          remember.  But I can't think, *much
          less plan*, with all that racket out
          there.

Larry leans back in his chair.

                    MAYOR KLINE (CONT'D)
          So, if you don't mind -- why don't
          you just do your job... flash your
          little gold badge...

The Mayor pops the cigar in his mouth.

                    MAYOR KLINE (CONT'D)
          And get rid of them.

FWOOM!  The Mayor lights his cigar.  And...

**EXT. STARCOURT MALL - ENTRANCE - DAY**

WHOOM!  HYDRAULIC BUS DOORS SHOOT OPEN AND --

A stream of people exit the bus, including...

Max and Eleven!  A look of worry spreads across El's

face. REVERSE TO REVEAL: STARCOURT MALL!

                    MAX
          What's wrong?

                    ELEVEN
          ... Too many people.  Against the
          rules.

Max shoots her a look.

                    MAX
          Seriously?  You have *superpowers*.
          What's the worst that can happen?

Off Eleven...

**INT. STARCOURT MALL - LOWER LEVEL - DAY**

Max excitedly leads Eleven through the mall.

We SPIN AROUND Eleven as she surveys her dizzying new
surroundings.  The teenagers, the fountain, the escalators --
it's all very overwhelming!  But also -- oh so VERY exciting!

                    MAX
          So what should we do first??

Max looks at Eleven, who seems, well, overwhelmed.

                    MAX (CONT'D)
          You've never been shopping before
          have you?

Eleven shakes her head.  *No.*  Max grins.

                    MAX (CONT'D)
          Then we'll just have to do
          everything.  Come on -- !!!

Max grabs Eleven, dragging her into THE GAP just as --

Lucas and Mike and (annoyed third wheel) Will stride past --
a near miss!!  Lucas leads the way, walking fast, on a mission.

                    MIKE
          I don't even understand what we're
          looking for --

                    LUCAS
          Something pretty and shiny that says
          "I'm sorry" --

                    MIKE
          You mean -- something that *literally*
          says "I'm sorry" -- ?

                    LUCAS
          No!  God you're *so lucky* you have me --

Lucas leads Mike and Will deeper into the mall as --

**INT. THE GAP - DAY**

Eleven inspects mannequins in the Gap.

                    MAX
          ... Do you like that?

                    ELEVEN
          ... How do I know -- what I like?

                    MAX
          You just -- try things on.  Until you
          find something that feels... like
          *you.*

                    ELEVEN
          Like... me?

                          MAX
          Yeah -- not Hopper.  Not Mike.
               (beat)
          *You*.

As Eleven takes in this *radical* new idea...

AN ENERGETIC POP SONG BEGINS AND --

**WE NOW MOVE INTO A FAST-PACED MONTAGE AS...**

Eleven tries on VARIOUS GAP OUTFITS, one after the next!

**INT. ZALES - DAY - MONTAGE**

Our boys shop for "shiny" jewelry at Zales.

Mike eyes a TINY SILVER BEAR.  Calls to a SNOOTY SALESMAN.

                          MIKE
          Excuse me, sir?  How much for this
          little teddy bear here?

Off the Snooty Salesman --

**INT. STARCOURT MALL - OUTSIDE ZALES - DAY - MONTAGE**

The boys storm out of the store, pissed!

                          LUCAS
          -- Eight hundred?!

                          MIKE
          -- I should've shoved that little
          bear right up his tight ass --

**INT. THE GAP - DAY**

Eleven finds the perfect outfit.  Max gives it a *THUMBS-UP!*

**INT. STARCOURT MALL - DAY**

The girls stride out of the Gap.

An excited Eleven swings a bag in her arms, and is wearing
her new outfit!  Max wears a new pair of sunglasses!  They
look so cool!

**INT. LOVELACE LINGERIE - DAY**

The boys confidently stride into LOVELACE LINGERIE.

But then take one look at the SEXY LINGERIE and --

Abruptly exit.  EMPTY-HANDED.

**INT. FLASH STUDIO - DAY**

Our excited girls race into Flash Studio and --

**INT. FLASH STUDIO - DAY - MONTAGE**

CHOOM!  Max and Eleven have photos taken by a PHOTOGRAPHER!

They try on various SILLY ACCESSORIES, striking a series of
ridiculous poses, having *a blast* as --

**INT. STARCOURT MALL - PERFUME KIOSK - DAY - MONTAGE**

Our miserable boys test out VARIOUS PERFUMES at a mall kiosk.

Lucas sprays a puff right into Mike's face.

Mike stumbles back, waving his arms, gagging, as --

**INT. KAUFMAN'S SHOES - DAY - MONTAGE**

Eleven tries to walk in heels.  Topples over.  Max laughs!

A GANG OF MEAN GIRLS (including STACEY, the jerk who rejected
Dustin at the Snow Ball) shoots Eleven *dirty* looks.

Max and Eleven share looks of their own, then --

**INT. STARCOURT MALL - FOOD COURT & ESCALATOR - DAY - MONTAGE**

Max and Eleven hide behind a column, now spying on --

The Mean Girls.  They're flirting with some CUTE ORANGE
JULIUS EMPLOYEES.  Eleven narrows her eyes, focusing her
powers, and --

BOOM!  Stacy's Orange Julius BURSTS EXPLOSIVELY, showering
the Mean Girls with juice.  The Mean Girls SCREAM and --

**MOMENTS LATER**

Max and Eleven race away, laughing --

                    MAX
          What'd I tell you???  There's more to
          life than --

                    ELEVEN
          *Stupid boys.*

They smile, hold hands, having the best day ever, as they pass right by --

OUR STUPID BOYS, moping on a bench, empty-handed, having --

*THE. WORST. DAY. EVER.*

> WILL
> ... Can we *please* play D&D now?

> MIKE/LUCAS
> NO!

OUR POP SONG NOW CRASHES TO AN END AND --

**EXT. DOWNTOWN HAWKINS - DAY - ESTABLISHING**

Silence.  Main Street is a depressing ghost town.

**INT. MELVALD'S GENERAL STORE - DAY**

WE DRIFT PAST A GIANT STACK OF SCIENCE LIBRARY BOOKS to find...

Joyce at the front counter, reading a book titled --

*THE ELECTROMAGNETIC FIELD*

Her eyes narrow as she reads.  This hurts her head.  WE CUT TO HER POV and reveal the reason *why*: The page she's reading is full of crazy diagrams and math... *lots of math.*

Off Joyce, baffled, we SMASH TO:

**EXT. COUNTRY ROAD - DAY**

VROOOM!  Joyce's Gremlin TEARS down the road.

**EXT. UNKNOWN HOUSE - DAY**

An elbow JABS a doorbell: DING DONG!

WIDEN TO REVEAL: Joyce is now standing outside an unfamiliar house.  The giant stack of science books teeters in her arms. She can hear the sound of BOMBASTIC CLASSICAL MUSIC COMING FROM SOMEWHERE WITHIN.  Someone is *clearly* home. But...

Nobody comes to the door.  She leans her elbow in again.

*DING DONG!*

                    JOYCE
        Hello???   HELLO?!?!?!

**INT. GARAGE - DAY**

A paintbrush sweeps across a LEGOLAS MINIATURE.

TILT UP TO REVEAL: A MAN is painting the figurine.  We can't
make out _who_ he is, because his face is hidden behind HEAD
MAGNIFYING GLASSES.  As he finishes painting the
miniature...

He hears something beneath his music.  *A voice.*

                    JOYCE
        HELLO????   HELLOOOOO???

**EXT. GARAGE - DAY**

DING DONG!  Joyce tries the bell one more time, then --

Gives up.  She starts to shuffle back to her car when --

VROOM!  A LOUD CHURNING NOISE.  She turns to find...

The GARAGE DOOR rising dramatically with the rising CLASSICAL
MUSIC to reveal...

MR. CLARKE??!!  He's wearing a T-shirt and short shorts.
_Very_ short shorts.  He slides off his head magnifying glass.

                    MR. CLARKE
        ... *Missus Byers?*

Off Joyce, clutching her wobbling stack of science books, we
SMASH TO --

**BLACK**

As the CLASSICAL MUSIC rings out, we hear a voice call out:

                    BILLY (PRE-LAP)
        *... WHAT DO YOU WANT FROM ME -- WHAT
        DO YOU WANT -- ???*

**EXT. COUNTRY ROAD (THE UPSIDE DOWN) - NIGHT (FLASHBACK)**

*We're suddenly back in time.  Back in the Upside Down.*

*Billy screams at the APPROACHING SHADOWY FIGURES.*

                    BILLY
        *WHAT DO YOU WANT????*

The LEAD SHADOW emerges from the fog.  It's...

BILLY.  A MIRROR IMAGE.  THE LEADER OF THIS... ARMY.

He steps right up to Billy.  He's calm.  Composed.

> BILLY 2
> ... To build... I want you to
> build...

> BILLY
> ... Build -- build what -- ?

> BILLY 2
> What you see.

> BILLY
> I -- I don't understand --

But before he can ask more questions, BRIGHT RED LIGHTNING
SCARS THE SKY and --

**EXT. COUNTRY ROAD - NIGHT (FLASHBACK)**

Billy is suddenly back on the country road in the REAL WORLD.

No more spores, no more fog, no more ARMY.

Billy stares, shaken, scared, alone.  He steps into the
middle of the road, calls out into the darkness.

> BILLY
> I -- I don't understand -- I DON'T
> UNDERSTAND -- I DON'T UNDER --

**EXT. HAWKINS POOL - DAY (PRESENT)**

WHOOM!  Billy suddenly jerks awake on the lifeguard stand.

Something is wrong.  His body is soaked in sweat.  His ears
are ringing.  And he's in pain.  Real pain.

He looks down at his right arm.  It hangs out of the shadow
of the umbrella, exposed to the sunlight.

The skin is dark red.  PEELING.  Badly BURNT.

He yanks it out of the sun and --

**EXT. HAWKINS POOL - DAY**

Billy staggers across the crowded pool.

Heather sees him, calls out:

                        HEATHER
            -- Billy?  Are you okay?

Billy ignores her, explodes into the MEN'S LOCKER ROOM.

**INT. HAWKINS POOL - MEN'S LOCKER ROOM - DAY - A MINUTE LATER**

CLOSE ON: A cold knob twists, full blast as --

Billy stands under a shower in an empty shower stall.  He lets the cold water wash over his body.  Sweeping away the sweat, cooling him down.  He sighs with relief, but --

His arm -- his arm still *fucking hurts like hell.*

He lifts it up, examining it, rotating it.

> BILLY
> *Jesus...*

The skin is red, wrinkled, peeling, *gross.*  And something else.  *Something worse.*  Through the damaged skin:

BLACK VEINS.  PULSATING EVER SO SLIGHTLY.  *WHAT.  THE.  FUCK?*

He touches an exposed black vein and --

A QUICK FLASH OF THE MIND FLAYER!  SHRIEKING!

Billy SCREAMS, drops to the tile floor in pain.

That HIGH-PITCHED RINGING fills his ears again.  Then...

> VOICE
> *Billy...  Billy...*

He looks up.  Through the curtain of falling water, he sees --

HEATHER.  WALKING OVER TO HIM.  ODDLY CALM.  DREAM-LIKE.

She kneels down, just inches away from him now.

She reaches out.  Takes his head in her hand.

Then whispers:

> HEATHER
> Take me to him.

Billy pulls away.  Startled, confused.

> BILLY
> ... *W-what -- ?*

> HEATHER
> I said, *Are you hurt??*

Heather is now back to her normal self.

That awful ringing sound is now gone.

                    HEATHER (CONT'D)
          What's going on?  I -- I heard a
          scream --

Billy catches his breath.  Not sure what to say.

                    HEATHER (CONT'D)
          Should I call an ambulance?  Billy?

Billy doesn't answer.  He just stares at Heather through the
falling water.  And then, slowly but surely, it happens...

His face relaxes.  His breathing slows.  His pupils contract.

The shift is subtle.  But unsettling.

He locks eyes with Heather.

*And...*

**INT. DRISCOLL FARMHOUSE - BASEMENT - DAY**

SNAP!  A bright light flashes as --

A crouched Jonathan takes a photograph with his camera.  As
he takes more photos, we DOLLY AROUND HIM to reveal...

THE RAT.  It's trapped in a small cage.  It looks more or
less like a regular rat except that it seems oddly aggressive
-- repeatedly slamming its body into the cage.  It wants *out*.

                    JONATHAN
          We're going to have to keep doing
          this until you stop moving you little
          shit...

SNAP!  Jonathan takes another picture and --

**INT. DRISCOLL FARMHOUSE - FIRST FLOOR - DAY**

CLOSE ON: A PHONE BOOK.  A "Pest Control" ad is circled.

TILT UP: Nancy paces on a corded phone.

                    NANCY
          Hi, yes -- this is Nancy Wheeler from
          the Hawkins Post...  I have a bit of
          a... weird question.  I was seeing if
          you had any calls lately about...
          uh... rabid rats?
               (muffled voice)
          *Rabid* rats -- rats with rabies?
               (muffled voice)
          What about rats -- just in general??
               (MORE)

103

                    NANCY (CONT'D)
               (muffled voice)
          Oh, okay, thank--

The line goes dead.  Nancy sighs.  Hangs up.

                    MRS. DRISCOLL (O.S.)
          You're quite the little detective,
          aren't you?

Nancy turns to find Mrs. Driscoll hobbling over to her from
the kitchen.  She carries an ICE-COLD GLASS OF LEMONADE.

                    MRS. DRISCOLL (CONT'D)
          Lemonade?  It's fresh squeezed.

                    NANCY
          Sure, thanks --
               (takes the lemonade)
          Do you mind if I make -- just a few
          more calls?

                    MRS. DRISCOLL
          Not at all.  I enjoy the company.

Nancy smiles, returns to the phone book page, flips to --

"BLACKBURN'S FARM SUPPLY."  She dials the number.

                    NANCY
               (into phone)
          Hi -- um -- I have a bit of a...
          weird question --

INT. DRISCOLL FARMHOUSE - BASEMENT - DAY

CHOOM!  CHOOM!  Jonathan takes two more snaps then --

SNAP-CLICK!  The camera roll runs out.

                    JONATHAN
          *Shit...*

MOMENTS LATER - BASEMENT CORNER

Jonathan grabs a new roll of film from his backpack.

He loads the film into the back of the camera, snaps the door
shut, then -- pauses, realizing something: *It's suddenly
quiet in here.*  He turns around, looks back at the dark cage.

Something is... wrong.  The rat isn't moving at all.

Jonathan walks over to the cage.  His face drops.

                         104

The rat is *sick,* curled up on the cage floor, shivering.

*It's just like those rats in the factory.*

                    JONATHAN (CONT'D)
          ... You feeling bad, little buddy?

Jonathan kneels down right by the cage.  His eyes narrow.

The rat's skin is moving a little bit.  *Bubbling.*

The rat makes a pained WHIMPERING sound and --

WHOMP!  A LOUD SOUND startles us as --

                    NANCY
          -- Jonathan!

Nancy bounds to the bottom of the stairs.  Excited.

                    NANCY (CONT'D)
          I got a lead!

                    JONATHAN
          Yeah, okay -- I think there's
          something *really* wrong with this rat --

                    NANCY
          Yeah, no shit.  *Come on.*

Nancy races back up the stairs.  Jonathan takes one last look
at the sick rat, then hurries up the steps after Nancy.

But we don't follow them; instead, OUR CAMERA DRIFTS BACK TO
THE RAT.  It's still shivering.  Faster and faster and then --

SPLAT!  IT IMPLODES LIKE THE OTHERS.  BLOOD AND MUCUS SPRAYS.

But this time we don't cut away from the horror.  We HOLD on
the disgusting mess of rat blood and guts.  We're going to
call this THE GOOP.  The GOOP begins to move... slinking
across the cage... slipping *through* the bars... *escaping.*

THE GOOP NOW BEGINS TO COALESCE ON THE OTHER SIDE, FORMING
INTO A KIND OF SHAPE.  INTO A... *BODY.*  LEGS SPROUT.  THEN --

EEEEEEE!  THIS *GORE-SPIDER* SUDDENLY DARTS AWAY --

SKITTERING ACROSS THE BASEMENT FLOOR *AND* --

**INT. STARCOURT MALL - DAY - ESTABLISHING**

The mall bustles with activity.

PRE-LAP: THE SOUND OF A RUSSIAN VOICE.

**INT. SCOOPS AHOY! - BACK ROOM - DAY**

Robin paces, listening intently as --

Dustin plays the RECORDING. It's low quality and in Russian, so *very* difficult to decipher. But Robin is determined.

> ROBIN
> That last part, just one more time --

Dustin rewinds, plays the tape again.

> ROBIN (CONT'D)
> Okay, that word, that sounded like --
> like "d-linny." Pronounced "D" --

Dustin scurries over to the alphabet board, translates. In Russian, the D is a:

> DUSTIN
> *Chair-looking thingy* --

Robin scrawls this down and --

**INT. SCOOPS AHOY! - FRONT COUNTER - DAY - MOMENTS LATER**

WHOOM! Robin flings open the pass-through window, breathless.

> ROBIN
> We got our first sentence!

Steve, scooping ice cream into a cone, turns to her, amazed.

> STEVE
> *Seriously?*

> ROBIN
> (bad Russian accent)
> "The week is long."

> STEVE
> Wow. That's... thrilling.

> ROBIN
> I know. But -- *progress*.

As Robin slides the pass-through window shut --

Steve turns back to his customers: Max and Eleven!

                         STEVE
          Alright.  Here ya go, one vanilla
          chocolate swirl, one strawberry --

He suddenly pauses.  Eyes Eleven skeptically.

                         STEVE (CONT'D)
          -- Are you allowed to be here?

Off Eleven...

**EXT. STARCOURT MALL - ENTRANCE - DAY**

WHOOM!  The mall doors shoot open and --

Max and Eleven skip out, laughing, licking and loving their
ice cream cones.  It's the perfect end to a perfect day.

                         MAX
          Wanna trade?

Eleven nods.  They switch cones, smiling, when --

Max's smile sharply drops.

                         MAX (CONT'D)
          Oh.  You have got to be shitting me.

Eleven follows her gaze and our CAMERA REVERSES to find --

THE BOYS.  Retrieving their bikes from the bike rack.  Not
twenty feet away.

The girls share looks.  And then...

**EXT. STARCOURT MALL - BIKE RACKS - DAY - A MINUTE LATER**

The boys are climbing on their bikes when...

                         MAX (O.S.)
          -- Isn't *this* a nice surprise?

The boys whirl to find the girls striding toward them.

Mike is so shocked he drops his bike.  It CLATTERS LOUDLY.

He looks at Eleven's new look, stunned --

                         MIKE
          Wh-- what are you doing here??

                         ELEVEN
          Shopping.

                    MAX
          This is her new style.  What do you
          think?

Mike glares at Max.

                    MIKE
          What's *wrong* with you?  You *know* she
          can't be here --

                    MAX
          What is she, *your little pet* -- ?

                    ELEVEN
          Yeah am I *your pet* -- ?

                    MIKE
          *What* -- NO -- !

                    ELEVEN
          Then why do you treat me like
          garbage?

                    MIKE
          *What* -- ?

                    ELEVEN
          You told me "*Nana was sick*" --

                    MIKE
          She *is* -- she *is sick* -- !

                    LUCAS
          *Super* sick.  It's true.  That's --
          why we're here actually --

                    MIKE
          *Yeah!*  We've been shopping too, not
          for ourselves -- for *Nana* --

                    LUCAS
          For flowers --

                    MIKE
              (to El)
          And also... for *you*.  We just...
          didn't find anything we... liked.
          For you.  I mean -- I only had --
          five dollars, so -- it's hard --

                    LUCAS
          *Super hard.*

Eleven stares at Mike.  *Hurt.*

                              ELEVEN
                    You lie.  Why do you lie?

Mike hesitates.  He knows how bad this looks.  But he's not
sure how to respond.  *Not even sure where to begin.*  When --

THE BUS RUMBLES UP BEHIND THEM.  IT'S TIME TO LEAVE.

Eleven looks to Max.  Then back to Mike.  *Then:*

                         ELEVEN (CONT'D)
                    I dump your ass.

Mike stares --

                              MIKE
                    *What -- ?*

The girls whip around and stride toward the bus.

Mike stares, dumbfounded and --

**INT. BUS - DAY**

The girls drop into bus seats.  Max holds up an open hand.

Eleven gives her a high-five.  And --

**EXT. STARCOURT MALL - BIKE RACKS - DAY**

VROOM.  The bus rumbles away, passing our dumbfounded boys.

                              WILL
                    ... *Now* can we play D&D?

Off Mike, *miserable*, we SMASH TO:

**EXT. HAWKINS TOWN HALL - DAY**

WHAM!  Handcuffs SNAPPING over the wrists of --

THE ANGRY PROTESTOR!  Hopper is dragging him away --

                         ANGRY PROTESTOR
                    He raised my property taxes, Jim --
                    forced me off my land -- !!

                         HOPPER
                    You can protest all you want, Henry --
                    but you've gotta go through the
                    proper channels first --

ANGRY PROTESTOR
Nothin' *PROPER* about what that man
did to us -- to our town -- !!!

Hopper shoves the Angry Protestor into the back of --

POWELL'S POLICE CAR, where there are already two more ANGRY
PROTESTORS. Hopper slams the door shut, shares a look with
Powell. Both men are *exhausted* from this. When suddenly --

FLORENCE
Special delivery!!!

Hopper looks up to find FLORENCE, ambling over toward him
from her parked car. She hands him a bag from JCPENNEY.

Hopper pulls out a BRIGHT BLUE 80s-PATTERNED SHIRT.

FLORENCE (CONT'D)
That the right one -- ?

Hopper looks the shirt over. Pleased.

HOPPER
*Yup*, this is the one --

POWELL
That's *a lotta* color for you, Chief --

HOPPER
Hey -- this is cutting-edge stuff.
*Cutting edge.*

Off Powell, clearly *skeptical*, we now begin the first notes
of a CLASSICAL SUITE and...

**INT. ENZO'S ITALIAN RESTAURANT - NIGHT 4**

A BOW flies up and down a *VIOLIN*. PULL OUT TO REVEAL:

A MUSICAL QUARTET playing at ENZO'S -- the fanciest joint
in Hawkins!

Hopper swaggers in -- he's wearing his new shirt, jeans,
and a white blazer. With his mustache, he looks *exactly*
like Tom Selleck in *Magnum PI*! Cutting edge *indeed*!

**ENZO'S ITALIAN RESTAURANT - LATER**

CLOSE ON: A romantic candle flutters on a table.

WIDEN OUT: Hopper is now sitting at a table.  Joyce has not
yet arrived, but a SNOBBY WAITER has.  He waits with his
hands behind his back while Hopper reads the drink menu.

                    HOPPER
          ... I'll start with a scotch, make it
          a double --

                    SNOBBY WAITER
          Very good, sir --

                    HOPPER
          -- And I'm thinking I'll get us a
          bottle of red --

                    SNOBBY WAITER
          Very good, sir --

                    HOPPER
          Is this... uh -- cheeantee good?

                    SNOBBY WAITER
               (wincing)
          Yes our Key-AHN-tee is *quite good* --
          medium bodied with just a hint of
          cherry --

                    HOPPER
          Who doesn't like cherries?  *I'll take
          it.*  And two glasses -- one for me
          and one for the lady.

                    SNOBBY WAITER
          Very good, sir.

The Snobby Waiter heads off, wiping past a HAPPY COUPLE
sitting across from Hopper.  They're holding hands, enjoying
their dinner.  Seeing them makes Hopper feel *very alone*.

His eyes move to the front door.  Looking for Joyce.

*Where is she??*  As his impatience grows, CUT TO:

**EXT. MR. CLARKE'S GARAGE - NIGHT**

Joyce's car.  It's parked outside... *Mr. Clarke's house*.

Oh no!!  She's still here!!!

Light spills out from the garage door windows.

                    JOYCE (PRE-LAP)
          ... And okay -- *what* is that again?

**INT. MR. CLARKE'S GARAGE - NIGHT**

Mr. Clarke is carefully hooking wires to a copper coil --

> MR. CLARKE (PRE-LAP)
> *... This is a SOLENOID*. It's a coil
> wrapped around a *metallic core* and
> when electricity passes through it --

> JOYCE
> It creates <u>an electromagnetic field</u>.

Mr. Clarke looks up at Joyce. Pleased by his new pupil.

> MR. CLARKE
> *Exactamundo.*

Mr. Clarke runs the wires around a TOOLBOX SMOTHERED IN
MAGNETS, then hooks them up to an AC TRANSFORMER.

> MR. CLARKE (CONT'D)
> Now for the fun part. Shall we?

Joyce nods. Eager. Mr. Clarke flips ON the transformer. As
it HUMS to life, an AMP meter slowly rises, measuring the
electrical voltage. But... nothing else happens.

That was, well... anticlimactic.

Joyce stares. Confused. She waves her hand over the table.

> JOYCE
> ... I don't see anything --

> MR. CLARKE
> Nope. You can't see it. But it's
> <u>there</u>. I assure you. Our very own
> Clarke-Byers electromagnetic field.
> Pretty neato, huh?

> JOYCE
> Yeah --

> MR. CLARKE
> And this magnetic field, it affects
> *any charged object* in its vicinity --

> JOYCE
> ... Just like my magnets.

> MR. CLARKE
> *Just like your magnets.*

Joyce leans in closer, staring at the magnets on the toolbox.

                    JOYCE
        ... Then why's nothing happening?


                    MR. CLARKE
        Because our field is stable.  But if
        we reduce our current...

Mr. Clarke lowers the transformer voltage back to zero and --

WHOOM!  The magnets suddenly de-magnetize, falling off the
toolbox, clattering to the table!  Just like at Joyce's
house!

Joyce looks at Mr. Clarke -- amazed! She picks up a fallen
magnet and tries to stick it back onto the toolbox, but sure
enough, it slides right back off.

She looks back up at Clarke.  Eyes wide.

                    JOYCE
        ... *How -- ?*


                    MR. CLARKE
        The magnetic dipoles try to orient
        according to the field but since it's
        changing they become randomized and --

                    JOYCE
            (interrupting)
        No, no, I mean -- how did this happen
        *in my house?*

Mr. Clarke scratches his mustache.

                    MR. CLARKE
        You want my honest opinion?

                    JOYCE
        Yes --


                    MR. CLARKE
        One of your kiddos got up in the
        middle of the night, bumped into the
        fridge, and knocked the suckers
        loose --

                    JOYCE
        And the magnets at Melvald's -- ?

                    MR. CLARKE
        Apophenia.

                    JOYCE
        Sorry -- ?

                    MR. CLARKE
          Apophenia.  You're seeing patterns
          that aren't there.  _Coincidence_.

Joyce considers this.  Examines the magnet.

                    JOYCE
          But what if... it _wasn't?_

Mr. Clarke drops into his chair as he considers.

                    MR. CLARKE
          Well... theoretically speaking... I
          suppose some large version of this AC
          transformer could exist -- a machine
          of some kind --

                    JOYCE
          A "_machine_" -- ?

                    MR. CLARKE
               (nods)
          -- But to reach both your house _and_
          downtown -- _gosh_ -- _that_ would take
          _billions_ of volts of electricity and
          cost _tens_ of millions of dollars --

Joyce drops down closer to Clarke.

                    JOYCE
          But _is it possible_?

Mr. Clarke can't help but grin at this question.

                    MR. CLARKE
          We cured polio in fifty-three.
          Landed on the moon in sixty-nine.  As
          I tell my students -- once you open
          up that curiosity door...
               (beat)
          _Anything is possible_.

Off Joyce, taking in this lesson, we SMASH TO --

**INT. STARCOURT MALL - VARIOUS - NIGHT**

Silence.  Various lonely shots of the empty mall.

**INT. SCOOPS AHOY! - NIGHT**

Scoops is empty too.

**INT. SCOOPS AHOY! - BACK ROOM - NIGHT**

Dustin, Robin, and Steve in the back.  Staring at the white board.  Their eyes narrow as they read the translation aloud:

> STEVE/ROBIN/DUSTIN
> "The week is long --  the silver cat feeds -- when blue and yellow go south..."

We PUSH IN on Robin as these words race through her head and --

**INT. STARCOURT MALL - OUTSIDE SCOOPS - NIGHT**

WHOOM!  The Scoops gate crashes down.  They're closing up.

> STEVE
> I mean it just -- it *can't* be right --

> ROBIN
> It's *right.*

**INT. STARCOURT MALL - NIGHT - A LITTLE LATER**

Steve, Dustin, and Robin stride through the empty mall.

> DUSTIN
> Honestly, I think it's *great* news --

> STEVE
> *How is that great news?*  We'll never be heroes now, it's total *nonsense* --

> DUSTIN
> It's not nonsense.  It's too specific.  It's *obviously* a code.

> STEVE
> A code -- ?

> DUSTIN
> A *top-secret spy code* --

> STEVE
> That's a *stretch* dude --

> ROBIN
> I don't know.  *Is it?*

Steve shoots Robin a stunned look.

> STEVE
> You're buying into this -- ?

115

                    ROBIN
I mean listen -- just for kicks let's
say this IS a secret Russian
transmission.  What did you think
they were gonna say, "Fire the
warhead tomorrow at noon" -- ?

                    DUSTIN
*Exactly --*

                    ROBIN
My translation is correct, I know
that much at least.  *"The silver cat
feeds"?*  I mean -- why would anyone
talk like that UNLESS they were
trying to mask the true meaning of
their message --

                    DUSTIN
*Exactly -- !*

                    ROBIN
And why would they mask the meaning
of their message unless that message
was sensitive --

                    DUSTIN
*Exactly -- !*

                    ROBIN
Which seems to confirm his suspicions
--

                    DUSTIN
*Evil Russians --*

                    ROBIN
I mean, I can't believe I'm agreeing
with this strange child -- but yeah.
Totally.  *Evil Russians.*

Dustin beams.  Validated.  But Steve has crashed to a stop.

Robin and Dustin keep walking, unaware.

                    DUSTIN
-- How do we crack it?

                    ROBIN
I guess we translate the rest -- and
hopefully a pattern emerges.

                    DUSTIN
          A pattern, *right* -- like "Silver Cat"
          could be a meeting place --

                    ROBIN
          Or a *person* --

                    DUSTIN
          Or a *weapon* ---

                    ROBIN
          It will probably take a super genius
          to break it, but --

Robin suddenly pauses, realizing:

                    ROBIN (CONT'D)
          ... Where's Steve?

They turn back around to find --

Steve, fifty yards back, standing in front of a MECHANICAL
HORSE, frantically digging around in his pockets.

Dustin and Robin share looks.  *Uhhhhh...*

                    ROBIN (CONT'D)
          *Steve*, what are you doing -- ??

Steve thrusts out a hand, urgent:

                    STEVE
          Quarter -- do you have a quarter??

Dustin and Robin cross over to him --

                    ROBIN
          Aren't you a little old for that?

                    STEVE
          *Quarter!*

Robin sighs.  She fishes into her pocket and flips Steve a
QUARTER.  He pops it into the horse.  It jolts to life,
rocking up and down.  A TINNY SONG begins to PLAY.

Robin crosses her arms, impatient --

                    ROBIN
          Would you like help getting on,
          widdle Stevie -- ?

Dustin chortles at this but --

                    STEVE
          Just shut up and listen.

The TINNY MUSIC begins to take on a *familiar quality*.

It hits Dustin like a lightning bolt.

                    DUSTIN
          Oh shit -- *the music* --

                    ROBIN
          What -- ?

                    DUSTIN
          THE MUSIC!!

Dustin drops to his knees, unzips his backpack, grabs the
tape recorder, fast-forwards, then punches play, and --

THE SAME TINNY MUSIC PLAYS ON THE TAPE.

                    ROBIN
          I don't understand --

                    DUSTIN
          This *exact song* is on the recording --

                    ROBIN
          Maybe they have horses like this in
          Russia --

Steve motions to the horse's name:

                    STEVE
          "Indiana Flyer?"  I don't think so.
          That code didn't come from Russia.
               (beat)
          It came from here.

Robin stares.  Stunned.  She looks back at Indiana Flyer.

The TINNY MUSIC now takes on a menacing quality as...

The horse rocks up and down.  Up and down.  Up and --

**INT. ENZO'S ITALIAN RESTAURANT - NIGHT**

The QUARTET rocks a wild number!!  We're back at Enzo's!

Hopper is still alone at his table, now with an empty glass
of scotch and a half-drunken bottle of Chianti.  He is
looking quite miserable... *and quite drunk*.

He looks over, sees the HAPPY COUPLE now *FEEDING EACH OTHER DESSERT LIKE NEWLYWEDS*. It makes Hopper *SICK*.

> SNOBBY WAITER
> ... Would you like to order your
> entree sir?

Hopper snaps out of it, looks up at the Snobby Waiter.

> HOPPER
> ... You know what Enzo -- ?

> SNOBBY WAITER
> My name is not En --

> HOPPER
> I've lost my appetite.

WHAM! Hopper slams a WAD OF CASH down to the table.

> HOPPER (CONT'D)
> You can keep the change --

He stands, grabs up the BOTTLE OF CHIANTI --

> SNOBBY WAITER
> -- Sir, I'm afraid no alcohol is
> allowed off the premises --

Hopper shoots "Enzo" a look. Jabs the wine bottle at him.

> HOPPER
> I can do anything. I'm the *Chief of
> Police*.

With that, Hopper turns and stumbles his way out of the restaurant, passing through --

THE RESTAURANT BAR. The TALL MAN from town hall is having a drink, motorcycle helmet by his side. His back is turned to us, but then a drunken Hopper bumps into him, causing him to turn toward the camera. It's...

GRIGORI. STEPANOV'S RIGHT HAND. *HERE*. *IN HAWKINS*.

As Grigori watches Hopper stumble out of Enzo's --

Our JAZZ TUNE CRASHES OUT and --

**EXT. COUNTRY ROAD - NIGHT**

VROOOM! Billy's Camaro *TEARS* down an empty road.

**EXT. ABANDONED FACTORY - NIGHT**

It *SKIDS* to a stop outside the factory.  A beat, then...

Billy steps out.  He slowly walks around to the back of the car and opens up the trunk.  We now REVERSE ANGLE to reveal:

HEATHER.  INSIDE THE TRUNK.  UNCONSCIOUS.

Her mouth is duct-taped.  Her head bleeds.

> HEATHER (O.S.)
> *(filtered)*
> -- Billy -- ?  Billy?

**INT. HAWKINS POOL - MEN'S LOCKER ROOM - DAY (FLASHBACK)**

*We're back in time.  Heather is looking at Billy with concern.*

> HEATHER
> *Should I call an ambulance?*

*Billy locks eyes with her.  Then he pushes to his feet in the shower.  Heather watches, confused as --*

*He reaches past her -- and closes the curtain.*

*We don't see what happens behind the curtain.*

*But we hear SCREAMING -- a STRUGGLE --*

*The curtain SNAPS to and fro and --*

**EXT. ABANDONED FACTORY - NIGHT**

Billy carries Heather's limp body toward the factory.

**INT. ABANDONED FACTORY - STAIRS - NIGHT**

Billy carries her down the steps.

**INT. ABANDONED FACTORY - BASEMENT - NIGHT**

Billy lays her down in the wet basement.  In this... *lair.*

Her eyes blink.  Her consciousness returning.  She's alive.

She takes in her surroundings.  It's dark, hard to see much.

She tries to call out, but her cries are muffled by the duct tape.  She flails, desperate to escape, only to find her hands and feet are tightly bound.

Billy crouches in front her.  Calm.  Unemotional.

He watches her struggle for a beat.

Then, as her energy wanes...

> BILLY
> Don't be afraid.  It will be over
> soon.

He removes the duct tape from her mouth.

> BILLY (CONT'D)
> Just... try and stay very still.

Billy now stands up and steps out of the way.  Behind him...

IN THE SHADOWS: *SOMETHING* STIRS.  SOMETHING LARGE.  *INHUMAN*.

Heather's tear-stained eyes go wide.  She starts to SCREAM as
this SHADOWED MONSTROSITY lumbers toward her.  Each step it
takes is wet, heavy.  Just as it's about to emerge from the
shadows, we CUT AWAY to...

Billy watching.  We don't see what he sees, but we hear it:

The sound of SCREAMING, of flesh TEARING, *a nightmare*.

And through it all, Billy remains calm.

Because Billy is not here anymore.

<u>Billy is gone</u>.


<u>END EPISODE</u>

# CHAPTER THREE:
# THE CASE OF THE MISSING LIFEGUARD

WRITTEN BY **WILLIAM BRIDGES**

**EXT. CABIN - NIGHT 4 CONT'D**

We open on the cabin.  Quiet.  Peaceful.

VROOM!  Hopper's Blazer suddenly slams into frame.  Then --

HOPPER stumbles out, carrying that fancy wine from Enzo's.
He's still clearly angry about being stood up by Joyce.

He GRUMPILY STOMPS up the cabin steps, wine sloshing, and --

**INT. CABIN - CONTINUOUS**

WHOOM!  Hopper staggers inside.  Freezes.  His eyes narrow.

He hears LOUD MUSIC.  GIGGLING.  The noise is coming from
Eleven's room.  But the door is shut.  Which can only mean --

*Mike!!!*

>                    HOPPER
>          -- HEY!  What did I tell you?!  Huh?!
>          Three inches!!!  *THREE INCHES*!

Hopper storms across the cabin, throws open the door, and --

**INT. CABIN - ELEVEN'S ROOM - CONTINUOUS**

His anger promptly vanishes because --

ELEVEN is here not with Mike -- she's with <u>MAX</u>!

The girls are sprawled side by side on the bedroom floor,
their feet kicked up in the air, reading TIGER BEAT.

They look up at Hopper, *annoyed*.

>                    MAX
>          -- Do you *knock*?  *Jeez*.

>                    ELEVEN
>          Yeah.  *Jeez*.

Hopper stares, completely taken off guard.

>                    HOPPER
>          Oh, uh, sorry, I thought --

>                    MAX
>          Mike isn't here.

                              ELEVEN
          Max wanted to have a...
                    (remembering new word)
          "Sleepover."  Is it okay?

                              HOPPER
          Oh -- uh -- sure, yeah -- I mean...
                    (to Max)
          Your parents know?

                              MAX
          Yep.

                              HOPPER
          Right.  Cool.  *Very cool*...

An awkward beat.  The girls stare at him.  *Uhhhhh...*

                              MAX
          Did you... *need* something?

                              HOPPER
          Oh, uh, no... no -- sorry -- I'll
          just, uh -- leave you girls to it!

**INT. CABIN - MAIN ROOM - CONTINUOUS**

Hopper exits.  Shuts the door.  And... *smiles*.

NEEDLE DROP: "ANGEL" BY MADONNA!

**INT. CABIN - MAIN ROOM - NIGHT**

WHOOSH!  Wine pours into a coffee mug.

Hopper settles onto the couch and hits on the TV.  He then
takes a big sip of the fancy wine.  *Goddamn, it tastes good.*

He smacks his lips, kicks up his feet, happy, as --

**INT. CABIN - ELEVEN'S ROOM - NIGHT**

Max dances to Madonna, *happy*.  She bobs her head, sings:

                              MAX
          *"-- OOOOO -- YOU'RE AN ANGEL -- OOOOO
          YOU'RE AN ANGEL -- "*

Eleven's eyes go wide -- she holds up *Tiger Beat*.

It's open to a PHOTO SPREAD of --

TEEN IDOL RALPH MACCHIO!  Max smiles --

                    MAX (CONT'D)
     Oh!  You found Ralph Macchio!!

                ELEVEN
     Matchy-o?

                MAX
     *Mock-ee-oh.*  He's the Karate Kid.  Hi-
     YA!!!!

Max chops the air, then kicks!  Eleven laughs.

                MAX (CONT'D)
     He's so *hot*, right?!  I bet he's an
     amazing kisser too.

Max drops back down by Eleven.

                MAX (CONT'D)
     ... Is Mike a good kisser?

                ELEVEN
     I don't... know.  He is my first --
     boyfriend.

                MAX
     *Ex*-boyfriend.

Eleven nods, feigns a smile.  But she looks a little sad.

Max gently nudges her.

                MAX (CONT'D)
     *Hey*.  Don't worry about it, okay?
     He'll come crawling back to you in no
     time, begging for forgiveness --

                ELEVEN
     Yes -- ?

                MAX
     Yes!  *Just* -- trust me on this, okay?
     I *guarantee you* him and Lucas are,
     like, totally wallowing in like
     misery and self-pity right now --
          (shakes head)
     God, what I wouldn't give to see
     their stupid faces!!

Max giggles.  But Eleven doesn't.  She's had an idea.

                MAX (CONT'D)
     ... What is it?

Eleven looks at Max.  A mischievous smile forms.

> MAX (CONT'D)
> ... What? WHAT??

Eleven's smile grows, and --

**INT. CABIN - ELEVEN'S ROOM - NIGHT**

CHHHH!  Static blasts from the BOOMBOX.  We DROP to find...

Eleven cross-legged on the floor, tying on a black blindfold.

Max kneels beside her, excited.

> MAX
> Is this really gonna work -- ?

Eleven nods.  Yes.

> MAX (CONT'D)
> Holy shit this is *insane* --

> ELEVEN
> *Max* --

> MAX
> *Quiet*, yeah, sorry, sorry...

We PUSH IN on Eleven.  Moving toward that black blindfold.  A CACOPHONY OF VOICES overwhelm us, overlapping, multiplying, and before we know it the BLACK overtakes us and we're in --

**THE BLACK VOID**

Eleven stands in this vast nothingness.  All alone.  *Wait.*

She hears something.  LOW VOICES.  *Familiar ones.*  She turns around.  About thirty feet off in the distance, she sees:

THE BOYS.

**INT. CABIN - ELEVEN'S ROOM - NIGHT**

Eleven speaks to Max in the real world.  Low.

> ELEVEN
> ... I see them.

Max leans in, wide-eyed.  *Whoaaa.*

> MAX
> ... What are they doing?

                    ELEVEN
        ... *Eating*.

                    MAX
        Eating *what*?

                    ELEVEN
        ... *Junk*.

**THE BLACK VOID**

Eleven grimaces as she nears the boys.  Sure enough --

They're eating the *junkiest* of junk.  DOMINO'S PINEAPPLE
PIZZA, SKITTLES, JELLY BEANS, COCOA PUFFS, NACHO CHEESE
DORITOS, all washed down with CANS OF NEW COKE.

Will sets up a D&D game on the card table, while Lucas and
Mike sit on the couch, depressed and moping just like Max
said they would be:

                    MIKE
               (whiny)
        I just -- I still don't understand
        what I did to deserve this --

                    LUCAS
        NOTHING.  NOOOOTHING.  That's my whole
        point -- you're the victim here --

                    MIKE
        Yeah but then why --

                    LUCAS
        Stop Mike.  Stop asking *rational*
        questions.

                    MIKE
        Right, right.  Because girls act on
        emotion, not logic --

                    LUCAS
        Precisely.  It's a totally different
        species --

**INT. CABIN - ELEVEN'S ROOM  - NIGHT**

Eleven frowns.

                    ELEVEN
        ... They say we're... "a species."

                    MAX
        What -- ?

                        ELEVEN
        "Emotion, not logic."

                        MAX
        *WHAT?!*

**THE BLACK VOID**

Will looks back from the D&D game, suddenly excited.

                        WILL
        Guys, it's ready -- !

                        LUCAS
        Not right now, okay, Will --

                        WILL
        They broke up with you, what else is
        there to talk about -- ??

                        LUCAS
        *Tons* --

                        MIKE
        Yeah we're trying to solve the great
        mystery of the female species here --

On that note, Mike suddenly opens his mouth wide and --

BURRRRPSSS!  He seems *very* impressed with himself.

                        MIKE (CONT'D)
        *Dude.*  You can smell the ranch *and*
        the pineapple --

                        LUCAS
        Eh, I've got that beat --

                        MIKE
        No -- *don't* --

Lucas lifts up his leg --

                        MIKE (CONT'D)
        Lucas <u>DON'T</u> -- !

Too late!  Lucas lets *ONE RIP*.  PFFFFFFFFT!

The FART echoes out across the void and --

**INT. CABIN - ELEVEN'S ROOM - NIGHT**

WHOOM!  Eleven rips off her blindfold.  Her eyes WIDE.

She looks at Max.

> MAX
> What?? What happened??

Eleven bursts out laughing --

> MAX (CONT'D)
> WHAT?! *WHAT??*

Eleven falls over in a FIT OF HYSTERICS and --

**INT. CABIN - LIVING ROOM - CONTINUOUS**

LAUGHTER from both girls now drifts out into the living room.

Hopper beams. He pours himself another glass and --

**INT. CABIN - ELEVEN'S ROOM - NIGHT**

EXTREME CLOSE ON: Names scribbled down on paper.

*--MR. WHEELER. --MRS. WHEELER  --MR. CLARKE --DUSTIN*

*--STEVE  --NANCY  --BILLY*

WIDEN OUT TO REVEAL: The names have been written down on something that resembles a pie chart. It's labeled: "SPY LIST." In the center of this spy list: <u>AN EMPTY GLASS BOTTLE</u>.

It's like a twisted version of spin the bottle!

The girls share looks. Excited.

> ELEVEN
> Ready?

> MAX
> *Ready.*

Eleven cocks her head and... WHOOSH! The bottle spins around and around and around! The girls watch anxious, excited --

But their excitement *deflates* as the bottle lands on --

> ELEVEN/MAX
> "Mister Wheeler."

Max sticks out her tongue.

> MAX
> Boring.

                    ELEVEN
          Boring.

                    MAX
          Spin again.

                    ELEVEN
          Against the rules?

                    MAX
          We make our own rules.

Eleven nods.  *Totally*.  She cocks her head again and --

WHOOSH!  The bottle spins again.  It spins and spins and --

It finally lands on:

                    MAX/ELEVEN
          ... *Billy*.

Eleven and Max share looks.  Now *THIS* is interesting.

**INT. CABIN - ELEVEN'S ROOM - MOMENTS LATER**

Max turns up the STATIC on the boombox as --

Eleven sits cross-legged, pulls on her blindfold.

                    MAX
          -- I should just warn you, if he's
          with a girl or doing something gross,
          just get out of there right away
          before you're *scarred for life* --

                    ELEVEN
          Max --

                    MAX
          I'm just saying --

                    ELEVEN
          *Max* --

                    MAX
          Okay, okay.  Shutting up now...

Eleven focuses.  Slows her breathing.  And...

**THE BLACK VOID**

WHOOM.  Eleven's eyes snap open.  She's back in the void.

She hears a RUMBLING SOUND.  Like a growl.  *Turns*.

                    131

IT'S BILLY'S CAMARO.  ENGINE STILL RUNNING.  TRUNK OPEN.

Eleven slowly walks up to it.  Looks into the trunk --

Inside, she sees some DUCT TAPE and ROPE.  *That's odd...*

And that's when she hears it: A WHIMPERING SOUND.

She turns.  And she sees him.  *BILLY.*  He's further away than the boys were, kneeling on the dark wet floor, his back turned to her, heaving slightly.

Eleven's breath *catches*.  Something about this unsettles her.

*It doesn't feel like fun and games anymore.*

**INT. CABIN - ELEVEN'S ROOM - NIGHT**

Eleven shifts her body in the real world.

> ELEVEN
> ... I found him.

> MAX
> ... What's he doing?

> ELEVEN
> I... don't know.  He's... on the floor.  *Talking to someone.*

**THE BLACK VOID**

Bare feet splash through water as... Eleven slowly approaches Billy.  With every step, her sense of unease grows.

She still can't see his face, but she can hear him now:

> *BILLY*
> *... It's going to be okay.  Don't be afraid.  Just... stay very still.  It will all be over soon....*

Billy reaches out a hand and touches someone... someone who *isn't there*.  We know it's Heather, but Eleven can't see her.

She can, however, *hear* her.  And she sounds scared to death. WHIMPERING, CRYING, SEEMINGLY IN SOME KIND OF GREAT PAIN.

The water in front of Billy begins to ripple and then --

Billy turns sharply and -- <u>LOOKS DIRECTLY AT ELEVEN</u>.

Eleven GASPS, her eyes shooting wide, then --

WHOOM!  Billy *DISSOLVES* into SMOKE -- VANISHING *and* --

**INT. CABIN - ELEVEN'S ROOM - NIGHT**

WHOOM!  Eleven suddenly rips off her blindfold.

She's breathing hard, scared.

> MAX
> -- What is it??  What happened??
> (no answer)
> *What happened???*

Eleven looks at Max.  Their eyes lock.  And...

**INT. ABANDONED FACTORY - BASEMENT - NIGHT**

Billy pushes to his feet in the dark factory basement.

He walks forward a few steps, looking exactly where Eleven just stood.  But... it's just an empty basement.  Stairs. As he continues to stare, we hear HORRIBLE NOISES behind him.

Heather's SCREAMS grow LOUDER and LOUDER and then --

We hear something wet and loud and monstrous and --

Her SCREAMS ABRUPTLY SILENCE.  *Is she dead?*

We don't know.  We just hold on Billy.

His eyes burn with anger.

And right here we SMASH TO --

## MAIN TITLES

**EXT. WHEELER HOUSE - MORNING 5 - ESTABLISHING**

We FADE UP on dark clouds gathering.  *A storm is coming.*

We TILT DOWN to reveal TED mowing the lawn in a rain slicker and short shorts.  This man is ready for anything!

**INT. WHEELER HOUSE - BASEMENT - MORNING**

THE "CONAN THE BARBARIAN" SOUNDTRACK CASSETTE slots into a BOOMBOX.

A finger hits play.  DRUMS POUND and TRUMPETS BLARE and --

Mike and Lucas jolt awake, startled by the music!  They look around, confused, only to be *more confused* when they see:

Will. He's now dressed up as a PURPLE WIZARD! He's got a
hat, a staff, a fake beard, the whole works!

                    LUCAS
               (groggy)
          -- *What* are you doing -- ??

                    MIKE
          Yeah, Will, turn that down --

                    WILL
          Please address me by my full name.

                    MIKE
          What -- ?

Will SLAMS down his staff.

                    WILL
          My FULL NAME.

Mike and Lucas share looks.

                    MIKE
          Okay, um... "Will the Wise"...? Can
          you please turn down the music?

                    WILL
          That is not music.  That is the sound
          of... *destiny*.
               (waves staff)
          I have *seen* into the future.  And I
          have seen that today is a new day.
               (dramatic beat)
          A day FREE OF GIRLS.

Lucas and Mike share looks --

                    LUCAS
          Whoa wha -- ?

                    MIKE
          Will, *come on* --

Will points his staff at them --

                    WILL
          A tribe of villagers, the Qu'azar,
          are under threat from an evil force
          from the Swamps of Kuzatan.

Will now sits down at the table, where --

THE D&D GAME is still set up.  It's all ready to go!


                         134

                    MIKE
        Will, seriously, it's *way* too early --

                    WILL
        Tell that to the villagers crying for
        your help.  To the children so
        frightened they cannot sleep.  Are
        you truly going to let them perish?
        Or are you going to come to their
        rescue and become... the heroes you
        were always meant to be.

Mike grumbles, still trying to wake up, while --

Lucas smells himself.  Wrinkles his nose.

                    LUCAS
        ... Can I at least -- *shower first*?

Off Will, HARD CUT TO:

**INT. CABIN - BATHROOM - MORNING**

WHOOSH!  A STREAM OF SHOWER WATER spraying down onto --

HOPPER.  He rubs his temples.  Grumbles.  *Hungover.*

**INT. CABIN - MINUTES LATER**

Hopper exits the shower in a TOWEL.  As he ambles across the
cabin, our camera clocks the wine bottle from last night.

It's toppled over.  Empty.

**INT. CABIN - KITCHEN - MOMENTS LATER**

Hopper throws open a cabinet, grabs a BOTTLE OF TYLENOL.

He pops three pills, swallows them dry, then -- his eyes
narrow.  He's noticed a NOTE stuck to the fridge door.

He snatches it up.  Messy handwriting reads:

*"GONE TO MAX'S.  SLEEPING OVER -- EL."*

Just as Hopper takes this in --

BAM!  BAM!  BAM!  Someone POUNDS on the front door -- *and
directly into his brain.*  He winces.  A familiar voice belts:

                    JOYCE (O.S.)
        Hopper?!  You in there?  HOPPER?!

Hopper's irritation turns to *anger* at the sound of Joyce.


                    135

**INT. CABIN - MOMENTS LATER**

WHOOM!  Hopper throws opens the front door to find --

JOYCE standing on his porch.  She looks wild, frazzled, dark rings around her eyes.  She clearly hasn't slept a wink.

> HOPPER
> Well *well* look who it is --

She strides inside, on edge.

> JOYCE
> We need to talk --

> HOPPER
> Yeah, I'd say so --

Hopper slams the door behind her, pissed.

> HOPPER (CONT'D)
> I haven't been stood up like that
> since Alice Gilbert in the ninth
> grade --

Hopper's voice suddenly catches.  His eyes narrow.

> HOPPER (CONT'D)
> -- What are you doing?

REVERSE: Joyce is emptying out her purse onto the kitchen table.  ALL OF HER MAGNETS FALL OUT.  She grabs up a handful.

> HOPPER (CONT'D)
> Joyce? *Hello* -- ?

> JOYCE
> Just *watch*.  WATCH.

Joyce places a magnet on his fridge.  It doesn't stick and --

WHOMP!  It slides and falls to the floor.  She grabs another magnet and slaps it on the fridge.  It falls too.

She stares at Hopper.  Hopper stares back.

> HOPPER
> Okay, you're freaking me out here --

She tosses him the magnet from Melvald's --

> JOYCE
> Remember when you slipped on this??

Hopper catches the magnet, looks it over.

                    HOPPER
          Yeah -- ?

                    JOYCE
          It fell in the night.  It lost its --
          its *magnetism*.  And the same thing --
          the exact *same thing* happened at my
          house the day before.  So I thought
          that was weird -- right?  Why are all
          these magnets suddenly losing their --
          their magnetism -- ?

                    HOPPER
          Uh huh  --

                    JOYCE
          So I went to see Scott --

                    HOPPER
          *Scott?*  Who is Scott --

                    JOYCE
          Scott Clarke --

                    HOPPER
          *Your child's science teacher -- ?*

                    JOYCE
          He's -- he's pretty brilliant
          actually.  And I asked how this could
          happen -- and -- so, he created this
          magnetic field by connecting an AC
          transformer to --

                    HOPPER
          Whoa whoa whoa, *slow down* --

Hopper rubs his temples.  His headache is getting unbearable.

                    HOPPER (CONT'D)
          I just -- I want to get this
          straight.  You stand me up, no phone
          call, no apology -- because you were
          at *Scott Clarke's house* --

                    JOYCE
          Yes --

                    HOPPER
          Oh.  Oh, Joyce -- I have to say,
          you've outdone yourself this time --
          you've _REALLY_ outdone yourself.

Hopper stomps away, starts collecting his clothes from all
over the house.  Joyce follows him --

                    JOYCE
          You're not listening to me -- Scott --
          he was able to de-magnetize some
          magnets -- so he thinks --

                    HOPPER
          I DON'T *CARE* what Scott thinks --

                    JOYCE
          -- *He thinks* a large scale magnetic
          field could have been created by some
          kind of -- machine --- or, or
          experimental technology --

                    HOPPER
          You're right, he *really is brilliant*,
          this Scott -- is he single too -- ?

                    JOYCE
             (sharply)
          *What if it's them*?

Now *this* -- this stops Hopper dead in his tracks.

He turns back to Joyce.

                    HOPPER
          What are you talking about?

                    JOYCE
          To make a machine like this --
          you'd need resources -- scientists --
          funding -- tens -- *TENS* of millions
          of dollars --

                    HOPPER
          Joyce --

                    JOYCE
          It *can't be coincidence* -- it *has* to
          be them --

                    HOPPER
          JOYCE, stop --

                    JOYCE
          It *has* to be the lab --

                    HOPPER
          That's *impossible* --

                    JOYCE
            *How do you know --?*

                    HOPPER
          Because I KNOW --

Joyce steps toward him.

                    JOYCE
          Then prove it to me.

                    HOPPER
          Prove it?

                    JOYCE
          I want to go back there --

                    HOPPER
          To the lab -- ?

                    JOYCE
          Yes --

                    HOPPER
          Because some magnets fell off your
          fridge -- ?

                    JOYCE
          Yes.

Hopper absorbs this.  Nods his head.

                    HOPPER
          It makes sense, Joyce.  It makes
          total sense.  Listen -- I'm a little
          busy today, but how about...

He checks his watch.

                    HOPPER (CONT'D)
          We meet there later -- shall we say
          seven o'clock?  That is -- unless
          something else comes up, which --
                    (beat)
          It will.

WHOOSH!  He shuts the curtain to his room, closing his "door"
on Joyce's face.  And she *can't fucking believe him.*

                    JOYCE
          This is all -- all some *joke* to you?


                              139

**INT. CABIN - HOPPER'S ROOM - CONTINUOUS**

Hopper rants as he gets dressed.

>                    HOPPER
>          -- No it's not a joke, Joyce.  Jokes
>          are funny.  This is just -- *sad.*  You
>          wanna know what *I* think is really
>          going on here?  I think when I asked
>          you out, I *scared you.  So* now you're
>          *inventing things* to get worked up
>          about -- to push me away -- because
>          *God forbid* you move on -- God forbid
>          any of us move on!  Because that
>          would be too much, wouldn't it?
>          *Wouldn't it?*

Hooper suddenly realizes it's very quiet.

>                    HOPPER (CONT'D)
>          ... Joyce?

He flings open the curtain to reveal --

An EMPTY CABIN.  <u>Joyce is gone.</u>

**EXT. CABIN - DAY**

WHOOM!  The front door to the cabin explodes opens and --

Hopper stumbles out, still pulling on his clothes.

His eyes dart, scanning the porch, the forest --

>                    HOPPER
>          Joyce??  *Joyce?*

There's no sign of her.  *Wait.*  He hears a CRASHING NOISE.
It's coming from --

A SMALL WOODSHED.  What in the world?

He starts to walk over to it, baffled, but just as he nears
it, the shed door suddenly flies open and --

Joyce BURSTS OUT.  She's carrying <u>BOLT CUTTERS.</u>

>                    HOPPER (CONT'D)
>          *What* are you doing -- ?

>                    JOYCE
>          I need to borrow these.

She walks right past him.  Marching toward her car.

                    HOPPER
          You're not really going in there, are
          you?  Joyce?

Joyce ignores him, keeps walking.

                    HOPPER (CONT'D)
              *JOYCE!*

She doesn't stop.  Doesn't even turn back.

                    HOPPER (CONT'D)
              *Sonofabitch...!*

Hopper hurries after her, still pulling on his clothes, and --

**EXT. LOWER-CLASS NEIGHBORHOOD STREET - DAY**

Foliage blows in the growing wind.  *The storm is close.*

TILT DOWN TO FIND: Max and Eleven, walking together through a
lower-class neighborhood, moving fast.  Max is looking up at
the sky, concerned, and a little frustrated --

                    MAX
          -- It's gonna start pouring like any
          second, we should be at the mall or
          watching a movie or something --

Eleven shoots her a look.

                    ELEVEN
          You don't -- believe me?

                    MAX
          I believe you saw some super weird
          stuff, totally.  But you said Mike
          has sensed you in there before,
          right?

Eleven nods.

                    MAX (CONT'D)
          So maybe it was just like that?
          Maybe Billy just... sensed you
          somehow?

                    ELEVEN
          But the screams --

                        MAX
          I know.  The thing is -- when Billy's
          alone with a girl they make like
          really crazy noises...

                        ELEVEN
          They... *scream*?

                        MAX
          Sometimes?  But, like, happy screams.

                        ELEVEN
          *Happy* screams?  What is -- happy
          scream?

                        MAX
          It's...
              (how to put this...??)
          How about I just lend you my mom's
          *Cosmo*?

Before a confused Eleven can ask more questions --

Max crashes to a stop.  They've arrived at her house.

                        MAX (CONT'D)
          ... His car's not here.

Sure enough, the driveway is empty.

She looks at Eleven.

                        MAX (CONT'D)
          ... You *really* still want to do this?

Eleven looks at Max.  Nods.  And --

**INT. MAX'S HOUSE - BILLY'S ROOM - DAY**

Max opens the door to BILLY'S ROOM.

                        MAX
          Why do I get the feeling we're going
          to find *all kinds of wrong* in here?

Eleven ignores this, heads inside.  Max follows, reluctant.
It's a mess, and, *oh yes*, there are all sorts of "wrongs":

BEER CANS, CIGARETTES, HALF-NAKED LADIES ON POSTERS.

Max opens up a drawer, finds a *PLAYBOY*.

                    MAX (CONT'D)
          *Oh gag me with a spoon* --

She quickly shuts the drawer as --

**INT. MAX'S HOUSE - BILLY'S BATHROOM - DAY**

Eleven opens the door to the bathroom.  Freezes.

She's looking at something off-screen.  Something unsettling.

                    ELEVEN
          ... *Max.*

Max walks in and steps up beside her.  Her eyes narrow.

REVERSE TO REVEAL: A BATH TUB.  ODDLY ENOUGH -- IT'S FILLED
WITH PLASTIC BAGS, FLOATING LIKE SKIN IN CLOUDY WATER.

Max lifts up one of the bags.  Bold red letters read:

                    MAX
          "*ICE.*"  It's just *ice*.  It's probably
          for his muscles or something -- he
          works out like a maniac --

She tosses the bag back, turns to Eleven.

                    MAX (CONT'D)
          I mean, what, you think he kept that
          girl's *corpse* in here or something?

Max giggles at the thought -- but Eleven isn't laughing.
She's noticed something:

A TINY SMEAR OF BLOOD ON THE CABINET DOOR.

                    MAX (CONT'D)
          ... What is it?

Eleven doesn't answer.  She just kneels down by the cabinet
and swings it open.  Inside: a small trash can.  She reaches
inside the trash can, pulls out a LIFEGUARD BUM PACK, and...

A YELLOW LIFEGUARD WHISTLE.

Eleven holds it up.  As it unfurls, RACK FOCUS TO:

The side of the plastic whistle.  It's spotted with --

                    ELEVEN
          ... *Blood.*

Eleven turns back at Max.  Their eyes lock.

As Max finally begins to *believe*...

**EXT. HAWKINS POST - DAY**

Thunder RUMBLES in the dark sky.  TILT DOWN TO...

THE HAWKINS POST: *COURAGE IN JOURNALISM SINCE 1931!*

**INT. HAWKINS POST - PHOTOGRAPHY ROOM - DAY**

A RAT comes into focus.  It's... *frozen in time*.  Then --

WHOOM!  The rat is suddenly yanked *out of frame* as JONATHAN
plucks it off a drying line.  *It was a photograph*.  He passes
the photo to NANCY, who is holding a STACK OF PHOTOS.

As she re-shuffles the photos, ordering them:

                    JONATHAN
      ... You sure about this?

                    NANCY
      You really are your mom's son you
      know?

                    JONATHAN
      What does that mean?

She finishes ordering the photos, looks up.

                    NANCY
      It means you *worry* too much.  I've
      got this okay?

Nancy leans forward and kisses Jonathan, then hurries out.

Jonathan watches her go, still worried as...

                    TOM (PRE-LAP)
      Okay, so...

**INT. HAWKINS POST - CONFERENCE ROOM - DAY**

... The NEWSPAPER MEN are now passing the photos around.

                    TOM
          What exactly are we looking at here?
          This is the Driscoll lady's stuff?

                    NANCY
          No, no, see -- that's the thing.
          I mean, listen, I thought Missus
          Driscoll was crazy too --

                    NEWSPAPER MAN #1
          That old bag once told me Johnson
          killed Kennedy --

The room CHUCKLES.  Nancy ignores this, keeps going:

                    NANCY
          But it turns out she's not alone --
          Blackburn's Supply, Hawkins Farming,
          the Hess's -- they've all had some
          supplies go missing.  All in the past
          few days.  And not just fertilizer.
          Pesticides, cleaning supplies, diesel
          fuel --

Sure enough, we see PHOTOS OF CHEWED-THROUGH SUPPLIES.

                    NANCY (CONT'D)
          And that's just from one day of
          calling around.  I mean, there's got
          to be more --

                    BRUCE
          Wait wait wait --

BRUCE holds up his hand, interrupting Nancy.  He rubs his
nose.  He's clearly having some trouble containing himself.

                    BRUCE (CONT'D)
          Let me just make sure I've got this
          story of yours straight.  So these...
          little *rodents*, they've gone...
               (he twirls finger around ear)
          Cuckoo in their furry little heads --

Some chuckles from the room --

                    BRUCE (CONT'D)
          --- and now they're running 'round
          Hawkins, dinin' out on chemicals??

More laughter from the room.

                    NANCY
          Yeah I know how it sounds but --

Bruce holds up the photograph --

                    BRUCE
          BUT YOU'VE GOT PROOF!!

More laughter.  Bruce looks around at his friends.

                    BRUCE (CONT'D)
          You have to admit -- it does have one
          *helluva* headline: "Hawkins' Rats
          Prefer Poison, Nutbag Tells All!!!"

The room erupts now with laughter.  Tom holds up a hand --

                    TOM
          Guys, guys, enough!  THAT'S ENOUGH!

The group settles down, their laughter fading.  Tom grabs up
the photo of the rat.  He studies it, carefully considering.

                    TOM (CONT'D)
          I think this is... big.  Bigger than
          one article, in fact.

Nancy exhales, relieved.  *Finally someone gets it.*

                    TOM (CONT'D)
    I think this has *got to* be a *book*.
        (he looks up)
    "The Mysterious Case of the Missing
    Fertilizer. *A Nancy Drew Mystery*!"

THE ROOM EXPLODES WITH A SECOND WAVE OF LAUGHTER.

Tom smirks at Nancy. *Couldn't help himself.*

                    TOM (CONT'D)
    Next time a call comes in, do what we
    hired you for, and let us know, yeah?
    We'll decide what's a real story --
    and what's not.

Tom tosses the photo back over to Nancy and --

**INT. HAWKINS POST - BULLPEN - DAY**

WHOOM!  Nancy bursts back out of the conference room, the
stack of photos in hand.  Jonathan crosses to her, worried --

                    JONATHAN
    What'd they say?  Nancy?  Nancy -- ?

But Nancy just blows past him.  Too hurt to talk.  *Shit.*

Jonathan turns to look at the men in the conference room.

Their LAUGHTER GROWS, echoing through the bullpen.

Off Jonathan, red with embarrassment, SMASH TO:

**INT. STARCOURT MALL - DAY**

Starcourt Mall bustles with life.

**INT. MALL - SCOOPS AHOY! - DAY**

CLOSE ON: A TAPE spins in a MICRO CASSETTE PLAYER.  BOOM UP
TO FIND...

ROBIN, listening on headphones, concentrating hard as she
flips through the Russian-to-English dictionary, when --

                    VOICE (O.S.)
    Excuse me -- I SAID *EXCUSE ME!*

Robin lowers her headphones, looks up to find --

ERICA AND HER ARMY OF FRIENDS.  *Of course.*

                    ERICA
          I'd like to try the peanut butter
          chocolate swirl *please* --

                    ROBIN
          <u>No</u>.  No more samples today --

                    ERICA
          Why not -- ?

                    ROBIN
          Because you're *abusing* our policy.

Erica glares.  Looks around.

                    ERICA
          Where's the Sailor Man?

                    ROBIN
          He can't help you.  Sorry.  He's
          busy --

                    ERICA
          Busy with *what* -- ?

A beat as Robin considers, then:

                    ROBIN
          ... *Spycraft.*

Robin flashes a knowing smile and --

**INT. STARCOURT MALL - LOWER LEVEL - DAY**

WHOOSH!  BINOCULAR GLASSES poke out from behind THICK PLANT
LEAVES.

BINOCULAR POV: We sweep around the mall, moving from shopper
to shopper.  They all look... well... like *shoppers*.

                    DUSTIN (O.S.)
          ... You see anything?

REVERSE TO REVEAL: STEVE and DUSTIN hiding behind the plant.

Steve sweeps the binoculars around.  Frowns.

                    STEVE
          ... I guess I don't totally know what
          I'm looking for --

                    DUSTIN
          *Evil Russians.*

                    STEVE
          Yeah exactly, I don't know what a
          Russian looks like --

                    DUSTIN
          Tall, blonde, not smiling.  Also look
          for earpieces, camo, duffel bags,
          that kind of thing.

                    STEVE
          Right, right, *duffel bags...*

Steve re-doubles his focus, adjusts the focus, and --

BINCOCULAR POV: Steve locks onto something of great interest:
THE CUTE GIRL FROM EPISODE 301??  She's talking to a real
DOUCHE-Y LOOKING GUY!

                    STEVE (CONT'D)
          -- You have *GOT* to be kidding!
          Anna Jacobi is with that meathead
          Mark??

Dustin stares at Steve in disbelief.

                    DUSTIN
          Dude!  If you can't focus, just give
          me the binoculars --

                    STEVE
          What happened to standards??  Mark
          never even *came off the bench* -- !!!

Dustin yanks the binoculars away from Steve.  Annoyed.

                    DUSTIN
          You're a *terrible* spy, you know that?

He starts to canvass the mall for Russians himself.

                    DUSTIN (CONT'D)
          Also -- I don't even get why you're
          *looking* at girls when you've got the
          perfect girl *right in front of you* --

                    STEVE
          If you say Robin again --

                    DUSTIN
          Robin Robin Robin Robin --

                    STEVE
          No no no NO!  She's *NOT* my type dude,
          okay??  She's not even, like, in the
          ballpark of what my type is --

                    DUSTIN
          What's your type again?  *Not awesome?*

Steve sighs.  *Dustin is relentless.*

                    STEVE
          For starters, she's still in school,
          okay?  And she's weird.  And hyper.
          I don't like that.  And she was in
          drama and *band* --

Steve sticks out his tongue.  *GROSS.*

Dustin lowers his binoculars, shoots Steve a look.

                    DUSTIN
          Okay, now that you've graduated, and
          you're *technically* an "*adult*," I
          think it's time you move on from
          primitive constructs such as
          "popularity" --

                    STEVE
          "Primitive constructs?"  Is that some
          shit you learned from Camp Know-
          nothing --

                    DUSTIN
          It's Camp *Know Where,* and no -- it's
          shit I *learned from life.*  Instead of
          dating girls to make yourself *look
          cool,* try dating girls you *actually*
          like being around.  Like me with
          Suzie --

                    STEVE
          Oh yeah, Suzie who looks like Phoebe
          Cates, only hotter?  *That* Suzie?

Dustin rolls his eyes, goes back to the binoculars.

                    STEVE (CONT'D)
          -- And how did you score this perfect
          chick, huh?  Huh?  Oh right!  With <u>MY</u>
          advice.  Because <u>that's</u> how this
          works.  I give *you* advice.  You
          follow through.  NOT the other way
          around.  You hear me, Henderson?
          *Henderson*?

But Dustin isn't listening.  He's focused on the crowd.

> DUSTIN
> I've acquired a target.

> STEVE
> *Seriously*?

Dustin passes Steve the binoculars.

> DUSTIN
> Ten o'clock -- Sam Goody's.

Steve raises up the binoculars.  BINOCULAR POV: We swivel to Sam Goody, where we find A TALL MUSCULAR MAN WITH LONG BLONDE HAIR.  He's walking with a sense of purpose.

He's not smiling.  And, yep, he carries a --

> STEVE (O.S.)
> *... Duffel bag.*

Steve lowers the binoculars.  Looks at Dustin.  Eyes wide.

> STEVE/DUSTIN
> *Evil Russian.*

Steve and Dustin scramble to their feet and --

**EXT. WHEELER HOUSE - DAY**

PLOP.  PLOP.  PLOP.  The first drops of rain begin to fall outside the Wheeler house.  *The storm is almost here...*

As distant thunder *GROWLS*...

> WILL (O.S.)
> Do you guys hear that?  It sounds
> like thunder... but *no* -- wait...
> that's not thunder...

**INT. WHEELER HOUSE - BASEMENT - DAY**

We DRIFT PAST THE BOOMBOX, that CONAN music still blaring, to find...

Will, Lucas, and Mike playing Dungeons & Dragons!  Will is still in his wizard costume, and he's *really* into the game.

> WILL
> It's... a HORDE OF JUJU ZOMBIES!!!!

WHAM!  Will slams FIVE ZOMBIE MINIATURES onto the table.

Mike and Lucas don't react.  Clearly _not_ into the game.

> WILL (CONT'D)
> Sir Mike -- your action!

Mike looks at Lucas.  Apathetic.

> MIKE
> ... What should I do?

> LUCAS
> ... Attack?

Mike turns back to Will.

> MIKE
> Okay, I attack.  With my Greatsword.

Mike rolls the dice.  And --

> WILL
> WHOOSH!  You miss!  Your sword "CLANKS
> against the stone"!  The zombie horde
> lumbers toward you _and_ --

Will rolls the dice.

> WILL (CONT'D)
> A juju bites your arm!!!  Flesh
> _TEARS_!  RRRARGHGHGHG!

Mike gives a half-hearted reaction:

> MIKE
> AHHHHH.  My arm -- my arm.

Lucas laughs.  But Will does not, clearly hurt by this
mockery.  But he powers forward, staying in character:

> WILL
> Okay, Sir Lucas: the zombie horde
> ROARS.  Do you fight back -- or do
> you run?

Lucas is about respond when --

BRRRRRRRING!  The basement phone rings, interrupting.

Mike and Lucas share excited looks.  _Could it be... them?_

> WILL (CONT'D)
> That's a distraction -- a trap -- do
> not answer it -- !!

The boys ignore Will, scramble away from the table and --

Mike answers the phone, excited --

                    MIKE
          El???
               (his excitement drops)
          Sorry, no, no... I'm not interested.

Mike hangs up the phone.  Deeply disappointed.

                    MIKE (CONT'D)
          *Telemarketer.*

                    LUCAS
          Maybe we should just... call them --

                    MIKE
          Can we do that -- ?

                    LUCAS
          I mean I think so --

                    MIKE
          But what would we say -- ?

                    WILL (O.S.)
          YOU WILL SAY NOTHING!

Lucas and Mike snap back to Will.  He strides over.

                    WILL (CONT'D)
          Did you not heed my calling?

Will STOMPS his staff.

                    WILL (CONT'D)
          This is a day FREE OF GIRLS!  The
          Qu'azar tribe still need your help!

                    MIKE
          Alright, then... I use my torch to
          set fire to the chamber, sacrificing
          ourselves to kill the Jujus and save
          the Qu'azar, and we live on as heroes
          in the memories of the Kalamar!

                    LUCAS
          VICTORYYYYY!

Mike and Lucas high-five.

Will's face falls.  Dropping character.  *Giving up.*

                              WILL
                    Okay.  Fine.  You guys win.
                    *Congratulations.*

Will rips off his wizard hat.  Clearly upset.

Mike suddenly feels bad. He knows he went too far.

                              MIKE
                    Hey.  I'm just messing around, Will --

Will ignores Mike, removes his beard and his cape.

                              MIKE (CONT'D)
                    Come on.  We'll finish for real,
                    okay?  How much longer is the
                    campaign  -- ?

                              WILL
                    Just *forget it, Mike* --

                              MIKE
                    We want to keep playing, right Lucas?

                              LUCAS
                         (nope)
                    Totally --

                              MIKE
                    We'll just -- we'll call the girls
                    after the game --

Will suddenly explodes:

                              WILL
                    I said FORGET IT!  Okay, Mike???  *I'm
                    GOING HOME.*

Will grabs up his backpack and races away up the steps.

Mike stares, shocked by this outburst, and --

**EXT. WHEELER HOUSE - GARAGE**

WHOOM!  The basement door flying open as --

An angry Will stomps into the garage.

Mike hurries out after him --

                              MIKE
                    Will, come on, you can't leave, it's
                    raining --

Will ignores Mike.  Mounts his bike.

                    MIKE (CONT'D)
          -- I said I'm *sorry*, okay?  It's a
          cool campaign, it's super cool, we're
          just not really in the mood --

Will turns to Mike.  Upset.

                    WILL
          Yeah, that's the problem -- Mike.
          You guys are *never* in the mood
          anymore.  <u>You're ruining our party</u> --

                    MIKE
          What?  That's <u>*not true*</u> --

                    WILL
          No?  Where is Dustin right now?

Mike hesitates.  *Not sure.*

                    WILL (CONT'D)
          See -- you don't know *and you don't
          even care.*  And obviously he doesn't
          either -- and I don't blame him.
          You're destroying everything, and for
          what?  So you can swap spit with some
          STUPID GIRL --

                    MIKE
          El's NOT stupid, okay??  It's not my
          fault you don't like girls --

Will flinches.  *That stings.*

                    MIKE (CONT'D)
          I don't want to be a jerk, alright,
          but... we're not kids anymore.  I
          mean, what did you think, really?
          That we weren't ever going to have
          girlfriends?  That we were just going
          to play games in my basement the rest
          of our lives?

Will can't fight back his tears anymore.

                    WILL
          ... Yeah.  I guess I did.  I *really
          did.*  Pretty stupid, huh?

Will turns away and bikes out into the rain.

                         MIKE
            Will, come on!  Will -- Will!!!

But Will is already gone.  THUNDER BOOMS as --

**EXT. COUNTRY ROAD - DAY**

VROOM!  Hopper's Blazer speeds through the rain.  *Fast.*

**INT. HOPPER'S BLAZER - DAY**

*EEEE.  EEEE.  EEEE.*  Windshield wipers swipe the rain away.

Hopper is driving, Joyce sits passenger.  Neither speak, but
Hopper GRUMBLES, clearly not happy about this "adventure."

                         JOYCE
            ... Would you please stop that?

                         HOPPER
            Stop what?

                         JOYCE
            Making noises.

                         HOPPER
            I'm not "making noises."

                         JOYCE
            You're *grumbling.*

Hopper rolls his eyes.  Then grumbles *again.*

                         JOYCE (CONT'D)
            You know who you remind me of?
            Jonathan.  When he was <u>*six years old*</u>.

                         HOPPER
            Yeah?  You know who you remind me of?
            My mother.  Nasty and mean and
            batshit crazy --

                         JOYCE
            You know I could've done this myself --

                              156

                    HOPPER
          Yeah, well, how could I turn this
          down?  I mean, a date at Enzo's
          woulda been nice.  But breaking and
          entering government property on a
          rainy Monday afternoon?  *Even better*.

                    JOYCE
          You said it *wasn't a date* --

                    HOPPER
          It wasn't.  It most definitely
          *wasn't*.

Hopper cranks the volume on the radio and --

AN OLDIES SONG BLASTS.  Smothering the tension.  And --

**EXT. HAWKINS LABS - BARRICADED DOORS - DAY**

Our MUSIC CONTINUES as the Blazer crashes to a stop outside --

The Hawkins Lab entrance.  The barricaded doors read:

                TRESPASSERS WILL BE PROSECUTED.

We move into a SERIES OF QUICK SHOTS as --

-- Grumpy Hopper exits the car --

-- Removes his bolt cutters from the trunk --

-- Chops his way through the chain locks and --

**INT. HAWKINS LABS - MAIN LOBBY - DAY**

BOOM!  Hopper kicks open the lab door.  Our music ends.

Hopper and Joyce cross into the lobby.

We hold on a CLOSE-UP of Hopper as he looks around the lab.

His eyes go wide.

                    HOPPER
          You were right, Joyce.  They're
          back... they're *really back*....

WIDEN TO REVEAL: Hopper is just being a *dick*.  The lobby is
empty.  It's clear that no one's been in here in some time.

He cups a hand to his mouth, hollers:

                    HOPPER (CONT'D)
          Helllooo???   *HELLOOOOO???*

His voice echoes through the empty corridors.

                    HOPPER (CONT'D)
          IS ANYONE HERE???   WE COME IN PEACE!

As Hopper continues to strut through the lobby and call out,
being generally obnoxious, we turn our attention to Joyce.

She looks uneasy.  *Bad memories triggered by this place.*  Our
camera PUSHES IN ON HER FACE and...

***WE FLASHBACK TO***

*BOB SMILING AT HER, RELIEVED, WHEN -- THE DEMODOG LEAPS INTO*
*FRAME -- SLAMMING HIM TO THE GROUND -- JOYCE SCREAMS AS --*
*THE DEMODOG KILLS BOB -- HOPPER DRAGS JOYCE AWAY -- AND --*

                    HOPPER (O.S.) (CONT'D)
          Joyce?  *Joyce?*

**BACK TO SCENE**

Joyce snaps out of to this dark memory to find --

Hopper looking back at her with concern.

He can tell she's shaken.  Softens.

                    HOPPER (CONT'D)
          ... You alright?

                    JOYCE
          I -- I'm fine --

                    HOPPER
          You wanna wait in the car?

                    JOYCE
          I said *I'm fine*.

Joyce continues forward, marching past Hopper, pushing
through a set of double doors.  Hopper sighs, then follows.

**INT. HAWKINS LABS - HALLWAY - DAY**

As they venture deeper into this *tomb*, we MOVE UP to find...

A SMALL CAMERA ANCHORED TO THE HIGH CEILING.

We almost wouldn't have noticed but for --

A small red light. *Recording*. We push into...

The GLASS OF THE LENS. Which becomes....

**EXT. HAWKINS POOL - DAY**

A *PUDDLE* on the ground.

WHOOSH-SPLASH! Bike tires *blow* through the puddle as --

Eleven and Max bike up to the Hawkins pool. But they're the only ones *arriving*. Families are *leaving* en masse, sprinting to their cars, driving off. *Not a good day for swimming.*

A CRASH OF THUNDER rumbles overhead and --

**INT. HAWKINS POOL - POOL HOUSE - DAY**

Eleven and Max enter the pool house, dripping wet.

There are a FEW KIDS in here, waiting out the storm. Our camera swings past a GROUP OF GIRLS playing patty cake, settles on --

A MEATHEAD POOL MANAGER, lounging behind the front desk. His bare feet are kicked up and he's reading MAD MAGAZINE.

> MAX
> Excuse me --

He doesn't even look up from his magazine.

> POOL MANAGER
> No one in the water until thirty
> minutes after the last strike and
> *don't* try and argue with me. You
> wanna get electrocuted go climb a
> tree --

> MAX
> Yeah we don't care, we're not here to
> swim. Or get electrocuted.

> ELEVEN
> We found this.

Eleven tosses Heather's BUM PACK up on the desk.

The Pool Manager looks up.

> MAX
> Does that belong to someone here?

The Manager takes the pack, looks it over.

                    POOL MANAGER
          Oh yeah -- this is Heather's -- I'll
          get it back to her --

                    ELEVEN
          We could give it to her --

                    POOL MANAGER
          You *could*, 'cept she's not here.
          Bailed on me today.

Max and Eleven share knowing looks.

                    POOL MANAGER (CONT'D)
          What is this?  You girls want a
          reward or something?

                    MAX
          Nope.  We're just... good samaritans.

Max flashes a smile.  The Pool Manager just shakes his head,
*could give a shit,* and goes back to reading his magazine.

Eleven's eyes narrow, clocking something.  She walks away
from the desk, moving past the patty cake girls, and up to...

**THE OTHER SIDE OF THE ROOM**

Max joins her, following her gaze to find --

A PHOTOGRAPH OF HEATHER.  "LIFEGUARD OF THE MONTH."  A
FAMILIAR BUM PACK AROUND HER WAIST, A <u>YELLOW WHISTLE</u> AROUND
HER NECK.

                    MAX (CONT'D)
               (low)
          ... That's her.  *Heather.*

Eleven nods, yes.

                    MAX (CONT'D)
          Do you think... you can find her?

Eleven considers.  She looks look back at the Pool Manager,
finds him still reading the magazine.  *Not watching.*

She turns back to the photo of Heather.  Then --

WHOOM!  She snatches it off the wall and --

**INT. HAWKINS POOL - LOCKER ROOM - DAY**

WE'RE NOW RACING THROUGH A SERIES OF FAST TIGHT SHOTS AS:

-- Eleven's hand grabs SWIM GOGGLES off a hanger --

-- Max spins on a SHOWER KNOB, turning on a shower --

-- She spins ANOTHER KNOB, another, *another* as --

-- Eleven covers the goggles up with DUCT TAPE --

-- She places the PHOTO OF HEATHER on the floor --

AND WE NOW WIDEN OUT TO REVEAL:

Eleven sitting cross-legged on the tiled floor.  The photo of
Heather is laid out in front of her and the showers are all
running behind her, creating a SUSTAINED STATIC-LIKE SOUND.

Max crouches beside Eleven.  On edge.

                    MAX
          ... Will this work?

                    ELEVEN
          ... I think so.

Eleven takes one last look at Heather's photo, then slips the
duct-taped goggles over her eyes, takes a deep breath, and...

THE SOUND OF THE RUSHING WATER TRANSFORMS... BECOMING THE
SOUND OF VOICES... OVERLAPPING... GROWING LOUDER... AND...

**THE BLACK VOID**

SILENCE.  We're back in the watery void.

Eleven looks across the eerie vastness.  Sees...

A VERTICAL OBJECT jutting up out of the dark water.

She slowly approaches.  It's a MAILBOX.  1438 Oak Street.  As
Eleven reaches out and touches it, something materializes:

A RED DOOR.  TEN FEET AWAY.  STRIKING AGAINST THE BLACK.

**INT. HAWKINS POOL - LOCKER ROOM - DAY**

Max leans in.  Nervous.  Low:

                    MAX
          ... What do you see?

                    ELEVEN
          A house.  A... door.  A *red door*.

**THE BLACK VOID**

Eleven approaches this red door.  Opens it.

**ON THE OTHER SIDE OF THE DOOR,**

A LARGE WHITE BATHTUB. She approaches....

Lying within the tub, under the water and CHUNKS OF ICE...

HEATHER.  Still dressed in her bright red lifeguard swimsuit.

She's not moving.  Seemingly dead?  When suddenly --

WHOOM!  She bursts up out of water.  Breathing hard.  Alive.

But she does not look good.  She's shaking, her breathing is
shallow, and her skin is very pale.  Her eyes lock onto
Eleven... like Billy, it seems that she can *see* her.

Then, through shallow breaths, she says:

> HEATHER
> ... *Help... me* --

Eleven opens her mouth, about to respond, when --

WHOOM!   HEATHER IS SUDDENLY SUCKED BACK DOWN INTO THE ICY
WATER!   THE TUB AND THE WATER VANISH IN A *SWIRL OF SMOKE* --

AND HEATHER IS GONE!

> ELEVEN
> HEATHER??   HEATHER -- ??!

Eleven drops to her knees.  Her eyes shoot wide.

She can still see Heather!  She is being dragged down JAWS-
like *BELOW THE DARK SURFACE OF THE VOID, DOWN DOWN DOWN.*

Eleven reaches for her, plunging her hand through the surface
of the void floor, reaching into the dark water, desperate.

Heather reaches back.  But she's too far away already.

Eleven can only watch helplessly as she is dragged further
and further away, until she is but a speck in the dark --

And we SMASH BACK TO:

**INT. HAWKINS POOL - LOCKER ROOM - DAY**

WHOOM!  Eleven rips off the goggles.  Breathing hard.

                         MAX
          ... What happened??   *EL???*

Eleven looks at Max.  Scared.  And...

**EXT. STARCOURT MALL - DAY**

BOOM!  Another CRASH OF THUNDER outside the mall.

Shoppers race in and out, carrying umbrellas.

**INT. STARCOURT MALL - UPPER LEVEL - DAY**

CLOSE ON: Sneakers squeak, moving fast across the tile floor.

WIDEN OUT: We're with Dustin and Steve, moving through the
mall, trailing the Evil Russian.  They weave through the
crowd, desperately trying not to lose sight of him.

                         DUSTIN
          Slow down -- *slow down* --

                         STEVE
          I don't want to lose him --

                         DUSTIN
          You're getting too close --

                         STEVE
          No I'm not --

                         DUSTIN
          Yes you are --

                         STEVE
          NO I'm --

WHAM!  Steve slams into a HIP TEENAGER.

                      HIP TEENAGER
          Watch it, dickwad!!

                         STEVE
          Sorry, sorry --

*Too late.*  The Evil Russian heard the commotion, *turns* --

Steve quickly looks away, eying a window display of
CHILDREN'S TOYS, while Dustin grabs up a PAYPHONE.

                         DUSTIN
          Hello how are you yes I'm fine --

It's official: <u>THEY ARE THE WORST SPIES EVER</u>.  But...

The Evil Russian *somehow* doesn't seem suspicious!  He turns
back around, continues on his way, and then enters --

A JAZZERCISE GYM!!

Dustin and Steve share confused looks and --

**INT. MALL - OUTSIDE THE GYM - MOMENTS LATER**

The boys race up the glass window.   Their eyes narrow.

**INT. GYM - THROUGH THE GLASS - BOYS' POV - CONTINUOUS**

A GROUP OF SPANDEX-CLAD WOMEN excitedly greet the Russian.

                    JAZZERCISE WOMEN
          Hey Dougie!

                    EVIL RUSSIAN
          Hey ladies!  How we doing this
          morning???

                    JAZZERCISE WOMEN
          GREAT -- !

"DOUGIE" opens his duffel bag and removes...

A BOOMBOX?!?!  He hits play.  AN EIGHTIES FUNK TUNE BLARES.

                    DOUGIE
          Alright!  Who's ready to sweat???

                    JAZZERCISE WOMEN
          WE ARE!!!

Dougie removes his jacket to reveal a COLORFUL TANK TOP!

Steve and Dustin share stunned looks.  Wait a *minute*... this
guy isn't an Evil Russian -- he's a Jazzercise instructor!!

                    DOUGIE
          OH -- okay!!  And nice and easy now!
          Starting with the head.  And.  HERE!
          WE!  GO!

Dougie begins to lead them in an exercise.  *Smiling* big.

Off Steve and Dustin, slack-jawed, CRASH TO:

**INT. SCOOPS AHOY! - DAY**

Robin, sitting at the counter, still working on translation.

She's finished a new sentence:

                    ROBIN
          ..."*If you tread lightly...*"

She reads back over everything she has.  Trying to crack it.

                    ROBIN (CONT'D)
          ... "The week is long --  the silver
          cat feeds -- when blue and yellow
          meet in the west -- a trip to China
          sounds nice -- if you *tread
          lightly* -- "  *Tread lightly*???

She shakes her head.  It's nonsense.  When --

BAM BAM!  A KNOCKING interrupts her concentration.

She drops her headphones, sighs, and...

**INT. SCOOPS AHOY! - BACK ROOM - MOMENTS LATER**

Robin swings opens the back door.  It's --

A DELIVERY MAN.  He lifts a package off a PUSHCART, hands it
to her.

                    DELIVERY MAN
          Delivery for ya --

                    ROBIN
          Thanks --

He passes Robin a clipboard to sign.  She quickly signs,
hands the clipboard back, then... her eyes narrow.  Noticing:

The Delivery Man's HAT.  It reads: *LYNX*.

                    DELIVERY MAN
          Have a nice day.

                    ROBIN
          ... You too.

He turns, walks away.  Off Robin, smile fading...

**INT. MALL - DELIVERY CORRIDOR - MOMENTS LATER**

Robin steps out into the delivery corridor.  She watches the
Delivery Man push his cart away.  The back of his jacket
reads *LYNX TRANSPO*.  And it features a logo of a --

                    ROBIN
          Silver cat.  *Silver cat.*

**INT. SCOOPS AHOY! - MOMENTS LATER**

Dustin and Steve burst back into the store --

>                    STEVE
>          Robin, oh man -- you won't believe
>          who Dustin thought was a Russian --

>                    DUSTIN
>          You thought it too -- !

>                    STEVE
>          Did not -- !

>                    DUSTIN
>          *Did too* -- !

Robin ignores their childish bickering, races out the store.

Dustin and Steve stare, watching her go, baffled as --

**INT. MALL - BALCONY - MOMENTS LATER**

Robin races out into the middle of the mall.  Talking to
herself.

>                    ROBIN
>          "A trip to China sounds nice -- "   "A
>          trip to China sounds nice -- "

Her eyes dart to the food court.  To a restaurant called:

IMPERIAL PANDA.  *Chinese.*  Then --

>                    ROBIN (CONT'D)
>          "If you tread lightly," if you tread,
>          tread, tread  -- "

She locks on an upstairs store called KAUFMAN SHOES.  Then --

>                    ROBIN (CONT'D)
>          "When blue and yellow meet in the
>          west -- "

She spins around.  Her eyes to the MALL CLOCK.  Its hands are --

BLUE AND YELLOW.  Holy shit.  *Holy shit.  Holy* --

>                    STEVE (O.S.)
>          Robin!

She whirls around with a start to find --

Steve and Dustin, racing up to her, confused.

                    STEVE (CONT'D)
        ... What are you doing?

She takes a beat to catch her breath.  Then --

                    ROBIN
        I -- I cracked it.

She holds up the notepad.

                    ROBIN (CONT'D)
        I cracked the code.

Off Dustin and Steve, gobsmacked, SMASH TO --

**EXT. HAWKINS POST - DAY**

BOOM!  RAIN POURS outside Hawkins Post.

**INT. HAWKINS POST - KITCHEN - MOMENTS LATER**

Nancy opens up the coffee maker, removes its filter (filled
with used grounds), and dumps it into the trash.  She then
opens up the cabinet to get more coffee, and --

WHOOOM!  A LARGE RAT SUDDENLY LEAPS OUT!!

Nancy gasps in terror and leaps back but --

It's just a RUBBER RAT!  It swings from a string which has
been tied to the cabinet door.  Just as Nancy takes this in --

A CHORUS OF LAUGHTER ERUPTS.  She whips around to find --

Bruce and the men in the bullpen watching, laughing.

                    BRUCE
        Watch out!!!  It might have rabies!!!

Bruce makes a rat face.  Gnashes his teeth.

More laughter erupts.

                    NEWSPAPER MAN #1
                        (to Bruce)
              You're sick, man, *SICK* --

Nancy burns.  She turns back to the rubber rat.  Still
swinging from that string.  Rips it off the cabinet.

Her eyes narrow.  *An idea forming.*

**INT. HAWKINS POST - PHOTOGRAPHY ROOM - DAY**

WHOOM!  Nancy bursts into Jonathan's dark room, once again
flooding it with light, obliterating his work.

                        JONATHAN
                  Hey -- *come on -- !*

Nancy tosses him the rubber rat.

Jonathan startles, catches it.

                        JONATHAN (CONT'D)
                  What is this??

                        NANCY
              *Proof.*

                        JONATHAN
                  Proof -- ?

                        NANCY
                  That's what they said they need,
                  right?  So let's give it to them.

Jonathan looks at this rubber rat, still confused.

                        JONATHAN
                  A rubber rat?

                        NANCY
                  The *real one.*  Missus Driscoll's *rat.*
                  You said yourself it looked sick --
                  if we take it to an animal control
                  center, they can run blood tests,
                  find out what's wrong with it and --

                        JONATHAN
                  Whoa whoa, slow down -- Tom didn't
                  ask for proof, Nancy.  He told us to
                  drop it --

                        NANCY
                  That's only because he doesn't
                  believe us --

                    JONATHAN
     Nancy --

                    NANCY
     I _know_ I'm right --

                    JONATHAN
     That's not the point --

                    NANCY
     What's the point --?

                    JONATHAN
     The point is you should have thought
     about this _before_ you talked to them.
     They're assholes, okay, I get it --
     but at the end of the day, it's just
     some silly story --

                    NANCY
               (_wow_)
     It's "_silly_"?

                    JONATHAN
               (rephrasing)
     It's... a _silly_ thing to get fired
     over --

                    NANCY
     _No one's_ going to fire us.  Not when
     they realize I'm right.  If you
     don't want to come, that's fine.
     _Really_.  Just -- give me the keys.

Nancy holds out her hand.  Jonathan sighs --

                    JONATHAN
     You're _relentless_, you know that?

On that note, he heads out the door.  Nancy smiles, follows.

As the door swings shut behind them --

**EXT. HAWKINS LABS - NIGHT**

BOOM!  Thunder cracks, rain pours outside the lab.

**INT. HAWKINS LABS - STAIRWELL - NIGHT**

WHOOM!  A FLASHLIGHT PUNCHES through darkness as --

Hopper and Joyce make their way down the dark, winding lab
stairwell.  They've clearly been at this for some time.

Hopper pauses at a landing to take a breath.  Sweating
bullets.  Hands on knees.  *A mess.*

Joyce stares at him.

> JOYCE
> Are you alright?

> HOPPER
> You know -- there was an elevator for
> a reason.

He takes another breath, then continues on his way, and --

**INT. HAWKINS LABS - LOWER FLOOR - NIGHT**

BOOM!  A HEAVY METAL DOOR bangs open as...

Hopper and Joyce step out into a dark hallway.  Hopper steps
out, wipes his brow, relieved.  They've finally made it.

> HOPPER
> This way.

Hopper pushes forward.  Heaving.  Joyce follows.  And...

**INT. HAWKINS LABS - RIFT LAB - NIGHT**

SLASH!  A knife slices through a plastic seal as --

Hopper and Joyce enter the rift control room.  Hopper sweeps
his flashlight around.  It's dark, eerie.  It looks like the
remains of some long-lost alien spacecraft.

Hopper runs his hands along the control panel, pressing
buttons at random like some toddler.

> HOPPER
> Beep, boop, beep!

It's dead.  Just like everything else in here.

He continues into...

**INT. HAWKINS LABS - THE RIFT ROOM - MOMENTS LATER**

He walks up to the far wall, where the Rift once was.

It's solid concrete.  He RAPS the concrete with his fist.

> HOPPER
> Knock, knock, who's there?
> (waits a beat)
> Nope.  Nobody home.

He walks over to the floor and SMACKS it with his foot.  His
shoes THUD dully against the cement floor.  *Sounds solid.*

                    HOPPER (CONT'D)
          Just like I said -- all cavities have
          been filled.

He looks back up at Joyce.  She still looks uncertain.

                    HOPPER (CONT'D)
          I watched them do it, Joyce.  *I
          watched them.*

Joyce walks up to the Rift wall.  Places a hand on it.
Remembering back.  As our camera MOVES IN ON HER...

*WE ONCE AGAIN FLASHBACK, THIS TIME TO...*

*HOPPER AND JOYCE MOVING THROUGH THE UPSIDE DOWN -- FINDING
WILL -- REVIVING HIM -- POSSESSED WILL SCREAMS IN THE CABIN --
THE MIND FLAYER PARTICLES RUSH OUT OF HIM -- AND --*

                    HOPPER (CONT'D)
          <u>Hey</u>.

Joyce turns back to Hopper.  Shaken.  He walks over to her.

                    HOPPER (CONT'D)
          It's over, Joyce.  Okay?  *It's over.*

Deep down, Joyce knows he has to be right.  *He has to be.*

She sits down on the concrete steps.  Emotional.

                    JOYCE
          ... I think I'm losing my mind.

Hopper sits down beside her.  He's softening now.

                    HOPPER
          You're not losing your mind, okay?  I
          mean -- no more than I am.  The other
          day, I nearly *shot* Betsy Payne's dog.
          It charged at me from behind this
          fence and I swear to God I thought it
          was one of those... *things.*

He laughs a bit.  Joyce can't help but smile a bit.

                    HOPPER (CONT'D)
          Listen... you know I'm keeping a
          close eye on things, right?

                    JOYCE
          Yeah -- I -- I know --

                    HOPPER
          Because it's important to me that you
          feel safe here.  You and your family.
          I want you to feel that...
                    (a tad emotional)
          This can still be your home.

Joyce gives him a surprised look.  Hop smiles a bit.

                    HOPPER (CONT'D)
          What?  You didn't think I'd find out?
          Gary called me, said he's been fixing
          up your place, getting it ready to
          put on the market.

Joyce looks away.  She's not denying it.

                    HOPPER (CONT'D)
          Do the kids know yet?

Joyce shakes her head.  Hopper nods.  He gets it.

                    HOPPER (CONT'D)
          ... After Sarah, I had to get away.
          Had to get the hell out of that
          place, outrun those -- *memories* I
          guess.  I mean -- why do you think I
          came back to this shithole?

He smiles, then softens again.

                    HOPPER (CONT'D)
          ... But you have something I *never*
          *had*, Joyce.  You have people who know
          what you've been through.  Who care
          about you.  A support system.  And
          they're all right here.  In Hawkins.

Joyce takes this in.  Looks at Hopper.

                    JOYCE
          You mean, people like... Scott
          Clarke?

Hopper stares.

                    JOYCE (CONT'D)
          That was a joke.

Hopper can't help but smile.  Joyce wipes away a tear.  A
real moment between them here.  And that's when it happens:

A SMALL METALLIC SOUND ECHOES IN THE DISTANCE.

She turns.  Her eyes narrow.

> JOYCE (CONT'D)
> ... Did you hear that?

Hopper hesitates.  Not sure.  *When* --

ANOTHER NOISE.  LOUDER THIS TIME.  *UNDENIABLE*.

Hopper and Joyce both stand.  Eyes wide.  And...

**INT. HAWKINS LABS - HALLWAY OUTSIDE RIFT - NIGHT**

BOOM!  Hopper steps back into the hallway.

There's no one out here.  But wait --

He hears another sound.  FOOTSTEPS.  He races forward and --

**INT. HAWKINS LABS - LOWER FLOOR - NIGHT**

Swings back around the hallway, only to find --

The door to the stairwell swinging shut.

> HOPPER
> Hey -- HEY!!!

Hopper draws his gun, breaks into a run.

> JOYCE
> Hopper -- wait!!!

> HOPPER
> Stay back!!!

Hopper flies through the stairwell door, *gun raised*, and --

**EXT. BYERS HOUSE - NIGHT**

Pedals spin around and around, fast, as --

Mike and Lucas speed up to the Byers house on bikes.

**MOMENTS LATER**

Mike POUNDS the door, RINGS THE DOORBELL, but no one answers.

He shouts over the drone of the storm.

                    MIKE
          Will?  I'm sorry, man, okay?  I was
          being a total asshole -- please --
          can we just talk?

Still no response.  Lucas joins in the knocking.

                    LUCAS
          Hey Will -- come on, man -- we're
          sorry -- !!

As the boys pounds in unison, calling out, worried, we CUT:

**INT. BYERS HOUSE - NIGHT**

Inside the house.  It's empty.  <u>Will is not in here.</u>

**EXT. WOODS - NIGHT**

Our CAMERA now pushes toward: CASTLE BYERS.

It's caught in the downpour.  The flag is limp, <u>soaked</u>.

**INT. CASTLE BYERS - NIGHT**

The tarp is taking a pounding from the rain.  Tiny streams of
water drop through some holes.  We SLOWLY TILT DOWN to find:

Will.  He's huddled inside.  <u>All alone.</u>  He's flipping
through an old comic book.  Tosses it.  Looks around.

There are toys, magazines, tons of comics,  his own drawings
all over the walls, old movie tickets, D&D miniatures.

There was so much fun had in here.  *This was his childhood.*

As his eyes start to well up, we MOVE INTO....

**A CASCADE OF EMOTIONAL MEMORIES:**

*THE GANG TOGETHER PLAYING D&D IN MIKE'S BASEMENT --*

*MIKE AND WILL LAUGHING TOGETHER --*

*EVERYONE WATCHING DUSTIN PLAY DRAGON'S LAIR --*

*THE BOYS AT SCHOOL DRESSED AS GHOSTBUSTERS --*

But then we hear Mike's words from earlier echoing in.

                    *MIKE (V.O.)*
          *... I don't mean to be a jerk,*
          *alright?  But we're <u>not kids anymore</u>.*

*MIKE AND ELEVEN WALK DOWN THE HILL TOGETHER HAND IN HAND.*

> MIKE (V.O.)
> *... I mean, what did you think?  That
> we would never have girlfriends --*

*MIKE AND ELEVEN WALK AWAY FROM CEREBRO -- AWAY FROM WILL --*

> MIKE (V.O.)
> *That we were just going to play games
> in my basement the rest of our lives?*

*WILL TEARS OFF HIS WIZARD COSTUME AND --*

**BACK IN CASTLE BYERS,**

Will's eyes harden.  Sadness replaced by anger.

But it's not anger at Mike.  *It's anger at himself.*

His eyes lock onto a drawing of WILL THE WISE.

> WILL
> Stupid... so *stupid*..

He grabs the DRAWING and RIPS IT UP.

> WILL (CONT'D)
> *SO STUPID -- SO STUPID -- SO STUPID -*

He rips up another drawing.  Another.  Another.  Then --

He stops.  Breathing hard.  His eyes have locked onto...

A WOODEN BASEBALL BAT.  A FLASH OF LIGHTNING then --

**EXT. CASTLE BYERS - NIGHT**

Will steps outside into the rain, baseball bat now in hand.

He takes one look at Castle Byers through tears, then --

WHAM!  He swings the bat into a wall of the fort.  Wood
splinters, smashes, spraying rain.  But it's not enough.

He keeps attacking the fort.  *Demolishing it.*

He CRIES OUT IN ANGER with every hit as --

The fort crashes down around him.

Thunder BOOMS and --

**INT. MALL - SCOOPS AHOY! - NIGHT**

WHAM!  A GATE *RATTLES* as --

Erica kicks the gate of Scoops.  It's *been closed*.

> ERICA
> AHOY SAILORS!!  WE KNOW YOU'RE IN
> THERE!!  AHOY!!!

> ERICA FRIEND #1
> What is this *BULLSHIT*?!!

As Erica and Friend continue to kick and rattle the gate, our camera swings away, leaving them behind, DRIFTING TOWARD...

THE MALL CLOCK.  It's EIGHT FORTY-THREE PM.  *When blue and yellow meet in the west.*

PRE-LAP: THE SOUND OF BEEPING.  *EEEE EEE EEEE*.  It's...

**EXT. MALL - LOADING DOCK - NIGHT**

The SOUND OF A LYNX DELIVERY TRUCK, reversing through rain.

The truck backs up to a LOADING DOCK DOOR and...

**EXT. MALL - LOADING DOCK - ROOF - NIGHT**

We're now in a BINOCULAR POV, watching as LYNX WORKERS begin to unload boxes from the back of the truck.  Several GUARDS supervise the unloading.

Steve, Robin, Dustin are lying on the roof directly above the loading dock.  Dustin has the binoculars, spying.

> ROBIN
> (low)
> Okay, look for *Imperial Panda* and
> *Kaufman Shoes*.

Dustin PANS AROUND, scanning various boxes, until he finds --

A STACK OF BOXES MARKED "IMPERIAL PANDA" AND "KAUFMAN SHOES."

A WHISTLING MAN is pushing them on a LOADING CART.

> DUSTIN
> (low)
> -- They're with that whistling guy,
> ten o'clock --

Steve and Robin find him.  Watch those boxes, uneasy.

176

                    STEVE
        ... What do you think's in there?

                    DUSTIN
        Guns?  Bombs?

                    ROBIN
        Chemical weapons?

                    STEVE
        Great... that's all just... *great*.

The Whistling Man pushes the boxes up to a LARGE METAL DOOR.
Unlike all the other doors in this loading dock, it has an
ELECTRONIC CARD READER.  A SCARY-LOOKING GUARD walks over to
the card reader, slides a KEYCARD through it and --

WAHHHH!  The doors open up vertically.

                    ROBIN
        ... What's in there -- ?

                    DUSTIN
        Just more boxes --

                    STEVE
        Okay -- let me look --

Steve reaches for the binoculars --

                    STEVE (CONT'D)
        *Let me look* --

As Steve attempts to take the binoculars from Dustin --

The binoculars *SLIP*, dropping onto the roof with a CLANG!

**DOWN BELOW IN THE LOADING DOCK,**

The Scary Guard *hears it*.  His eyes snap up to the roof --

But he sees no sign of our heroes --

**EXT. MALL - LOADING DOCK - ROOF - NIGHT**

Because they're hiding beneath the lip of this roof, trying
not to breathe.  Steve looks down -- Robin's hand is
squeezing his own.  *Whoa.*  But there's no time for romance
now as --

**DOWN BELOW IN THE LOADING DOCK,**

                    SCARY GUARD
            (in Russian, to Guard #2)
        <Stay here.  Watch the door.>

He unholsters an SMG and starts walking fast and --

**EXT. MALL - LOADING DOCK - ROOF - NIGHT**

WHOOM!  A door explodes open as the Scary Guard bursts out
onto the roof.  His eyes scan the area like he's the
Terminator but --

REVERSE: The roof is empty.

**INT. MALL - DELIVERY CORRIDOR - LATER**

The "Scoops Troop" races through the delivery corridor
down below.  They're exhilarated.  But also *terrified*.

>                    ROBIN
>          .... Well... I think we found your
>          Russians.

As our TENSE MUSIC builds, we RETURN TO --

**EXT. MALL - LOADING DOCK - NIGHT**

The Whistling Man.  He finishes loading boxes into the
MYSTERIOUS ROOM.  GUARD #2 swipes his keycard and --

VROOM!  The door slams shut.  They walk away.  But...

We STAY, keeping our gaze fixed on the door to this room.  We
begin to hear a BIZARRE RUMBLING sound from within and then --

The door itself begins to *shake*.  As if from an earthquake.

Something is happening behind this door.  Something *bad*.

THE SOUND OF RUMBLING GROWS LOUDER -- AND LOUDER --  *AND* --

**INT. HAWKINS LABS - FIRST FLOOR - NIGHT**

BOOM!  A door explodes open as --

Hopper bursts out onto the first floor.  Gun raised.  He's
sweating bullets, barely able to breathe, but this is not the
time to rest.  He swings his flashlight around, but there's
so sign of the intruder, no sign, no --

*Wait*.  On the floor, A TRAIL OF WET FOOTPRINTS.

He follows the footprints, tracking them down --

**A HALLWAY -- CONTINUOUS**

The trail of footprints stops outside an OFFICE DOOR.

Hopper pauses outside, shouts through heavy breaths:

                    HOPPER
          -- THIS IS THE HAWKINS CHIEF OF
          POLICE!  COME OUT -- WITH YOUR HANDS
          UP, YOU HEAR ME?  HANDS UP!

No answer.  No sound of movement.  Hopper sighs.  *Fuck.*

He takes a beat, gathers his composure, then --

BOOM!  He kicks open the door and --

**INT. HAWKINS LABS - EMPTY OFFICE ROOM - NIGHT**

Hopper sweeps inside, swinging his gun around, but --

The intruder has fled.  The window is open, the wind blowing
rain inside.  Hopper hurries to the window, looks outside,
and --

BOOM-CRACK!  Lightning suddenly flashes, revealing...

THE INTRUDER STANDING BEHIND HOPPER.  IT WAS A TRAP.

Hopper senses him, turns --

*Too late.*  The Intruder slams him with A CLENCHED FIST --

Hopper stumbles back, dazed.  Blood spits from a GASH above
his eye.  He takes a wild, blind swing at the Intruder but --

The Intruder ducks, easily dodging, then WHAM-WHAM-BAM!  The
Intruder attacks Hopper with a SERIES OF VERY RAPID BLOWS.
This fucker is fast and STRONG.  We hear a DULL CRACK and --

Hopper goes down, flipping backwards onto tile floor as --

**INT. HAWKINS LABS - HALLWAY - NIGHT**

BOOM!  Joyce explodes out of the stairwell.

                    JOYCE
          *Hopper?!*  HOPPER??!

She spots the trail of water, follows it, bursts into --

**INT. HAWKINS LABS - EMPTY OFFICE ROOM - NIGHT**

The Intruder is gone -- Hopper lies flat on the ground.

She races over to him.  Drops to his side.  She shakes him.

                         JOYCE
          HOPPER -- *HOPPER* -- !!

But he's not moving.  Not responding.  Unconscious.  Dead?

VROOOOM!!  A LOUD ENGINE ROAR causes Joyce to look up.  She
scrambles over to the window.  Through it, she sees:

The Intruder starting up a MOTORCYCLE.  As he starts to put on
a familiar helmet, he turns *just* enough so that we can see
his face.  It's...

GRIGORI.  He slips on the helmet and --

Speeds off.  Vanishing into the rain.

Off Joyce, watching him shaken, we CRASH TO:

**EXT. DRISCOLL FARMHOUSE - NIGHT**

Another car: *Jonathan's.*  It speeds toward THE DRISCOLL FARM.

**EXT. DRISCOLL FARMHOUSE - PORCH - MOMENTS LATER**

DING DONG!  Nancy rings the doorbell.  But no one comes to
the door.  She tries the doorbell again.  Still nothing.

                         NANCY
          Missus Driscoll?  Doris?  *Hello?*

She raps on the door, but --

                         JONATHAN
          ... She must not be home --

                         NANCY
          -- She's eighty years old and it's
          pouring.  Where else would she be?

Nancy tries the doorknob.  It turns.

                         JONATHAN
               *Nancy --*

                         NANCY
          What if she fell or something?

Jonathan sighs.  *Relentless.*

**INT. DRISCOLL FARMHOUSE - FOYER - NIGHT**

Nancy steps into the foyer.  Jonathan follows, reluctant.

Nancy looks around.  The house seems empty.

                         NANCY
            Missus Driscoll?  It's Nancy -- from
            the Hawkins Post?  Are you okay?

There's no response.  *Wait.*  She hears something.  But it's
not a voice.  It is an odd WET and CRUNCHY NOISE.  Sounds of
someone eating something.  Nancy tracks the sound up to...

The basement door.  It's open.  *Of course it is.*

She calls into the darkness below:

                      NANCY (CONT'D)
            ... Missus Driscoll...?

No response.  Just more of that *AWFUL EATING SOUND.*

This is a classic "*don't go down there*" *moment*, but --

Nancy goes down there.

                       JONATHAN
                      (low)
            Nancy -- *Nancy!!*

Too late.  She's already gone.

Jonathan stares.  *Fuck!*  He quickly follows.

**INT. DRISCOLL FARMHOUSE - BASEMENT - NIGHT**

WOOD GROANS as Nancy and Jonathan descend into the basement.

They reach the bottom.  It's too dark to see down here.
Nancy finds the chain, yanks it, and --

BBZZZ!  The light bulb buzzes on, humming, revealing:

The floor is littered with FRESHLY TORN BAGS OF FERTILIZER --
There are no sign of rats.  But *THAT* sound.... *That* sound is
coming from the basement storage room, just out of view.

                       JONATHAN
                      (whisper)
               Nancy...

Nancy's eyes go to the work bench.  Above it: A WALL OF
TOOLS.  She snatches up a HAMMER.  Jonathan grabs a WRENCH.

The teens take a moment, then continue forward...

With each step, the sound grows LOUDER...

And *LOUDER*.  And *LOUDER*...  *And...*

**INT. BASEMENT - STORAGE ROOM - CONTINUOUS**

Our teens <u>freeze</u>. Jonathan lowers the knife. Because...

It's not a rat. It's not a monster. It's...

<u>MRS. DRISCOLL. SHE'S STANDING IN THE DARK CORNER OF THE
BASEMENT, HUNCHED OVER A TABLE, HER ARCHED BACK HEAVING AS --</u>

<u>SHE RAPIDLY SHOVELS FERTILIZER INTO HER MOUTH.</u>

THE TEENS CAN'T MOVE. CAN'T SPEAK. CAN ONLY WATCH AS --

MRS. DRISCOLL DEVOURS MORE AND MORE -- AND MORE -- AND --

> NANCY
> Missus ... Driscoll?

Mrs. Driscoll slowly turns. Looks at our teens.

Black liquid drools down her cold lips and --

Her eyes are dead. *Zombie-like.*

As our teens stare in shock --

Thunder BOOMS and --

**EXT. NEIGHBORHOOD STREET - NIGHT**

*WHOOSH*! Rain *FLIES* off metal spokes as...

Max and Eleven speed through the rain on Max's bike. Their
rain jackets fly, shimmer. They look like *superheroes*.

**EXT. 1438 OAK STREET - NIGHT**

They pull to a stop outside a TWO-STORY UPPER-CLASS HOUSE.

The mailbox reads 1438 OAK STREET.

> MAX
> ... Is this it?

Eleven looks from the mailbox to the house. The DOOR IS RED.

She nods. "*Yes.*" And...

**INT. 1438 OAK STREET - MOMENTS LATER**

CA-CHUNK! A DEAD BOLT "MAGICALLY" UNLOCKS and --

*EEEEEEEE.* The front door inches open. Eleven and Max enter.

There's PLEASANT MUSIC PLAYING. *Beethoven*. The girls share looks. That's odd....

Max's eyes narrow. She walks up to --

A FRAMED PORTRAIT. IT FEATURES A HAPPY-LOOKING FAMILY.

A MOM, A DAD... AND HEATHER. Suddenly it hits Max:

> MAX
> (low)
> ... This is her house --

> ELEVEN
> What -- ?

> MAX
> *Heather's house.*

Before Eleven can respond to this revelation, there is --

A BURST OF LAUGHTER. COMING FROM NEARBY.

The girls share surprised looks, then --

**INT. 1438 OAK STREET - CORRIDOR - MOMENTS LATER**

They track the laughter down a corridor and into...

**INT. 1438 OAK STREET - LARGE DINING ROOM - CONTINUOUS**

Billy is in here. He's eating a fancy dinner with --

HEATHER'S BOURGEOISE MOTHER AND FATHER. The mother, JANET, is new to us. But we recognize the father. It's --

TOM, the newspaper editor-in-chief. They laugh along genially to some joke that Billy has just made. Our girls barely have time to register what they're seeing when --

Billy sees our girls. His laughter dies.

> BILLY
> (surprised)
> ... *Max*??

Tom and Heather's mom now turn. All eyes are now on --

Max and Eleven. The girls look fucking crazy, standing in this fancy dining room in their soaking wet raincoats.

                    MAX
          -- We -- we didn't mean to barge in --
          we tried to knock, maybe you couldn't
          hear it over the storm --

                    TOM
          -- I'm sorry, *who are you*?

A CHAIR SCOOTS as Billy stands up, explaining:

                    BILLY
          I'm sorry -- Janet, Tom, this is my
          sister, Maxine --

                    JANET
          *Oh* --

Billy walks over to the girls.  He seems *genuinely* concerned.

                    BILLY
          -- What are you doing here?  Is
          something wrong?

                    MAX
          We wanted to see if -- if everything
          was okay --

Billy smiles, confused.

                    BILLY
          Okay?  Why wouldn't it be okay?

Max hesitates.  Unsure of what to say here.  But --

                    ELEVEN
               (firm)
          Where is she?

Billy looks at Eleven.  Taking her in for the first time.

                    BILLY
          I'm sorry... where is *who?*

Eleven is about to respond when --

WHOOM!  A door suddenly flies open and --

                    HEATHER (O.S.)
          They're a little burnt, so sorry -- !

HEATHER ENTERS FROM THE KITCHEN.  To the shock of our girls,
she looks perfectly normal, smiling and happy and unharmed.

She's carrying a tray of FRESHLY BAKED COOKIES.

She freezes when she sees the girls, confused.

The girls stare back. *Equally confused.*

> BILLY
> Heather -- this is my sister Maxine,
> and...
> > (to Eleven)
> I'm sorry, I didn't catch your name?

> ELEVEN
> El.

> BILLY
> *El.* Now what is it you were saying --
> El? You were looking for someone?

Eleven can't take her eyes off Heather.

*FLASHCUT TO HEATHER GETTING DRAGGED BELOW THE VOID --*

> ELEVEN
> ... I ... saw --

> MAX
> > (rescuing)
> *Your manager.* At the pool. He said
> you didn't come in to work and we got
> worried --

> BILLY
> Oh. *Oh shoot.*

Billy looks at Heather.

> BILLY (CONT'D)
> We forgot to call Chad, didn't we?

> HEATHER
> Oh yeah. We did forget!

Billy turns back to the girls, explaining:

> BILLY
> ... Heather wasn't feeling well, so
> we took the day off to... nurse her
> back to health. But she's feeling
> much better now. Aren't you,
> Heather?

> HEATHER
> Yes. Much better.

Heather smiles, then walks over to the girls. She holds out her tray of cookies.

                    HEATHER (CONT'D)
          You girls want one?  They're fresh
          out of the oven!

Off our girls, staring, baffled...

**EXT. 1438 OAK STREET - NIGHT**

BOOM!  THUNDER CRASHES as the girls hurry back out into the rain.  OUR CAMERA SLOWLY ROTATES AROUND TO REVEAL...

Billy, watching them through the foyer window.  His eyes are fixed intensely on *Eleven*.  TIME SEEMS TO SLOW as his pupils dilate -- his breathing quickens -- his heart pounds -- and --

WE'RE SUDDENLY BOMBARDED WITH A SERIES OF FLASHBACKS:

-- *WE FLY TOWARD ELEVEN AS SHE THRUSTS OUT HER HAND IN THE SUSPENDED CAGE -- SHE'S FIGHTING BACK THE MIND FLAYER -- SHE'S FIGHTING BACK US -- SHE LEVITATES -- SCREAMS -- SHOVING US BACK -- CLOSING THE GATE ON US --*

-- *THE MONSTER IN THE FACTORY SHRIEKS IN ANGER AND --*

**EXT. WOODS - CASTLE BYERS - NIGHT**

WHOOM!  WE SUDDENLY PULL OUT OF ANOTHER EYE.  IT'S...

Will.  He's standing amongst the rubble of Castle Byers.

The bat drops out of his hand.  He's sensed something again. *Something bad.*  His breaths quicken, his heart races, and --

A ROW OF GOOSEBUMPS rise on the back of his neck.

He drops to his knees.  *Weak.*  When --

                    VOICES (O.S.)
          WILL??  WILL?!

Mike and Lucas hurry toward him through the rain.

Mike drops down beside him.

                    MIKE
          -- What happened?  *Are you okay?*  ARE
          YOU OKAY???

Will looks up at Mike.  Shaking.  Their eyes *lock*.

                              WILL
                    ... He's back.

And right here ANOTHER BOOMING CRASH OF THUNDER takes us...

**INT. HEATHER'S HOUSE - NIGHT**

Back to Billy.  Watching as Eleven bikes away.

His breaths slow.  His heart rate returns to normal.  And --

**INT. HEATHER'S HOUSE - LARGE DINING ROOM - NIGHT**

Billy drops back into his seat at the dining table.

The CLASSICAL MUSIC returns to the foreground.

*As if nothing was ever wrong...*

The mother is eating her cookie.

                              HEATHER
                    Is everything alright?

                              BILLY
                         (smiles)
                    Yes.  Everything is fine.

                              JANET
                    Your sister really didn't want to
                    stay?

                              BILLY
                    No.  She's just -- not really a
                    people person.

                              JANET
                    I just don't like the idea of them
                    out there in the storm like that --

                              TOM
                    They'll be fine.

Janet reaches for her drink to wash down her cookie, but she
misses it, knocking the glass over.  Wine goes everywhere.

                              TOM (CONT'D)
                    I told you to slow down on that
                    wine  --

                              JANET
                    *Yes* darling --

                              187

Janet grabs a napkin and begins to clean up the mess of wine.
And that's when we realize: her hands are shaking.

> HEATHER
> ... Are you okay Mommy -- ?

> JANET
> Yes -- I'm fine.  Just --  feeling a
> bit lightheaded is all --

> TOM
> It's *all that wine* Janet --   --

But Janet doesn't seems *drunk*.  She seems... sick.  Her
breathing is labored.  She's sweating, blinking rapidly.

> JANET
> I'm sorry -- if you'll excuse me --

She smiles halfheartedly, abruptly stands.

> JANET (CONT'D)
> I'm gonna just -- go lie down for a
> bit --

She starts to walk away when her knees suddenly buckle and --

SHE COLLAPSES TO THE GROUND.

A shocked Tom leaps to his feet.

> TOM
> Janet??   *JANET* -- ??

He races over, drops to her side, shakes her --

> TOM (CONT'D)
> JANET???   *JANET* -- ?!

She's not responding.  Tom spins, panicked --

> TOM (CONT'D)
> *Call nine-one-one* -- !!!

His voice suddenly catches.  Heather is standing behind him.
There is not an ounce of worry or compassion in her eyes and
she has the WINE BOTTLE raised like a weapon.

Before Tom even has a chance to say anything --

Heather SWINGS the wine bottle and --

WHAM!  It SLAMS Tom across the head and --

TOM SPIRALS TO THE FLOOR.  HE GASPS ON THE GROUND.  IN PAIN.

HE BEGINS TO TRY TO CRAWL AWAY.  TRYING TO ESCAPE.

Billy calmly removes a CLOTH... methodically dabs it with
chloroform... then passes it over to --

Heather.  She looks down at her father.  He is still crawling
away.  She slowly walks up to him --

WHAM!  Steps on his back with her heel, pinning him back onto
ground.  She kneels beside him.  Emotionless.  *Gone.*

                    HEATHER
          ... I'm really sorry about this
          Daddy.  But it will all be over soon.
          I promise.

She slams the cloth over his mouth --

Stifling a BLOOD-CURDLING SCREAM --

And right here we --


                    END EPISODE

# CHAPTER FOUR:
## THE SAUNA TEST

WRITTEN BY **KATE TREFRY**

**EXT. MAX'S HOUSE - NIGHT 5**

The storm still rages: Foliage sways, thunder GROWLS.

A single light shines from Max's house.

**INT. MAX'S HOUSE - BATHROOM - NIGHT**

Rain beats against a window.  We PULL BACK to find...

ELEVEN, dressed in pajamas, brushing her teeth in Max's bathroom.  She is lost in deep thought.  *In memory.*

WE'RE BOMBARDED WITH FLASHBACKS FROM HER DAY:

*-- ELEVEN FINDS BILLY IN THE VOID -- HE LOOKS AT HER --*

*-- ELEVEN FINDS THE WHISTLE -- IT UNFURLS -- BLOODY --*

*-- ELEVEN FINDS HEATHER -- SHE CRIES FOR HELP --*

*-- HEATHER IS SUCKED UNDER THE WATER AND --*

SPLAT!  Eleven spits the toothpaste out into the sink.

She looks back up in the mirror.  Unnerved.

**INT. MAX'S HOUSE - MAX'S ROOM - NIGHT**

As Eleven climbs into bed with MAX...

Max holds up TWO COMIC BOOKS: SPIDER-MAN and WONDER WOMAN.

                    MAX
          Which one?

                    ELEVEN
          I don't -- know.

Max can tell El is bothered, lowers the comics.

                    MAX
          Hey.  There's *nothing* to worry
          about anymore, okay?

Eleven hesitates.  Not so sure about this.

                    ELEVEN
          It... doesn't make sense --

                    MAX
          What doesn't make sense?

                    ELEVEN
          Heather.  The blood -- the ice --

                    MAX
          Heather had a fever, so she took a
          cold bath, but she's better now.
          That *has* to be it.  I don't know
          where that blood came from.  But we
          saw her, *we both saw her*.  She's
          totally fine.

Eleven knows this is true, but...

                    ELEVEN
          ... What about Billy?

                    MAX
          What about him?

                    ELEVEN
          Did he seem...
               (how to put this?)
          Wrong to you?

Max can't help but smile a bit at this.

                    MAX
          "Wrong" is, like, *his default*.  But
          it's nice to know he's not a
          murderer.  Because that would have
          totally *SUCKED*.

Max chuckles.  Even Eleven smiles softly, feeling a bit
better now.  Her eyes shift to WONDER WOMAN, curious.

                    ELEVEN
          Who is... that?

                    MAX
          *See* -- this is why you can't just
          hang out with Mike all the time!
          This is Wonder Woman, aka Princess
          Diana -- she's from Paradise
          Island, which is like this hidden
          island where there are only Amazon
          woman warriors, and...

As Max continues, WE PUSH PAST OUR GIRLS TO THE WINDOW.
Slanted rain BATTERS the glass, harder and harder *and* --

**INT. DRISCOLL FARMHOUSE - BASEMENT - NIGHT**

MRS. DRISCOLL SCREAMS.

WHOOM!  A cloth strap yanks across a frail body as --

TWO PARAMEDICS secure her to a STRETCHER. But she's not
cooperative: she flails, desperate to escape, screaming in
anguish, tears in her eyes, her mouth smeared with black
fertilizer.

                    MRS. DRISCOLL
          LET ME GO, LET ME GO -- !!

                    PARAMEDIC #1
          Doris, we need you to stay calm for
          us, okay? *Stay calm --*

But Doris is not calm; tears begin to stream from her eyes.

                    MRS. DRISCOLL
          I HAVE TO GO BACK!! I HAVE TO GO
          BACK!!! I HAVE TO GO BACK!!!

JONATHAN, NANCY, and a clearly very disturbed OFFICER
CALLAHAN look on as the Paramedic yanks and tightens another
strap over the screaming Mrs. Driscoll, pinning her body to
the stretcher, and --

**EXT. DRISCOLL FARMHOUSE - NIGHT**

BOOM! Thunder crashes outside the Driscoll farm as --

The Paramedics carry her out on a stretcher. An OXYGEN MASK
is now strapped to her black-smeared mouth.

Nancy and Jonathan watch from the porch as they load her into
the back of the ambulance. They look stunned, *confused*.

Callahan steps beside them. Equally baffled.

                    CALLAHAN
          Okay so... you two wanna explain to
          me what in *the name of Jesus*
          happened here?

Off Jonathan and Nancy, not sure where to even <u>begin</u> --

**EXT. COUNTRY ROAD - NIGHT**

VROOM! The Ambulance speeds down a country road.

Its SIRENS BLARE as it *PUNCHES* through the torrential rain.

**INT. AMBULANCE - NIGHT**

We're now *inside* the jostling ambulance.

Mrs. Driscoll's eyes drift to the SIDE OF THE AMBULANCE. Her raspy breathing quickens beneath the oxygen mask as she reaches out a hand, *stretching* for someone... *or something.*

**EXT. COUNTRY ROAD - NIGHT**

WOO-WOO-WHOO! The ambulance races past camera to reveal --

THE FACTORY. Scarier than ever in this violent storm.

**EXT. ABANDONED FACTORY - NIGHT**

Billy's Camaro is parked out front in the tall weeds. Tears of rain drip down its cracked windshield. Another CRASH OF THUNDER and --

**FLASHBACK TO THE NIGHT OF THE ATTACK**

*HEATHER SLAMS the wine bottle into her father and --*

**FLASHBACK TO**

*Billy dragging a now unconscious Tom down the same hallway. His limp body catches on the rug, twisting it, as --*

**FLASHBACK TO**

*Billy and Heather tie up Tom and JANET -- gag their mouths --*

**FLASHBACK TO**

*Billy tosses them in his trunk. Slams it shut. And --*

**INT. ABANDONED FACTORY - BASEMENT - NIGHT**

WHOOM! A SHARP GASP AS A PAIR OF EYES SNAP OPEN.

It's TOM. He's weak and bleeding from the cut on his head. He tries to call out, *can't* -- his mouth is GAGGED. Tries to move, *can't* -- a rope binds him to a RUSTY BEAM. He hears a DESPERATE MOAN, looks over to find --

His wife, JANET. She's also gagged and bound, crying. They share a terrified look, and that's when they hear it.

FOOTSTEPS. They look up as --

HEATHER emerges from shadow. BILLY is not far behind.

Heather kneels down beside her dad.

> HEATHER
> Hi, Daddy.

She removes the gag. Tom gasps, his voice is choked, raspy --

                    TOM
     He-heather -- Heather -- wh-whatever
     this is -- whatever he's got you
     into -- you -- you don't have to do
     it -- _you can stop this_ --

                    HEATHER
     No.  There's no stopping it, Daddy.
     You'll see.  I promise.

Heather wipes a stray tear from her dad's cheek as --

Billy rips off Janet's gag.  Through sobs --

                    JANET
       _PLEASE -- HEATHER -- PLEASE -- !_

                    BILLY
     Try not to move.

Billy and Heather both stand and walk away, calmly headed
back up the stairs -- leaving Tom and Janet down here.

                    TOM
     HEATHER!  _HEATHER!!!  HEATHER!!!_

As Tom stops screaming, out of breath, he hears:

A HEAVY, WET BREATHING.  His eyes snap to the far end of the basement.  Something stirs in the shadows.  Something big...

THE MONSTER.  As it lumbers toward them, it catches some light, giving us our best look at it yet.  Its shape is spider-like, its skin wet and bloody and composed of gore.

FLESHY TENTACLE-LIKE APPENDAGES swing from its body.

> TOM (CONT'D)
> Jesus -- *JESUS CHRIST* --

Janet SCREAMS and Tom THRASHES, trying to escape, when --

WHOOO!  TWO FLESHY TENTACLES STRIKE OUT LIKE COBRAS AND --

SPLWAP!  THE TENTACLES LATCH ONTO TOM'S AND JANE'S MOUTHS, LIKE GAS MASKS MADE OF HUMAN FLESH.  The tentacles attached to these gas mask begin to throb and undulate horribly as --

They PUMP DARK PARTICLES into their mouths.  Now it *hits us*:

Tom and Janet are being *force-fed* Mind Flayer particles.

As more and more particles pump into them...

Their eyes flag... Their heads loll...

*And we make a HARD CUT TO:*

## MAIN TITLES

## EXT. CABIN - DAY 6

The rain has finally stopped.  The sun is shining.

## INT. CABIN - MAIN ROOM - DAY

CLOSE ON: A pair of eyes flutter open.

It's HOPPER.  He blinks, groggy, looks around.  He's on the sofa with a blanket over him.  *What the hell is going on? How did he get here?*  He starts to sit up, when --

> JOYCE
> Careful, *careful* --

Hopper looks up to find JOYCE walking over to him from across the cabin.  She's blurry at first, but comes into focus. She's carrying a GLASS OF WATER and a BOTTLE OF ADVIL.

                    HOPPER
          ... Joyce -- ?

Hopper is suddenly hit with a wave of nausea.  He doubles
over --

But Joyce is ready!  She grabs a tin pan from the floor and
slides it over to Hopper just in time to catch his vomit.

                    HOPPER (CONT'D)
          ... *Jesus*...

Hopper wipes some stray vomit from his mouth.

                    HOPPER (CONT'D)
          ... How long have I been out?

                    JOYCE
          A while.  You've been drifting in
          and out.

Hopper downs a handful of Advil.  Groggy.

                    HOPPER
          How'd I get here...?

                    JOYCE
          *Slowly*.  What's the last thing you
          remember?

                    HOPPER
          Some... *thug* attacked me --

Hopper starts to slide out of bed --

                    JOYCE
          You need to rest --

                    HOPPER
          I'm fine --

                    JOYCE
          You're *not* fine --

Hopper stands.  As he does, his bedsheet drops to reveal --

HE'S NAKED!  He catches the falling sheet *just* before his
privates are exposed.  He shoots Joyce a shocked look.

                    HOPPER
          Where are my clothes -- *?!*

**EXT. CABIN - PORCH**

WHOOM!  The cabin door flies open as --

Hopper stumbles onto the porch, his bedsheet haphazardly wrapped around him.  He squints in the light, then locates his uniform, which hangs limply from the porch railing.

He lifts it up.  IT'S SOPPING, MUDDY, BLOODY.

                    JOYCE
          They were soaked.
               (off Hop's look)
          I *didn't look*.

                    HOPPER
          Yeah.  *I bet*.

Hopper tosses the clothes back over the railing, and --

**INT. CABIN - DAY**

Hopper waddles back inside.  The bedsheet trails behind him like a dress train.  Joyce follows close behind him --

                    JOYCE
          Did you recognize him -- ?

                    HOPPER
          Who -- ?

                    JOYCE
          This thug --

                    HOPPER
          No, I didn't get a good look --

                    JOYCE
          He has to be government, right?

Hopper grabs up some dry clothes.

                    HOPPER
          Maybe.  But if he's government,
          why's he slinking around like that?
          Why's he running?  And why didn't
          we find anything down there?

                    JOYCE
          I don't know.  Let's ask him.

Joyce shoves a piece of scrap paper in Hopper's face.

HASTILY SCRIBBLED LETTERS read: *89---YB.*

                    HOPPER
          What's this?

                    JOYCE
          His license plate --

                    HOPPER
          What are these dashes -- ?

                    JOYCE
          Blanks.  It might be W Y at the
          end.  Or Z Y.  There was definitely
          a Y.

Hopper shoots Joyce a look, tosses the paper.

                    HOPPER
          You should stick to sales.

WHOOSH!  He slides the curtain "door" to his bedroom,
shutting Joyce out.  Joyce stands right outside, not letting
up:

                    JOYCE
          -- Why can't you run a search?

**INT. CABIN - HOPPER'S ROOM - DAY**

Hopper explains as he puts on the clothes --

                    HOPPER
          I never said I couldn't -- I just
          think you should lower your
          expectations --

                    JOYCE
          What does that mean -- ?

                    HOPPER
          It means it's not a simple process.
          I have to a file a request with the
          Motor Vehicle Department -- I'll
          push it, but keep in mind we're
          talking state government here.
          It's gonna take them weeks to get a
          match --

                    JOYCE
          *Weeks* -- ??

                    HOPPER (CONT'D)
          *If* we're lucky.  And the odds this
          guy purchased a car under his name,
          his *real name*, I mean, just forget
          it --

                    JOYCE
          It wasn't a car --

WHOOSH.  Hopper throws back open the curtain to reveal --

**INT. CABIN - OUTSIDE HOPPER'S ROOM - CONTINUOUS**

He's now dressed in his "SEXY" DATE OUTFIT!

Joyce can't help but startle a bit.

                    JOYCE
          *What* are you wearing??

Hopper doesn't react to this.  His mind racing.

                    HOPPER
          What do you mean it wasn't a car?

Off Joyce, SMASH TO:

**EXT. MAX'S HOUSE - ESTABLISHING**

WE PUSH IN on Max's house.

                    LUCAS VOICE (OVER WALKIE)
          Do you copy?  I repeat: this is a
          *CODE RED* --

**INT. MAX'S HOUSE - MAX'S ROOM - DAY**

A sleepy Max sits up in bed.  She's been woken by --

Lucas's voice, which is coming from her WALKIE-TALKIE at the
foot of the bed.

                    LUCAS VOICE (OVER WALKIE)
          This is a code red -- do you
          copy???  Max?  Do you copy??

As Eleven stirs awake, woken by the voice now too, an annoyed
Max crawls over a carpet of Wonder Woman comics and --

                    MAX
          Shut... UP...!

CLICK!  She switches off the walkie.  As she flops back into bed with a GROAN --

**INT. WHEELER HOUSE - BASEMENT - DAY**

A stunned LUCAS looks at MIKE.

> LUCAS
> *She turned it off.*

Mike considers this dilemma for a beat.  Then -- screw it. He storms over to the phone.  Quickly dials a number and --

**INT. MAX'S HOUSE - MAX'S ROOM - DAY**

Max's eyes snap back open as --

Her bedroom phone now begins to RING.

> MAX
> Oh.  You have *got* to be kidding.

Max flings off the covers, slides off the bed, and angrily grabs the phone --

> MAX (CONT'D)
> I'm sleeping go awayyyy -- !

> MIKE VOICE (OVER PHONE)
> This is Mike -- DON'T HANG UP.

Max freezes.  She's surprised to hear Mike -- and even more surprised by his tone.

**INT. WHEELER HOUSE - BASEMENT - INTERCUT**

We PUSH IN ON MIKE as he lays it out for her:

> MIKE
> Just listen to me, okay?
> Something's happened... something
> bad, and... our very lives may be
> at stake.

> MAX
> What are you talking about??

Mike glances at WILL, sitting on the couch, *scared*.

> MIKE
> Just come to my house and we'll
> explain everything.  And *hurry*.

Before Max has a chance to debate, Mike hangs up.

**INT. MAX'S HOUSE - MAX'S ROOM - DAY**

DIAL TONE.  Max lowers the phone, stunned.

Eleven sits up in the bed behind her, groggy.

> ELEVEN
> What... did he say?

Max looks back at Eleven, worried, as --

**INT. WHEELER HOUSE - BASEMENT - DAY**

Lucas looks at Mike, worried --

> LUCAS
> Dude she really doesn't like when
> you hang up on her --

Mike ignores this, strides back over to him.

> MIKE
> Try Dustin again.

> LUCAS
> He's not answering --

> MIKE
> *Try again*.

Lucas switches the walkie channel and --

**EXT. STARCOURT MALL - DAY**

WHOOSH!  A LYNX WORKER pushes boxes toward the secret room.

**ON THE ROOFTOP ABOVE,**

We find DUSTIN, lying on his belly, spying with binoculars.

BINOCULAR POV: AN ARMED GUARD swipes a KEYCARD through the
card reader.  The reader BEEPS, a light turns green, and...

The secret door grinds open.

> DUSTIN (PRE-LAP)
> ... That keycard opens the door.
> But unfortunately the Russian with
> this keycard also has a *massive*
> *gun*...

**INT. SCOOPS AHOY! - BACK ROOM - DAY**

Dustin is now pacing in the back room of Scoops, de-briefing.

STEVE and ROBIN listen, on edge.

> DUSTIN
> ... All I know is -- whatever's in
> that room -- whatever's in those
> boxes -- they _really_ don't want
> anyone finding it.

> ROBIN
> There's _gotta_ be a way in --

> STEVE
> What if I... take him out?

Robin shoots Steve a look.

> ROBIN
> Take _who_ out_?_

> STEVE
> This Russian guard.  I sneak up,
> knock him out, steal his keycard --

> DUSTIN
> Did you not hear the part about his
> _massive gun_ -- ?

> STEVE
> That's why I _sneak up_ on him --

> DUSTIN
> Steve -- be honest -- have you ever
> won a fight in your life?

> STEVE
> Okay, that was _one time_ dude --

> DUSTIN
> Didn't Jonathan beat you up too?

> STEVE
> That -- that was _different_ --

> DUSTIN
> How was that different -- ??

As the boys continue to argue, Robin's eyes narrow.  We track
with her as she walks away from them.  Her eyes move up to --

A VENTILATION GRATE BY THE CEILING.  The grate blows out air.
As she studies the vent, her mind races and... _an idea forms._

                    ROBIN
          (low, to herself, excited)
     That might work -- *that just might
     work* --

Robin turns, races past the bickering boys, and --

**INT. SCOOPS AHOY! - FRONT COUNTER - DAY**

-- Up to the front counter.  Robin grabs the TIP JAR and
upends it.  A PILE OF CASH AND COINS spills onto the counter.

She gathers it all up, quickly shoving it into her pockets

Steve approaches, confused --

                    STEVE
     The hell are you doing??

                    ROBIN
     I need cash --

                    STEVE
     Half that's mine --

Robin shoots him a look.  *Really?*  Then --

She leaps over the counter, makes for the exit.

                    STEVE (CONT'D)
     Where are you going??

                    ROBIN
     To find us a way into that room --
     a safe way.

She turns around, backpedaling now as she talks --

                    ROBIN (CONT'D)
     In the meantime -- no getting beat
     up.  Just... sling ice cream and
     *behave* -- I'll be back in a jiff.

And with that, Robin spins and *sprints* away down the mall.

Steve sighs, annoyed with her as always, while --

Dustin watches her -- *infatuated*.

                    DUSTIN
     I swear -- if I wasn't already
     taken...

Off Steve, staring at Dustin...

**EXT. HAWKINS POST - DAY**

We PUSH IN on the Hawkins Post.  PRE-LAP: *A TICKING CLOCK*.

*TICK TOCK.  TICK TOCK.  TICK TOCK.*

**INT. HAWKINS POST - BULLPEN - DAY**

We DRIFT through the bullpen door to find...

Nancy and Jonathan.  They're sitting by the closed door to
the EDITOR-IN-CHIEF'S OFFICE.  They look like guilty kids
waiting outside of the principal's office.

Nancy notices BRUCE eyeing them from his desk.  He makes a
hanging gesture.  Sticks out a sideways tongue.  *Then* --

WHOOM!  The door opens up and Callahan exits the office.

He looks unusually serious.  A half-beat later --

TOM EMERGES FROM THE OFFICE.  STILL ALIVE.

But he doesn't look happy.

                    TOM
          Nancy.  Jonathan.

He opens the door wide for them.  Off our tense teens --

                    TOM (PRE-LAP) (CONT'D)
          I've worked at this paper for
          twenty-five years.  Twenty.  Five.
          Years.

**INT. HAWKINS POST - TOM'S OFFICE - DAY**

Tom is now pacing in his office.  Sleeves rolled up.

Now that we're closer to him, we see that his skin is quite
pale and he's sweating like he's in a 90s Oliver Stone movie.

A fan spins, cooling the office.

                    TOM
          -- Now we're a small town paper...
          but we've got something the bigger
          papers don't have.  *Trust*.  The
          *trust of our community* --

                    NANCY
          Tom -- if you just let me explain --

                    TOM
              (talking over her)
     You want to know how I built that
     trust?  By placing my faith in
     something you two don't seem to
     value a whole lot: facts.  *Facts.*

Tom stops pacing, wipes his brow.

                    TOM (CONT'D)
     So, if you don't mind, I'd like to
     go over the *facts* here.

He lifts a finger for each fact.

                    TOM (CONT'D)
     *Fact one.*  You disobeyed my direct
     order to stop pursuing this "story" --
              (lifts second finger)
     *Two.*  You falsely identified
     yourself as reporters, repeatedly
     lying to an elderly woman --
              (third finger)
     *Three.*  You broke into her home,
     committing trespass --
              (fourth finger)
     *Four.*  She nearly died en route to
     the hospital --

Nancy can't take it anymore, interrupts:

                    NANCY
     She *would've* died if we hadn't
     shown up.  Whatever disease that
     rat had, it passed to her ---

                    TOM
     *FIVE.*  Missus Driscoll is a
     paranoid schizophrenic.

Nancy, for once, is speechless.  Jonathan looks stunned.

                    TOM (CONT'D)
     You didn't know that did you?  Now:
     disease carrying rats... the second
     coming of the plague... does that
     sound credible to you?  Or,
     perhaps, does it sound more like
     the delusions of a very sick old
     lady --

                    NANCY
     I -- I didn't know --

                    TOM
          The family is furious -- so
          furious, in fact, they've
          threatened litigation --

                    JONATHAN
          *Litigation* -- ??

                    NANCY
          That -- that's *crazy* --

                    TOM
          For once we agree.  This is
          "crazy."  In fact, in my entire
          professional career, I've never
          dealt with anything quite like it.

Tom pushes up off his desk, crosses to the door.

                    TOM (CONT'D)
          But hopefully you've learned
          something valuable here.  Learned
          how in the workplace -- in the *real
          world* -- there are consequences to
          your actions.  To your behavior.
          Which brings me to my sixth and
          final *fact*.

Tom opens the office door.  Turns back to the teens.

                    TOM (CONT'D)
          You're fired -- both of you.

Off Nancy and Jonathan, shaken, SMASH TO:

**EXT. WHEELER HOUSE - DAY**

WHOOSH!  Bike wheels cut across pavement as --

Max and Eleven bike toward the Wheeler house.

                    WILL (PRE-LAP)
          ... I didn't think it was anything
          at first... I mean, I think I
          just... didn't *want* to believe
          it...

**INT. WHEELER HOUSE - BASEMENT  - DAY**

Max and Eleven are now in the basement with the boys.

The kids sit on sofas, chairs, the floor, making a campfire-
style circle, all listening intently as Will explains:

                        WILL
            ... The first time I felt it was at
            *Day of the Dead* --

*WE FLASHBACK TO THE MOVIE THEATER -- WILL REACHES UP AND*
*TOUCHES THE BACK OF HIS NECK --*

                        MIKE
            The power went out that night too --

                        LUCAS
            Which could be coincidence --

                        MIKE
            Or not.

The girls share looks as Will continues:

                        WILL
            Then... I felt it again the next
            day.  At the field near the Wilson
            Farm.

*WE FLASHBACK TO THE KIDS WALKING UP THE HILL -- WILL PAUSES --*
*TOUCHES HIS NECK -- FINDS MORE GOOSEBUMPS --*

                        WILL (CONT'D)
            And then again, yesterday, outside
            Castle Byers --

*WE FLASHBACK TO LAST NIGHT AT CASTLE BYERS -- MORE GOOSEBUMPS*
*RISE ON HIS NECK -- MIKE CALLS OUT TO HIM --*

                        MAX
            What does it... feel like...?

                        WILL
                (finding the words)
            It's almost like... you know when
            you drop on a roller coaster?

                        MAX
            Yes --

                        ELEVEN
            No --

                        WILL
            It's like... everything inside your
            body is... sinking, all at once.
            Except... this is worse.  Your body
            goes cold.  You can't... breathe.
                (beat)
                        (MORE)

                    WILL (CONT'D)
          I've felt it before.  Whenever...
          he was close.

WE FLASHBACK TO SEASON 2 -- WILL IS AT HIS HOUSE -- FEELS
GOOSEBUMPS AS THE DOOR OPENS -- RED LIGHTNING FLASHES --

                    MAX
          ... When... *who* was close?

A beat, then...

                    WILL
          The Mind Flayer.

A SUDDEN AND VIOLENT FLASHBACK AS THE MIND FLAYER RISES UP
ABOVE WILL AT THE SOCCER FIELD -- WILL SCREAMS THROUGH TEARS:

                    WILL (FLASHBACK) (CONT'D)
          *GO AWAY!  GO AWAAAAY!!!!*

A chill goes through the entire room.

After a beat, Eleven breaks the silence --

                    ELEVEN
          I *closed The Gate.*

                    WILL
          I know, but...

Will locks eyes with Eleven.

                    WILL (CONT'D)
          What if he never left?  What if we
          locked him out here with us?

Off Eleven, unnerved...

**MOMENTS LATER**

WHOOM!  A BLANK PIECE OF PAPER hits the card table.

The kids crowd around Will as he draws on the paper with a
black charcoal crayon, creating a quick, crude sketch of the
Mind Flayer, all gangly arms, swirly lines, dark shapes --

                    WILL (CONT'D)
          This is him.  All of him.  But that
          day on the field -- *a part of
          him...* attached itself to me...

Will touches the drawing, getting black charcoal on his hand.
As the black smears across his palm, CUT TO:

*A FLASHBACK OF THE TORNADO-LIKE ARM SWOOPING OVER WILL AT THE FIELD -- PARTICLES SUCK INTO HIS MOUTH -- MORE AND MORE AND --*

> WILL (CONT'D)
> My mom got it out of me...

*FLASHBACK TO THE PARTICLES SHOOTING OUT OF WILL -- NANCY WATCHES THEM SOAR AWAY -- VANISHING INTO THE NIGHT SKY --*

> WILL (CONT'D)
> And then Eleven closed the Gate --

Will flips the paper upside down, slapping it down hard onto the table and here we --

*FLASHBACK TO ELEVEN CLOSING THE GATE.*

> WILL (CONT'D)
> But the part of him that was in me
> -- what if it's still in our world?
> *In Hawkins?*

Will touches the blank piece of paper, smearing black charcoal across it. The girls take this in, shaken, confused.

> MAX
> I, I don't understand. The
> Demodogs died when El closed the
> Gate. If the brain dies, <u>the *body*
> dies</u> --

> WILL
> I know. Maybe I'm wrong. I *hope*
> I'm wrong --

> MIKE
> But we can't take any chances. We
> have to assume the worst. <u>The Mind
> Flayer is back</u>.

> WILL
> And if he is, he would want to
> attach himself to someone again. A
> new "me" --

> LUCAS
> *A new "<u>Host</u>."*

We PUSH IN on Eleven as she takes all this in, her eyes narrowing. She's been struck by a thought.

Finally she looks up at the others.

                    ELEVEN
          ... How can you tell if someone is
          a... "Host?"

As all eyes go to Eleven, we SMASH TO:

**EXT. HAWKINS TOWN HALL - DAY**

WHAM!  A tire smashing over a PROTEST SIGN as --

HOPPER'S BLAZER speeds up to Town Hall.

**INT. HAWKINS TOWN HALL - OUTSIDE MAYOR'S OFFICE - DAY**

WHOOM!  The lobby door flies open.

Hopper marches in, on mission.  Joyce is close behind.

The MAYOR'S SECRETARY looks up at them, smiles.

                    HOPPER
          Hey, is Larry in?

                    MAYOR'S SECRETARY
          Yes, he's busy at the moment, but --

Hopper ignores her, makes a beeline for the Mayor's office.

Joyce hangs back, flashes the Secretary a friendly smile as --

**INT. HAWKINS TOWN HALL - MAYOR'S OFFICE - DAY**

Hopper heads into the Mayor's office.  Shuts the door.

MAYOR KLINE looks up from a phone call, surprised.

                    MAYOR KLINE
          Hold on, Tony -- uh -- let me -- uh
          -- let me call you back --

He hangs up the phone.

                    MAYOR KLINE (CONT'D)
          Jim --

                    HOPPER
          I know, I know -- you're busy --
          I'll make this fast, *promise*.

Hopper drops down into the chair opposite Larry.

                    MAYOR KLINE
          There some kind of a problem -- ?

                    HOPPER
          You might say that, yeah.  I'm
          trying to find out the name of a
          guy --

                    MAYOR KLINE
          "The *name of a guy* -- "

                    HOPPER
          Yeah.  I think you might know him --

                    MAYOR KLINE
          Alright --

                    HOPPER
          He was here the other day.  Rides a
          motorcycle -- big build, square
          jaw, dark hair.  Looks maybe
          military, ex-military -- this
          ringing any bells?

Larry considers, but...

                    MAYOR KLINE
          ... No, don't think so --

                    HOPPER
          You sure about that?  This was just
          two days ago -- right before I saw
          you --

Larry suddenly SNAPS his finger --

                    MAYOR KLINE
          Oh, you know what?

                    HOPPER
          What -- ?

                    MAYOR KLINE
          Maybe he's that maintenance man!

                    HOPPER
          "Maintenance" -- ?

                    MAYOR KLINE
          Yeah, yeah -- can't remember his
          name -- Gary or John or something --
          but we've had trouble with the
          plumbing   -- clogged toilets,
          sinks with minds of their own --

                    HOPPER
          You meeting with a lot of plumbers,
          Larry -- ?

                    MAYOR KLINE
          Sorry -- ?

                    HOPPER
          This guy, when I saw him, he was
          coming *out of your office* --

                    MAYOR KLINE
          Okay I don't remember that --

                    HOPPER
          What about that time I found you
          passed out in the Hideaway with
          powder all over your nose?  You
          remember that?

Larry laughs off the tension --

                    MAYOR KLINE
          Jim!  Jim, *come on now* --

                    HOPPER
          How about the time my boys found
          you and Candice going at it like
          rabbits in your Cadillac?  You
          remember that?  Does *your wife?*

Larry's friendly facade now drops, giving way to something
much darker.

                    MAYOR KLINE
          You really want to play this game
          Jim -- ?

                    HOPPER
          It's not a game, Larry.  It's just
          the truth --

                    MAYOR KLINE
          -- which *cuts both ways*.  Those
          pills you used to gobble like candy
          -- can't remember, did you have a
          prescription for those?

Hopper stills here.

                    MAYOR KLINE (CONT'D)
          How about drinking on duty -- I've
          got a few *fun stories* about that.


                              214

Larry leans in.

> MAYOR KLINE (CONT'D)
> One call to Tom at the Post --
> you're *done*. Gone. Oh, and *please*
> don't give me that dead daughter
> sob story -- I don't care.

Hopper burns. Larry relaxes a bit, smiles smugly. *He knows
he's won this round.*

> MAYOR KLINE (CONT'D)
> Now, if you don't mind, Jim -- I
> *really* am rather busy.

Larry pushes to his feet, crosses to the door.

> MAYOR KLINE (CONT'D)
> Our parade director is about to
> have a breakdown -- seems a
> shipment of fireworks got lost en
> route and --

Just as Larry reaches the door to his office, Hopper suddenly
grabs him by the back of the head and --

WHAM! SLAMS HIS HEAD FORWARD *INTO THE CLOSED DOOR.*

**INT. HAWKINS TOWN HALL - OUTSIDE MAYOR'S OFFICE - DAY**

Candice looks up sharply as the door shudders!

**INT. HAWKINS TOWN HALL - MAYOR'S OFFICE - DAY**

Mayor Kline stumbles back, dazed, holding his now bleeding
nose.

> MAYOR KLINE
> MY NOSE -- YOU BROKE MY GODDAMN NOSE!

> HOPPER
> Yeah, well, your new friend almost
> killed me last night, so I'd say
> we're still not even --

WHOOM! Hopper grabs Larry, throws him against a shelf.

**INT. HAWKINS TOWN HALL - OUTSIDE MAYOR'S OFFICE - DAY**

The Secretary races to the rescue --

> MAYOR'S SECRETARY
> -- LARRY?!

She tries to open the door to his office, but it's locked.

MAYOR'S SECRETARY (CONT'D)
*LARRY -- ??!  LARRY???*

**INT. HAWKINS TOWN HALL - MAYOR'S OFFICE - DAY**

Hopper leans into a hurt, gasping Larry.

HOPPER
Let's cut the bullshit, Larry,
shall we.  Who is he really?
Government?  Military -- ?

MAYOR KLINE
Jim -- you -- *you don't want to do
this --*

HOPPER
Is he government -- ?

MAYOR KLINE
*JIM --*

HOPPER
*WHO IS HE -- ?!*

MAYOR KLINE
... Arnold ... Schwarzenegger.

An unamused Hopper sucker punches Larry right in his broken
nose.  As Larry lets out another PAINED YELP --

**INT. HAWKINS TOWN HALL - OUTSIDE MAYOR'S OFFICE - DAY**

The Secretary races back to her desk only to find --

Joyce yanking the phone cord out of the wall.

JOYCE
Who were you going to call anyway?
The police?

Joyce tosses the cord to the ground as --

**INT. HAWKINS TOWN HALL - MAYOR'S OFFICE - DAY**

Hopper hauls the now weakened Larry across the office, back
over to his desk, then --

WHAM!  Hopper slams Larry's hand flat on the desk.

                    HOPPER
          That's a real nice ring you got
          there, Larry.

Hopper forces Larry's ring finger into the cigar cutter.

                    MAYOR KLINE
          *ARE YOU INSANE -- ?!?!?!*

                    HOPPER
          *Let's find out --*

He starts to squeeze but --

                    MAYOR KLINE
          *WAITWAITWAITWAIT -- !!!*

Kline is terrified now.  Sobbing.  He sputters:

                    MAYOR KLINE (CONT'D)
          I don't know his name -- I SWEAR --
          I SWEAR --

                    HOPPER
          But you *know* him -- ?

                    MAYOR KLINE
          He -- he -- he just -- brings me
          things sometimes --

                    HOPPER
          Things?  What kinds of things -- ?

                    MAYOR KLINE
          Money -- presents -- gifts --

                    HOPPER
          Who is this guy, *Santa Claus* -- ?

                    MAYOR KLINE
          Starcourt -- he works for Starcourt --

                    HOPPER
          Starcourt?  The mall?  *Nice try* --

Hopper starts to squeeze, drawing blood -- Larry screams
through tears:

                    MAYOR KLINE
          I SWEAR!!  I, I SWEAR!!  Starcourt
          -- they -- they own the mall -- but
          I don't know who they are, okay??
                         (MORE)

                    MAYOR KLINE (CONT'D)
          They want to expand to East
          Hawkins, they needed property --
          some land -- some people didn't
          want to sell -- so I leaned on 'em
          a little -- !!  THAT'S ALL -- I
          SWEAR -- THAT'S ALL!

                    HOPPER
          Why do they want this land -- ?

                    MAYOR KLINE
          I -- I don't know --- !

                    HOPPER
          Do you have records of these
          purchases -- these land purchases?

                    MAYOR KLINE
          Jim -- you -- you don't wanna mess
          with these people --

                    HOPPER
          I think you should worry about
          yourself right now, Larry.  Not me.
                    (beat)
          The records.  Where are they?

Off Larry, sobbing, *breaking* --

**INT. TOWN HALL - OUTSIDE MAYOR'S OFFICE - A LITTLE LATER**

WHOOM!  The door flies open as Hopper strides back into the
lobby -- and he's dragging Mayor Kline with him!

                    MAYOR'S SECRETARY
          Larry -- !

                    HOPPER
          Don't worry, he just bumped his
          head.  A little boo boo.  Isn't
          that right, Larry?

                    MAYOR KLINE
          Uh huh --

Hopper yanks Larry out of the room.  Joyce smiles at the
Secretary.  As if nothing were the matter at all.

                    JOYCE
          Have a nice day.

She follows Hopper.  Off the stunned Secretary...

**INT. HAWKINS POST - BULLPEN - DAY**

Nancy and Jonathan carry Bankers Boxes filled with their belongings through the office. *A walk of shame.*

It's awkward as hell. Everyone is staring.

Bruce leans over to Newspaper Man #1.

> BRUCE
> ... I hate to see her leave, but I do _love_ to watch her go...

As Newsman #1 cackles, the teens push out the door and --

**EXT. COUNTRY ROAD - DAY**

VROOOM! Jonathan's car TEARS down the road.

> NANCY (O.S.)
> It's bullshit -- _total bullshit_ --

**INT. JONATHAN'S CAR - DAY**

Jonathan drives while Nancy rants --

> NANCY
> ... I mean -- so *according to Tom* --
> Driscoll's just some schizophrenic?
> That rat was just a rat? And it's
> all -- *what* -- some big coincidence
> -- ?

Nancy turns to Jonathan.

> NANCY (CONT'D)
> You know what I think? I think Tom
> was on drugs --

                    JONATHAN
          What -- ?

                    NANCY
          I mean, did you see him?  He was
          sweating like crazy, his hands were
          all clammy, he looked *awful* --

Jonathan laughs a bit to himself.

                    NANCY (CONT'D)
          ... This is *funny* to you -- ?

                    JONATHAN
          No, it's just -- sort of
          incredible.

                    NANCY
          *"Incredible"* -- ?

                    JONATHAN
          Yeah, incredible how you just...
          continue to convince yourself --

                    NANCY
          What's *that* supposed to mean --

                    JONATHAN
          I mean did it occur to you that
          maybe, *just maybe,* you've been
          wrong about all this -- ?

                    NANCY
          Are you serious right now -- ?

                    JONATHAN
          Are *you?*

Jonathan shoots a look at Nancy.

                    JONATHAN (CONT'D)
          From the beginning, I've told you
          over and over to drop this story,
          that it was BAD idea, but you
          refused -- and now I'm screwed --

                    NANCY
          It's *a summer job* Jonathan, your
          life is hardly over --

                    JONATHAN
          You don't get what it's like,
          Nancy.
                    (MORE)

                    JONATHAN (CONT'D)
          I don't live in a nice two-story
          house on Maple Street -- my dad
          doesn't earn six figures -- he
          isn't *even around*.

                    NANCY
          Oh God here comes the "Oliver
          Twist" routine --

Jonathan shoots Nancy a dirty look.

                    JONATHAN
          Really?  *"Oliver Twist"?*  College
          tuition -- *mortgage* -- these are
          *real* things, Nancy -- things you
          don't care about only because you
          don't *have to*.

                    NANCY
          I didn't realize I still lived in a
          bubble --

                    JONATHAN
          Well *you do*.  You want everything
          handed to you on a silver platter.
          We were interns, Nancy -- *interns*.
          What did you expect -- you'd be
          star reporter in a month?  Crack
          the big case -- !

                    NANCY
          You sound *just* like them, you
          realize that, right?  *Just like*
          Bruce and those *assholes* --

                    JONATHAN
          Those *"assholes"* gave us jobs --

                    NANCY
          Is that what that was?  It was
          humiliating -- *humiliating* --

                    JONATHAN
          Yeah, the real world *SUCKS*.  Now
          deal with it like the *rest of us*.

Nancy shakes her head in disgust.

                    NANCY
          You don't know what it's like.

                    JONATHAN
          Neither do you.


                         221

                    NANCY
          Then I guess we just don't
          understand each other anymore.

                    JONATHAN
          Yeah.  I guess not.

As the teens stop speaking, fuming, feeling further apart
than ever, Jonathan PUNCHES the accelerator and --

**INT. WHEELER HOUSE - DAY**

WHOOM!  The door to the Wheeler house flies open as --

An upset Nancy races inside, clutching her sad box.  _Alone_.

KAREN hits off a vacuum cleaner, calls out with a smile:

                    KAREN
          Hey you're home early --

                    NANCY
          Yeah -- light day.

Nancy flashes a fake smile as she pounds up the stairs.

Off Karen, knowing something is wrong, CUT TO:

**EXT. STARCOURT MALL - DAY**

WHOOSH!  A bike flies toward the mall.  It's --

Robin, wearing a BACKPACK and HELMET!  She slams to a stop,
hops off the bike, and races excitedly to the mall entrance.

                    ROBIN (PRE-LAP)
          ... It's _fascinating_ what twenty
          bucks will get you at the County
          Recorder's Office...

**INT. SCOOPS AHOY! - BACK ROOM - DAY**

Robin removes large rolled-up papers from her backpack.

She flattens them on a table to reveal:

                    ROBIN
          Starcourt Mall.  The complete
          blueprints.

Dustin and Steve lean in, eyes wide.

                    DUSTIN
          Not bad, _not bad_ --

Robin grabs a RED MARKER, circles a room.

                    ROBIN
          Okay, so this is us, *Scoops*. And
          *this*...

She circles a room on the opposite side of the map.

                    ROBIN (CONT'D)
          ... Is where we want to get.

                    STEVE
          I don't see a way in --

                    ROBIN
          There's not.  If you're talking
          exclusively about *doors*.

Robin flips to a SECOND BLUEPRINT.  This one looks different,
with an intricate drawing of maze-like tubes.

                    DUSTIN
          ... *Air ducts*.

Robin nods.  *Bingo.*

                    ROBIN
          Turns out this secret room needs
          air just like any old room.  And
          these air ducts...

She draws a line from the top secret room, tracing a winding
path through the air ducts...

                    ROBIN (CONT'D)
          Lead all the way...

She circles another entrance to the air ducts.

                    ROBIN (CONT'D)
          Here.

She now points up with the marker.  All eyes go to --

The SCOOPS AHOY AIR DUCT.  Blowing cold air.  *Holy shit.*

**A LITTLE LATER**

CLOSE ON: A SCREWDRIVER twists as...

Steve -- now standing on a table -- unscrews the vent cover.

POP!  He removes the grate.  Holds out a hand.

                    STEVE
          Flashlight.

Dustin passes him a FLASHLIGHT.  WE NOW CUT INSIDE THE VENT
as Steve swings the flashlight around.  His eyes narrow.

                    STEVE (CONT'D)
          Yeah, I don't know... it's like,
          super tight in here.  I don't think
          you can fit.

                    DUSTIN
          I can fit.  I don't have
          collarbones, remember?

                    ROBIN
          What?

                    STEVE
          It's a disease.  Cryto --
          something.

Dustin hops up on the table and shoves his head into the vent
and pushes, hard, trying to squeeze his body in but... no go.

                    STEVE (CONT'D)
          He's missing bones and stuff.  He
          can bend like Gumbo and --

                    DUSTIN
          Steve, shut up and push me -- !

                    STEVE
          What -- ?

                    DUSTIN
          PUSH ME!

Steve sighs, reluctantly grabs Dustin by the butt, and starts
to push, but Dustin still isn't going anywhere.

                    DUSTIN (CONT'D)
          PUSH HARDER!!

                    STEVE
          I'm PUSHING!

The boys both groan with effort -- it sounds like two men
giving birth.  And it's not working.  Dustin can't fit.

As Robin watches this doomed effort from below --

DING DING DING DING!!!  A BELL RINGS off-screen.

Robin looks toward the front counter to find ERICA.

                    ERICA
          AHOY SAILORS!  AHOY!!!  ALL HANDS
          ON DECK!!!!!  AHOY!!

We PUSH IN on Robin, *an idea forming*, as --

Erica continues to ring that bell.  DING DING -- !!!

**EXT. HAWKINS POOL - DAY**

*SPLASH!!!*  KIDS SCREAM WITH JOY as they leap into the pool.

We're watching them from a binocular POV.  The binoculars
swivel, pan and tilt to find --

BILLY.  He's in his regular spot on the lifeguard stand,
sprawled out.  But today he looks *full* LOST BOYS: long-
sleeved shirt, dark sunglasses, hands white with sunscreen.

He CHUGS liquid from a giant cup, chewing the ice.

**EXT. WOODS BY HAWKINS POOL - CONTINUOUS**

Max is the one spying on him through the binoculars.  She's
in the woods a few hundred yards away, hiding behind foliage.

Behind her, the rest of the gang: Eleven, Mike, Lucas, Will.

                    MAX
          ... I don't know -- he looks pretty
          normal to me --

                    LUCAS
          *Normal?*  How many times have you
          seen him with a shirt on?
          Seriously.  I'm asking.

                    MAX
          It's a *little* weird.

                    MIKE
          More than a little.  And he was in
          a tub with ice -- the Mind Flayer
          likes it cold -- plus everything El
          saw --

                    MAX
          But he's *lounging at the pool*,
          which is, like, the *least* Mind
          Flayer thing ever --

                    WILL
          Not necessarily.

All eyes now go to Will.

                    WILL (CONT'D)
          The Mind Flayer... likes to hide.
          He only used me when he needed me.
          It's like... you're dormant -- but
          then... when he needs you...
          you're... *activated*.

A beat as everyone takes this in.

                    MAX
          Okay... so then -- we wait until he
          gets "activated" --

                    MIKE
          Yeah but what if he hurts someone --

                    WILL
          Or *kills* someone.

                    MIKE
          We can't take the risk.  We need to
          find out if he's the Host.

Mike abruptly stands, pushes through the foliage.

                    ELEVEN
          Where are you -- going?

                    MIKE
          I have an idea.  But boys only.

                    MAX
          *Seriously -- ?*

                    MIKE
          Just -- *trust me on this one*.

Mike continues toward the pool house.

Will and Lucas stand and hurry after him, leaving --

Max and Eleven.  The girls share confused looks, then --

**INT. HAWKINS POOL - POOL HOUSE - DAY**

We PUSH IN on a MEN'S BATHROOM SIGN.  It swings open as --

**INT. HAWKINS POOL - MEN'S LOCKER ROOM - DAY**

Mike, Lucas, and Will weave through the men's locker room.

All around them -- PEEING in urinals, showering, dressing.

*Definitely boys only.*

> MIKE
> -- We wait until after the pool
> closes, when everyone is gone.
> Then all we have to do is somehow
> get him through here --

Mike walks down a hall, through a door, into --

**INT. HAWKINS POOL - THE GYM - CONTINUOUS**

> MIKE
> -- And into *here.*

Mike grabs some wooden handles and throws open --

**INT. HAWKINS POOL - THE SAUNA ROOM DOOR - CONTINUOUS**

WHOOM! Our boys are suddenly face to face with:

A GAGGLE OF GROSS HAIRY MEN, lounging in the sauna like
seals, staring back at them! Just the *tiniest* of towels
cover their privates.

> GROSS HAIRY MAN
> HEY SHUT THE DOOR!!!

> MIKE
> Sorry, sorry -- !

Mike quickly shuts the door --

**INT. HAWKINS POOL - THE GYM - DAY**

Lucas looks horrified.

> LUCAS
> I think I just threw up in my
> mouth --

Mike's eyes move to a SAUNA TEMPERATURE DIAL.

He walks over to it, excited.

> MIKE
> And look -- *look* -- the controls
> are here. It's perfect.

227

Will walks over to him.

                    WILL
          How hot does it get?

                    MIKE
          Two hundred and twenty degrees.

Mike turns back.  More certain now of his plan.

                    MIKE (CONT'D)
          We just have to figure out how to
          get him in there --

                    WILL
          Then we lock him in --

                    LUCAS
          Turn up the heat --

                    MIKE
          And whatever happens -- we'll know.
               (beat)
          We'll know for sure.

Off Will and Lucas, on board now, we SMASH TO:

**INT. STARCOURT MALL - ESTABLISHING**

WHOOSH!  The fountain shooting up water in the mall.

**INT. SCOOPS AHOY! - VENTILATION SHAFT - DAY**

An empty ventilation shaft hums with air.  Then...

Erica's head suddenly pops up into view!  She raises up a
flashlight and sweeps it around.  She frowns, then --

**INT. SCOOPS AHOY! - BACK ROOM - DAY**

WHOOM!  Erica drops down to the floor where --

Robin, Dustin, Steve are waiting anxiously.

                    ERICA
          Yeah... I don't know.

                    DUSTIN
          You don't know if you can fit?

                    ERICA
          Oh, I can fit.  I just don't know
          if I want to.

                    ROBIN
          You're claustrophobic -- ?

                    ERICA
          I don't have phobias --

                    STEVE
          Then what's the problem?

                    ERICA
          The problem is, I still haven't
          heard what's in this... *for Erica.*

Shared looks.   Then...

**INT. SCOOPS AHOY! - A LITTLE LATER**

Steve slides a GIANT ICE CREAM SUNDAE over to --

Erica, now seated in the big corner "boat" booth.  There is
already an ASSORTMENT OF ICE CREAM TREATS laid before her:
BANANA SPLIT, ROOT BEER FLOAT, ICE CREAM CAKE, *the works.*

She slides the sundae back to Steve, displeased.

                    ERICA
          More fudge please --

Steve fights the urge to snap.  As he goes to the counter to
fulfill the demands of his new "boss" --

Robin tries to get the ice cream-obsessed Erica to focus on
the blueprints, which are now spread out over the table...

                    ROBIN
          See this, Erica -- ?

                    ERICA
               (eating ice cream)
          Mmmm hmmm --

                    ROBIN
          This is the route you'd take -- we
          just wait until after the last
          delivery tonight, then you just
          have to knock out the grate, drop
          down, and open the door --

                    ERICA
          Then you find out what's in those
          boxes?

                    ROBIN
          Exactly --

                    ERICA
Mmm hmmm.

Erica licks ice cream off her spoon.

                    ERICA (CONT'D)
          And you say this guard is armed?

                    DUSTIN
          Yeah but the guard won't be there --

                    ERICA
          But what if there's another guard
          *in* the room -- ?

                    DUSTIN
          There's... not --

                    ERICA
          And what about booby traps -- ?

                    ROBIN
          Booby traps?

                    ERICA
          Lasers or spikes in the wall --

                    ROBIN
          *What -- ?*

                    ERICA
          You know what this half-baked plan
          of yours sounds like to me?
                    (beat)
          Child endangerment.

                    ROBIN
          We'll be in radio contact with you
          the *whole time* --

                    ERICA
          Child.   Endangerment.

Erica returns to her ice cream.

Dustin tries a new tactic, leans in --

                    DUSTIN
          Erica... these Russians -- we think
          they want to do harm to our
          country.  *Great harm.*  Don't you...
          love your country?


                         230

                    ERICA
           Can't spell America without Erica.

Erica sips loudly on her root beer float.

                    DUSTIN
                (mind blown by this)
           Right yeah.  Totally.  You...
           totally can't.  So then... forget
           about *us*.  Do this for *your*
           *country*.  Do it for your fellow
           man.  For America.  *Erica*.

Erica stops sipping, looks up.

                    ERICA
           I just got the chills -- from this
           float, not your speech.

She licks her lips.

                    ERICA (CONT'D)
           You know what I love most about
           this country?

Blank looks.

                    ERICA (CONT'D)
           *Capitalism*.

Um, not what they were expecting.

                    ERICA (CONT'D)
           Do you all know what capitalism is?

                    DUSTIN/ROBIN
           Yes --

                    ERICA
           It means this is a free market
           system.  Which means people get
           paid for their services depending
           on how *valuable* their contributions
           are.  And it seems to me my ability
           to fit into that little vent is
           *very valuable* to you all.  So...
           you want my help?

She clanks the edge of her now empty bowl of ice cream.

                    ERICA (CONT'D)
           This banana split better be the
           first of many.
                (looks up)
                (MORE)

ERICA (CONT'D)
I'm talking free ice cream.  *For
life*.

She plucks up a cherry, pops it in her mouth.

Off Dustin and Robin, left *speechless* by this crazy child...

**EXT. MAYOR KLINE'S HOUSE - DAY**

SCREECH!  Hopper's Blazer squealing up to MAYOR KLINE'S
HOUSE.  It's a pompous two-story McMansion.

**INT. MAYOR KLINE'S HOUSE - DAY**

The beat-up Mayor leads Joyce and Hopper inside.  He's got
some bloody Kleenex stuffed up his broken nose.

Hopper looks around.  It's proper eighties tacky in here.
We're talking chandeliers, statues, fur rugs -- *yuuuuck*.

                    HOPPER
          Nice place you got here Larry --
               (re: fur rug)
          I love this rug -- how many zebras
          you kill to make this?

                    MAYOR KLINE
          That -- that's not real --

                    HOPPER
               (fake shock)
          *No* shit?!

Larry sniffles, ignores the mockery.

                    MAYOR KLINE
          This way --

**INT. MAYOR KLINE'S HOUSE - HALLWAY - DAY**

Larry leads them down a GRAND HALLWAY.  Joyce clocks an OLD
TIMEY MAP OF HAWKINS on the wall as they continue into --

**INT. MAYOR KLINE'S HOUSE - MASTER BEDROOM - DAY**

This is somehow the tackiest room yet, with a CANOPY BED and
a CEILING MIRROR.  As Joyce and Hopper look up at the mirror
in disgust, Larry crouches by a SAFE.  Three spins, then --

CLICK!  It opens.  He pulls out a STACK OF PAPERS, passes
them to Hopper.

Hopper thumbs through it all; Joyce reads over his shoulder.

                    HOPPER
          Alright, so -- what exactly are we
          looking at here Larry?

                    MAYOR KLINE
          Land deeds, transfers of property --

                    HOPPER
          So your buddies at Starcourt,
          they're suddenly buying up all this
          property -- they tell you why
          exactly -- ?

                    MAYOR KLINE
          I *told you* they don't tell me
          *anything* --

                    HOPPER
          They're just using you, I get it.
          But what I don't get is -- why
          you're keeping land deeds in a safe
          in your bedroom?

                    MAYOR KLINE
          I told you, Jim, these people, Jim
          -- they're -- they're bad news --

Hopper holds up the papers.

                    HOPPER
          So this is what?  *Blackmail*?

                    MAYOR KLINE
          Protection.

Before Hopper can respond to this --

Joyce abruptly yanks the papers out of Hopper's hands and --

**INT. MAYOR KLINE'S HOUSE - HALLWAY - MOMENTS LATER**

She carries them over to the FRAMED HAWKINS MAP in the
hallway.  As she looks from the deeds to the map, eyes
darting, mind racing, Hopper crosses to her side --

                    HOPPER
          ... What is it?

                    JOYCE
          The Hess farm, Henry's place,
          Bullock's -- look -- they're,
          they're all here, in Southeast
          Hawkins.

She taps a BODY OF WATER on the map --

> JOYCE (CONT'D)
> Right by Jordan Lake.  And -- what
> else is near Jordan Lake -- ?

Hopper suddenly realizes --

> HOPPER
> ... Hawkins Power & Light.

Joyce nods.  *Exactly.*  She turns to Hopper.

> JOYCE
> Four nights ago, there was the
> power outage and that *next day* --

> HOPPER
> Your magnets fell --

> JOYCE
> And Scott, he said this machine
> would need a lot of power to run --

> HOPPER
> Yeah --

> JOYCE
> So what if this -- this *machine*
> he's talking about really does
> exist?  And what if we didn't find
> it at the lab because it *isn't* at
> the lab --

She holds up the land deeds.

> JOYCE (CONT'D)
> It's at one of these properties?

Hopper takes this in, impressed.

> HOPPER
> You know what?  Forget sales.  How
> about joining the Hawkins police?

> JOYCE
> And have to see you every day?  I
> don't think so.

Hopper can't help but smile.  They share a moment.  A team
now.  Perhaps... *more?*  When --

A THUDDING NOISE SHATTERS THE MOMENT.

**INT. MAYOR KLINE'S HOUSE - MASTER BEDROOM - DAY**

Hopper and Joyce head back into the bedroom to find --

Larry, frantically struggling to get out his window.

> HOPPER
> Where do you think *you're going*?

Hopper grabs Larry, *DRAGS* him back inside.  As Larry YELPS --

**EXT. HAWKINS - DAY**

We're soaring over Hawkins now.  The sun sets over pylons.

We crest a hill to find ourselves soaring toward the Wheeler house.  We PRE-LAP the sound of RAPPING KNUCKLES as --

**INT. WHEELER HOUSE - UPSTAIRS HALLWAY - DAY**

Karen KNOCKS on the door to Nancy's room.

> KAREN
> Nancy...?  Nance?

No answer.  Her daughter clearly doesn't want to talk.  *Of course she doesn't.*  Defeated, Karen turns around and starts to walk away when the door suddenly opens behind her and --

Nancy steps out.  Her eyes red from crying.

As mother and daughter lock eyes...

> NANCY (PRE-LAP)
> ... I mean, maybe Jonathan's
> right...

**INT. WHEELER HOUSE - KITCHEN - DAY**

Nancy and Karen are now sitting at the kitchen counter, drinking tea.

As Joyce would say, they're having a *heart to heart.*

> NANCY
> ... The truth is... I *wasn't*
> thinking about him... I wasn't
> thinking about *anyone really*... I
> just -- I wanted to be right.  I --
> wanted to be right *so* badly...

                    KAREN
And were you?

                    NANCY
Was I -- ?

                    KAREN
Right?  About this Driscoll woman?

                    NANCY
... I thought so.  But... maybe I
just don't want to admit that I'm
wrong, because if I admit I'm
wrong, then --

                    KAREN
You're what everyone thinks you are --

                    NANCY
A kid who doesn't know what she's
doing.

Karen nods.  She knows this feeling too well.

                    KAREN
It's not easy out there, Nance.
People are always saying you *can't*.
That you *shouldn't*.  That you're
not smart enough.  Not good enough.
This world --
     (shakes head)
It just -- it beats you up again
and again, until eventually, most
people, they just... stop trying.

Nancy looks at her emotional mom, realizing now that she is
talking about herself.  *About her own regrets in life.*

                    KAREN (CONT'D)
... But you're *not like that*,
Nance.  You're a fighter.  You
always have been.  I honestly don't
know where you get it from...

                    NANCY
... Dad?

Mother and daughter share a look, then a laugh.

                    KAREN
I think you were swapped at the
hospital, to tell the truth!

Nancy takes her mother's hand, squeezes.

                    NANCY
         No.  I get it from you Mom.

Karen smiles through her tears.

                    KAREN
         Well -- wherever you got it from...
         I'm proud of you.

                    NANCY
         Proud that I got fired -- ?

                    KAREN
         That you stood up for yourself.
         That you stood up to those...
         shitheads --

                    NANCY
         Mom -- !

                    KAREN
         They are!  And if you really
         believe in this story -- finish it.
         Then go -- sell it to the
         Indianapolis Star or something!  I
         mean, can you imagine their faces,
         reading a story about their own
         town in a big paper like that?!

Nancy can't help but smile at the thought.

                    NANCY
         That'd be... kind of amazing.

                    KAREN
         Right?  So why not?  Why not??

Nancy looks up at her mom.

                    NANCY
         Yeah.  Why not.

Off Nancy, feeling better, stronger --

**EXT. HAWKINS POOL - GROUNDSKEEPER'S SHED - DAY**

Lucas and Will head toward a groundskeeper's shed.

Will stomps a few feet ahead, clearly avoiding conversation.

**INT. GROUNDSKEEPER'S SHED - DAY**

WHOOM! Will throws open the door to the shed. It's dark in here. He motions toward the corner of the shed.

The boys spread out as they gather a bizarre assortment of items: FISHING LINE, DUCT TAPE, SCREWDRIVER, PADLOCKS...

> LUCAS
> Hey, Will...

Will glances back at Lucas.

> LUCAS (CONT'D)
> You know... about yesterday --

> WILL
> It's fine, Lucas. You don't have
> to say anything. Really.

Will looks back, continues to search for things --

> LUCAS
> I know. It's just -- it was a
> really cool campaign and --

> WILL
> I don't care anymore, Lucas. I
> really don't. We have bigger
> things to worry about now.

Before Lucas has a chance to even respond, Will removes...

A HEAVY DUTY CHAIN FROM A BOX. As it unfurls...

> WILL (CONT'D)
> This should hold him.

**EXT. HAWKINS POOL - POOL HOUSE - DAY**

BOOM! A padlock suddenly EXPLODES off a door as --

**INT. POOL HOUSE STORAGE ROOM - DAY**

Eleven enters the pool house storage room. Her eyes scan the shelves until she finds what she's looking for: a CPR DUMMY.

As she picks up the dummy, examining this weird thing --

Mike enters, out-of-breath.

                    MIKE (O.S.)
          -- I found the breakers -- !

As Eleven turns to meet him, Mike sees the dummy --

                    MIKE (CONT'D)
          Whoa, that's... *super creepy.*

He takes the dummy from El, checks it out.

                    MIKE (CONT'D)
          Yeah. This'll work -- this'll
          *totally work* --

Mike smiles. But the smile is not returned. El takes the
dummy back from Mike and starts to leave without a word.

She is almost out the door when --

                    MIKE (CONT'D)
          ... El?

She turns back. Mike takes a few awkward steps toward her.

He's clearly nervous about this. El stares, impatient.

                    ELEVEN
          ... Yes?

Mike hesitates. Then -- *screw it.*

                    MIKE
          My Nana *wasn't sick* the other day.
          That was... a lie --

                    ELEVEN
          I know.

                    MIKE
          Oh. Right. Yeah. It's just -- I
          think it's important you know the
          context --

                    ELEVEN
          Con--text?

                    MIKE
          *Why* I lied. Hopper, you see, he
          went all crazy on me and said we've
          been spending too much time
          together.
                    (MORE)

                    MIKE (CONT'D)
          He MADE me lie -- I mean you're *the
          most* important thing to me in the
          whole world and --

                    ELEVEN
               (interrupting)
          What if he is right?

                    MIKE
          *What -- ?*

                    ELEVEN
          Hop.

Mike is APPALLED by this suggestion.

                    MIKE
          He -- he's NOT.  He's just a crazy
          angry old man who -- who *hates joy*.

                    ELEVEN
          But I only see you.  And I am a
          different species than you.  And
          maybe I should be with my species
          more.

Mike stares.  Confused.

                    MIKE
          What are you talking about?

Mike's eyes suddenly narrow.  Realizing.

                    MIKE (CONT'D)
          Did you *spy* on me?

Eleven doesn't answer.  Doesn't need to.

                    MIKE (CONT'D)
          That's against the rules!

                    ELEVEN
          I make my own rules.

And with that, Eleven stomps away with her dummy.

Mike watches her leave, dumbfounded, when --

CHHH!  His radio blasts.  It's Max:

                    MAX VOICE (OVER WALKIE)
          Where are you guys??

                    MIKE
          We're -- *we're coming.*  Stand by.

As a dumbstruck Mike races out of the storage room --

**EXT. WOODS BY HAWKINS POOL - DAY**

Max lowers her walkie-talkie.  She is still stationed in the
hiding spot in the woods.  She raises back up the binoculars.

BINOCULAR POV: BILLY IS IN HIS CHAIR.  STILL "DORMANT."

                    MAX
               (low)
          ... God, I hope it's not you... I
          really *hope it's not you...*

**EXT. HAWKINS POOL - DAY**

We're with Billy now.  Sitting there.  *Calm.*  We SLOWLY PUSH
in on him, closer and closer, until we MOVE *INTO* the frames
of his dark sunglasses, and the screen goes completely --

**BLACK**

**EXT. STARCOURT MALL - NIGHT 6 - ESTABLISHING**

Stars stab through the black.  We TILT DOWN to find...

STARCOURT MALL.  It's night now.  The neon sign glows bright.

**EXT. STARCOURT MALL - ROOF - LOADING DOCKS - NIGHT 6**

BINOCULAR POV: We survey the loading dock.  It's empty.

Dustin, Steve, and Robin are lying on the roof of the mall,
overlooking the loading dock; Robin raises up her walkie.

                    ROBIN
          Erica -- do you copy?

**INT. SCOOPS AHOY! - BACK ROOM - INTERCUT**

CLOSE ON: Erica, speaking into a familiar headset.

                    ERICA
          Mmmm hmmm I copy.

PULL OUT TO REVEAL: Erica is now *geared for action.*  She's
wearing Dustin's headset, Robin's bike helmet with a
FLASHLIGHT strapped to it, and roller skating elbow pads.

As she snaps on her helmet and pulls on a PINK BACKPACK...

                    ERICA (CONT'D)
          You nerds in position or what?

                    ROBIN
          Yeah, we're in position.  It's all
          quiet here, so you've got the
          greenlight --

                    ERICA
          Greenlight.  Roger that.

Erica hops up on onto the work desk.

                    ERICA (CONT'D)
          Commence Operation Child
          Endangerment.

                    ROBIN
          Can we maybe _not_ call it that?

Erica ignores Robin, kicks on her flashlight, then --

                    ERICA
          See you on the other side nerds.

Erica squirms her way into --

**INT. VENTILATION SHAFT - NIGHT**

It's real tight in here, but sure enough -- she fits!

She begins to shimmy her way through the vent.  And she moves
_fast_, really fast -- she's like a pint-sized John McClane!

As she flies forward --

**INT. MAYOR KLINE'S HOUSE - NIGHT**

A door opens and...

A TACKY FAUX-RICH WOMAN enters the Mayor's House.  Wait, _we
know her_!  This is Mom #1 from the pool!  She's dressed in a
tight and bright Jazzercise jumpsuit.  She puts down her keys
when --

She hears something.  A FAMILIAR, _WHINY_ VOICE:

                    VOICE (O.S.)
          -- WINNIE?!?!?!  WINNIIEEEEE!!!!!

WINNIE's eyes shoot wide and --

242

**INT. MAYOR KLINE'S HOUSE - MASTER BEDROOM - NIGHT**

WHOOM! Winnie races into the bedroom. --

> WINNIE
> Larry -- oh my God, baby?!!!

REVERSE TO REVEAL: Larry is now <u>*handcuffed* to the bed</u>.

> MAYOR KLINE
> Get me a phone -- !

> WINNIE
> Baby, what happened -- !!!

> MAYOR KLINE
> GET ME A GODDAMN PHONE WINNIE!!!!

As a horrified Winnie sprints away to get a phone, SMASH TO:

**EXT. ABANDONED HOUSE - NIGHT**

PLUMES OF DIRT kicking back up at camera as --

Hopper's Blazer now speeds along a STRETCH OF DIRT ROAD toward a house. It's isolated. Abandoned.

**MOMENTS LATER**

Hopper unholsters his gun as he steps up to the door.

He checks the handle. *It's locked*.

A beat of consideration. Then --

**INT. ABANDONED HOUSE - NIGHT**

BOOM! Hinges fly inward as Hopper KICKS open the door and --

WE CUT WIDE: THE HOUSE IS EMPTY. DARK. NOTHING HERE.

**INT. ABANDONED HOUSE - VARIOUS - NIGHT**

Joyce moves through the house, checking rooms as --

**INT. ABANDONED HOUSE - VARIOUS - NIGHT**

Hopper searches the opposite side of the house, but finds nothing.

**INT. ABANDONED HOUSE - FOYER**

Hopper and Joyce meet back at the foyer.

They've circled the house.  Joyce sees his face.

>                     JOYCE
>           Anything -- ?
>
>                     HOPPER
>           This place is dead.

They look around for a beat, stumped, then --

**INT./EXT. HOPPER BLAZER - ABANDONED HOUSE**

They climb back into the Blazer.  As Hopper revs the ignition, Joyce consults a notepad where she's scribbled a list of properties.  She scratches out this property, the third one they've checked... leaving just two houses left.

>                     HOPPER
>           Where to now?
>
>                     JOYCE
>           -- The Hess Farm.

Hopper nods, shifts into DRIVE, and --

They speed off into the night.

**EXT. HESS FARM - NIGHT**

CLOSE ON:  A mailbox that reads <u>HESS</u>.

We PUSH PAST IT to find an ISOLATED FARMHOUSE.

The windows are boarded up, and a STRANGE MECHANICAL NOISE emanates from inside the house -- it sounds like a tractor-like growling... something is in here.

Could it be *OUR MACHINE?*

Through the cracks in the boards, we see the lights inside the house begin to PULSE and --

That GROWLING grows louder. And *LOUDER*. And --

**INT. VENTILATION SHAFT - NIGHT**

BAM! Elbow pads DRUM HARD AGAINST METAL as --

Erica continues to make her way through the tiny vents, sweating from the effort. She swings a hard left then --

Her crawl comes to a stop. Straight ahead: <u>A VENT GRATE</u>.

She catches her breath, presses a finger to her ear:

> ERICA
> Alright nerds -- <u>I'm there</u>.

**EXT. STARCOURT MALL - ROOF - LOADING DOCKS - NIGHT**

Dustin and Steve share looks. Robin raises her walkie.

> ROBIN
> ... Can you see anything?

**INT. VENTILATION SHAFT - INTERCUT**

Erica sticks her face right up the vent. She can make out a medium sized room with blank cement walls. It's empty save for a FEW DOZEN BOXES (Imperial Panda and Kaufman Shoes).

> ERICA
> Yeah I see those boring boxes
> you're so excited about.

> ROBIN
> Any guards?

> ERICA
> Negative.

> ROBIN
> Booby traps, lasers -- ?

> ERICA
> If I could see them they'd be
> pretty shit traps wouldn't they?

Erica pulls off her My Little Pony backpack --

                    ERICA (CONT'D)
          I know you're joking by the way.
          But just remember, I blow up into
          little pieces, it's on *your*
          *conscience*.

                    ROBIN
          Yeah yeah I got it...

Erica reaches into her backpack and removes --

DUSTIN'S SLAMMER (the electric hammer from Camp Know Where!)

                    ERICA
          Initiating "The Slam."

**EXT. STARCOURT MALL - ROOF - LOADING DOCKS - NIGHT**

Steve shoots Dustin a look.

                    STEVE
          Your little contraption *better work* --

                    DUSTIN
          It'll *work*.

**INT. VENTILATION SHAFT - NIGHT**

Erica lifts The Slammer to the edge of the vent, presses the
button, and... BAMBAMBAMAMBAMBAM!  The hammer begins to POUND
WILDLY against the edges of the grate and --

**INT. SECRET ROOM - NIGHT**

POP!  The vent cover suddenly EXPLODES off the wall in a
shower of DRIED PAINT and SCREWS.  A brief moment later --

WHOOM!  Erica drops into frame -- like a fucking ninja!

                    ERICA
          *I'm in*.

**EXT. STARCOURT MALL - ROOF - LOADING DOCKS - NIGHT**

Our Scoops Troop share impressed looks as --

**INT. SECRET ROOM - NIGHT**

Erica confidently struts over to the door --

She SLAMS a GREEN OPEN DOOR button, and --

**EXT. LOADING DOCKS - NIGHT**

Erica steps outside, tiny and silhouetted on the loading
dock.  She looks up at the teens on the roof, victorious.

>                    ERICA
>          Ice cream.  *For life.*

**EXT. HAWKINS POOL - NIGHT**

The pool is now closed.  Everyone is gone.

**INT. HAWKINS POOL - MEN'S LOCKER ROOM - NIGHT**

WHOOSH!  COLD WATER streams from a shower head.

Billy is showering, cooling off from his day in the heat.

**INT. HAWKINS POOL - MEN'S LOCKER ROOM - NIGHT**

Billy, now showered and wearing a towel, walks over to his
LOCKER.  He spins a combination on a MASTER LOCK when --

He freezes.  He heard something -- a FAINT SHUFFLING NOISE.

He looks around. *Is someone else in here?*

CUT WIDE: <u>THE LOCKER ROOM IS EMPTY.</u>

Billy shakes it off -- *must have been nothing* -- and opens
his locker.  He grabs his jeans, slips them on, when --

ANOTHER NOISE.  This time from behind him.

Billy turns.  The door to the locker room shudders a bit.

> BILLY
> HEY!  POOL IS *CLOSED*!!

In response, a BURST OF VOICES, a FLURRY OF FOOTSTEPS.

> BILLY (CONT'D)
> HEY!!  DID YOU HEAR ME???

Billy storms over to the door.

> BILLY (CONT'D)
> POOL.  IS.  *CLOSED* -- *!!*

Billy yanks on the door to confront whoever this is but --

CHOOM!  The door catches.  Stuck.  *What in the hell???*  As
Billy continues to yank the door, harder and harder, CUT TO --

**THE OPPOSITE SIDE OF THE DOOR**

The door is LOCKED WITH A HEAVY CHAIN and PADLOCK.

**INT. HAWKINS POOL - MEN'S LOCKER ROOM - NIGHT**

CHOOM!  THE LIGHTS IN THE LOCKER ROOM SUDDENLY <u>SHUT OFF</u>.

As Billy whips around, a DISEMBODIED VOICE calls out:

>                    DISEMBODIED VOICE
>                     (filtered, hazy)
>               ... *Billy...!!  Billy...!!*

Billy scans the darkness.  A little freaked out now.

>                         BILLY
>               ... Who's there??  *WHO'S THERE??*

No answer.

>                         BILLY (CONT'D)
>               You think this is funny??  I find
>               you, IT'S YOUR FUNERAL.  YOU HEAR
>               ME ASSHOLE??

Still no response.  Billy's eyes swivel and lock onto --

THE DOOR TO THE GYM.  IT'S OPEN.  *JUST A HAIR.*

Billy takes this in a beat, then...

**INT. HAWKINS POOL - THE GYM - MOMENTS LATER**

WHOOM!  Billy throws open the door to the gym.

He steps in, looks around, quietly scanning.  He sees --

WEIGHT-LIFTING EQUIPMENT and LOCKERS and BENCHES and --

A SHADOWY FIGURE.  HIDING IN THE SAUNA.  *JUST* VISIBLE THROUGH
THE SAUNA'S SQUARE GLASS WINDOW.

>                         BILLY
>                          (low)
>                     ... *Got you.*

**INT. HAWKINS POOL - SAUNA - CONTINUOUS**

WHOOM!  Billy hurls open the door to the sauna and --

Freezes.  The FIGURE is not moving.  Not *human*.  It's...

THE CPR DUMMY.  HANGING FROM FISHING WIRE LIKE A MARIONETTE.

Billy yanks it off the string.  Looks it over.

A WALKIE-TALKIE is duct-taped to the dummy's chest.

>                         CPR DUMMY (OVER WALKIE-TALKIE)
>                     *Behind you.*

Billy drops the dummy and whips around just as the lights
kick back on to reveal:

ELEVEN.   STANDING BEHIND HIM.

> ELEVEN
> Hi.

Eleven thrusts out a hand and --

WHOOM!  Billy HURTLES backwards into the sauna.  His back slams into the wall so hard tile shatters.  As his body *folds* to the ground --

> MIKE (O.S.)
> -- NOW!!

Our other kids burst out of dressing rooms with various items: Will has his BAT, Max has the WALKIE-TALKIE (she was the voice!), Mike and Lucas have the CHAINS AND LOCKS.

Eleven swipes her hand again and WHAM!  The sauna door SLAMS SHUT on Billy!

The boys wrap the chains around the sauna door handles --

**INT. HAWKINS POOL - SAUNA - CONTINUOUS**

A stunned Billy staggers to his feet.

He charges the door just as --

**BACK OUTSIDE,**

Will SNAPS the padlock over the chains and --

**INT. HAWKINS POOL - SAUNA - CONTINUOUS**

WHAM!  Billy slams into the door a *half-second too late.*

The door shudders but won't open.  The chains <u>hold</u>.  *Billy's locked in here.*  As Billy continues to shake the door --

**BACK OUTSIDE,**

Our kids back away from the shuddering door.  They did it!

**INT. HAWKINS POOL - SAUNA - CONTINUOUS**

Billy clocks Max through the small sauna window.

A look of surprise, confusion flashes across his face.

> BILLY
> ... <u>Max</u>...?

Max looks back at him.  Speechless.  Scared.

                    BILLY (CONT'D)
        What are you doing?  What is this??
        WHAT IS THIS??!

Max doesn't answer.  She just turns to Mike.  And nods.

                    MAX
            Do it.

Mike twists the TEMPERATURE GAUGE *all the way* up and --

**EXT. HAWKINS GENERAL HOSPITAL - NIGHT**

WHOOSH!  Car tires *SPIN* past camera as --

KAREN'S STATION WAGON pulls up to HAWKINS GENERAL HOSPITAL.

**INT. HOSPITAL LOBBY - NIGHT**

Nancy heads into the lobby carrying a BOUQUET OF FLOWERS.

She steadies her nerves as she approaches a RECEPTIONIST.

                    RECEPTIONIST
            Hi --

                    NANCY
            Hi.  I'm here to see Doris
            Driscoll?  She was admitted late
            last night?

The Receptionist consults some paperwork.

                    RECEPTIONIST
            Name and relation?

                    NANCY
            Nancy.  Nancy Driscoll.  I'm her --
            granddaughter --

The Receptionist smiles, slides over a clipboard --

                    RECEPTIONIST
            Alright -- just need your John
            Hancock right here --

As Nancy signs, *so far so good*, CUT TO:

**INT. HOSPITAL CORRIDOR - NIGHT**

A CHEERY VISITOR STICKER READS: "NANCY DRISCOLL."

WIDEN: Nancy is now walking down a corridor with her flowers.

**INT. HOSPITAL CORRIDOR - MOMENTS LATER - NIGHT**

She arrives at ROOM 211. *This is it.* She takes a deep breath, turns the knob. The door opens to reveal:

**INT. HOSPITAL ROOM - NIGHT**

MRS. DRISCOLL. She's sleeping in a hospital bed. IV pumps fluids into her old body; *she's heavily sedated.*

Nancy walks over, places down the flowers, then retrieves the medical chart from the foot of the bed. She flips through the charts, scans them rapidly. We don't show what Nancy sees -- but whatever she's reading, it's surprising -- *validating.*

Nancy pulls out a notepad and begins to make furious notes.

As she scribbles, our CAMERA DRIFTS BACK UP to Mrs. Driscoll.

Her breathing is quickening, her skin percolating with *SWEAT*... we PUSH IN to the HEART RATE MONITOR...

It's rising rapidly. *Beep beep BEEP-BEEP-BEEP* --

**INT. SECRET ROOM - NIGHT**

SWOOSH! AN EXACTO KNIFE *SLASHES* THROUGH HEAVY TAPE.

Steve is opening up one of the Imperial Panda boxes. Dustin, Robin, and Erica crowd around him, anxiously watching as --

Steve opens the box. Inside, a LARGE METAL CASE.

> STEVE
> Yeah... that doesn't exactly look
> like Chinese food...

Steve snaps opens the case. He is about to open it when...

> STEVE (CONT'D)
> Maybe you guys should... stand
> back?

Robin and Erica take a few steps back, but --

Dustin holds his ground.

> DUSTIN
> If you die -- *I die.*

Steve considers.

                         STEVE
          Okay.

He turns back to the case and WHOOM!  Pops it open.

His eyes shoot wide.

                         STEVE (CONT'D)
               ... *The hell...?*

INSIDE: A DOZEN METAL CYLINDERS, safely protected by some
CUSHY FOAM.  Think BACK TO THE FUTURE'S PLUTONIUM.  Some
steam rises out, looks like dry ice.

Steve reaches in and very carefully removes A CYLINDER.

It's filled with a STRANGE GREEN SUBSTANCE.

Erica and Robin step closer.  Eyes wide.

                         ROBIN
               ... What *is that* -- ?

As if in response: A LOUD RUMBLING SOUND.

Dustin looks around.

                         DUSTIN
               Was that just me -- or did the room
               *move*?

                         ERICA
               *Booby traps.*

ANOTHER RUMBLE and --

                         ROBIN
                    (to Steve)
               Just take that and let's go --

As Steve quickly shoves the cylinder into his backpack, Robin
races to the door and slams the OPEN DOOR button, but --

The door doesn't open like before.  She tries again.  No go --

She shoots a panicked look to Erica.

                         ROBIN (CONT'D)
               How did you open this -- ??

                         ERICA
               Hit the button -- !!!

Erica pounds the button again, the same way, only this time --

WHOOM!  A GUILLOTINE-STYLE DOOR suddenly shoots down, trapping them in here.  They back away in horror, just as --

THE ROOM ITSELF JERKS DOWNWARD!  Everyone loses their balance, and that's when Steve sees it:

The cement wall is *RAPIDLY DROPPING*.  *Wait a sec --*

This isn't a room.  This is a GODDAMN ELEVATOR!

As our GANG SCREAMS --

**INT. ELEVATOR SHAFT - NIGHT**

WHOOSH!  The elevator RUSHES down, traveling *deep underground!*

As the elevator recedes from camera, *falling* rapidly --

**INT. HAWKINS POOL - THE GYM - NIGHT**

The temperature gauge *rises* rapidly.  We're at 210 degrees!

**INSIDE THE SAUNA,**

WHAM!!  Billy SLAMS the door in anger.

                    BILLY
          MAX -- let me out of here!!  LET ME OUT!!

His panicked eyes dart, swiveling across the kids.

                    BILLY (CONT'D)
          You kids think this is funny???
          This some kind of -- sick prank???

The kids stare at him.  Not saying anything.

                    BILLY (CONT'D)
          What is this??  *WHAT IS THIS*???

No answer.

                    BILLY (CONT'D)
          OPEN THE DOOR!!  OPEN THE DOOR!!
          OPEN THE *GODDAMN DOOR!!*

Billy slams the door again and again, but the chains hold firm.  Defeated, exhausted, he drops down onto the back bench, right by the SMASHED TILE WALL.

**BACK OUTSIDE,**

Mike walks over, checks the temperature gauge.

                    MIKE
          We're at two twenty --

**BACK INSIDE,**

Sweat pours from Billy to the floor -- so hot it HISSES as it
strikes the floor.  Then something surprising happens:

He begins to cry.

                    BILLY
          ... It's not my fault... it's not
          my fault... it's not my fault...

**BACK OUTSIDE,**

The kids share looks.

Max takes a small step toward the glass.

                    MAX
          Billy, what's not your fault?

                    BILLY
          ... I... I've done things Max...
          terrible things...

More shared looks from our kids.  They're getting something
very unexpected from Billy here: a confession.

                    BILLY (CONT'D)
          ... But... he... he made me do
          them...

                    MAX
          Who made you do it?

Billy looks up now at Max.  Tears are rolling down his
cheeks.  He's full-on sobbing now.

                    BILLY
          I don't know -- it -- it looked
          like a... a shadow.  A -- a giant
          shadow.

Our kids can barely breathe.  Holy shit -- they were right.

Max steps toward the door.  She's scared, fighting tears.

                    MAX
          What did he make you do Billy --
          what things did he make you do??

                         BILLY
                It's not my fault... it's not my
                fault... I tried to stop him... I
                tried to stop him...

Billy shakes his head, sobbing. CLOSE ON: His right hand
inches across the bench, starts closing up, tightening.

                         MAX
                ... Billy... it's going to be
                okay... we want to help you... but
                you have to *talk to us*, okay? You
                have to talk to us...

As Max tries to reach Billy, we turn our attention to --

Will. Ten feet away. Something is wrong. *Very wrong.* He
slowly reaches up and touches the back of his neck as...

**BACK INSIDE THE SAUNA,**

We reveal that Billy's hand is in fact curling around...

A SHARP PIECE OF BROKEN TILE.

**BACK OUTSIDE,**

CLOSE ON: THE BACK OF WILL'S NECK. COVERED IN GOOSEBUMPS.

                         WILL
                    (low)
                I feel him --

Mike hears this, turns to Will. The boys lock eyes.

                    WILL (CONT'D)
                He's *activated*.

Mike spins back to Max. Standing right by the door.

And suddenly it hits him --

                         MIKE
                *Max -- get away from the door --*

                         MAX
                What -- ?

                         MIKE
                GET AWAY FROM THE DOOR -- !

WHOOM! BILLY SUDDENLY LAUNCHES OFF THE BENCH -- SMASHES A
HAND THROUGH THE GLASS WINDOW OF THE SAUNA AND --

WHOOM!  MAX JUMPS OUT OF THE WAY JUST AS --

Billy SLASHES at her with the tile, *just missing* her neck.

> BILLY
> LET ME OUT YOU BITCH!!!  LET ME
> OUT!!!  LET ME OUT OR I'LL CUT YOU
> TO PIECES!!!!  I'LL CUT YOU TO
> PIECES!!!

Max backpedals, scared, tears falling now --

Billy reaches down a bloody hand and *YANKS* at the chains.

Mike swings his bat, crushing Billy's hand, but --

Billy keeps pulling at the chains, undeterred --

Lucas draws back his LOADED SLINGSHOT and --

> LUCAS
> MIKE -- GET DOWN!!!!!

Mike ducks out of the way as --

Lucas fires!  WHOOSH!  THE ROCK *SOCKS* BILLY IN THE EYE AND --

**INT. HAWKINS POOL - SAUNA - NIGHT**

Billy stumbles backwards, SCREAMING, holding his eye --

<u>A QUICK FLASH OF THE MIND FLAYER!  IT SHRIEKS IN PAIN!</u>

Billy lets out a GUTTURAL SCREAM and --

**INT. HOSPITAL ROOM - NIGHT**

Mrs. Driscoll SCREAMS.  Guttural.  Painful.

Nancy leaps to her feet, startled.  She now sees something is
VERY wrong with Mrs. Driscoll; she's covered in sweat and the
heart rate monitor is rapidly rising.  *BEEPBEEPBEEPBEEP!*

Nancy looks up as the lights above her begin to flicker --

> NANCY
> *Oh my God* --

Nancy races over, smacks an EMERGENCY CALL BUTTON as --

**INT. HAWKINS POOL - THE GYM - NIGHT**

The lights flicker in the gym now too as --

**INT. HAWKINS POOL - SAUNA - NIGHT**

Billy drops to his knees.  He's now in *SEVERE PAIN* as --

He begins to undergo a TERRIFYING TRANSFORMATION.  His muscles THROB and BULGE... DARK, PULSATING VEINS climb up his naked torso... then his neck... taking him over... as...

**INT. HOSPITAL ROOM - NIGHT**

DARK VEINS form on Mrs. Driscoll, rising up her pale white skin.  As Nancy watches in growing horror, we FLASHBACK TO:

*THE VEINS RISING ON WILL LAST YEAR -- WILL SCREAMS AND --*

WHOOM!  The hospital door flies open and a NURSE races into the room.  Nancy spins to her, panicked, tears in her eyes --

> NANCY
> DOCTOR -- GET A DOCTOR -- !!!

**INT. HAWKINS POOL - SAUNA - NIGHT**

CLOSE UP: Billy, still on his hands and knees, looks toward the sauna door.  We now see his face for the first time.  Or at least what remains of it.  It's grotesque, covered in nasty veins, twisted by rage, by madness.  He looks like a monster.  His breathing quickens, faster and faster, then --

He suddenly *LUNGES* at the door like a charging bull and --

BOOM!  *SLAMS* his whole body into the sauna door --

**INT. HAWKINS POOL - THE GYM - NIGHT**

The chains SHUDDER but hold firm --

Lucas loads his slingshot, Mike pulls back his bat.

> MAX
> He can't get out, can he -- ?!

> WILL
> No way -- no way -- !

**INT. HAWKINS POOL - SAUNA - NIGHT**

But Billy throws his weight into the door again and again --

His attacks are fast, violent, *superhuman,* and --

**INT. HAWKINS POOL - THE GYM - NIGHT**

The sauna door handles BEND and GROAN under the pressure --

**INT. HAWKINS POOL - SAUNA - NIGHT**

One more charge from Billy and --

**INT. HAWKINS POOL - THE GYM - NIGHT**

BOOM!  The sauna room door handles SNAP RIGHT OFF!!!

The kids dive out of the way, narrowly evading Billy as --

He EXPLODES out of the sauna room.  *Finally free.*

He rises to his feet, turns toward our terrified kids --

WHOOSH!  Lucas fires his slingshot.  The rock strikes Billy across the head, but he keeps coming, undeterred, and --

> ELEVEN
> -- BACK!!!!

Eleven SCREAMS, thrusts out a hand and sends him HURTLING backwards at high speed!  Billy's back SLAMS into the wall.

Then, in a flash, Eleven swings her second hand and sends a BARBELL WITH TWO HEAVY WEIGHTS flying through the air and --

WHAM!  The barbell slams into Billy's neck, *PINNING HIM TO THE WALL*.  As he begins to *CHOKE* under the weight of it --

**INT. HOSPITAL ROOM - NIGHT**

Mrs. Driscoll begins to breathe heavier, *flail* --

The DOCTOR finally races into the room.  His eyes go wide when he sees what's happening.  Nancy shouts, desperate --

> NANCY
> Do something -- *DO SOMETHING* -- !

But the Doctor is frozen, shocked, not sure _what_ to do.

As Mrs. Driscoll's back *arches upward...*

**INT. HAWKINS POOL - THE GYM - NIGHT**

Billy continues to gag beneath the barbell, *face turning red.*

He reaches up, grabs hold of the barbell, and -- with a GUTTURAL SCREAM -- he pushes back against it.  His huge muscles strain and the veins on his forehead pulse and --

HE STARTS TO PUSH THE BARBELL AWAY.  *OVERPOWERING ELEVEN*!

Eleven keeps her hand raised, focused, blood rushing down her nose, veins forming around her eye sockets too, but then --

Billy releases a FEROCIOUS SCREAM and --

The barbell flies _back_ at Eleven!

                    MAX
          WATCH OUT -- !!!

Max pushes Eleven out of the path of the barbell just in the nick of time. As the barbell smashes into the wall, exploding brick --

Billy _LUNGES_, SLAMS MAX, KNOCKING HER BACK, THEN --

HE GRABS ELEVEN and DRIVES HER across the room and against a wall with _incredible force_. He's choking _her_ now -- _the tables have turned_. His eyes bore into her. As she struggles to free herself, staring into those crazed eyes of his, we --

_FLASHCUT TO THE MIND FLAYER ROARING AT ELEVEN AS SHE CLOSES THE GATE -- HIS LONG ARM REACHES FOR HER -- ANGRY -- AND --_

WHAM! The baseball bat cracks Billy across the back of the head this time, _hard_, so hard it causes him to release El.

As El drops, clutching her throat, gasping for air --

A dazed Billy spins around to find --

Mike. Wielding the bat. _Brave._

                    MIKE
          GO TO HELL YOU PIECE OF SHIT -- !!!

Mike swings again, but Billy _CATCHES_ the bat, rips it away from Mike with ease. He tosses the bat across the room.

Billy steps toward Mike, moving to attack, when --

WHOOM! Billy suddenly lifts up into the air!

REVERSE TO REVEAL: Eleven, standing back on her feet, hand out. She gathers her strength, SCREAMS FEROCIOUSLY, and --

FWOOM!!!! SENDS BILLY FLYING BACKWARDS WITH ALL HER POWER --

HE _EXPLODES THROUGH THE WALL_ WITH INCREDIBLE FORCE AND --

**EXT. HAWKINS POOL - POOL HOUSE - NIGHT**

CRASH!  Billy tumbles outside in a SHOWER OF DUST AND
BRICKS!!

**INT. HAWKINS POOL - THE GYM - NIGHT**

The kids all share stunned looks.  *Mother.  Of.  God.*

Eleven's knees weaken and she slumps back to the floor.

Mike races to her side.

> MIKE
> El -- you okay??  *El?!??!*

As Mike tends to her, the others turn to the hole in the
wall.  Beyond it... darkness.  *Is Billy still out there?*

Max grabs up the bat, Lucas his slingshot, and...

**EXT. HAWKINS POOL - POOL HOUSE - NIGHT**

Will, Max, and Lucas step up to the busted wall.

WIDEN OUT: The only thing out here: bricks, debris.

Billy is gone.  *Wait.*

> WILL
> *There.*

Max and Lucas follow Will's gaze to find --

Billy, dimly lit in the moonlight, fleeing into the woods.
He looks almost like a werewolf -- his back hunched, his body
bruised, bloody, limping.  As our kids watch him go...

Eleven and Mike now step outside, joining them.  Eleven
pushes her way to the front of the group.  She watches as...

Billy vanishes into foliage.  *Into darkness.*  *Escaping.*

We PUSH IN on Eleven as she realizes that the real battle
still lies ahead.  As her expression *hardens*, PRE-LAP:

> FEMALE VOICE (PRE-LAP)
> *... The girl... was it her?*

> BILLY (PRE-LAP)
> *Yes.  It was her.*
> (beat)
> *She knows now.  She knows about me.*

261

**INT. ABANDONED FACTORY - NIGHT**

CLOSE ON: Billy's bruised, cut, bleeding face.  A pair of slender hands reach into frame, carefully mending his wounds with a washcloth and water.  SLOWLY WIDEN OUT TO REVEAL...

It is Heather who is mending him.

                    BILLY
          ... She could have killed me.

                    HEATHER
          Yes...  But not us.  _Not us_.

As Heather continues to heal Billy, we PULL BACK FURTHER to reveal that she is not the only one here with Billy.

There is TOM... JANET... and another TWO DOZEN we don't recognize, all lit by moonlight in this eerie factory.

It's a human army.  An army we will soon come to know as...

THE FLAYED.

Behind them, the monster looms.

And off this haunting image, we --

                    END EPISODE

262

# CHAPTER FIVE:
## THE FLAYED

WRITTEN BY **PAUL DICHTER**

**DARKNESS.**

We hear RUMBLING.  It grows louder and louder and --

**INT. ELEVATOR SHAFT --**

WHOOM! An elevator flies down a cement shaft.

Thick cables slashing at camera.  SCREAMS fill the air. And --

**INT. ELEVATOR**

STEVE watches the wall plummet, eyes wide --

> STEVE
> We're going down -- !!!

> ROBIN
> Yeah *no shit* -- !

DUSTIN races over to control panel, but --

> DUSTIN
> Why don't these buttons have
> labels??!

He starts to mash the buttons at random, but nothing happens.

ERICA joins in, mashing more buttons, but --

The cement wall keeps dropping as --

**INT. ELEVATOR SHAFT**

The elevator continues to rocket down the elevator shaft,
faster, *faster*, almost to the floor now, when suddenly --

EEEEE-SHUNK!  A PULLEY CATCHES -- BRAKES LOCK -- *AND* --

**INT. ELEVATOR**

KA-WHAM-WHOOM!  The elevator SLAMS to a VIOLENT STOP!

The Scoops Troop jolts on impact, grabbing one another to
steady themselves.  Then... silence. *Calm.*

They share stunned looks.

> ROBIN
> ... Is everyone okay?

> STEVE/DUSTIN/ERICA
> ... Yeah/yes/uh-huh.

                    STEVE
          Okay so -- apparently Russians can't
          design elevators --

Steve punches more buttons.

                    ROBIN
          Steve, I think we've now *clearly*
          *established* those buttons don't
          work --

                    STEVE
          They're buttons, they've gotta do
          *something* --

                    ROBIN
          *If* we had a keycard --

                    STEVE
          What -- ?

Robin walks over to a slot in the door.  Smacks it.

                    ROBIN
          *It's an electronic lock*.  Same as the
          loading dock door.  If we don't have
          a keycard this won't operate,
          meaning --

                    DUSTIN
          We're *stuck* in here.

                    ERICA
               (fast)
          Just so you nerds are aware, I'm
          supposed to be spending the night at
          Tina's -- and Tina always covers for
          me -- but if I'm not home for Uncle
          Jack's party tomorrow and my mom
          finds out you three are responsible?
          She's gonna hunt you down one by one
          and Slit.  Your.  Throats.

                    STEVE
          Yeah well she can't kill us if she
          can't *find us*.

Dustin's eyes go up to the hatch.

                    DUSTIN
          ... Maybe we can climb.

Shared looks.  And --

**INT. ELEVATOR ROOF**

WHOOM!  The hatch door SHOOTING open to reveal --

Dustin standing on a stack of boxes below.  He reaches up and hoists himself onto the elevator roof.  Steve follows close behind.  As he clambers up, he follows Dustin's gaze skyward.

>             STEVE
> ... What were you were saying about climbing...?

Dustin doesn't answer.  *Doesn't have to.*  We now RISE UP, revealing they are at the bottom of this massive elevator shaft, SEVERAL HUNDRED FEET UNDERGROUND.  The walls are solid on all sides.  No scaffolding... no ladders... *NO WAY OUT*.

As our CAMERA CONTINUES TO RISE, faster and faster, SMASH TO --

**EXT. COUNTRY ROAD - NIGHT**

VROOM!  HOPPER'S BLAZER speeding down a dark country road.

**INT./EXT. HOPPER'S BLAZER - NIGHT**

JOYCE looks up from a MAP, clocks a mailbox.

>             JOYCE
> *Hess*, that's it -- left, turn left --

HOPPER pumps the brakes and swings left, careening past a decrepit wooden mailbox that reads HESS and onto --

**EXT. GRAVEL ROAD - HESS FARM - NIGHT**

The old Hess farmhouse sits at the end of this long gravel road.  A BLACK CAR AND LYNX VAN are parked along the side of the house.

>             HOPPER
> ... Looks like someone's home.

Hopper shares a look with Joyce.  *Bingo.*  Then...

**INT. HESS FARM - NIGHT**

EEEEE.  The front door inches open and...

Hopper slips inside, gun raised, but --

THE HOUSE IS EMPTY.  DARK.  QUIET.  NO ONE HERE.  *WAIT.*

The ceiling lights pulse, dimming and then brightening, accompanied by a LOW HUMMING SOUND.

                    JOYCE
               (low)
          ... You hear that?

Hopper listens.  Sure enough, he hears it too:  It sounds ALMOST LIKE A GROWLING JET ENGINE.  And it's coming from somewhere DEEP WITHIN THE BOWELS of this vacant house.

**INT. HESS FARM - NIGHT**

A ceiling light PULSES as Hopper and Joyce track the strange sound through the house.  With each CREAKING step, the sound grows just a little louder... a little *clearer*.

**INT. HESS FARM - BEDROOM - NIGHT**

They enter a bedroom.  The sound is much louder but --

The room is *empty too.*  Nothing in here but an OLD MURPHY BED, which has been built into the house.  *A dead end.*

Hopper looks around, confused --

                    HOPPER
               (low)
          The hell is that coming from...?

Joyce drops down to the ground and presses her ear to the floor.  The growl vibrates through the floorboards.

                    JOYCE
          ... *It's below us.*

Staying ground level, her eyes shift to the MURPHY BED in the corner.  A faint beam of orange light emanates from below.

Off Joyce, epiphany building...

**MOMENTS LATER**

CLOSE ON:  A pair of hands wrap around the bed posts, then...

Hopper and Joyce raise up the Murphy bed, heaving, and --

KA-WING!  Springs trigger and the entire bed swings upward, folding back into the wall to reveal:

A DOOR IN THE FLOOR.   STEPS LEAD INTO A HAZY ORANGE LIGHT.

Hopper and Joyce share looks.  *Holy shit.*  Then...

They *descend*.  As they recede from us, the GROWLING SOUND
builds in volume, then *shifts*, turning into --

**EXT. COUNTRY ROAD - NIGHT**

THE *GROWL* OF A MOTORCYCLE ENGINE as --

GRIGORI speeds down a country road.  He's wearing his sleek
black helmet; a LARGE ASSAULT RIFLE hangs from his back.

He turns past a familiar mailbox: <u>HESS</u>.

As he speeds toward the farmhouse.  *Toward a showdown...*

**INT. HESS FARM - GENERATOR ROOM - NIGHT**

BOOM!  Hopper's boot strikes cement as --

Hopper and Joyce reach the basement.  Unlike the rest of the
farmhouse, this room has been very recently constructed. It
has been built to hold --

TWO LARGE, GROWLING GENERATORS.  *The source of the noise.*
The audience will recognize these machines from the opening
in Russia.

TWO MEN are busily working on a generator, their faces hidden
behind an open metal panel, when --

> HOPPER
> Hey, *dipshits*.

The men startle, step out into view.  It's --

A MECHANIC and ALEXEI, our young Russian scientist!

They stare in shock and confusion at the sight of Hopper and
Joyce.  Hopper steps forward, gun raised, flashing his badge.

> HOPPER (CONT'D)
> Hawkins Police!  Hands in the
> air -- !

The Russians share confused looks.

> HOPPER (CONT'D)
> Don't make me ask me twice.  I said
> *HANDS IN THE AIR!*

The men share another look.  Then they begin to talk *RAPID-
FIRE*.  But they don't speak English, of course.  They
speak --

*MOTHERFUCKING* **RUSSIAN.**

Hopper stares in shock.  *What????*  He shoots a look at Joyce, who is equally baffled.  He snaps back to the Russians --

> HOPPER (CONT'D)
> English -- do you *speak English*??

The Russians start talking *at* Hopper now.

> HOPPER (CONT'D)
> -- I can't understand you!  *CAN*'T
> UNDERSTAND!  NO UNDERSTAND!

As Hopper's exasperation grows --

Joyce suddenly hears something, looks up.  Above her:

A FLOORBOARD GROANS, coughing dust.  *Someone is upstairs.*

> JOYCE
> *Hopper!*

Hopper stops yelling at the Russians, turns back to Joyce.

He follows her gaze to the ceiling.

As another floorboard BENDS and GROANS, CUT TO:

**INT. HESS FARM - FIRST FLOOR - NIGHT**

A HEAVY BOOT moving across the old floorboards.

It's <u>Grigori</u>, striding through the house with his GIANT ASSAULT RIFLE.

**INT. HESS FARM - BEDROOM - NIGHT**

Grigori enters the bedroom.  Pauses.  Sees --

The raised Murphy bed.  The open door in the floor.

He continues forward.  And...

**INT. GENERATOR ROOM - NIGHT**

... Enters the basement.  Ready to fire.  But...

REVERSE:  <u>THERE IS NO ONE IN HERE</u>.  *Wait*.  He sees a MOVING HUMAN SHADOW on the far wall.  The movement of the shadow is accompanied by what sounds like some kind of struggle -- MUFFLED VOICES, CLANKING METAL.

Grigori moves toward the shadow -- sweeps around the generator -- and --

IT'S THE MECHANIC.  He's been handcuffed to a pipe and gagged with his own sweaty bandana.  He is desperately trying to speak, *to warn*.  His wide eyes look *behind* Grigori where --

                    HOPPER
          *Don't move*.

Hopper emerges from the shadows.  Gun trained on Grigori.

                    HOPPER (CONT'D)
          Drop the gun.  *Drop it*.

As Hopper moves toward Grigori, our CAMERA DRIFTS --

**BEHIND ANOTHER GENERATOR,**

Where we find Joyce in hiding!  Alexei is nearby, sweating and scared, handcuffed to a pipe.  Joyce listens, tense, as --

**BACK ACROSS THE ROOM,**

Hopper walks up to Grigori, gun raised, ready.

                    HOPPER (CONT'D)
          Hey -- you understand what I'm
          saying, big guy?  DROP THE WEAPON --

                    GRIGORI
          ... Or *what*?  You going to shoot?

                    HOPPER
          Ah so you *do* understand me.  Good.
          And yeah, that's right, you don't put
          that away I'll blow some daylight
          through that thick skull of yours --

Hopper shoves his gun to the Grigori's head, but --

                    GRIGORI
          No.  You won't do that.

                    HOPPER
          Yeah, and *why's that?*

                    GRIGORI
          Because you are policeman.  Policeman
          *have rules* --

                    HOPPER
          Oh yeah?  Let's test out that theory.

Hopper clicks off his safety.

HOPPER (CONT'D)
                I'll give you three seconds.  One.
                Two.  Th--

Grigori suddenly *makes a move* -- rushing backwards at high
speed, driving Hopper's back into the wall *and* --

WHOOM!  Hopper's gun skips loose and scatters to the floor!

Joyce sees the fallen gun.  She scrambles for it as --

                HOPPER (CONT'D)
                AAAAAARGGGH -- !

Hopper fights back, climbing onto Grigori's back, squeezing
his neck, *strangling him*.  Grigori spins, trying to shake him
loose.  As he does, his assault rifle FIRES, spraying bullets
*EVERYWHERE* --

BAM BAM BAM!  Bullets HIT the Mechanic, killing him, and --

They almost hit Joyce too, but miss, just barely!  Phew!!
She grabs Hop's gun and, keeping low, scurries back --

**BEHIND THE GENERATOR,**

She covers her head, taking cover, as --

**BACK ACROSS THE ROOM,**

BANGBANGBANG!  Bullets continue to fly.  They drill into the
generators, which spark.  BANG!  An overhead light shatters!

Hopper and Grigori continue to fight.  Hopper, still holding
onto Grigori's neck, manages to knock away Grigori's rifle;
the rain of bullets ends but this fight is *far from over.*

Grigori grabs hold of Hopper's arm and --

WHAM!  Slings him off his back and onto the ground.

But Hopper is fast too -- he crawls away, grabs a wrench off
the floor, turns, SWINGS it with all his might, and --

WHAM-CRUNK!  SMACKS Grigori in the kneecap!

As Grigori stumbles back with a *GRUNT* --

Joyce leaps out from cover with Hop's gun --

                JOYCE
                HOPPER -- !!

She slides the gun to Hopper like she's in some action movie, but there's a little too much juice behind it and --

WHOOSH! Hopper misses the gun! It slides _past him_ --

<u>Right to Grigori</u>. He swoops it up.

> HOPPER
> -- _SHIT_ -- !

Grigori opens fire on Hopper. BANG BANG BANG!!

Hopper dives for cover --

**BEHIND THE GENERATOR - CONTINUOUS**

-- Where he joins Joyce and Alexei --

> HOPPER (CONT'D)
> _NICE TOSS_ -- _!!_

> JOYCE
> _NICE CATCH_!

**BACK ACROSS THE ROOM,**

_CLICK!_ Grigori is out of ammo. He throws away the gun as --

**BEHIND THE GENERATOR,**

Hopper unhooks one of Alexei's handcuffs, snaps it to his own wrist. They're now handcuffed together, _Midnight Run-style_!

> HOPPER
> Alright, Smirnoff, you're coming
> with us --

Hopper and Joyce leap to their feet and --

They make a break for the basement door, dragging poor Alexei with them. They stay behind their row of generators as --

**BACK ACROSS THE ROOM**

Grigori reclaims his assault rifle. Fires at them but --

BANG BANG BANG! Hopper, Joyce, and Alexei are shielded by a mounted control panel!

**INT. HESS FARM - BASEMENT STAIRWELL - NIGHT**

They sprint up the steps and --

**INT. HESS FARM - BEDROOM - NIGHT**

WHOOM! Burst through the hatch door and back into the bedroom. Hopper slams the Murphy bed back down over the door, a mere *split second* before --

Bullets *TEAR* through the mattress as --

**INT. HESS FARM - BASEMENT STAIRWELL - NIGHT**

Grigori opens fire from down below.

**INT. HESS FARM - BEDROOM - NIGHT**

COTTON erupts as the mattress is SHREDDED. Alexei SCREAMS IN RUSSIAN as --

Hopper grabs a bookshelf, slams it down over the bed --

> HOPPER
> LET'S GO -- !

**INT. HESS FARM - HALLWAY - NIGHT**

They race down the hallway as --

**INT. HESS FARM - BASEMENT STAIRWELL - NIGHT**

Grigori charges up the steps. He tries to open the door but --

It's held down by the heavy bookshelf. He drives his massive shoulder into the bottom of the bed, pushing it up, as --

**EXT. HESS FARM - NIGHT**

Hopper, Joyce, and Alexei <u>sprint</u> for the Blazer.

**INT. HESS FARM - BEDROOM - NIGHT**

BOOM-WHOOM! The bookshelf goes <u>FLYING</u> off the bed as --

A red-faced Grigori explodes upstairs. He looks *pissed*.

**INT./EXT. BLAZER - NIGHT**

Hopper tosses Joyce his car keys --

> HOPPER
> -- *Drive* -- !

Joyce leaps into the driver's seat, while Hopper yanks Alexei into the backseat with him as --

**EXT. HESS FARM - PORCH - NIGHT**

Grigori strides outside.  Raises his assault rifle.  And --

**INT./EXT. BLAZER - NIGHT**

> HOPPER
> *JOYCE DRIVE -- !!!!*

Joyce hammers the accelerator and spins the car around as --

**EXT. HESS FARM - PORCH - NIGHT**

Grigori opens fire.  BANGBANGBANGBANG!

**INT./EXT. BLAZER - HESS FARM - DRIVEWAY - NIGHT**

The back windshield *SHATTERS!*

Hopper and Alexei duck as they're showered with glass.

Joyce screams and spins the wheel hard to the left, squealing onto the country road, smashing *through* the Hess mailbox.

**EXT. HESS FARM - PORCH - NIGHT**

Grigori continues to fire.  BANGBANGBANGBANGBANG!

**INT./EXT. BLAZER - HESS FARM - DRIVEWAY - NIGHT**

Bullets *rip* through the car's hood and then --

**EXT. HESS FARM - PORCH - NIGHT**

CLICK!  Grigori is out of ammo.  He lowers the rifle as --

**INT./EXT. BLAZER - COUNTRY ROAD - NIGHT**

The Blazer *speeds* away.  Scott-free.  *Sorta.*  It's bullet-riddled, the engine hissing smoke.

Hopper catches his breath, looks at Joyce.

> HOPPER
> ... You still think it's our
> government?

Off a shell-shocked Joyce --

**EXT. HESS FARM - PORCH - NIGHT**

We PUSH IN on Grigori, scowling, angrier than ever.

And right here, we CRASH TO:

**MAIN TITLES**

**EXT. HAWKINS GENERAL HOSPITAL - MORNING**

A sign reads: EMERGENCY.  Our camera CRANES DOWN to find...

NANCY, dialing a number on a payphone outside the hospital.

**INT. BYERS HOUSE - KITCHEN - MORNING**

BRRRING!  BRRRRING!  The phone rings inside the Byers house.

**INT. BYERS HOUSE - JONATHAN'S ROOM - MORNING**

JONATHAN stirs awake in bed.  He looks at his clock.  It's
5:48 AM.  *Who the hell is calling here this damn early?*  He
shoves his pillow over his ears, rolls over, *and...*

**INT. BYERS HOUSE - KITCHEN - MORNING**

The phone stops ringing.  But then...

BRRRING!!  BRRRING!!  It starts up again!

**INT. BYERS HOUSE - JONATHAN'S ROOM - MORNING**

Jonathan sits up.  His eyes a little wild.  UGGGHH!

He throws off his covers and --

**INT. BYERS HOUSE - KITCHEN - MORNING**

Jonathan rips the phone off the hook, grumpy --

> JONATHAN
> *-- Hello?*

INTERCUT WITH:

**EXT. HOSPITAL - PAYPHONE - MORNING**

Nancy, relieved, urgent --

> NANCY
> *Jonathan, it's me, don't hang up* --

> JONATHAN
> Do you realize what time it is?

                    NANCY
          Jonathan just -- listen to me --

                    JONATHAN
          I'd really rather not - it's *six AM*
          and I had a late night with Fagin and
          the gang so --

                    NANCY
               (sharply interrupting)
          I'm at the hospital with Driscoll.

This shuts Jonathan up -- he can't believe his ears.

                    JONATHAN
          *What -- ?*

                    NANCY
               (almost manic)
          She's been sedated for a few hours
          now and the doctors are still running
          tests but --

                    JONATHAN
          Nancy *please* tell me you're joking --

                    NANCY
          No it's not a joke and yes I know I'm
          insane and irrational and out of
          touch but can you save your lecture
          for later because I really don't give
          a shit right now I just need you to
          put me on the phone with your
          brother --

                    JONATHAN
          *What -- ?*

                    NANCY
          Jonathan, *please* --

                    JONATHAN
          He's not here --

                    NANCY
          Where is he?  Is he safe?

Jonathan is starting to actually freak out now.

                    JONATHAN
          Why wouldn't he be safe??

Nancy hesitates.

> JONATHAN (CONT'D)
> Nancy, *why wouldn't he be safe*???

**EXT. MIDDLE OF THE WOODS - MORNING**

HISSSSS!!!  STEAM SPITS OUT OF AN ENGINE --

> HOPPER
> *SONOFABITCH*!!  *SONOFABITCH*!!

Hopper tightens a bolt, quickly cutting off the steam.

WIDEN TO REVEAL:  He's hunched over his Blazer's engine in
the middle of the woods.  The bullet-riddled car is now dead,
and from the looks of it, he has been trying to repair it for
some time.  He's drenched in sweat, oil, grease.  As he
continues to work, grumbling, our camera MOVES TO FIND...

Joyce, standing next Alexei, who has been handcuffed to a
tree.  She is talking to him -- or rather, she is *trying* to.

> JOYCE
> -- Maaaaag-net?  Do you know
> Maaaagnet?

She presses two rocks together, pretending they're magnets.
Alexei nods.

> ALEXEI
> Magneet, yes?

Joyce nods, excited.

> JOYCE
> Yes!  Magneet, yes!  They were on my
> fridge -- see -- the magnets, then --

She picks the rocks back up, then promptly drops them.

> JOYCE (CONT'D)
> They fell.  De-magnetized?
> Understand?

> ALEXEI
> Da --

> JOYCE
> Is that because of *machines* you were
> working on -- ?

> ALEXEI
> *Mahshina* -- ?

                    JOYCE
          Mashina, mashina, yes -- !

She makes noises like the generator.  Alexei gets it!

                    ALEXEI
          Da -- da -- machina -- machina!!

He points to the Blazer, then makes the gesture of cranking a
car!

                    ALEXEI (CONT'D)
          VROOM!  VROOOM!

Or rather -- *he doesn't get it.*

                    JOYCE
          No no -- *not the car*.  The machines --
          the *machines* in the Hess farm --

Hopper can't take it anymore --

                    HOPPER
          JOYCE!!!  Pleeease.  You're giving me
          a headache -- the *both of you.*

Joyce glares, stomps over to him.

                    JOYCE
          I'm *making progress* --

                    HOPPER
          *Progress?*  Let's see -- you've
          learned that Smirnoff over there --

                    JOYCE
          *Alexei* --

                    HOPPER
          *Smirnoff* is Russian and works for
          Starcourt, two things we *already*
          knew --

                    JOYCE
          We *thought* we knew and now I've
          *confirmed* --

                    HOPPER
          Okay, well...

Hopper finishes tightening a bolt.

                    HOPER
          Why don't you go *confirm* something
          useful --

Hopper tosses her the car keys.

                    HOPPER
          And see if this thing'll start.

                    JOYCE
          You fixed it?

                    HOPPER
          We'll find out, won't we?

Hopper flashes Joyce a big obnoxious smile.  Joyce smiles
back at him, then stomps off, her smile promptly *dropping*.

                    HOPPER (CONT'D)
          Make sure it's in neutral!!

**INT. HOPPER'S BLAZER - MOMENTS LATER**

Joyce climbs into the car, muttering to herself.

                    JOYCE
          *"Do something useful" -- "do*
          *something useful" --*

She shifts the car into neutral.

                    JOYCE (CONT'D)
          *Why don't you do something useful --*

She jams the key into the ignition, turns it, and --

CHUH-CHUH-CHUH-CHUH!  The engine tries but fails to catch.

                    JOYCE (CONT'D)
          It's *NOT* working!!

                    HOPPER
          *TRY AGAIN!*

Joyce sighs, tries again.

**EXT. MIDDLE OF THE WOODS**

The engine CHUGS, starts to make an ODD WHINING SOUND.

Alexei hears it, starts to call out.  He's speaking in
Russian of course, but there is *one word* that both our
languages share:

                         ALEXEI
          -- *STOP* -- *STOP!!*

Hopper snaps to him.

                         HOPPER
          Shut up, Smirnoff --  !

But Alexei keeps shouting.  He's trying to warn Hopper, but
Hopper is just getting pissed off.  He stomps toward Alexei --

                    HOPPER (CONT'D)
          Hey!  *What'd* I just tell you??  Shut
          your --

CHOOOOM!  THE ENGINE SUDDENLY ERUPTS IN SMOKE BEHIND HOPPER!

Hopper whips around --

                    HOPPER (CONT'D)
          *JESUS* --  !

                         JOYCE
          -- *SHIT!*

A panicked Joyce scrambles out of the car just as --

KA-BOOOM!  THE ENGINE EXPLODES INTO FLAMES!!!

As Joyce stumbles away from the burning car --

Alexei shoots Hopper a knowing look.

                         ALEXEI
               *Stop*.

Off Hopper...

**EXT. MIDDLE OF THE WOODS - LATER - DAY**

WHOOM!  Boots smash leaves as...

A sweaty Hopper and Joyce trudge through the dense woods,
dragging a reluctant Alexei with them.  They're clearly onto
plan B now -- and Joyce is *not* happy about it.

                         JOYCE
               -- I thought this friend of yours
               lived in Illinois --

                         HOPPER
               First of all, he's not my friend.
               He's more like an... *acquaintance*.

Alexei swats at a swarm of mosquitos, CURSES in Russian --

Hopper yanks him forward --

>                    HOPPER (CONT'D)
>          *Keep up* --

>                    JOYCE
>          But this "acquaintance," he lives in
>          *Illinois* -- ?

>                    HOPPER
>          Yeah --

>                    JOYCE
>          So we're *walking* to Illinois -- ?

>                    HOPPER
>          That's right.  I figured we'll get
>          there by Friday evening.  That work
>          for your schedule?

Joyce stares.

>                    HOPPER (CONT'D)
>          We're obviously not going to walk to
>          Illinois, Joyce, *Jesus* --

>                    JOYCE
>          So *WHAT* are we doing -- ?

>                    HOPPER
>          I don't know, I'll figure it out!

>                    JOYCE
>          There's got to be *someone* in Indiana
>          who speaks Russian --

>                    HOPPER
>          I'm all ears, Joyce.  *ALL EARS*!

As Hopper and Joyce continue to bicker, our CAMERA SLOWLY
PULLS BACK and *something unusual* begins to happen...

The TREES EVAPORATE, DISSOLVING INTO INKY BLACKNESS -- then
the forest floor EVAPORATES... then Alexei vanishes... then
*Joyce too*... until...

Hopper is walking ALONE THROUGH DARKNESS.

And suddenly it hits us.  We're now in --

**THE BLACK VOID!!**

We PULL BACK DEEPER into the void to reveal...

ELEVEN, watching Hopper.  Her eyes narrow.

>                         ELEVEN
>             I found him.

**INT. WHEELER HOUSE - BASEMENT - DAY**

Eleven is blindfolded, sitting cross-legged on the couch in
Mike's basement.  The nearby television blasts static.

Sitting around her: MIKE, LUCAS, MAX, and WILL.  They're
still wearing their clothes from the sauna fight and they
look exhausted -- they clearly haven't slept a wink.

>                    MAX
>         ... Where is he -- ?
>
>                    ELEVEN
>         ... Woods.
>
>                    LUCAS
>         *Woods --* ?
>
>                    ELEVEN
>         He's with... *Will's mom.*

Will sits forward, stunned.

>                    WILL
>         My *mom?*
>
>                    MAX
>         What are they doing?
>
>                    ELEVEN
>         Ill -- *annoy.*  They're *going* to...
>         Ill -- *annoy.*

Everyone shares confused looks, when --

KNOCKING ON THE BASEMENT DOOR INTERRUPTS.  IT'S --

>                    KAREN (O.S.)
>         MIKE!  BREAKFAST!
>
>                    MIKE
>         NOT NOW MOM!

Mike spins back to Eleven.

                    MIKE (CONT'D)
          *Illinois*?  Like the *state* Illinois?

Eleven pulls down her blindfold.  Nods.

                    ELEVEN
          Ill. Annoy.

More baffled looks, then --

**INT. WHEELER HOUSE - BASEMENT - BATHROOM - LATER**

WHOOSH!  Water streams from a faucet as --

Max washes the spilled blood from Eleven's nose with a
washcloth.  As she cleans, her eyes go to El's neck.  It's
bruised.  *Swollen.*

*FLASHCUT TO BILLY ATTACKING HER IN THE SAUNA -- STRANGLING
HER -- KILLING HER --*

                    MAX
          Does it still hurt?

Eleven shakes her head.

                    ELEVEN
          Only... when I talk.

                    MAX
          Good thing you're not Mike then.
          Blab blab blab blab -- you'd be in
          like constant pain --

Eleven smiles softly at this, our girls finding light in the
darkness, as --

                    MIKE (PRE-LAP)
          ... *Something is not right* --

**INT. WHEELER HOUSE - BASEMENT - DAY**

Mike is pacing in the basement, *blabbing just as Max said* --

                    MIKE
          ... I can't get Hopper off my back
          all summer, and now all of a sudden
          he's hiking with Will's mom to
          Illinois -- and Dustin's MIA too -- I
          mean -- it can't all be coincidence --

                    LUCAS
What does it matter?  The bottom line
is -- they're *not here*.  It's up to
us.

                    MIKE
"Up to us" -- to do *what* exactly --


                    LUCAS
Find Billy, and *stop him* --

                    MIKE
Yeah, okay, that's a real nice
sentiment, but even if El can find
him again, and that's a *pretty big if*
-- then what?

                    LUCAS
We *burn the shit out of him* -- and
make sure he can't escape this time --

                    MIKE
Yeah okay, *then what* --

                    LUCAS
THEN WE WIN --


                    MIKE
No.  See, that's the problem -- we
don't.  We don't win.  We got the
Mind Flayer out of Will before -- and
he just came right back.  We don't
just have to stop Billy -- we have to
stop the Mind Flayer --

                    LUCAS
That's a real nice *sentiment*, Mike --
but how exactly do we do that?

Mike hesitates.  Finally admits:

                    MIKE
... I don't know.

                    LUCAS
You "don't know" --

                    MIKE
No --

                    WILL
Maybe El does.

Mike takes this in.  Will may just be right.  His eyes swivel
to the closed bathroom door, *annoyed* --

                    MIKE
          What are they still doing in there?

                    LUCAS
          Girls like hanging out in bathrooms.

                    MIKE
          *Why?*

                    LUCAS
          I don't know.

                    MIKE
            (suddenly paranoid)
          They're conspiring against me.

                    WILL
          *That's* your concern right now?

                    MIKE
          It's not my main concern, it's just a
          *subconcern* --

                    WILL
          But I thought it was already over --

                    MIKE
          It's *not over*, we're just -- taking a
          break --

                    WILL
          She said she "dumped your ass" --
          that *doesn't* sound like a *break* --

                    MAX (O.S.)
          IT WASN'T.

The boys snap to the bathroom door, still closed, but --

**INT. WHEELER HOUSE - BASEMENT - BATHROOM - DAY**

                    MAX
          You guys DO realize we can hear
          everything you are saying, right???

**OUTSIDE THE BATHROOM,**

The boys stare awkwardly --

                         MIKE
                      (to Lucas)
          Told you.  *Conspiring.*

BAM BAM BAM!  MORE POUNDING ON THE BASEMENT DOOR.

                    MIKE (CONT'D)
                   (real pissed)
          Mom, NOT NOW -- !

But it's not Karen this time.  It's --

                    NANCY (O.S.)
          MIKE!  OPEN THE DOOR!

The boys share looks, then --

**MOMENTS LATER - TOP OF STEPS**

WHOOM!  Mike swings open the door to find --

Nancy and Jonathan.  They look *scared*.

As brother and sister *lock eyes*...

                    DUSTIN (PRE-LAP)
          This is a CODE RED!  I repeat -- a
          CODE RED!

**INT. ELEVATOR SHAFT - DAY**

WHOOSH!  Our camera SOARS down the immense elevator shaft.

                      DUSTIN
          DOES *ANYONE* COPY -- ??

We land on Dustin.  He's standing on the roof of the secret
elevator, holding his walkie up as high as he can, shouting:

                    DUSTIN (CONT'D)
          We are INNOCENT CHILDREN and we are
          trapped under Starcourt Mall -- THE
          RED ARMY HAS INFILTRATED HAWKINS AND
          IF WE ARE FOUND THEY WILL TORTURE AND
          KILL US AND --

                    STEVE (O.S.)
          *DUDE!*

Dustin looks over to find Steve climbing up onto the roof.

                    STEVE (CONT'D)
          You gotta *chill* out on that thing,
          you're gonna drain the battery --

                         DUSTIN
          The mall just opened --

                         STEVE
          So -- ?

                         DUSTIN
          *So* someone might be in range now --

                         STEVE
          Oh I can't wait for Petey the mall
          cop to save the day --

                         DUSTIN
          Why are you such a crankypants?
          After you got to spend the night with
          Robin --

                         STEVE
          Dude, give that creepy dream up --

                         DUSTIN
          I heard you two talking all night.

Steve walks over to the edge of the elevator --

                         STEVE
          Yeah, we were trying to get the door
          open while you children were napping.
          And eight hours later, we're exactly
          nowhere.  Which, for the record, is
          WHY I'M CRANKY.

Steve suddenly unzips his pants.

                         DUSTIN
                      (appalled)
          What are you doing??

                         STEVE
          Peeing.  Look away!  *AWAY*!

A horrified Dustin averts his gaze just as --

Steve begins to *URINATE*.

**INT. ELEVATOR - DAY**

His pee splashes outside the elevator window right near --

Robin, who is fiddling with control panel wires.  GROSS!

                         ROBIN
          CAN YOU REDIRECT YOUR STREAM PLEASE??

The stream of pee begins to move as --

BANG BANG!  A loud noise.  An annoyed Robin turns to find --

Erica.  She is slamming one of those green-liquid cylinders against the wall, trying to open it up.

>                     ROBIN (CONT'D)
>           HEY -- HEY!  *CAREFUL!*

Robin storms over, snatches the cylinder away --

>                     ROBIN (CONT'D)
>           We don't know what that is -- !

>                     ERICA
>           *Exactly*.  It could be useful.

>                     ROBIN
>           Useful *how* -- ?

>                     ERICA
>           We can survive down here a *long* time
>           without food.  But if the human body
>           doesn't get water it *will* die.

>                     ROBIN
>           Yeah, okay, well -- I hate to break
>           it to you but...
>                (holds up cylinder)
>           This *ain't* water.

>                     ERICA
>           No.  But it's a liquid.  And if it
>           comes down to drinking that shit or
>           dying of thirst...
>                (beat)
>           I drink.

Erica snatches the cylinder back.  Robin stares at this *insane* child, speechless, when --

Her eyes narrow.  She hears a DRONING SOUND.  *Now what??*

She walks away from Erica and crosses to the elevator door. The sound is coming from outside.  And it's GROWING LOUDER.

*Something* is coming their way.

**INT. ELEVATOR ROOF - DAY**

Robin pops her head up through the elevator panel.

                    ROBIN
          We've got company.

Off Dustin and Steve, SMASH TO:

**INT. UNDERGROUND TUNNEL - CONTINUOUS**

VROOOOM!  Rubber tires spinning rapidly as --

A LYNX MINI-TRUCK speeds down a tunnel.  A RUSSIAN WORKER
drives; ANOTHER sits beside him, dragging on a cigarette.

**INT. UNDERGROUND TUNNEL - DAY**

EEEEE!  The mini-truck pulls to a stop by the elevator.

The Russian Workers climb out.  Worker #1 approaches the
elevator door, removes a KEYCARD, and swipes it through an
electronic card reader.  The elevator door RISES to reveal:

**INT. ELEVATOR - DAY**

Dozens of boxes.  But no sign of our kids.

Worker #1 suddenly pauses, sniffs the air.

                    WORKER #1
          <You smell that?>

                    WORKER #2
          <What?>

                    WORKER #1
          <... Piss.>

Worker #2 sniffs.  Shrugs.  They enter the room and begin to
load boxes onto a hand cart.  We now reveal...

**INT. ELEVATOR ROOF - CONTINUOUS - DAY**

... Our gang hiding on the roof directly above them, trying
not to move, trying not to breathe.

Steve's gaze shifts to Erica.  She's still holding onto that
metal cylinder.  We PUSH IN on Steve, *an idea forming*, and --

**INT. OUTSIDE ELEVATOR - A LITTLE LATER - DAY**

VROOM!  The truck drives away, carrying away the boxes.

As it recedes from camera, we RETURN OUR GAZE to...

The elevator door.  It's closing.  Almost down when --

WHOOM!  The metal cylinder slides under the door just in the nick of time and --

Stops it from closing!

**INT. ELEVATOR - DAY**

Steve did it!!

>                         STEVE
>             Alright, *go go go* -- !

The others scramble under the door --

**INT. UNDERGROUND TUNNEL - A LITTLE LATER**

Erica makes it out first -- then Dustin -- but --

**INT. ELEVATOR - DAY**

EEEEE!  The glass begins to spiderweb under the pressure!

Robin slides through, then Steve scrambles under *just as* --

**INT. UNDERGROUND TUNNEL - A LITTLE LATER**

SMASH!  The glass SHATTERS -- the DOOR SLAMS DOWN -- and --

HISSSSS!  THAT GREEN LIQUID splashes everywhere.

Steve scrambles away as the liquid corrodes the floor, *EATING RIGHT THROUGH IT LIKE XENOMORPH BLOOD*!!!

>                         STEVE
>             Jesus *Christ* --

Robin shoots Erica a look.

>                         ROBIN
>             *Still* want to drink that?

Before Erica can respond, Dustin turns around and...

>                         DUSTIN
>             *Holy mother of God...*

The others turn, following his gaze.  WE PUSH OVER THEM TO REVEAL: A GIANT TUNNEL STRETCHING BEFORE THEM.  IT GOES ON FOR WHAT MUST BE MILES.  NO END IN SIGHT -- *LITERALLY.*

The mini-truck so far away now it looks like a *fucking ant.*

                         STEVE
          Well...  I hope you guys are in good
          shape.  *Lookin' at you Henderson.*

Steve starts walking down the tunnel.

Everyone shares looks, then --

<u>Scrambles after Steve</u>

**EXT. WHEELER HOUSE - DAY**

We PUSH toward the Wheeler house...

                         NANCY (O.S.)
          It was the same thing...  the *exact
          same thing* that happened to Will last
          year...

**INT. WHEELER HOUSE - BASEMENT - DAY**

WHOOM!  Nancy tosses down DRISCOLL'S MEDICAL RECORDS.

                         NANCY
          And look -- *look* at the body
          temperature.

Mike, Will, Lucas, and Max lean in to see.  Sure enough,
CLOSE ON: body temperature is an *extremely* low <u>95 DEGREES</u>.

                         WILL
          ... *He likes it cold.*

                         MIKE
          ... So this crazy old lady who ate
          the fertilizer --

                         NANCY
          *Missus Driscoll* --

                         MIKE
          Yeah.  Missus Driscoll.  What time
          did she have this... *attack?*

                         NANCY
          Last night --

                         MIKE
          Yeah I mean, what *time* last night?

                         NANCY
          Around nine --

This catches Jonathan by surprise.

                              291

                    JONATHAN
You waited *all night* to call -- ?

                    NANCY
I was waiting for them to run tests --

                    WILL
          (confused)
You weren't there --?

                    JONATHAN
Well I'm here now aren't I??

                    NANCY
*Hallelujah.*

The kids share looks.  This is... awkward.  Nancy pivots
back.

                    NANCY (CONT'D)
What time was your... "sauna test"?

                    ALL THE KIDS
Around nine.

                    NANCY
Okay, then that proves it -- proves
my theory.

                    MIKE
She's Flayed, just like Billy --

                    JONATHAN
"Flayed?"

                    MIKE
The Mind Flayer -- he flays people,
takes over their minds.  They
basically -- *become him* --

                    LUCAS
And if there are two Flayed --

                    WILL
We have to assume there are more.

A beat as this terrifying thought sinks in.  Then...

Eleven shares a look with Max.

                    ELEVEN
*Heather.*

Everyone turns to Eleven, surprised.


                         292

                    ELEVEN (CONT'D)
      Billy -- he was doing... *something* to
      Heather.  I -- I heard her --

*WE SUDDENLY FLASHBACK TO BILLY IN THE VOID FROM EPISODE #303.*

                        ELEVEN (CONT'D)
      She was... scared.  Screaming.
           (clarifying)
      *Bad screams.*

                        LUCAS
      What's a *good* scream -- ?

                        ELEVEN
      Max said --

                        MAX
           (quick)
      It doesn't matter --

                        NANCY
      I'm sorry -- I'm a little lost here.
      Who is "Heather"?

                        MAX
      She's a lifeguard at the pool --

                        NANCY
      Heather *Holloway?*

Max and Eleven nod.  "Yes."

Jonathan and Nancy share looks.  Simultaneously realizing --

                    JONATHAN/NANCY
           *Tom.*

**INT./EXT. STATION WAGON - WHEELER HOUSE - DAY**

The gang race outside to Karen's station wagon.

Nancy leaps behind the wheel.  Jonathan takes the passenger
seat.  Meanwhile, Lucas (carrying his backpack full of
supplies), Max, and Eleven climb into the back, leaving --

Mike and Will stranded outside.

                        MIKE
           *Seriously?*

                        WILL
      Welcome to my world.


                          293

**MOMENTS LATER**

Mike pulls down the rear door, shutting him and Will into the "way back."

Nancy kicks on the ignition, then turns to face the packed car like a soccer mom.

                    NANCY
          *Seatbelts*.

The kids buckle up.  As soon as the final seatbelt CLICKS --

SCREECH!  Nancy *tears* out of the driveway, toppling the boys' bikes, leaving burnt rubber in her wake, and --

**EXT. MIDDLE OF THE WOODS - DAY**

CLOSE ON:  FLAMES RAGING, licking the sky, spewing SMOKE.

WIDEN TO REVEAL: Hopper's Blazer.  Now burnt to a crisp.  We watching it burn for a bit, then --

WHOOM.  A LARGE FIGURE steps into our frame.  It's...

GRIGORI.  He's tracking them.  *Of course he is*.  He steps forward and calmly inspects the burnt vehicle, seemingly unbothered by the heat.  His eyes then scan the rest of the area, Terminator-like.  He locks onto something of interest.

He walks forward.  Kneels down.  It's...

A FOOTPRINT.  Pretty clear in the damp earth.

He looks up at the dense forest ahead.

As his eyes harden, SMASH TO...

**EXT. WOODS - DAY**

WHOOM!  Filthy white Keds trampling through thick underbrush.

WIDEN:  Joyce, Hop, and Alexei (still handcuffed) are still in the woods.  They're dirty, sweaty, exhausted, and above all: *grumpy*.

                    JOYCE
          Do you have to walk *so* close -- ?

                    HOPPER
          Sorry -- ?

                    JOYCE
I said <u>do you have to walk so close</u>?
You *stink* --


                    HOPPER
You know -- I get it, you're pissed
right?  'Cause I blew up the car --


                    JOYCE
With ME IN it -- !!


                    HOPPER
Let me remind you, Joyce, I am not a
mechanic --


                    JOYCE
Which is <u>*why*</u> you should've listened
to Alexei --


                    HOPPER
Oh, yes, your new Russian boyfriend --


                    JOYCE
Yes, yes, every man I speak to is now
my *boyfriend* --


                    HOPPER
You know, he *does* kinda look like a
Russian Scott Clarke --


                    JOYCE
Here it comes --


                    HOPPER
Maybe you two should go on a date.
Might I suggest -- Enzo's?


Joyce crashes to a stop --


                    JOYCE
You know what -- ?!


                    HOPPER
What -- ?!


                    JOYCE
I would MUCH rather go on a date with
him than a BRUTE like you --


                    HOPPER
Oh yeah -- ?!


                    JOYCE
Yeah -- !!

                                    HOPPER
                    Well he'd probably like you -- since
                    he _can't UNDERSTAND YOU_ --

Joyce is about to fire back when --

                                    JOYCE
                    Oh.

                                    HOPPER
                    What -- ?

                                    JOYCE
                    He's running.

Hopper follows her gaze.  Sure enough --

Alexei is _FLEEING THROUGH THE WOODS_!

                                    HOPPER
                    ... _SONOFA-- !_

Hopper gives chase and --

**EXT. WOODS - MOMENTS LATER**

Alexei sprints through the woods, shouting incoherently in
Russian, then --

**EXT. WOODS - CLEARING - MOMENTS LATER**

WHOOM!  Alexei bursts into a clearing and --

Crashes to a halt.  And points excitedly, smiling.

                                    ALEXEI
                    <Look, look!!!>

Hopper and Joyce crash to a stop behind him.  Breathing hard.
They follow his direction to find --

A 7-ELEVEN GAS STATION!!!

Hopper and Joyce share a look of _enormous relief_, then --

**INT. 7-ELEVEN - DAY**

DING!  The door to the 7-ELEVEN FLIES OPEN as --

Our BEDRAGGLED TRIO stagger into this _divine shelter_.  They
fling open a COLD DRINKS fridge and grab SODAS!  _Bubble Up,
New Coke, Jolt!_  As they CHUG down their chosen sodas --

A GAS STATION CASHIER eyes them warily.

                    GAS STATION CASHIER
          You all gonna pay for those?

They turn to look at him, still chugging, and --

**A FEW MINUTES LATER**

WHAM!  Hopper tosses a PACK OF SPICY BEEF JERKY, a SIX-PACK
OF NEW COKE, and a MAP OF ILLINOIS onto the gas station
counter.

As the Cashier rings him up, he glances at the handcuffed
Alexei, who is now making himself a GIANT CHERRY SLURPEE.

                    GAS STATION CASHIER
          ... So what are you anyway -- a
          bounty hunter or something?

                    HOPPER
          Cop actually.
               (off Cashier's skeptical look)
          *Undercover.*

Hopper tosses the Cashier a WAD OF MONEY.  And that's when he
hears it: BLARING 80S ROCK MUSIC.  Hopper turns to find --

A YELLOW CONVERTIBLE swerving into the gas station, music
blasting.  The driver is a RICH SUNGLASS-WEARING DOUCHEBAG.

Off Hopper, *an idea forming...*

**EXT. 7-ELEVEN - DAY**

As the Rich Douchebag starts to pump gas...

Joyce paces at a nearby PAYPHONE.

                    JOYCE
          Karen -- Karen, hi!  It's -- Joyce.
               (beat)
          Oh I'm... *fine.*  I was just checking
          on Will...  The movies -- ?

As Joyce continues to talk, OUR CAMERA SWINGS BACK OVER TO --

Hopper and Alexei (now sucking hard on that Cherry Slurpee)
stride toward the Douchebag's convertible.  Without a word,
Hopper throws open the side door, shoves Alexei in --

                    HOPPER
          ... *In ya go* --

The Douchebag looks up from pumping gas --

                         RICH DOUCHEBAG
             HEY -- !!

Hopper flashes his badge --

                         HOPPER
             Police emergency -- I need your car.

**BACK BY THE PAYPHONE,**

Joyce, still on the phone, clocks the commotion.  WTF?

                         JOYCE
             Karen, I, I, uh, I'm going to have to
             call you back --

As she hangs up the phone --

**BACK BY THE FILLING STATION**

WHOOM!  Hopper slots the gas nozzle back into the pump.

                         HOPPER
             -- What's your name, sir -- ?

                         RICH DOUCHEBAG
             Todd --

                         HOPPER
             Todd.  *Listen to me.*
                 (gestures to Alexei)
             This man may not look like it but
             he's one of the world's most
             dangerous men, he's --
                 (Hop's a terrible improviser)
             Murdered many children --

                         TODD
             -- *What* -- ??

                         HOPPER
             A true psychopath.  I've tracked him
             across two state lines   --

                         JOYCE
             What's going on -- ?

Hopper looks up to find Joyce walking over --

                         HOPPER
             Detective Byers!  This is Todd, he's
             agreed to lend us his car to
             transport our dangerous prisoner --

Joyce picks up on what's going on --

> JOYCE
> Yes, yes, thank God -- he's a very
> dangerous --
>     (also a bad improviser)
> Thief --

> HOPPER
> Child murderer --

> JOYCE
>     (what??)
> Child murderer --

> HOPPER
> We really should get going --

> JOYCE
> Yes --

Hopper and Joyce climb into the convertible; Todd remains as baffled as ever.

> TODD
> Hey -- how do I get my car back -- ?

> HOPPER
> Just call the station --

> TODD
> What station -- ?

Hopper cranks the ignition --

> HOPPER
> Love the sound of that Todd --

> TODD
> Hey -- what station?!

> HOPPER
> You did the right thing here Todd --

Hopper kicks into drive and SCREEECH! Squeals off, music blasting, leaving a slack-jawed Todd in the dust!

**EXT. ROAD OUTSIDE GAS STATION - MOMENTS LATER**

Hopper's hair blows in the wind, he looks like a madman!

                        JOYCE
          Detective Byers -- ??

                        HOPPER
          It's got a ring, no?

Hopper shifts into another gear --

                        HOPPER (CONT'D)
          God, I could get *used to this*.

He PUNCHES the gas and --

*VROOOOM!*  The convertible *ROARS* past camera and WE SMASH TO --

**INT. UNDERGROUND TUNNEL - DAY**

Feet.  Moving *slowly as...*

Steve, Robin, Dustin, and Erica stride down the never-ending
tunnel.

Dustin is doing his best to stay positive.

                        DUSTIN
          ... I mean, you have to admit, as
          just a feat of engineering alone,
          this is *impressive*...

                        STEVE
          You ask me, it's a fire hazard: no
          stairs, no exits, an elevator from
          hell --

                        ERICA
          They're commies.  You don't pay
          people?  They cut corners.

                        ROBIN
          To be fair to our Russian comrades, I
          don't think this tunnel was designed
          for walking.  I mean think about it --
          they've developed the *perfect*
          delivery system for transporting that
          cargo --

                        DUSTIN
          It all comes into the mall like any
          old delivery  --

                        ROBIN
          And then they load it up on those
          trucks -- and nobody is the wiser --

STEVE
You think they built a whole mall to
transport some -- *green poison* -- ?

DUSTIN
I very seriously doubt it's something
as boring as poison.  It's gotta be
more valuable than that.  Like
Promethium or something --

STEVE
"Promethium" -- ?

ROBIN
(jumping in)
It's what Victor Stone's dad used to
make Cyborg's bionic and cybernetic
components --

ERICA
You're all so nerdy it makes me
*physically ill.*

STEVE
Hey, watch who you call a nerd,
alright?

ROBIN
Why so sensitive, Harrington?  Don't
want to lose cool points with this
*ten-year-old child?*

STEVE
I'm just saying -- I don't know jack
shit about this *"prometheus"* --

DUSTIN
*Promethium.*  Prometheus is a Greek
mythological figure.  But whatever --
doesn't matter -- all I'm saying is,
I bet they're using it to make
something --

ROBIN
*Or power something* --

DUSTIN
Like a nuclear weapon --

ROBIN
Totally --

                    STEVE
          So then we might be walking toward a
          nuclear weapon -- that'd be great,
          that'd be *really great* --

                    ROBIN
          -- But if they *are* building something
          -- why *here*?  I mean -- Hawkins,
          *seriously*??  Of *all places*?

Dustin and Steve pause here, share loaded looks.

Robin keeps walking, unaware they've stopped...

                    ROBIN (CONT'D)
          At best, we're a toilet stop on your
          way to Disneyland.  But maybe that's
          the reason...  our very *lameness* is
          what drew them here --

As Robin continues to hypothesize, Dustin and Steve have
a private pow-wow, their voices hushed, urgent:

                    DUSTIN
          ... Do you think the Russians
          know -- ?

                    STEVE
          About the -- ?

                    DUSTIN
          They could -- ?

                    STEVE
          So it's connected -- ?

                    DUSTIN
          Maybe --

                    STEVE
          *How* -- ?

                    DUSTIN
          I don't know but it's --

                    DUSTIN/STEVE
          *Possible*.

                    ROBIN (O.S.)
          *I'M SORRY* --

The boys swivel to find --

Robin and Erica staring back at them.

                         ROBIN (CONT'D)
               -- But is there something you two
               would like to share with the group?

Dustin and Steve look at one another, speaking without words.
Should they... *tell them???*  They hesitate, not sure, when --

                         RUSSIAN VOICE (O.S.)
               Nedelya dlinnaya:  Serebryanyi kot
               yest --

A Russian voice seems to call to them from nowhere.

                         DUSTIN/STEVE/ROBIN
               *Walkie* --

All eyes swivel to Erica, who is already on it.  She drops to
her knees, flings off her backpack, unzips it, and removes --

DUSTIN'S SUPERCOMM.  We hear the Russian clearly now:

                         RUSSIAN BROADCASTER
               --- Kogda seeneeye vstretitsa s
               zhyoltym na zapade --

Robin knows the rest by heart:

                         ROBIN/RUSSIAN BROADCASTER
               -- *Poyectka vkitay zvuchit ni-plocha,
               yesli bit' ostorojnim.*

Everyone shares looks.  Their eyes wide.  It's --

                         STEVE/ROBIN
               The code.

                         DUSTIN
               Wherever they're broadcasting from --

                         ROBIN
               It's *close.*  And if there's *one thing*
               we know about that signal --

                         DUSTIN
               It can reach the surface.

Robin nods.  *Exactly.*  More shared looks, then --

The group scrambles to their feet and --

**EXT. HEATHER'S HOUSE - DAY**

TSK-TSK-TSK.  A sprinkler sprays water across a meticulously cut lawn.  We PAN TO FIND...

The Station Wagon pulling up to Heather's house.

**FRONT PORCH - A LITTLE LATER**

DING DONG!  Nancy rings the doorbell.  Again.  DING DONG!

No answer.  She turns to Eleven, nods.  And...

**INT. HEATHER'S HOUSE - FOYER**

FWOOM!  A bolt flies open, then --

Nancy pushes open the door, heads into the foyer.

> NANCY
> ... Tom?  ... Heather??

Her calls go unanswered.  The house is eerily quiet.  As the rest of the gang move inside, they clutch their arms.

> MAX
> ... Jesus, it's *freezing*.

Mike walks up to a THERMOSTAT.  It's all the way down.

> MIKE
> *... He likes it cold...*

> NANCY
> You guys smell that...?

Shared looks, then --

**INT. HEATHER'S HOUSE - KITCHEN - DAY**

The door to the kitchen opens...

Nancy enters first.  Covers her nose with her arm.

> NANCY
> *... God...*

The others step up behind her, equally repelled.

REVERSE TO REVEAL:  The fridge is toppled on its side.  It has been ripped open, dismantled, a puddle of NEON GREEN COOLANT on the floor.  But that's not all:  RANDOM CHEMICAL CONTAINERS are scattered about the kitchen -- *CLEANERS, CANNED FOOD, DETERGENT*...

As Nancy examines the mess, she shoots a look at Jonathan --

                    NANCY (CONT'D)
          More chemicals --

Jonathan holds up some AJAX.  Shakes it, flips it.  Empty --

                    JONATHAN
          You think they're *guzzling* this shit?

                    NANCY
          It's either that or they went on one
          helluva cleaning frenzy --

                    MAX
          But last year, Will didn't eat
          chemicals.
                    (*wait*)
          *Did you?*

                    WILL
          No.  This is something new --

                    MIKE
          Mister Clarke.  Fifth grade.  Posit:
          What happens when you mix
          chemicals -- ?

                    LUCAS/WILL
          "You create a new substance."

Mike nods.  *Precisely.*

                    MIKE
          Maybe they're making something.

                    MAX
          In themselves?  I mean, come on -- if
          you drank this crap it would *kill*
          *you* --

                    LUCAS
          Yeah.  *If* you're human.

On this unnerving note, Nancy's eyes narrow, seeing
something.  She crosses into...

**THE DINING ROOM - CONTINUOUS**

The scene of the crime.  The dinner plates are still laid
out... along with that now ominous plate of cookies.  But
Nancy is focused on something else.  She kneels down to the
floor...

There's a WINE BOTTLE. It is toppled on its side; red wine has spilled all over the carpet, ruining it.

A few feet from the wine... a different shade of red.

Nancy reaches out, touches it. It's --

                    NANCY
          ... *Blood.*

She turns back to Jonathan.

                    NANCY (CONT'D)
          ... Tom... yesterday... he had a
          bandage on his forehead --

**FLASHBACK TO ANOTHER SCENE FROM HAWKINS POST**

*TOM paces in his office, a BANDAGE ON HIS FOREHEAD.*

**INT. HEATHER'S HOUSE - DINING ROOM - DAY**

Nancy lifts up wine bottle. Inspects it.

The side is cracked, its label smeared with blood.

                    NANCY
               (realizing)
          ... He was attacked --

**FLASHBACK TO THE NIGHT OF THE ATTACK**

*HEATHER SLAMS the wine bottle into her father and --*

**INT. HEATHER'S HOUSE - DINING ROOM - DAY**

Nancy looks across the room. Finds MORE BLOOD.

She stands, tracks it into --

**A HALLWAY - CONTINUOUS**

As Nancy walks, she clocks a TWISTED-UP RUG.

**FLASHBACK TO**

*Billy dragging a now unconscious Tom down the same hallway.
His limp body catches on the rug, twisting it, as --*

**INT. HEATHER'S HOUSE - DINING ROOM - DAY**

Nancy continues past the twisted rug. Ahead --

A cracked door. She pushes through it into --

INT. HEATHER'S HOUSE - GARAGE - DAY

It's moody in here.  Scary.  But the blood trail ends.  *Wait.*

Jonathan spots A TANGLE OF ROPE lying on a nearby work table.
He walks over, holds it up.  It's been cut, its ends frayed.

>                    JONATHAN
>          ... They tied them --

**FLASHBACK TO**

*Billy and Heather tie up Tom and JANET -- gag their mouths --*

**THE PRESENT**

Everyone shares looks.

>                    JONATHAN
>          ... They must've taken them
>          somewhere --

**FLASHBACK TO**

*Billy tosses them in his trunk.  Slams it shut.*

**THE PRESENT**

Nancy's mind races.  *The puzzle pieces are clicking into
place.*

>                    NANCY
>          Missus Driscoll -- she kept
>          saying...  "I have to go back."

**FLASHBACK TO**

*MRS. DRISCOLL shouts at the paramedics.*

**TO THE PRESENT**

>                    NANCY
>          What if this "flaying" -- it's taking
>          place somewhere else -- ?  There must
>          be a place where all this started --
>          a Source --

>                    ELEVEN
>          ... Somewhere he didn't want me to
>          see --

**FLASHBACK TO**

*Billy turns, sees Eleven in the void, VANISHES --*

**INT. GARAGE - DAY**

Nancy nods. *Precisely.*

> NANCY
> If we can find the Source, maybe we
> can stop this, or at least, stop him
> from spreading and doing whatever the
> hell he's doing with those
> chemicals --

> ELEVEN
> But... *how* do we find it -- ?

> WILL
> *Missus Driscoll.*

All eyes turn to Will, standing behind them.

> WILL (CONT'D)
> If she wants to go back so badly...
> (beat)
> Why don't we let her?

Off our gang, finally having a plan, HARD CUT TO:

**EXT. WOODS - CLEARING - DAY**

BOOM! Boots smashing leaves as...

Grigori emerges from dense foliage and steps out into a
familiar clearing. His eyes narrow. Across the way --

The 7-ELEVEN. A FEW COP CARS now idle outside. TWO COPS are
talking to the Rich Douchebag.

**INT. 7-ELEVEN - DAY**

DING! Grigori enters the convenience store. He grabs a BOX
OF YANKEE DOODLES CUPCAKES off a shelf then --

**MOMENTS LATER**

WHAM! Drops Yankee Doodles onto the counter, some cash.

As the Cashier rings him up, Grigori motions to the cops.

> GRIGORI
> Busy day?

> GAS STATION CASHIER
> You could say that. Some psycho
> stole that dude's car.

The Cashier chuckles, but Grigori doesn't return the laugh.

                    GRIGORI
          What else?

                    GAS STATION CASHIER
          What -- ?

                    GRIGORI
          What else did he say?  This "psycho."

                    GAS STATION CASHIER
          Listen, man, no offense, but I just
          went over all this with the cops --

                    GRIGORI
          I'm not a cop.

                    GAS STATION CASHIER
          Yeah, no shit, Khrushchev --

WHOOM!  Grigori suddenly reaches out and grabs the Cashier's
arm, twisting it all the way around, slamming his head into
the Yankee Doodles, squishing the box!

                    GAS STATION CASHIER (CONT'D)
          Ahhhh shitshitshitshitshit -- !!!

The Cashier's eyes dart to the cops outside, praying they see
this, but --

                    GRIGORI
          Don't look at them.  <u>At me</u>.

The Cashier looks back to Grigori, his face twisted in pain.

                    GRIGORI (CONT'D)
          Tell me.  <u>About this psycho</u>.

Off the Cashier, WE PRELAP UPBEAT MUSIC as --

**EXT. ROAD - DAY**

VROOOOOM!  The Convertible *ZOOMS* past a sign that reads --

"WELCOME TO ILLINOIS!"

**EXT. MURRAY'S HOUSE - LATER - DAY**

WHOOM!  Gravel FLIES back at camera as --

The convertible speeds toward a house.  It looks oddly
*familiar.*  Satellites sit atop a crooked concrete roof.

**A MINUTE LATER**

Hopper and Joyce approach the front door.

Joyce eyes her surroundings warily.

> JOYCE
> ... I thought you said he was a
> journalist -- ?

> HOPPER
> Yeah, he was --

> JOYCE
> *"Was"* -- ??

Before Joyce can ask more questions, Hopper rings the buzzer.

WAHHHHHHHHHHHHH!  Sounds like a ship horn.

> DISEMBODIED VOICE (O.S.)
> LOOK AT THE CAMERA.

Hopper and Joyce startle.  *What the hell?*

> DISEMBODIED VOICE (O.S.) (CONT'D)
> *THE CAMERA.*  ABOVE YOU, TO *THE RIGHT*.

They look up and left.  Sure enough, there's a camera.

> DISEMBODIED VOICE (O.S.) (CONT'D)
> IDENTIFY YOURSELVES.

Hopper groans --

> HOPPER
> Jim Hopper, Joyce Byers, Smirnoff --

> JOYCE
> *Alexei* --

> HOPPER
> *Alexei.*

> DISEMBODIED VOICE (O.S.)
> SURNAME --

> HOPPER
> I don't know --   ?

310

                    DISEMBODIED VOICE (O.S.)
              FAMILY NAME --

                        HOPPER
              I said I don't know alright NOW CAN
              YOU JUST *OPEN THE GODDAMN DOOR*!

Silence.  Joyce looks at Hopper.  She's... *not feeling this.*

                        HOPPER (CONT'D)
              Don't worry.  He's just a little...
              eccentric.  But *totally harmless* --

WHOOM!  The heavy metal door suddenly *BURSTS* open and --

MURRAY lunges out wielding a DOUBLE-BARRELED SHOTGUN!!!!  He
swings the large gun past a startled Joyce and --

Shoves it right in Alexei's face.

                        MURRAY
              *NAME.*

                        ALEXEI
              <Get that out of my face you bald
              American *pig.*>

Murray smiles... and replies in FLUENT RUSSIAN:

                        MURRAY
              <I may be bald and American, but
              you're the one in handcuffs.  *Soviet
              scum.*>

Off Alexei, stunned, we SMASH TO --

**INT. MURRAY'S HOUSE - DAY**

WHAM!  Murray hits a button on the wall and --

WHOOM!  VERTICAL METAL SHUTTERS *slam* down over a window.

He walks to another window, hits another button.  WHOOM!
Another shutter down.  *His _entire house_ is a Panic Room!*

Joyce watches this unfold in growing bewilderment.

                        HOPPER
              Murray --

Murray holds up a hand --

                        MURRAY
              Please -- *stop talking.*

Murray retrieves a STRANGE GADGET FROM his closet.  It looks like a discarded prop from GHOSTBUSTERS.  This is --

A HOMEMADE BUG DETECTOR!  Murray begins to sweep it along Alexei's body.  It beeps with life.  BEEP BEEP BEEP BEEP!

He sweeps it across Alexei's privates.

> ALEXEI
> <Watch it -- !>

> MURRAY
> <Silence, scum!!>

Hopper and Joyce are growing impatient.

> HOPPER
> How long is this going to take?

> MURRAY
> NO!

> HOPPER
> No -- ?

> MURRAY
> _NO!_

Murray jabs the bug detector at Hopper.  Furious.

> MURRAY (CONT'D)
> You do _NOT_ get to question me.  You
> have dragged an enemy of the state
> into _MY HOME_ as carelessly as a child
> drags in _shit on his shoe_.  I _will_
> _SEARCH HIM UNTIL I AM SATISFIED_.

As Murray continues to sweep, Joyce pulls Hopper aside.

> JOYCE
> Okay.  This isn't going to work --

> HOPPER
> What do you mean -- ?

> JOYCE
> He's not eccentric, he's _certifiable_!

> HOPPER
> Glass houses Joyce --

> JOYCE
> What's _that_ supposed to mean?

                         HOPPER
              Pot calling the kettle --

                         MURRAY
              EXCUSE ME!!!!

They look up to find an impatient Murray.

                         MURRAY (CONT'D)
              Please do me a favor and move your
              lover's quarrel elsewhere --

                         HOPPER/JOYCE
              We're not --

                         MURRAY
              Oh -- SPARE ME!

Murray returns to searching Alexei.  Joyce glares at Murray.
She's getting FED UP.  She stomps over to him.

                         JOYCE
              ... What is your problem?

                         MURRAY
              Please, whoever you are, stop
              talking --

                         JOYCE
              NO.  I WILL NOT STOP TALKING.  We've
              had a VERY long day.  We've been shot
              at, nearly blown up, we've walked ten
              miles in hundred degree heat, stole a
              car, we're being chased by a, a giant
              psychopath, all so we could get HIM --
                   (jabs finger at Alexei)
              To YOU, since SOMEHOW you're the
              closest person who speaks Russian
              which I can't believe is true but now
              it's too late because unfortunately
              we're HERE.  So if you don't mind,
              put that THING AWAY -- stop behaving
              like such a JACKASS -- AND ASK HIM
              WHAT HE'S DOING THAT'S MAKING MAGNETS
              FALL OFF MY GODDAMN FRIDGE.
                   (beat)
              Please.

Hopper smirks.  Impressed with Joyce.

Off Murray, speechless for once, CUT TO --

**INT. UNDERGROUND TUNNELS - DAY**

VROOOOM! Tires explode past us as A MINI-TRUCK *ZOOMS* down a tunnel, zipping through a T-Junction. The second it passes --

Steve peeks his head out from behind a corner!

He surveys the area, then --

               STEVE
     *Clear.*

He heads out into the hallway. Right behind him --

The rest of the gang!

               ROBIN
     Okay, that was close --

               DUSTIN
     Too close --

               STEVE
     Relax, no one saw us --

Just as Steve says this, he rounds a corner and...

**AROUND THE CORNER - CONTINUOUS**

Crashes to a halt. Eyes shooting wide.

REVERSE TO REVEAL A LARGE TWO-STORY "HUB," THE DEATH STAR-STYLE BEATING HEART OF THIS RUSSIAN BASE. THERE ARE MULTIPLE DOORWAYS, BRANCHING HALLWAYS, METAL STAIRS, WORKERS, AND...

SOLDIERS. *LOTS OF SOLDIERS.*

Everyone stares. A moment of shock. Then --

Our gang backs away into --

**THE TUNNEL HALLWAY**

They shove their backs to the wall, terrified.

               STEVE
     Oh God, oh Jesus --

               DUSTIN
     ... *Red Dawn* --

Erica turns to the others, adrenaline pumping.

                         ERICA
              I saw it -- first floor.  Northwest.

The others stare.

                         STEVE
                    *Saw what*?

                         ERICA
                    The *comms room* --

                         STEVE
              You *saw* the comms room -- ?

                         ERICA
                    Correct --

                         DUSTIN
              Are you *sure?*

                         ERICA
                    *Positive* -- the door was open for a
                    second and I saw some weird machines
                    and lights and shit in there.

                         STEVE
              Machines and lights and shit -- ?

                         DUSTIN
              That could be a *hundred* things.

                         ROBIN
              ... I'll take those odds.

Everyone looks back at Robin, then...

**MOMENTS LATER**

Their four heads pop back out from cover, peering out.

POV:  They watch as a PAIR OF SOLDIERS march past them,
vanish down a hallway.  THREE more head into doors upstairs.
TWO MORE are repairing something -- their backs *turned to us*.

Shared looks.  Then...

                         STEVE
                    Alright... *keep low.*

                         ROBIN
                    *Why?*

Steve ignores Robin, heads out.  The others follow and...

**THE DEATH STAR "HUB" - CONTINUOUS**

They move quickly across the hub, keeping low for no good
reason, momentarily yet terrifyingly exposed.  But no one is
looking at them!  Steve throws open the northwest door and --

**INT. CONTROL ROOM - DAY**

The gang scrambles inside and slams the door behind and --

THEY MADE IT!!  But oh fuck --

There's a RUSSIAN TECHNICIAN IN HERE!!!  He's working on a
computer.  Or rather, *was*.  He swivels in his chair to find --

A child with a My Little Pony backpack.  Another in a Weird
Al Yankovic shirt.  And two teenagers in *sailor uniforms*.

He leaps to his feet, reaches for a handgun, but --

Robin thrusts out a hand --

> ROBIN
> <TREAD LIGHTLY!!!>

The Technician freezes upon hearing Russian.

> ROBIN (CONT'D)
> <TREAD LIGHTLY!!!>

> RUSSIAN TECHNICIAN
> <*Who -- who are you* -- ??!>

Robin, thinking fast, points to herself and her friends.

> ROBIN
> <Silver cat.  Silver cat -- >

> RUSSIAN TECHNICIAN
> <I, I don't understand  -- ??>

Robin stares, out of helpful vocabulary.

> ROBIN
> <... China?>

The Technician stares and --

> STEVE
> WAAAAAAAAAAAAHHH!!!!

Steve suddenly charges him at full speed and --

WHAM!  He slams the Russian backward, driving him into a
machine console.  His gun skips loose, scatters to the floor.

The Russian fights back, throws a punch, but Steve ducks and
evades!  Then, in one swift move, Steve grabs a PHONE off a
desk, swings with all his might, and --

WHAM-DING!  He *CLOCKS* the technician across the head with it!
HARD!  The technician spins, ricochets off the console,
then --

Folds to the floor.  Limp.  Unmoving.  *OUT COLD!!*

Steve breathes hard, adrenaline pumping.

                    DUSTIN (O.S.)
          ... Dude.

Steve turns to find the others staring at him.

                    DUSTIN (CONT'D)
          You did it.
              (beat)
          You won a fight.

Steve takes this in, *amazed with himself.*  Dustin drops down,
begins to riffle through the tech's pockets.

                    ERICA
          -- What are you doing?

                    DUSTIN
          Getting us our ticket out of here --

Dustin pulls out A KEY CARD.  *Bingo.*

                    ERICA
          You want to *walk* all the way back??

                    DUSTIN
          We don't have to -- we can hang out
          here for a bit, relax, have a picnic
          maybe --

As they continue to bicker, Robin opens up a door on the far
side of the room.  She's met by a PULSATING BLUE LIGHT and a
STRANGE ELECTRIC SOUND.

She turns back to the others, interjecting --

                    ROBIN
          *Hey guys...*

They look toward her...

                    ROBIN (CONT'D)
          I don't think this is the comms room.

Shared looks and...

**INT. ANTE ROOM - DAY**

The Scoops Troop ascends into...

A small room.  A pulsating blue-green light illuminates their
faces.  They slowly walk up to a set of windowed doors.

Their eyes grow wide.

                    DUSTIN
          ... *Holy shit.*

But we don't show what they're seeing.  *Not yet.*  Instead...

OUR CAMERA BEGINS TO SLOWLY PULL BACKWARDS, DRIFTING INTO...

**A LARGE OBSERVATION ROOM**

... Where a DOZEN RUSSIAN SCIENTISTS work on computers.

OUR CAMERA CONTINUES TO PULL BACK, SWOOPING THROUGH A LARGE
GLASS OBSERVATION WINDOW DAVID FINCHER-STYLE AND INTO...

**THE RIFT CHAMBER - CONTINUOUS**

Our camera now DROPS A FULL FLOOR to find a small army of
Workers in Hazmat suits.  We follow one of the Hazmat Workers
as he carries one of those strange green cylinders over to...

AN ENORMOUS MACHINE.  It looks very similar to the machine in
our first episode, only now it's souped up -- larger, more
complex, thousands of gears churning.

As the Worker loads the cylinder into the machine, *powering
it...*

OUR CAMERA CONTINUES, traveling along the machine's gun-like
barrel to reveal...

It's blasting the wall with A SURGE OF POWERFUL BLUE AND
GREEN ENERGY.

A RED-ORANGE CRACK HAS APPEARED IN THE WALL.  VINES ARE
GROWING OUT OF THIS CRACK, SPREADING ACROSS THE WALL.  IT'S --

A RIFT TO THE UPSIDE DOWN.  *OPENING.*

**INT. ANTE ROOM - DAY**

WE PUSH IN on our gang, staring at this jaw-dropping sight.

As BLUE-GREEN LIGHT dances off their wide eyes, HARD CUT TO --

**EXT. HAWKINS GENERAL HOSPITAL - NIGHT**

The moon in the sky. It's night now. All is quiet. Still.

WE TILT DOWN as the station wagon pulls up to the hospital.

**INT. HAWKINS GENERAL HOSPITAL - RECEPTION AREA - NIGHT**

Nancy and the gang walk through the lobby.

The RECEPTIONIST, who we recognize from last night, is busy
on the phone, having a lively conversation with a friend --

>                    RECEPTIONIST
>          -- Why would you invite her??? Well
>          there's a *reason* she had nothin' to
>          do --

She clocks Nancy and the gang, headed past her --

>                    RECEPTIONIST (CONT'D)
>          Hey hey -- excuse me!!

Everyone turns back.

>                    RECEPTIONIST (CONT'D)
>          Where do you think you're going?

>                    NANCY
>          Just -- wanted to see my grandmom
>          again. This is -- my family --

>                    LUCAS
>          *Extended* --

>                    RECEPTIONIST
>          I don't care who they are, you know
>          the rules. Two visitors at a time --

>                    NANCY
>          I know but --

>                    RECEPTIONIST
>          *Two.*

**INT. HAWKINS GENERAL HOSPITAL - ELEVATOR - NIGHT**

CLOSE ON: A FOURTH FLOOR button is pressed.

319

WIDEN: Nancy and Jonathan standing side-by-side in the elevator. There's a moment of awkward silence. Just the GENTLE HUM of the elevator. Then --

> NANCY
> You know... those things I said yesterday... I... didn't mean them.

> JONATHAN
> I know --

> NANCY
> You're not like those assholes, *at all*. I've <u>never</u> thought that. I was just --

> JONATHAN
> -- *Angry*. Which I still don't get. I mean -- I was just completely, utterly, *mortifyingly* wrong about -- <u>everything</u>.

Nancy can't help but grin. He shoots her a look.

> JONATHAN (CONT'D)
> <u>Don't</u> let it go to your head.

> NANCY
> I won't. I just look forward to you never doubting me again.

She smirks at him. Then --

DING! The elevator door opens. Nancy strides out.

Jonathan stares. Can't believe her! He races after her and...

## INT. HAWKINS GENERAL HOSPITAL - WAITING ROOM - NIGHT

THUNK! A QUARTER slots into a vending machine.

Mike and Lucas are purchasing some candy. Mike hits C5 for a KIT KAT bar. The metal coil inside the machine turns, opening, but --

The Kit Kat gets *stuck*, doesn't fall out!!!

> MIKE
> Aw come on you *piece of shit* --

WHUMP! Mike HITS the machine in frustration and --

SHOOM! The vending machine SHUDDERS VIOLENTLY and --

A SHIT-TON OF CANDY crashes into the bin below.

Mike and Lucas startle, look over to find --

Eleven.

>                         MIKE (CONT'D)
>           Thanks.

El nods, walks away.

As the boys drop down and grab the candy:

>                         LUCAS
>           Dude.  I think that was *it*.

>                         MIKE
>           That was *what?*

>                         LUCAS
>           The *olive branch*.

>                         MIKE
>           The *what?*

>                         LUCAS
>           Oh my God.  You're helpless.  I'll
>           distract Max, okay?  Get you an
>           opening.  And then -- *talk to her*.

A nervous Mike takes this in as --

Lucas scoops up another handful of candy and --

**INT. HALLWAY TO DRISCOLL'S ROOM - NIGHT**

Nancy and Jonathan stride down the fourth floor hallway.  It
is curiously quiet.  A lonely cup of hot coffee is left
behind on the empty nurses' station, and a "call light" above
one of the patients' rooms blinks.  It's all a little *off*.
Eerie.

**INT. HAWKINS GENERAL HOSPITAL - DRISCOLL'S ROOM - NIGHT**

Nancy opens the door to Driscoll's room.  Freezes.

The hospital bed is empty.

>                         JONATHAN
>           ... Where is she?

>                         NANCY
>           I -- don't know --

Nancy crosses to the bed --

> JONATHAN
> You're sure this is the right room?

> NANCY
> Yeah --

Nancy drops by the bed.  Grabs a clipboard to check when --

> VOICE (O.S.)
> She's gone home.

Jonathan and Nancy turn.  Their faces go pale.  It's...

TOM, standing in the doorway.  His face is pasty, sweating heavily, sleeves rolled up.  *Not looking good.*  Worse still --

There is a spattering of blood on his face, arms.

Off this awful image, WE PRE-LAP THE SOUND OF LAUGHTER...

**INT. HAWKINS GENERAL HOSPITAL - WAITING ROOM - NIGHT**

Lucas is tossing M&Ms into Max's mouth.  *Distracting her.*
She misses and it smacks her nose.  Another shared laugh.

A nervous Mike sits by Eleven.

> MIKE
> Hey.

> ELEVEN
> Hi.

An awkward beat.  Then...

> MIKE
> Does your species like... Skittles?

He holds up a bag of Skittles.  Eleven considers, then... nods.  She takes a few pieces, pops them in her mouth.

As they share a smile, we CUT BACK TO:

**INT. HAWKINS GENERAL HOSPITAL - DRISCOLL'S ROOM - NIGHT**

Tom.  Standing eerily in that doorway.

> TOM
> We were hoping you might come back.

> JONATHAN
> ... Whose blood is that?

Tom ignores this, walks toward the teens --

> NANCY
> Tom -- whatever you've done -- *this isn't you* -- he's <u>making you</u> do this --

But Tom keeps walking toward them -- closing in --

FUCK IT! -- Jonathan grabs a flower vase, swings it --

BOOM-SMASH! The vase shatters across the side of Tom's face --

As Tom recoils from the impact, Jonathan grabs Nancy, and --

They <u>*RUN*</u>, scrambling out of the hospital room, into --

**HALLWAY TO DRISCOLL'S ROOM**

They race back toward the elevator, only to --

Crash to a halt. Standing in their way:

<u>BRUCE</u>. <u>HE HOLDS THE SIDE OF HIS HEAD WHERE THE VASE HIT TOM</u>.

<u>THROBBING BLACK VEINS SPREAD OUT FROM "THE WOUND."</u>

> BRUCE
> ... Owie.

He looks up at Nancy and Jonathan.

> BRUCE (CONT'D)
> You shouldn't have done that.

Jonathan and Nancy go pale. Bruce is flayed -- he's FUCKING FLAYED!!!! They turn to flee in the opposite direction but --

Tom is right behind them, rounding the corner. He's bleeding from his head. *Angry*.

Jonathan grabs Nancy's hand, pulls her down --

**A SMALL HALLWAY**

As they run, they clock a DEAD NURSE, pale and bloody, just visible through a cracked door. But there's no time to linger on this horror. They keep running, burst through a door and into --

**A NARROW STAIRWELL**

Quick shots as our teens BOLT down the staircase and --

**INT. HAWKINS GENERAL HOSPITAL - WAITING ROOM - NIGHT**

SWOOP!  Max catches an M&M!  Lucas CHEERS, APPLAUDS!

Nearby, Mike and Eleven continue to bond over Skittles.

> MIKE
> I like the new look, by the way.

> ELEVEN
> ... Thanks.

> MIKE
> How did you... *pay for it*?

> ELEVEN
> American Express.

**INT. HAWKINS GENERAL HOSPITAL - SECOND FLOOR - NIGHT**

WHOOM!  Jonathan and Nancy explode out of a stairwell door --

They SPRINT down a long hallway, then bank left, shoving
through a Visqueen curtain and into --

**A HOSPITAL HALLWAY - UNDER RENOVATION - CONTINUOUS**

The atmosphere is dark and gritty in here: construction tools
and equipment scattered about, hospital equipment stacked to
the hallway.  But this place is a maze -- *no exit in sight*.

**INT. NARROW STAIRWELL - NIGHT**

Bruce moves down the stairwell and exits out into --

**THE SECOND FLOOR HALLWAY**

He quickens his pace, coming for them as --

**INT. OPERATING ROOM HALLWAY - NIGHT**

Jonathan runs up to an intercom, smashes it --

> JONATHAN
> Hello -- is anyone there -- *HELLO* --

Nancy's eyes dart, lock onto something --

> NANCY
> *Here* -- !

She leads Jonathan into  --

**INT. HAWKINS GENERAL HOSPITAL - OPERATING ROOM - NIGHT**

As Jonathan closes the doors behind them, locks them --

Nancy sprints over to a PHONE, grabs it up.

She dials a button for RECEPTION and --

**INT. HAWKINS GENERAL HOSPITAL - LOBBY - NIGHT**

A light flashes on the receptionist's phone, but she doesn't notice, too busy chatting with her friend.

>                    RECEPTIONIST
>          -- Just call her in the morning and
>          tell her my shift went late and it's
>          been canceled -- she won't find out!!
>          Who would tell her you're her only
>          friend -- I'm not being mean I'm
>          being honest!

**INT. OPERATING ROOM - NIGHT**

BRRRRING BRRRRING --

>                    NANCY
>          *Come on come on come on -- PICK UP!!*

SMASH! A HAND SUDDENLY BREAKS THROUGH THE GLASS WINDOW OF THE DOOR. THE HAND REACHES IN, TWISTS THE LOCK, OPENS THE DOOR. IT'S BRUCE.

>                    BRUCE
>          Hi there.

Nancy drops the phone as Bruce moves toward her, fast, but --

Jonathan charges him, swings a punch, and BAM! Lands it. But Bruce doesn't even seem to feel it. He grabs Jonathan, headbutts him, then throws him with amazing strength, and --

Jonathan flies over the operating table --

>                    NANCY
>          JONATHAN -- !!!

He hits some hospital equipment on the far wall. His body crumples. But Bruce doesn't let up. He strides over to him, fast, grabbing up a METAL STOOL on the way.

Nancy's eyes snap to SURGICAL SCISSORS on a table. She races for them as --

**ACROSS THE ROOM,**

WHAM!  Bruce BRINGS THE STOOL CRASHING DOWN ONTO his back, driving him back down on the floor.  Jonathan SCREAMS.

Bruce raises the stool up for another hit when --

Nancy charges, swings the scissors, and --

THUNK!  THE BLADES PLUNGE INTO BRUCE'S BACK!!!

Bruce ROARS in pain, spins to Nancy.  She backpedals, clearly a little stunned by what she's just done.

Bruce reaches a hand around his back.  Grabs the scissors. *RIPS* them out.  Black veins bulge on his forehead.

He is *PISSED*.

> BRUCE
> ... You *BITCH*.

He tosses the bloody scissors, then -- <u>lunges</u>.

Nancy throws an IV pole into his path, escapes into --

**INT. OPERATING ROOM HALLWAY - CONTINUOUS**

She looks around the dark hallway, screams:

> NANCY
> HELP!!!  IS ANYBODY HERE??!!
> *HELP -- !*

Bruce explodes out the door -- Nancy races away, turns left down --

**OPERATING ROOM HALLWAY**

There is an EMERGENCY EXIT.  She pushes it but --

**ON THE OTHER SIDE OF THE DOOR**

A pile of wooden pallets and a ladder obstruct the door and --

**HALLWAY**

It won't open.  She slams it again.  Still stuck.  And --

Bruce is coming!  She can't stay here.  She flees into the only room she has available for her.  At its entrance, not visible to Bruce, she sees --

A FIRE EXTINGUISHER.  She rips it off the wall as --

**OPERATING ROOM**

Jonathan blinks, groggy. *Very hurt*. He grabs onto a nearby stool, uses it to lift himself up off the floor, when --

WHOOM!  A SHOE SUDDENLY KICKS THE STOOL out from under him.

As Jonathan collapses back to the ground, we reveal --

TOM.  TOWERING ABOVE HIM.

>                    TOM
>          Where are you going?

**INT. OPERATING ROOM HALLWAY - NIGHT**

Bruce calmly walks toward the room where Nancy fled.

>                    BRUCE
>          Yoo hoo Nancy Drew, where are you???

As he heads for the only door available, CUT TO:

**INT. HOSPITAL ROOM - NIGHT**

Nancy, searching for a place to hide.  Her eyes go to a row of dividing curtains as...

**INT. OPERATING ROOM - NIGHT**

Tom lifts up the weak Jonathan, and --

WHOOM!  Flings him back into more equipment.

**INT. HOSPITAL ROOM - NIGHT**

Bruce enters the hospital room.  Looks around.

The curtains have all been recently closed, swaying with movement. *Nancy is clearly hiding behind one.*

He opens the first curtain.  SHOOM!  No one behind it.

**INT. OPERATING ROOM - NIGHT**

Tom walks up to Jonathan.  Jonathan tries to fight him off, but Tom slams his head down into the floor.  *Hard*.  Again.

Jonathan stops struggling.  His consciousness beginning to fade.

Tom grabs up those BLOODY SCISSORS as --

**INT. HOSPITAL ROOM - NIGHT**

SHOOM!  Bruce opens a second curtain.  Nothing.

**INT. OPERATING ROOM - NIGHT**

Tom raises up the scissors, ready to _finish Jonathan_.

He starts to bring bloody scissors down just as --

**INT. HOSPITAL ROOM - NIGHT**

SHOOM!  Bruce throws opens the third curtain and --

Nothing.  But then --

WHOOM!  A CLOSET door flies open behind him and --

NANCY EMERGES.  Bruce turns and sees her just as --

She swings the fire extinguisher and --

BAM!  IT SMASHES BRUCE IN THE FUCKING FACE!

HIS HEAD <u>SNAPS BACKWARD</u> AND --

**INT. OPERATING ROOM - NIGHT**

Tom's head suddenly jerks backward -- _feeling the same impact_ -- his hand jerks open and the scissors fly loose.

Tom touches his face, confused, _hurt_.

Black veins _branch out_ from his nose as --

**INT. HOSPITAL ROOM - NIGHT**

Black veins _branch out_ from Bruce's broken nose.

Nancy SCREAMS, then swings the extinguisher again, _right_ into his broken nose.  BAM!  His head snaps, his knees buckle and --

**INT. OPERATING ROOM - NIGHT**

Tom SHRIEKS as more black veins climb up his face.

He staggers to his feet, stumbles back in pain --

Jonathan, now free, reaches out, grabs the scissors as --

**INT. HOSPITAL ROOM - NIGHT**

Nancy towers over Bruce, breathing hard.

She pulls back the fire extinguisher as...

**INT. OPERATING ROOM - NIGHT**

Jonathan pushes to his feet behind Tom.  *Angry.*

**INT. HOSPITAL ROOM - NIGHT**

Nancy hardens.  *Angry.*

                    NANCY
          <u>GO</u>. <u>TO</u>. ***HELL***.

She brings the extinguisher crashing down just as --

**INT. OPERATING ROOM - NIGHT**

Jonathan swings the scissors.

The sharp blades PLUNGE into Tom's neck.

**INT. HOSPITAL ROOM - NIGHT**

Bruce collapses, <u>DEAD AT THE FEET OF NANCY</u>, as --

**INT. OPERATING ROOM - NIGHT**

Tom collapses, <u>DEAD AT THE FEET OF JONATHAN</u>.

**INT. HOSPITAL ROOM - NIGHT**

Nancy, finally finished, fighting tears and exhaustion, drops
the extinguisher.  It clanks to the floor.  Stained in blood.

It's over... it's <u>FUCKING OVER</u>.

But the relief is short-lived as --

THE LIGHTS IN THE ROOM BEGIN TO FLICKER.

**INT. OPERATING ROOM - NIGHT**

The lights flicker in here too...

**INT. WAITING ROOM - NIGHT**

And *downstairs too.*

Will is the first to notice.  He stands.

As the other kids take notice...

**INT. OPERATING ROOM**

Jonathan backs away in horror.  Something is happening to...

Tom.  His corpse is *shivering* very rapidly on the ground (think *THE THING*) as thick dark veins overtake him.

**INT. HOSPITAL ROOM - NIGHT**

The *exact same thing* is happening to Bruce's corpse.

Nancy steps away as his skin begins to darken and *ROT*...

**INT. OPERATING ROOM**

Tom's flesh *rots* too... then it begins to soften, erode...

MELT.  *It's just like the rat in 302.*

**INT. HOSPITAL ROOM**

Bruce's flesh MELTS too, dissolving into a PILE OF GORY GOOP.

Horribly, THE GOOP now begins to *MOVE*, slinking across the linoleum floor as...

**INT. OPERATING ROOM**

TOM'S GOOP SLINKS its way across the operating room floor, leaving a disgusting trail of blood and gore in its wake.

**INT. OPERATING ROOM HALLWAY - NIGHT**

Nancy and Jonathan step out into the flickering hallway.

They are on opposite ends.  Between them...

THE BRUCE GOOP MEETS THE TOM GOOP.  THERE IS A HORRIBLE SHRIEKING SOUND AS THEY FUSE IN THE FLICKERING LIGHT, *MUTATING, GROWING* TOGETHER INTO SOME KIND OF...

HORRENDOUS GORE FLESH MONSTER.  AMORPHOUS.  NO EYES.  SNARLED BONES JUT FROM SKIN LIKE BLADES.  PURE NIGHTMARE FUEL. AND...

IT'S *LOOKING* RIGHT AT NANCY.

THE FLESH ON ITS FACE MOVES, THEN --

*PEELS OPEN*.  *ROARING*.

AND *RIGHT HERE* WE --

END EPISODE

# CHAPTER SIX:
# E PLURIBUS UNUM

WRITTEN BY **CURTIS GWINN**

**DARKNESS.**

A GUTTURAL ROAR FILLS THE SOUNDSCAPE.

It sounds like the monster.  But it's not.  It's...

**INT. UNDERGROUND RUSSIAN BASE - RIFT CHAMBER - NIGHT**

THE RUSSIAN MACHINE.  Firing that wild blue electricity into the wall.  The wall SPLINTERS, VINES growing into our world.

It's beautiful.  *And horrifying.*

**INT. ANTE ROOM - NIGHT**

We PUSH IN on our Scoops Troop, still staring at this jaw-dropping sight.  DUSTIN shares a stunned look with STEVE.

> DUSTIN/STEVE
> ... The Gate.

ROBIN shoots them a baffled look.  And --

**INT. STEPS DOWN TO CONTROL ROOM**

CLOSE ON FEET as the gang scurry back down the steps.

> ROBIN
> -- I don't understand -- you've seen
> this before -- ??

> STEVE
> *Not exactly --*

> ROBIN
> Then WHAT *exactly* --

> DUSTIN
> All you need to know is it's bad --

> STEVE
> *Really bad --*

> DUSTIN
> Like end of *the human race as we know
> it kind of bad --*

> ROBIN
> And you know about this _HOW_ -- ???

**THE CONTROL ROOM - CONTINUOUS**

Our kids are about to respond when they crash to a halting stop --

                         ERICA
              Uh, Steve.  Where's your friend?

Sure enough, the guard that Steve knocked out is no longer
there.  They barely have time to takes this in before --

WAH WAH WAH WAH WAH!  AN ALARM BEGINS TO SOUND.

Steve races over, throws open the door --

**INT. UNDERGROUND RUSSIAN BASE - THE HUB - STEVE POV**

And *yup*.  A SHIT-TON OF SOLDIERS are racing their way.

                         GUARD #1
              *<HALT!!  HALT!!!>*

**THE CONROL ROOM - CONTINUOUS**

Steve quickly slams the door on the soldiers and --

**INT. STEPS - NIGHT**

The Scoops Troop RUN, racing back up the steps and --

**INT. OBSERVATION ROOM - NIGHT**

They *SPRINT* through the observation room.  Scientists leap
from their chairs, gawking at these kids and teens in shock,
confusion.  Soldiers race after them -- giving chase!!

                    RUSSIAN SOLDIER #1
              <STOP!!!  *STOP THEM!!!!!>*

**INT. RIFT CHAMBER - NIGHT**

WHOOM!  Sneakers fly down metal steps as --

The Scoops Troop races down into the experiment room.  That's
right -- they're now in the room with the enormous machine!

                         DUSTIN
              HOLYSHITHOLYSHITHOLYSHIT -- !!

They whirl around, taking it all in.  POWERFUL BLUE ENERGY
PUMPS THROUGH THE AIR ABOVE THEM, MEN IN SCARY HAZMAT SUITS
stare at them, the GATE *ROARS*.  It's all surreal, dizzying,
but there's no time to gawk --

The soldiers are flying down the steps, almost on them --

Robin's eyes snap to a door behind them --

                    ROBIN
          *HERE -- !*

She races forward, throws open the door, leads them into --

**INT. MECHANICAL ROOM - NIGHT**

WHAM!  Steve SLAMS the door shut behind them, just as --

**INT. RIFT CHAMBER - NIGHT**

The soldiers reach the door.  Slam their bodies into it.

**INT. MECHANICAL ROOM - NIGHT**

The door SHUDDERS but doesn't open, because STEVE is holding
it shut -- putting his whole back into it as --

The gang frantically survey this room.  There are churning
gears, metal pipes, and lots of steam, but --

No way out.  *A DEAD END*.

Making matters worse -- Steve can't hold the door much
longer.  *They're too strong.*  It starts to open when --

WHOOM!  Robin throws her weight into it, joining him--

The door slams back shut thanks to their combined weight --

                    STEVE
          *Thanks -- !!*

                    ROBIN
          *Any time -- !!*

Erica drops to the floor.  She's found something:

A SMALL GRATED PANEL.  She lifts it up to reveal AN AIR DUCT.

                    ERICA
          HERE!!!

Erica drops into the air duct, ninja-like --

               ERICA (CONT'D)
          LET'S GO -- COME ON!!!

A panicked Dustin looks back at Steve and Robin --

They're still holding that door shut, unable to follow.

                    STEVE
          DUDE GO!  GET OUT OF HERE -- !!

But Dustin can't bear to leave his friends --

                    STEVE (CONT'D)
          *GO!!!! GET HELP!!!*

                    DUSTIN
          I WON'T FORGET YOU -- !

                    ROBIN/STEVE
               (angry now)
          GO!!!!

Fuck it!!! Dustin finally *goes*, dropping down into the
shaft with Erica. He pulls the grate back down over him just
as --

BOOM! The door explodes open with such force that --

Steve and Robin are flung backward onto the ground. The
soldiers swarm inside, guns trained on our teens, screaming:

                    SOLDIERS
          <DON'T MOVE!!! HANDS UP! HANDS UP!>

Steve and Robin don't need a translation.

They throw up their hands. *Surrendering.*

Off our captured teens, we SMASH TO:

**INT. HAWKINS GENERAL HOSPITAL - WAITING AREA - NIGHT**

BZZZZZZ!!!! Lights flickering like crazy in the waiting
room. WE DROP DOWN FROM THE LIGHTS TO FIND...

Our kids, gathering together, looking up at these flashing
lights. WILL touches the back of his neck. *Goosebumps.*

                    WILL
          *... He's here.*

We PUSH past Will to find ELEVEN --

As her _resolve_ hardens, MAKE A SHARP CUT TO --

**INT. HAWKINS GENERAL HOSPITAL - OPERATING ROOM HALLWAY**

THE TOM-BRUCE MONSTER *ROARING* at NANCY.

We're now _right_ where we left off.

Nancy is now _trapped_.

                         NANCY
          *Shit.*

The monster begins to lumber toward Nancy, its limbs still
not fully formed -- but it's still *fucking terrifying.*

With nowhere to turn, Nancy turns and drives her shoulder
into the stuck emergency exit door but --

**ON THE OTHER SIDE OF THE DOOR,**

It's still obstructed by those fucking wood pallets!!  The
pallets begin to budge, but *only a bit* --

**BACK IN THE HALLWAY,**

As Nancy continues to throw her weight into the door --

JONATHAN'S eyes snap to an IV POLE.  He grabs it up, then
races toward the monster with this pole, SNAPPING it in half
to use it as a weapon --

But he's too late.  The monster is <u>on</u> Nancy, about to devour
her, when --

BAM!  Nancy slams into the door one more time and --

**ON THE OTHER SIDE OF THE DOOR,**

The pallets finally crash *down* and --

Nancy slips through the door, escaping just in time!

**BACK IN THE HALLWAY**

The monster lunges after her -- blasting through that door
with a FEROCIOUS ROAR and --

**RECEPTION AREA - NIGHT**

The kids *RACE* past the reception desk, El in the lead --

<u>THE CHASE IS ON</u>!

                      RECEPTIONIST
          *-- TWO AT A TIME!!!*

**INT. HAWKINS GENERAL HOSPITAL - HALLWAY 2**

<u>*SNEAKERS FLY*</u> as Nancy continues down another hallway.

The Monster is right on her tail.  She leaps into --

**EMPTY HOSPITAL ROOM**

And slams the door behind her, locking it *just as* --

**INT. HAWKINS GENERAL HOSPITAL - HALLWAY 2**

WHAM!  The monster slams its heavy flesh body into the door, but --

Its locked.  *No problem*.  It slinks over to a window of glass near the bottom of the door.  The window is small -- too small for our monster -- but its body transforms, *reshaping* itself as --

**ACROSS THE HALL**

JONATHAN rounds the corner with his makeshift weapon.  His face falls, watching in horror as the re-formed flesh monster smashes through the small window of glass on the bottom of the door and --

**INT. EMPTY HOSPITAL ROOM - NIGHT**

*SLITHERS* its way into the hospital room!

Nancy backpedals, watching in horror as the GOOP BEGINS TO REFORM INTO THE ORIGINAL MONSTER.

**INT. HOSPITAL - ELEVATOR BANK - NIGHT**

The kids reach the elevator.  Mash the button.  But --

*It's taking too long.*

> MIKE
> *Stairs* -- !!

They race for the stairs as --

**INT. HALLWAY 2 - NIGHT**

Jonathan reaches the door, tries to open it, but --

> JONATHAN
> Nancy!!!  NANCY!!!

It's <u>locked</u>, which means --

**INT. EMPTY HOSPITAL ROOM - NIGHT**

Nancy is *trapped* in here with this awful *thing*.  It finishes re-forming into its final shape, then begins to move toward Nancy, its deformed feet GROTESQUELY SLAPPING the floor as --

**INT. HAWKINS GENERAL HOSPITAL - HALLWAY 2 - NIGHT**

WHAM!  Jonathan throws his shoulder into the door --

> JONATHAN
> -- NANCY!  NANCY -- !

The door shudders but doesn't open and --

**INT. EMPTY HOSPITAL ROOM - NIGHT**

The monster moves toward Nancy, but --

She grabs a TWO-BY-FOUR and swings it at the monster as hard as she can.  But the monster is too strong and just BLOWS right through the wood and then   --

WHACK!  It LASHES at her with its tentacles.  Nancy is flung backward, landing hard onto some CONSTRUCTION MATERIALS as --

**INT. HAWKINS GENERAL HOSPITAL - HALLWAY 2 - NIGHT**

Jonathan slams the door again.  This isn't working.  His eyes snap to a ROW OF OXYGEN TANKS.  He grabs the closest tank then --

WHAM!  Begins to HAMMER it into the door handle as --

**INT. EMPTY HOSPITAL ROOM - NIGHT**

The monster lunges toward the dazed, fallen Nancy and --

THWACK!  It pins her to the floor with its WRITHING TENTACLES.  It leans down toward her -- its horrible face peels open, flashing GNARLED HUMAN BONES FOR TEETH.  Nancy SCREAMS -- turning her face as it goes to devour her -- *and* --

BOOM!  The door suddenly explodes off its hinges.

The Monster spins.  To our surprise, it's not Jonathan --

It's Eleven!!!  Standing like a badass in the doorway.  Hell. Yes.  Jonathan and the others crowd behind her, the kids' eyes shoot WIDE as they take in this AWFUL NEW CREATURE.

> MIKE
> Jesus -- !

> MAX
> What the fu -- ?!!!

THE MONSTER ROARS IN ANGER -- AN EVEN MORE *FEARSOME* ROAR THAN BEFORE -- ELEVEN HAS PROVOKED QUITE THE REACTION FROM THIS FUCKER!!  IT LUNGES WITH INCREDIBLE, HORRIFIC SPEED BUT --

ELEVEN SNARES IT WITH HER PSYCHIC ENERGY *AND* --

WHOOM! SLINGS IT INTO A WALL. WHOOM! *ANOTHER WALL.* THEN INTO THE CEILING. *SMASHING IT AROUND LIKE THE FUCKING HULK.*

The weakened Monster staggers back to its feet, not giving up. It lets out a horrific ROAR OF DEFIANCE but --

Eleven SCREAMS RIGHT back at it, even angrier, and --

THE MONSTER SOARS THROUGH THE AIR --

*EXPLODES* OUT A WINDOW -- AND --

**EXT. HAWKINS GENERAL HOSPITAL**

The monster flies outside in a HAIL of glass and --

**EXT. PARKING LOT**

SPLAT! It hits the pavement, SHRIEKING, ITS FLESH *SPLATTING* --

**INT. EMPTY HOSPITAL ROOM - NIGHT**

The kids share stunned looks, then --

**INT. HOSPITAL - FIRST FLOOR**

The kids race out of the hospital, Eleven in the lead.

**EXT. HOSPITAL - NIGHT**

They crash to a stop. REVERSE TO REVEAL:

The Monster is still alive -- and it is escaping, its disgusting amorphous body twisting, mutating itself, as --

It slurps its way down into a GRATED STORM DRAIN. Its bones won't fit through the grate, so it leaves *those* behind.

As the last of the flesh *squirms away...* escaping...

We PUSH IN on our gang, staring in horror.

> MAX
> (out of breath)
> Okay. What the *hell was that*?

> JONATHAN
> ... Our bosses.

> NANCY
> *Ex-bosses.*

Everyone shares looks.  Stunned.  And then --

**INT. ABANDONED FACTORY - BASEMENT - NIGHT**

The TOM-BRUCE MONSTER slithers out through rusty metal bars, finding its way into...

The factory basement.  It slinks across the damp floor and joins up with the BIG MONSTER, its flesh *folding* into the Big Monster, becoming *part of it*.  The big monster heaves, grumbles, satisfied with this addition to itself.

And if we're not mistaken... its size GROWS a little.

HEATHER and BILLY watch this stomach-wrenching display from the far end of the basement.  A beat of silence between them. Then --

                    BILLY
          ... It's time.

Heather doesn't answer.  She simply continues to watch the heaving, *growing* monster.  It lets out a GROTESQUE ROAR and --

**MAIN TITLES**

**EXT. UNKNOWN - DAY**

We open up on a beautiful blue sky.  And then suddenly --

WHOOSH!  An enormous and tacky banner, held up by two large poles, is dramatically lifted into view.  It reads:

          *MAYOR KLINE'S JULY 4TH SPECTACULAR!!!!*

Our CAMERA now CRANES UP and over the banner to reveal --

**EXT. FAIRGROUNDS - MAYOR KLINE'S SPECTACULAR - DAY**

... DOZENS OF WORKERS toiling to put together this fair. This so-called "biggest bash Hawkins has ever seen" has all the classic stuff, including a FERRIS WHEEL, a THREE-STORY FUNHOUSE, A GRAVITRON, GAME STALLS, FOOD STATIONS.

And organizing all of this, of course, is...

MAYOR KLINE HIMSELF!  He's wearing big sunglasses and lots of makeup to hide his battered face.  He seems pleased.

Until, suddenly, *he isn't*.

He storms over to a CORN DOG STAND.

                    MAYOR KLINE
        -- No no no NO, what is this doing
        here??

                    WORKER
        Huh -- ?

                    MAYOR KLINE
        Your stand -- it's right in the main
        thoroughfare!

                    WORKER
        Wh-- where do you want it, sir -- ?

Kline jabs a finger --

                    MAYOR KLINE
        OVER THERE with the rest of the
        goddamned food stalls!!!  This isn't
        ROCKET SCIENCE!!

As the Worker begins to move his stand, Kline sighs.  It's
hard to be surrounded by such... *incompetence*.  Then --

His expression abruptly shifts.  His face pales.  It's --

GRIGORI.  Standing less than thirty feet away, in front of
the GRAVITRON ride.  *Watching him*.  Off Kline...

                    MAYOR KLINE (PRE-LAP) (CONT'D)
        ... I -- I've talked to everyone --

**INT. GRAVITRON - DAY**

Kline paces around the colorful interior of the Gravitron.

It look like they're inside a low-rent spaceship.

                    MAYOR KLINE
        ... My friends in state PD -- the
        highway patrol -- they're all on the
        lookout.  I've got eyes *everywhere*.
        The second he pops up, I get a call --

                    GRIGORI
        A "call" -- ?

                    MAYOR KLINE
        Yes "a call."  I mean, what more do
        you people want me to do??

                    GRIGORI
        We want you to <u>find him</u> --


                        341

                    MAYOR KLINE
          This man is a *moron* -- okay?  He's
          driving around in a yellow
          convertible for chrissakes!!  He
          sticks out like a sore thumb.  I *will*
          find him -- and when I do, may I
          suggest you bring some back-up with
          you this time -- ?

                    GRIGORI
          "Back-up"?

                    MAYOR KLINE
          Some help, some *comrades,* since last
          time he got the better of you --

WHAM!  Grigori suddenly lunges, striking as fast as a
rattlesnake.  He slams Kline into the controls of the
Gravitron, turning on the machine, then --

WHAM!  Back against the railing.  The ride begins to spin,
rotating around them.  Colored lights swirl, dizzying, and --

Grigori's hand *tightens* around Kline's throat.  Kline croaks:

                    KLINE
          Pl-please -- I, I didn't mean that --
          you, you can do what you want -- you,
          you don't need back-up --

Grigori glares, unmoved by this pleading.  We can tell he
would enjoy nothing more than to *kill this clown*...

                    GRIGORI
          This man is your fault, your problem.
          You are lucky you still breathe.

                    MAYOR KLINE
          Yes yes I, I know -- very lucky --

FWOOM!  Kline's sunglasses suddenly suck off his face and fly
through the air, sticking against the wall!!!  Kline stifles
a scream -- HOLY SHIT!

                    MAYOR KLINE (CONT'D)
          Please -- I -- I'm sorry -- I -- have
          a bad temper -- I'm going to
          therapy --

                    GRIGORI
          You have one day.  One day to find
          this man for me.  Nod if you
          understand.

Kline, face now bright red, *nods,* terrified, as --

**EXT. GRAVITRON - DAY**

The Gravitron spins around, faster and faster.

It sounds almost like a SCREAM, *and* --

**EXT. MURRAY'S HOUSE - DAY**

It's quiet outside Murray's house.  Then...

VROOM!  The stolen convertible *ROARS* into view.

HOPPER slams it to a stop.  We don't know what is going on yet, but Hopper seems to be in... a *mood*.  He reaches into the back of the car, removes a BROWN BAG FROM BURGER KING and a GIANT SLURPEE and then...

**INT. MURRAY'S HOUSE - DAY**

WHOOM!  Hopper throws it all onto a coffee table in front of --

ALEXEI, sitting comfortably on a cushioned chair.  He's watching LOONEY TUNES alongside MURRAY and JOYCE!

> HOPPER
> -- Two Whoppers, no mustard, extra
> ketchup, a large fries, Marlboro
> Reds, and...

He slams down the Giant Slurpee.

> HOPPER (CONT'D)
> ONE EXTRA LARGE SLURPEE.

He shoots Murray an irritated look --

> HOPPER (CONT'D)
> The Burger King is *nowhere near* the
> Seven-Eleven by the way.

> MURRAY
> Never said it was.

As Alexei starts to devour his Whopper, Hopper grabs some fries, drops into a chair.

                        HOPPER
             Okay, let's try this again.  Joyce?

As Hopper tosses a few fries into his mouth --

Joyce turns to Alexei:

                        JOYCE
             Alexei.  Those generators -- what are
             they powering?

                        HOPPER
                   (mouth full, interrupting)
             -- And tell him we KNOW it's _not_ the
             mall so don't try selling us that
             crap again --

Murray nods, then gives his translation.  Alexei swallows a
big bite of burger, washes it down with his Slurpee, then --

Winces.  He says something in _disgust_.

Joyce and Hopper exchange looks.

                        HOPPER (CONT'D)
             What'd he say?

                        MURRAY
             He says it's...  strawberry.

                        HOPPER
             I'm sorry -- _?_

                        MURRAY
             His Slurpee.  He says it's
             strawberry.

                        HOPPER
             So what -- ?

                        JOYCE
                   (irritated)
             So he ordered _cherry_ Hopper -- !

                        HOPPER
             Well they _DIDN'T HAVE_ cherry and it
             all tastes the same anyway -- it's
             just sugar on ice.  Go on, _tell him_ --

                        MURRAY
             Tell him _WHAT_ -- ?

                    HOPPER
          TELL HIM IT ALL TASTES <u>THE GODDAMN
          SAME</u>.

Murray tells Alexei, but Alexei shakes his head.

                    MURRAY
          He respectfully disagrees -- it's not
          the same <u>at all</u> and he would like
          cherry --

                    HOPPER
          YEAH WELL TELL HIM TO *FORGET IT*.

Alexei looks at Hopper.  Says something firm in Russian.

                    MURRAY
          He says no cherry...  *No deal*.

Hopper stares at Alexei.  Anger rising.  Then suddenly --

Hopper LUNGES and GRABS ALEXEI, ripping him off the couch --

                    JOYCE
          *Hopper STOP*!!!

Hopper ignores Joyce, dragging Alexei over the coffee table
through the house.  Alexei yelps, panicked, cursing in
Russian.

                    JOYCE (CONT'D)
          No violence -- !!!!

                    HOPPER
          Don't worry, I'm not gonna hurt him,
          I'm just giving him *AN OPPORTUNITY* --

Hopper starts to unlock the heavily locked front door --

                    HOPPER (CONT'D)
          <u>TO GET</u> ---

Another lock  --

                    HOPPER (CONT'D)
          -- <u>HIS OWN</u> --

Another --

                    HOPPER (CONT'D)
          -- <u>DAMN</u> --

Hopper throws open the front door --

                        HOPPER (CONT'D)
            -- *CHERRY SLURPEE!!!!*

WHOOM!  Hopper shoves Alexei and --

**EXT. MURRAY'S HOUSE - DAY**

Alexei flies outside and lands on the driveway.

As Alexei tumbles across the gravel, Hopper digs into his
pocket, pulls out TWO SETS OF KEYS.  He tosses the keys out
onto the driveway and then --

**INT. MURRAY'S HOUSE - DAY**

WHAM!  Hopper SLAMS the door, re-locks it.

                        JOYCE
            *WHAT* ARE YOU DOING???

                        MURRAY
            JIM THAT MAN IS AN ENEMY OF THE
            STATE -- !

                        HOPPER
            YEAH AND HE'S BEEN JERKING US AROUND
            FOR TWELVE HOURS NOW -- I get him his
            cherry Slurpee, next thing you know
            he wants a helicopter to charter him
            to his own private island -- I've
            dealt with assholes like this a
            *million times* --

**EXT. MURRAY'S HOUSE - LATER**

Alexei grabs up one of the keys.  They're for his handcuffs.
He unlocks them.  The cuffs fall off.  His eyes shoot wide.

*Holy.  Shit.*

**INT. MURRAY'S HOUSE - DAY**

                        JOYCE
            So that's it -- you just give up??

                        HOPPER
            Yesterday, in the woods, he could've
            escaped, but *HE DIDN'T*  -- he <u>stuck
            with us</u>.  Now why do you think that
            is??

**EXT. MURRAY'S HOUSE - LATER**

Alexei crawls on his hands and knees across the gravel, finds the second set of keys. He snatches them up. They dangle in front of his face. They're keys to THE CONVERTIBLE.

HOLY SHIT *PART TWO*!!

**INT. MURRAY'S HOUSE - DAY**

> HOPPER
> It's because he's *scared*, Joyce, he's scared! But not of us -- *of THEM*, of that seven foot Russian *freak* who could've killed him just as easily as us. If Smirnoff runs back to his comrades without a scratch on him, they're gonna assume he spilled his guts -- so whether he likes it or not, we're the best chance he's got.

Hopper checks his watch.

> HOPPER (CONT'D)
> I give it thirty seconds before he comes running right back into our arms with a new sense of *humility*.

**EXT. MURRAY'S HOUSE - LATER**

Alexei drops into the convertible. He jams the keys into the ignition, turns it. The engine ROARS to glorious life.

*HOLY SHIT PART THREE.*

**INT. MURRAY'S HOUSE - DAY**

THE SOUND OF THE ENGINE carries into the house.

> MURRAY
> Jim -- I, uh, believe he just started the car --

> JOYCE
> Hopper!!

Hopper suppresses a pang of concern.

> HOPPER
> He's just testing us, calling my bluff --

**EXT. MURRAY'S HOUSE - LATER**

Alexei kicks the car into reverse.  A deep breath.  Then --

He reverses the car.  Driving out of here!!!

**INT. MURRAY'S HOUSE - DAY**

> MURRAY
> I believe he is now driving away.

Joyce makes a move for the door, but Hopper obstructs her --

> JOYCE
> Hopper MOVE -- !!

> HOPPER
> JOYCE, *wait* -- !!!

But Joyce isn't waiting one *fucking second longer*.  She
shoves past Hopper, unlocks the door, throws it open, and --

**EXT. MURRAY'S HOUSE - DAY**

Joyce stumbles outside, crashes to a halt.  Eyes narrowing.

REVERSE TO REVEAL:  Alexei has only driven about twenty feet.

**INT./EXT. CONVERTIBLE - DAY**

Alexei sits there, deep in thought.  Then -- *FUCK IT*.  He
shifts gears, drives back, hits off the engine, and...

He exits the convertible.

He walks back toward the house, his spirit broken.  He
doesn't even make eye contact with his captors.

He just mutters something in Russian, hands Hopper the car
keys...  And enters the house.

Hopper looks at Murray.

> HOPPER
> What'd he say?

> MURRAY
> He says he likes strawberry too.
> (beat)
> And he'll need some pen and paper.

Joyce looks at a proud Hopper, impressed in spite of herself,
and --

**INT. UNDERGROUND RUSSIAN BASE - HUB - DAY**

BOOM!  CLOSE ON:  Dark boots marching across shiny floors
as...

RUSSIAN SOLDIERS patrol the base like stormtroopers.

We're back underground.

> DUSTIN (PRE-LAP)
> ... When we set fire to the hub, we
> drew the demodogs away -- so El
> could close the Gate...

**INT. VENTILATION SHAFT - DAY**

WHOOSHWHOOSHWHOOSH!  A METAL BLADE CUTS AIR.

WE PULL OUT TO REVEAL: A GIANT ROTATING FAN.  We're now even
deeper underground, in the cooling/air distribution ducts for
this Russian facility.  We PULL BACK FURTHER to reveal...

Dustin and Erica!!  They're cramped in this small space,
spattered in grease, clearly exhausted.

Dustin works to unscrew a PANEL with a tiny screwdriver...

> DUSTIN
> ... But now, for some *insane* reason,
> the Russians appear to be trying to
> re-open it, which is DESTROYING
> *everything* we risked our lives for --

> ERICA
> Okay and just to be clear, by _we_
> you're including Lucas -- ?

> DUSTIN
> Yes of course --

> ERICA
> So all that shit you told me -- Lucas
> was *there* --

> DUSTIN
> Yes --

> ERICA
> My brother, *Lucas Charles Sinclair* --

> DUSTIN
> YES!

                        ERICA
              I find that hard to believe --

Dustin POPS a screw loose, looks back at Erica.

                        DUSTIN
              So you believe everything about El
              and the Gate and the Demodogs and the
              Mind Flayer -- you just question
              Lucas's involvement in it?

                        ERICA
              That is correct.

                        DUSTIN
              Makes *total* sense.

Dustin shakes his head, returns to unscrewing.  Erica slides
to his side of the vent, watches him struggle with a screw.

                        ERICA
              You need help with that?

                        DUSTIN
              No --

                        ERICA
              It's taking a while.

                        DUSTIN
              Yeah *no shit*.

                        ERICA
              You know if we don't find a more
              efficient method to stop these fans,
              we're never gonna find help and your
              ice cream buddies are *screwed* --

                        DUSTIN
              Yeah with that *attitude* they are --

                        ERICA
              I'm just being *realistic*.  We've made
              it about point three miles in...
                   (consults her watch)
              Nine hours.  And we walked three
              hours down that tunnel, so I'd
              estimate it's ten miles back to the
              elevator -- which is gonna take us...

Erica does quick calculations in her head --

                        ERICA (CONT'D)
              Approximately twelve and a half days.


                          350

Dustin stares at Erica.  Stunned.

                         DUSTIN
             Did you just do that in your head?

                         ERICA
                    (shrugs)
             I'm good with numbers --

Dustin's jaw all but drops.

                         DUSTIN
             Holy shit.

                         ERICA
             ... What?

                         DUSTIN
             You're a nerd.

Erica stares.

                         ERICA
             Come again -- ?

                         DUSTIN
             You.  Are.  A.  NERD.

Dustin returns his focus to unscrewing the panel.

Erica can't believe her ears.  Scoots closer.

                         ERICA
             Okay, take that back, nerd --

                         DUSTIN
             Can't put the truth back in the box --

                         ERICA
             It's *not* the truth --

                         DUSTIN
             No?  Let's examine the facts, shall
             we?  Fact one:  You're a math whiz --

                         ERICA
             That was a *pretty* straightforward
             equation --

                         DUSTIN
             Fact TWO:  You're a political
             junkie --

                    ERICA
          Just because I don't agree with
          communism as an ideology -- ???

                    DUSTIN
          Fact THREE:  You LOVE My Little Pony.

                    ERICA
          What does THAT have to do with
          anything???

                    DUSTIN
          Hmmmm.  Let's recall the Ponies'
          latest adventure, shall we??  The
          evil _centaur_ demon Tirek turns
          Applejack into a _dragon_ at Midnight
          Castle, and then Megan and the other
          ponies have to use Moochick's _magic_
          to defeat his rainbow of darkness,
          saving them from a lifetime of
          enslavement.

He jabs a finger at Erica's pink My Little Pony backpack.

                    DUSTIN
          All the pink in the world can't
          disguise the _irrefutable fact_ that
          CASTLES and CENTAURS and DRAGONS and
          MAGIC are all standard NERD TROPES --
          ergo, My Little Pony is NERDY --
          ergo, YOU, ERICA, are a NERD.

Erica stares at Dustin, flabbergasted.  Then... it hits her:

                    ERICA
          ... Why do you know so much about My
          Little Pony?

                    DUSTIN
          BECAUSE I'M A NERD!!!

FRWOOM!  Dustin yanks off the panel cover.  Then he grabs a
handful of wires, rips them out, and --

BZZZZZZ!  The fan stops spinning.

                    DUSTIN (CONT'D)
          Let's go.
              (beat)
          _NERD_.

A stunned Erica watches Dustin crawl through the stopped fan.

Her eyes narrow with irritation, then --

She CRAWLS AFTER HIM *AND* --

**INT. UNDERGROUND RUSSIAN BASE - INTERROGATION ROOM - DAY**

WHOOSH!  A CURLED FIST flies through the air and --

<u>BAM!</u>  <u>SOCKS STEVE ACROSS THE JAW</u>!

> STEVE
> -- Okay that one *stung.*

WIDEN OUT:  He's being interrogated in a small room, his poor face is bruised and bloody for the third season in a row!

A RUSSIAN INTERROGATOR, OZEROV, talks, while a BRAWNY SOLDIER does the dirty work.

> OZEROV
> (thick accent)
> Who do you work for?

> STEVE
> For the *millionth time*, *Scoops Ahoy* --

WHOOMP!  Another punch, this time to the gut.

Steve catches his breath --

> STEVE (CONT'D)
> What <u>the hell</u> man!  Look at my outfit
> -- LOOK AT IT!  What do you think,
> I'm a spy in a SAILOR UNIFORM?  I
> just thought, hey, you know, maybe
> some stripes and a red neckerchief
> will help me really BLEND IN --

WHAM!  Another punch to the gut.  Steve doubles over in pain.

> OZEROV
> How did you get in?

Steve speaks between choked breaths --

> STEVE
> ... A -- a delivery didn't come... my
> friends... my friends and I went to
> see if maybe... it was left at the
> loading dock... we went in a room...
> turns out that room's an *elevator*...
> next thing I know -- we're here in
> this...
> (checking his words)
> Wonderful facility.

Steve looks at the Guards.  Pleading, desperate --

> STEVE (CONT'D)
> But NO ONE -- <u>NO ONE saw us</u>, I SWEAR
> TO GOD.  So if you just let us go,
> we'll forget we ever saw anything.
> Shit happens, right, life goes on --

The Russians stare at him, unmoved, but Steve persists --

> STEVE (CONT'D)
> And <u>ice cream</u> -- ice cream!  I'll
> give you and your friend free ice
> cream <u>*for life*</u>.  You guys do like ice
> cream right?  I mean who doesn't?
> You have *GOT* to try the USS
> BUTTERSCOTCH -- it's <u>out of this</u>
> <u>world</u>.

The Russians share skeptical looks, then --

BREAK OUT INTO LAUGHTER.  Steve laughs along with them --

> OZEROV
> I like this guy -- USS Butterscotch!!

More LAUGHTER.  Then, the laughter dies downs, and...

> OZEROV (CONT'D)
> Who do you work for?

Steve's smile drops.

> STEVE
> ... Come on.  Seriously?

WHAM!  The muscle PUNCHES STEVE AGAIN and --

**INT. UNDERGROUND RUSSIAN BASE - HALLWAY - DAY**

CLOSE ON:  Sneakers dragging down a hallway as...

The Russians haul a now *unconscious* Steve through the base.

**INT. UNDERGROUND RUSSIAN BASE - CREEPY MEDICAL ROOM - DAY**

WHOOM!  They toss his limp body into a CREEPY MEDICAL room.

A moment later, a door behind them opens up and --

WHOOM!  TWO MORE GUARDS toss Robin in!  She hits the floor.
She's clearly shaken, but unlike Steve, she's conscious,
unhurt --

                         ROBIN
                 Steve -- !!

She crawls over to Steve, shakes him.  Gets no response.

She looks up at Ozerov --

                    ROBIN (CONT'D)
          What have you done to him?!  WHAT
          HAVE YOU DONE -- ??

WHAP!  Ozerov *SMACKS* her across the face.

She drops to the floor, dazed from the hit.  The guards now
lift Robin and Steve up and place them down into these
strange, medical-style INTERROGATION CHAIRS.  As the Russians
work to secure leather straps over their wrists and legs --

Ozerov lifts Steve's face up, then lets it go.

It drops to his chest, *limp*.

                         OZEROV
          I think your friend needs a doctor.
          Good thing we have the very best.

For some reason, they all LAUGH HEARTILY at this.  Then --

SPLAT!  Robin spits in Ozerov's face.

His smile drops.  He wipes it away.

                    OZEROV (CONT'D)
          You're going to regret that.  *Cyka*.

Ozerov leads the others out of the room.

Robin shouts after them, desperate, fiery:

                         ROBIN
          LET US OUT OF HERE YOU BASTARDS!!!
          LET US *OUT*!!!!  LET US OUTTTTT!!!

The door slams on Robin and --

**DARKNESS**

We sit in this darkness for a beat.  Then...

A BARE FOOT steps into frame.  Water ripples outward.  And
now it hits us.  We're in --

**THE VOID**

Eleven is walking through the black void.  She looks around, searching, but everywhere all she finds is DARKNESS.

WE NOW CUT TO AN EXTREME WIDE TO REVEAL:

A very small Eleven.  All alone in here.

**INT. CABIN - ELEVEN'S ROOM - DAY**

We PULL OUT of the black blindfold to find...

Eleven sitting cross-legged in front of the static-blasting TV, a ROW OF PHOTOGRAPHS laid in front of her:  Tom, Bruce, Janet, Billy, Heather, Driscoll -- all the confirmed Flayed.

A DROP OF BLOOD spills from Eleven's nose.  Without removing her blindfold, she grabs up a tissue, wipes the blood away, then tosses the tissue atop --

A PILE OF BLOODY TISSUES.  *She's been at this for quite some time...*

**INT. CABIN - MAIN ROOM - DAY**

... And it's making Mike *very* nervous.  He paces in front of Eleven's bedroom door, ranting to Lucas and Max --

> MIKE
> ... It can't be good for her to be in there for this long...

> MAX
> Mike you *need to relax* --

> MIKE
> What if she gets brain damage or something -- ?

> LUCAS
> Oh shit -- is that, like, a real thing?

> MAX
> No!!  Mike made that up -- he doesn't know what the hell he's talking about --

> MIKE
> Oh -- and *you* do?

As they continue to bicker, our CAMERA DRIFTS PAST INTO...

**THE KITCHEN - CONTINUOUS**

Where we find Nancy on the phone, notepad in hand.  Jonathan
and Will listen nearby, anxious.  Jonathan holds a phonebook.

> NANCY
> ... Yes, from the Hawkins Post... I
> called the other day about -- uh huh,
> yes -- I was just following up to
> see if you've had anything else go
> missing or -- oh, okay -- sorry to --

DIAL TONE.  Nancy hangs up.

> JONATHAN
> Nothing?

Nancy turns to him -- shakes her head.  *Nothing.*

> NANCY
> Who's next -- ?

> JONATHAN
> There is no next.

He tosses the phone book.

> JONATHAN (CONT'D)
> Unless you want to start calling
> random people's homes -- other
> counties -- states -- ?

Nancy is baffled, frustrated.  She sits down by Jonathan.

> NANCY
> It just -- it doesn't make sense --

> JONATHAN
> Yeah well what about any of this
> makes sense -- ?

> NANCY
> There was a pattern, a consistency to
> their behavior.  They've been feeding
> on chemicals since this started.  And
> now they just *stop* -- out of the
> blue?

> WILL
> Maybe they have all the chemicals
> they need.  Maybe they've all turned
> into those... *things* --

                    NANCY
     But what about the Source?  I mean --
     did the Mind Flayer just suddenly
     stop infecting people?  And even if
     the Flayed are all monsters now, why
     can't El find them?

Before anyone can respond to these very good questions --

                    MAX (O.S.)
     Okay can you guys settle an argument
     for us???

Our threesome now looks up to find --

Max and Mike and Lucas stomping over to them.

                    MAX (CONT'D)
     Who do you guys think should decide
     limits for Eleven: Mike... or *Eleven?*

                    MIKE
     Okay the way you framed that is SUCH
     BULLSHIT --

                    MAX
     It's not bullshit Mike, this is your
     whole problem and it's also precisely
     the reason she dumped your ass --

                    NANCY
     El dumped you -- ??

                    MIKE
     Yeah because Max is conspiring
     against me, *corrupting her* --

                    MAX
     *Enlightening her.*  The fact is, she's
     not yours -- she's her own person,
     fully capable of making her own
     decisions --

                    MIKE
     She's risking her life, for no
     reason!

                    NANCY
     For "no reason"?  The Flayed are out
     there, doing God knows what --

                    LUCAS
     Killing, flaying --

                    WILL
*Transforming into monsters --*


                    NANCY
And El isn't stupid.  She knows her
own abilities better than any of us --


                    MAX
Exactly, thank you --


                    NANCY
She's her own person --


                    MAX
Exactly --


                    NANCY
With her own free will --


                    MAX
EXACTLY --


                    JONATHAN
If you believe in free will --


                    NANCY
What -- ?


                    JONATHAN
I said, IF you believe in free will --


                    NANCY
            (appalled)
You don't believe in free will -- ?


                    JONATHAN
I just think there's a real case to
be made that there isn't any --


                    NANCY
That is horrible and depressing and I
hate that you think that --


                    MAX
What's truly depressing is that after
El has saved the world TWICE, Mike
still doesn't trust her --


                    MIKE
You wanna to talk about TRUST --
REALLY???  You're the one that made
her spy on us --

                    LUCAS
Wait *WHAT* -- ??

                    MIKE
Oh she didn't tell you this -- ??

                    LUCAS
No -- ??

                    MIKE
Your girlfriend used El's power to
spy on us --

                    MAX
I didn't MAKE her it was HER idea and
are we seriously talking about this
right now -- ??

                    WILL
Yeah who cares --

                    LUCAS
I care -- !

                    MIKE
Apparently girlfriends don't lie --
THEY *SPY* --

                    MAX
We were just joking around -- !

                    MIKE
Yeah well it wouldn't have been so
funny if I was taking a massive shit
or something -- !

                    MAX
        (shocked by this)
You *weren't* -- !

                    MIKE
But what if I was -- ?!

                    MAX
Then *GROSS* -- !!

                    NANCY
Mike, seriously -- ??

                    MIKE
          I'm just trying to demonstrate how
          careless Max is with El's powers --
          IN fact how careless ALL OF YOU ARE --
          you're taking her for granted and
          treating her like -- like some kind
          of machine -- but she's not a machine
          and I don't want her to die looking
          for Flayed who have clearly vanished
          off the face of the earth and we
          really just need to come up with
          another plan because I LOVE HER AND I
          CAN'T LOSE HER AGAIN!!!

Everyone suddenly and abruptly goes silent.  They share
stunned looks.  *Did he just say...*  Mike catches his breath.
Stunned himself this came out of him.  And that's when --

EEEEEE.  The SOUND OF A DOOR opening behind them.

Mike, startled, whirls to find --

ELEVEN.  FINALLY EMERGING FROM HER BEDROOM.  Her blindfold is
removed now, hanging around her neck.  She looks a little
pale and dazed, like she just emerged from a long nap.

She clearly didn't hear what Mike just said.

                    ELEVEN
          What's... going on?

                    MIKE
          NOTHING!  Nothing.  We we were just --

                    LUCAS
          Having a family discussion.

                    ELEVEN
          Oh.

A beat.  Then --

                    ELEVEN (CONT'D)
          I found him.

                    NANCY
          Found... who?

                    ELEVEN
          Billy.

As everyone shares stunned looks, SMASH TO --


                           361

**EXT. MURRAY'S HOUSE - DAY**

We PUSH IN on Murray's house...

> MURRAY (O.S.)
> ... He calls it... "The Key."  And
> this Key emits a great... *energy*.

**INT. MURRAY'S HOUSE - LIVING ROOM - DAY**

CLOSE ON: AN ELABORATE DRAWING OF THE RUSSIAN MACHINE.  "The
Key."  Complex math equations are scribbled in the margins.

We PULL BACK further to reveal this is not the only drawing;
there are also drawings of the generators, maps of their
placement in the town, etc.  Real *Beautiful Mind* shit here.

> MURRAY
> ... It requires much strength --
> (correcting)
> *Power*...

WE CONTINUE TO PULL BACK to find Hopper and Joyce sitting at
Murray's living room table, smoking, watching anxiously as
Murray focuses hard, doing his best to translate Alexei...

> MURRAY (CONT'D)
> ... Those houses -- like the one you
> found -- they're located near, uh
> transformers -- they're stealing --
> from your town's power grid --

> HOPPER
> Yeah okay but why build this Key
> here?  Why not play in their own
> backyards?  Are they trying to blow
> us to smithereens or what?

Murray translates.  Alexei nods, responds in Russian.

> MURRAY
> ... There were many of these -- uh --
> Keys before.  In Russia.  But they
> turned out... wrong.  They had to
> come to where the, where the, uh --

> HOPPER
> Where the what?

> MURRAY
> I don't understand what he's saying.

                    JOYCE
         I thought you were fluent?

                    MURRAY
         Oh.  I'm SORRY.  Are my free
         translation services not good enough
         for you?  Because you can just go
         ahead and file your complaint RIGHT
         UP MY ASS!!!

Alexei, realizing he's not understood, grabs up a Burger King
wrapper, then yanks out the Slurpee straw...

                    HOPPER
         What's Smirnoff doing?

                    MURRAY
         He, he's -- showing me... oh *okay* --

                    JOYCE
         Okay what -- ?

                    MURRAY
         He says this straw -- they're using
         it to... penetrate... a hole... in
         a... box.

Hopper and Joyce share looks, ummm...

                    MURRAY (CONT'D)
         Oh okay -- sorry -- sorry --
              (beat)
         The straw represents the, uh, the Key
         -- which emits a very powerful
         energy --  And they're using this
         energy to -- *break through* a -- a
         barrier -- to open... a doorway.
              (beat)
         A *doorway between worlds.*

Alexei presses the straw against a french fry box, but the
straw doesn't punch through, it just bends along the side of
the carton.  Off an EXTREME CLOSE UP of the bending straw --

**FLASHBACK TO**

THE OPENING SCENE OF THE SEASON -- THE POWERFUL BLUE ENERGY
IS PUSHED BACK INTO THE MACHINE -- IT EXPLODES -- AND --

**BACK TO SCENE**

MURRAY (CONT'D)
... But it seems this Key was only
half the equation.  *Location* --
location was the other half...

Alexei grabs up a Burger King wrapper, explaining...

MURRAY (CONT'D)
... In Hawkins -- this door had been
opened once.  It was... *still
healing*.

Alexei stretches out the thin wrapper, then STABS it with the
straw.  THUNK!  This time the straw PUNCHES through and we --

**FLASHBACK TO**

THE MACHINE TURNING ON IN HAWKINS -- THE POWER DROPS OUT
ACROSS THE ENTIRE TOWN -- MAGNETS FALL -- TOPPLING -- AND --

**BACK TO SCENE**

Hopper and Joyce go pale.  He's talking about *the Upside
Down*.

HOPPER
Jesus Christ --

Joyce grabs up the Burger King wrapper, points at it --

JOYCE
This -- this *door*.  It's open now?

Murray asks; Alexei responds.

MURRAY
He says it is... *opening*.

**FLASHBACK TO**

THE MIND FLAYER PARTICLES RISE IN THE BASEMENT -- RATS
SCATTER -- WILL FEELS GOOSEBUMPS IN THE MOVIE THEATER *AND* --

**BACK TO SCENE**

Joyce flies up off her chair, races away --

HOPPER
Where are you going -- ?

JOYCE
Calling <u>our children</u>.

Hopper snuffs out his cigarette, then pushes to his feet, and
walks off.  But he doesn't follow Joyce as we expect him to.
Instead he makes a beeline into --

**THE KITCHEN**

He rummages through some cabinets, urgent.

> MURRAY
> Can I help you with something -- ?

> HOPPER
> Whiskey -- you got any whiskey?

> MURRAY
> No.  But I _do_ have vodka.

Hopper shoots Murray a look.  *You've got to be kidding.*

Murray isn't.  He throws open a cabinet, grabs his
favorite STOLICHNAYA VODKA, and pours two glasses.

Both men throw back their vodka, gulp it down.

As Murray pours out two more glasses...

> HOPPER
> I mean -- if there's a way to start
> this Key -- there's gotta be a way to
> stop it, yeah?  Turn it off?

> MURRAY
> Right.

> HOPPER
> Right.

The two men throw back their drinks, then --

**INT. MURRAY'S HOUSE - LIVING ROOM - DAY**

Murray and Hopper drop back down by Alexei, side by side.

Murray asks Alexei this question, then translates the
response:

> MURRAY
> ... He says *of course* he could turn
> it off.  Could Edison not turn off a
> lamp?  Could Bell not hang up a
> phone?  *Cocky bastard.*  But --

Alexei says one more sentence.

365

                              HOPPER
                    But what --

                              MURRAY
                    But he is now naked --

Hopper stares --

                              MURRAY (CONT'D)
                    Sorry -- exposed -- _compromised_ --

Hopper leans forward, not worried, _confident_ --

                              HOPPER
                    Tell him I'll get him there -- I'll
                    get him to his goddamn Key.

Murray does, but Alexei responds to this with a hint of a
smile.

                              HOPPER (CONT'D)
                    Can you please tell me what THE HELL
                    is so funny about that?

                              MURRAY
                    He says... he likes your courage.
                    You remind him of a... fat Rambo.
                    But he says even thin Rambo could not
                    get there.  This Key -- it is in an
                    underground fortress designed by the
                    greatest Russian minds -- guarded by
                    their greatest warriors.  Breaking in
                    is... put simply...
                         (beat)
                    Impossible.

As Hopper takes this in, WE SMASH TO:

**INT. UNDERGROUND RUSSIAN BASE - STORAGE ROOM - DAY**

WHOOM!  A VENT GRATE in the floor swings open and...

Dustin's head pops out!  Impossible, HA!

Erica pops up right after him.  They share looks.

                              DUSTIN
                    _Jackpot._

Dustin and Erica climb up into the room.  As they stand up,
our camera SWINGS AROUND to reveal they've infiltrated --

A LARGE STORAGE ROOM.  There are shelves lined with stacks and stacks of those bizarre green canisters.  But that's not what interests Dustin.  He's making a beeline for --

A MINI-TRUCK.  PARKED IN THE CORNER.

                    ERICA
          Do you even *know* how to drive?

WHOOM!  Dustin flings open the truck door, climbs in --

                    DUSTIN
          How hard can it be?  Max did it.

His spirit drops -- there are no keys in the ignition.

                    DUSTIN (CONT'D)
          Aw come on, *come on*...

                    ERICA
          You seriously thought they'd just
          *leave keys in there* -- ?

                    DUSTIN
          There must be a spare.

He opens the center console, riffles through some papers.

                    DUSTIN (CONT'D)
          You gonna just stand there or you
          gonna help look?

Erica sighs, walks away.

**MOMENTS LATER**

Erica walks down an aisle, turns.  Her eyes go wide.

*What... the... hell?*  She calls out:

                    ERICA
          Hey, Dustin... how big did you say
          that Demogorgon was...??

Dustin doesn't look up, he's still searching the car, now trying to jam open the glove compartment with his mini screwdriver --

                    DUSTIN
          Big.  Nine feet tall or so -- why?

We now reveal what Erica is looking at: A LARGE TEN FOOT JURASSIC PARK-STYLE CAGE.  Clearly designed to contain... *something*.  *Oh boy*.  Her eyes now shift from the cage to...

Something else.  Something we don't show.  But whatever it is, it's caught her interest.  She walks toward it and...

**BACK BY THE TRUCK**

BAM!  Dustin finally gets that glove compartment open.

A bunch of shit spills out, including a SET OF KEYS!!!

> DUSTIN
> Found 'em!  Erica let's go!!

He looks up.  No sign of Erica.

> DUSTIN (CONT'D)
> ... Erica?

ZZZZZ!  A SHARP SOUND startles him.  He whirls to find --

Erica, jabbing at him with a WEAPON that looks like a souped-up CATTLE PROD.  A powerful blue current courses across its forked prongs.

> DUSTIN (CONT'D)
> Jesus what is that -- ??

> ERICA
> A deadly weapon.  Could be useful --

> DUSTIN
> For *what* -- ?

> ERICA
> What do you think?  Taking out some
> commies.  <u>Saving your friends</u>.

Dustin sighs.  He wishes, but...

> DUSTIN
> I thought you were more *realistic*
> than that, nerd.  We don't know where
> they are and even if we did there are
> a million guards with weapons *way*
> more deadly than that thing.

Erica seems disappointed by this, and so does Dustin, but --

> DUSTIN (CONT'D)
> Listen -- the best thing we can do
> for them is to get out of here and
> <u>get help</u>.  Our probability of living
> -- and theirs -- rises substantially.
> Just... trust me on this, okay?

Erica considers, then hits off the cattle prod and climbs
into the truck.  As she settles in, buckling up, Dustin slots
the keys into the ignition, but then -- he pauses, feeling a
pang of guilt.  *Is he really going to do this -- leave his
friends?*

No choice.  He turns the ignition.  As the engine FIRES UP,
CUT TO --

**INT. HALLWAY - DAY**

An empty hallway.  A half-beat of silence.  Then --

> VOICE (O.S.)
> (distant)
> *HELP!!!  HEEEEEELP!*

**INT. UNDERGROUND RUSSIAN BASE - CREEPY MEDICAL ROOM**

ROBIN.  She's still shouting her lungs off, pulling hard
against her restraints, trying to free herself:

> ROBIN
> HELPPPP!!!!  HEEEEELP!!!  HEEEEELLP --

A WEAK VOICE SUDDENLY INTERRUPTS --

> STEVE (O.S.)
> Will you *please* stop yelling...  I've
> got a splitting headache...

Robin twists her head around.  Steve's moving -- awake!!

> ROBIN
> Steve!!!  Steve!!  Oh -- thank --
> *thank God* -- are you okay -- ??

Steve... well... doesn't look okay.  His face is bruised,
bloody, swollen.  It hurts him just to talk.

> STEVE
> -- Well other than the splitting
> headache, let's see... it hurts to
> breathe... my ears are ringing... my
> right eye feels like it's about to
> pop outta my skull... but other than
> all that I'm, uh... *swell*.

> ROBIN
> ... Well the good news is apparently
> they're getting you a doctor --

> STEVE
> ... This his place of work?

369

He looks around this _nasty_ medical room... It's more torture
chamber than doc's office.

>                    STEVE (CONT'D)
>          I really dig the... vibe.

>                    ROBIN
>          Yeah, yeah, tell me about it.  Now
>          listen, Steve -- _wait_ -- can you
>          move?

Steve pulls on his restraints.

>                    STEVE
>          Um... no.

>                    ROBIN
>          I mean, like, does your body still
>          function?  Are you paralyzed or
>          something?

Steve shuffles around, checking.

>                    STEVE
>          Nope, uh, not paralyzed --

>                    ROBIN
>          Okay, okay, _fantastic_.  Now -- see
>          that table over there --

Steve looks around, confused.

>                    ROBIN (CONT'D)
>          To your left, _other left_ --

Steve looks left.  Clocks it.  A metal table.

>                    ROBIN (CONT'D)
>          Okay, now see -- see those scissors --

Atop the table, in a bloody bowl, A NASTY-LOOKING PAIR OF
SCISSORS.

>                    ROBIN (CONT'D)
>          I've been thinking -- if we move at
>          the same time, maybe we can get over
>          there.  And if I can kick the table --
>          maybe I can knock them into your
>          lap --

>                    STEVE
>               (getting into it)
>          And I cut these binds --

                    ROBIN
          And then we're outta here.

                    STEVE
          Alright, yeah, *yeah*.  We can do that,
          we can totally do that.  Morons left
          us in here with scissors -- !

                    ROBIN
          Yeah, right?  Morons -- !

                    STEVE
          Morons!

                    ROBIN
          Alright, okay -- on the count of
          three we're gonna hop --

                    STEVE
          Hop on three.  Got it --

                    ROBIN
          Okay -- ready?  One...

                    STEVE
          Two...

                    STEVE/ROBIN
          THREE --

They HOP as best they can.  Their chairs thump a couple feet
closer to the table.  Holy shit that worked!!!

                    ROBIN
          Okay, okay!  Again!  One...  Two...

                    ROBIN/STEVE
          Three -- !!!

They HOP again, get another foot closer!

                    ROBIN
          Holy shit this is totally gonna work!
          Almost there!  Okay, one... two...

                    ROBIN/STEVE
          THREE -- !!!

They really throw their weight into it this time and --

FWOOM!  The chair loses its balance, tips over, and --

CRASHES to the floor.  Steve and Robin groan on impact.
*Ouch.*

                    ROBIN
          No no no no no no -- !

                    STEVE
               (not giving up)
          It's fine!  We're almost there!  Come
          on -- we can do this!  Just wriggle!

Steve tries fruitlessly to wriggle.

                    STEVE (CONT'D)
          You can do it!  Wriggle!

He tries more, but Robin has gone dead-weight.  She starts to
whimper softly.  Steve tries to console her.

                    STEVE (CONT'D)
          Hey.  Don't cry.  It's gonna be   --

Then it dawns on him -- she's not crying.

                    STEVE (CONT'D)
          Are you _laughing_?

She is.  Sort of hard now.  She tries to compose herself.

                    ROBIN
          I'm sorry.  I'm so sorry.  It's
          just... I can't believe I'm gonna die
          in a secret Russian base with Steve
          "the hair" Harrington.  It's... it's
          just too trippy, man.

Her laughter finally fades and the mood once more darkens.

Steve tries to be brave.  Reassuring.

                    STEVE
          Hey.  Listen.  We're _not_ gonna die,
          alright?  We're gonna get outta here.
          Somehow.  Just, uh, lemme think...

                    ROBIN
          Do you remember Missus Click's
          sophomore history class?

                    STEVE
               (confused)
          What?

                    ROBIN
          Missus Clickity-Clackity -- at least
          that's what us band dweebs called
          her.
               (MORE)

                    ROBIN (CONT'D)
It was first period Tuesdays and
Fridays, so of course you were always
late.  And you had the same breakfast
every time: bacon, egg, and cheese on
a sesame bagel.  I sat right behind
you two days a week for a year.
Mister Funny, Mister Cool.  The King
of Hawkins High himself.

She takes an emotional beat, then --

                    ROBIN (CONT'D)
Do you even remember I was in that
class?

Steve is silent.

                    ROBIN (CONT'D)
Of course you don't.

Steve's hurt by this.  He hates that he doesn't remember her,
and that surprises the HELL out of him.

                    ROBIN (CONT'D)
You were a real asshole you know
that?

                    STEVE
Yeah.  I know.

                    ROBIN
But it's like -- it didn't *matter*
that you were an asshole.  I was
still... weirdly obsessed.  Not in,
like, a creepy Michael Myers way or
anything.  It's just like  -- even
though all us losers pretend like
we're so above it all -- deep down we
actually all want to be... popular.
Accepted.  *Normal*.  It's freaking
depressing --

                    STEVE
Yeah well turns out being all those
things isn't so great.  Everything
that people tell you is important...
that you should care about... it's
all pretty much *total bullshit*.

Fuck, Steve is getting emotional now...

                    STEVE (CONT'D)
But I guess you've gotta mess up to
figure stuff out right?

                    ROBIN
          ... I hope so.  Because my entire
          life feels like... one big error --

                    STEVE
          Yeah same --

                    ROBIN
          But I guess the good news is -- can't
          ever get more messed up than this!!

They laugh together about this, then...

                    STEVE
          God, I really *wish* I had known you in
          Click's class.  You coulda helped me
          pass and I then woulda gotten into
          college --

                    ROBIN
          -- And I would have no idea that evil
          Russians were scheming beneath our
          feet and right about now I'd be
          happily slinging ice cream with some
          other schmuck --

                    STEVE
          Yeah.  Exactly.
               (beat)
          But I have to say... I did like being
          your schmuck.  It was... fun.

                    ROBIN
          Yeah.  It was.

Bittersweet smiles, then --

FWOOM!  The door opens.  Steve and Robin whirl to find --

TWO RUSSIANS entering -- it's OZEROV and a new villain for us
to hate: DOCTOR ZHARKOV.  He is wearing dark gloves, large
round glasses, a stained white lab coat.

Ozerov can't help but grin at Steve and Robin's predicament.

                    OZEROV
          Where were you two going?

He lifts them up and drags them back to their original
position.  He leans down to their height.

                    OZEROV (CONT'D)
          ... Try telling the truth this time,
          yes?  It will make your visit with
          Doctor Zharkov less... *painful.*

They look up to find this fucking Doctor Zharkov now filling
a GIANT HYPODERMIC NEEDLE with a strange cloudy blue liquid --

                    STEVE
          Hey -- hey -- what is that -- ?

                    DOCTOR ZHARKOV
          It will help you talk.

Zharkov walks over to Steve --

                    STEVE
          Hey man -- did you clean that --

The Doctor suddenly JAMS the needle deep into Steve's neck --

As Steve SCREAMS, SMASH TO --

**EXT. CABIN - ESTABLISH - DAY**

SLOW PUSH-IN on the cabin.

**INT. CABIN - MAIN ROOM - DAY**

The TV has been moved into the main room.  Eleven is sitting
cross-legged on the couch; everyone else is in a semi-circle
around her, watching, waiting.  It looks like a seance,
except with a television in the place of a candle.

Eleven rips off her blindfold.  Returning to our world.

                    MAX
          ... What's he doing now?

Off Eleven, CUT TO --

**INT. CABIN - KITCHEN - DAY - A LITTLE LATER**

WHOOSH!  Water shoots out of a faucet as --

Eleven fills a glass to the brim.  She chugs the water, fast,
like a racer after a marathon, *re-charging her battery as* --

**INT. CABIN - MAIN ROOM - DAY - A LITTLE LATER**

The rest of the group paces in the main room, *thinking.*

                    NANCY
          ... And that's not normal right --

                    MAX
Billy, staying in his room on July
fourth? No, I'd say that's not normal --


                    WILL
He *wants* us to find him --


                    NANCY
Yeah that's exactly what I'm worried
about.  If we go to Billy, the rest
of the Flayed will know where we
are --


                    MIKE
It's a trap, *I agree*.  They'll <u>ambush</u>
<u>us</u> --


                    LUCAS
-- An ambush is a surprise attack.
And we won't be surprised -- we'll
<u>know</u> they're coming and we'll kick
their Flayed butts --


                    MAX
You mean *El* will kick their butts --

**BACK IN THE KITCHEN,**

Eleven finishes her water, sets it down, then clocks --

A BOX OF LUCKY CHARMS.  As she stares at it, she's struck
with a thought.  WE PUSH IN on its rainbow design and --

**FLASHBACK TO**

ELEVEN WALKING UP TO HER "MAMA" IN THE VOID LAST SEASON --
TERRY SUDDENLY GRABS HER HAND AND EL IS BOMBARDED WITH
MEMORIES -- FOUR FIFTY -- SUNFLOWERS -- <u>A RAINBOW</u> -- *AND* --

**BACK IN THE MAIN ROOM,**

                    JONATHAN
It's too risky --


                    NANCY
And unnecessary.  Killing the Flayed
won't stop the Mind Flayer -- we have
to find where he's spreading from --
we have to find the Source --


                    ELEVEN (O.S.)
Billy knows it.

Everyone turns around, surprised, to find --


                    376

Eleven stepping in from the kitchen.

>                    ELEVEN (CONT'D)
>          Billy has been there.  To... the
>          Source.

A concerned Mike starts to speak, but El beats him to it.

>                    ELEVEN (CONT'D)
>          It's a... *trap*.  I know.  We can't go
>          to him.  But... I think... there's
>          another way.
>                    (beat)
>          A way for me to see... where he has
>          been.

Shared looks, then --

**INT. CABIN - MAIN ROOM - DAY - A LITTLE LATER**

CHHH!  TV is powered back on, STATIC BLASTING to life as...

Eleven sits back down on the orange couch, crosses her legs.

An anxious Mike sits beside her.

>                    MIKE
>          ... El, I know  you think you have to
>          do this -- but *you don't* --

Max, overhearing this, bites her tongue.

>                    MIKE (CONT'D)
>          It's just... you've only done this
>          once... and your mom is someone who
>          loves you... who *wanted* to show you
>          what happened.  Billy -- his mind is
>          sick, *diseased.*  The Mind Flayer *is*
>          *in him* --

>                    ELEVEN
>          He can't hurt me.  Not in there.

>                    MIKE
>          We don't know that --

>                    ELEVEN
>          Mike.  I need you... to trust me.

Mike hesitates.  He can't help but glance back at Max.  She
shoots him a *TRUST HER YOU IDIOT* look.  He returns his gaze
to Eleven... takes a deep breath... and...

377

                         MIKE
              Just... be *careful*.

Eleven nods.  *She will*.  Mike steps away from the sofa,
leaving Eleven to it.  She starts to slip her blindfold on
when she senses something.  She looks up to find that --

EVERYONE IS STARING AT HER.  LOOKING *SUPER NERVOUS*.

                         ELEVEN
              The energy is... bad.

                    NANCY/MAX/LUCAS
              Sorry, sorry --

Everyone moves away, sits down, trying to stay calm for El.

Feeling more relaxed now, Eleven puts on her blindfold --

As she yanks it tight, we SMASH TO --

**INT. VOID**

WHOOM!  Eleven's eyes snap open.  <u>SHE'S BACK IN THE VOID</u>.

Straight ahead:  Billy.  He is sitting on the bed in his
room, unmoving.  Eleven takes a breath, slowly approaches.

She stops directly in front of him.

**INT. MAX'S HOUSE - BILLY'S ROOM - DAY**

Billy's breath seems to catch a bit.  *Does he sense her?*

**INT. VOID**

Eleven reaches out, takes Billy's hand, and...

<u>Nothing happens</u>.  Not like with Mama.

                         ELEVEN
              Billy -- are you there?  Can you hear
              me?  I... I want to see.  See what
              happened.

**INT. BILLY'S ROOM - DAY**

Billy slowly lifts his head and...

**INT. VOID - UNKNOWN**

He locks eyes with Eleven.  A flicker of recognition.

Eleven winces.  She looks down to find --

His hand now grips her arm, *squeezing tight* --

She tries to pull herself away, but Billy holds firm --

**INT. CABIN - MAIN ROOM - DAY**

Eleven's breathing quickens, blood slips down her nose --

> MIKE
> Something's wrong --

**INT. VOID**

WHOOM!  Billy suddenly *DROPS* out of existence *and* --

Eleven, now no longer held by him, TUMBLES BACKWARD.  As we
follow her fall in EXTREME SLOW MOTION, she's bombarded with--

RAPID-FIRE IMAGES FROM BILLY'S MEMORY BANK.  THE IMAGES ARE
HEAVILY DISTORTED, BLURRED, MORE COLORS AND ODD SOUNDS THAN
CONCRETE IMAGES.  A PAINFUL, ABSTRACT DISPLAY.  BUT IN THE
CHAOS WE MAKE OUT A FEW MOMENTS -- THE CAR CRASH -- BILLY
SCREAMING OUTSIDE THE PHONE BOOTH -- ATTACKING HEATHER --

THE MEMORIES RACE PAST US FASTER AND FASTER AS --

ELEVEN FALLS FURTHER AND FURTHER --

ALMOST TO THE GROUND NOW AND --

WHOOM-SPLASH!  <u>Eleven falls on her back</u>.  <u>Landing in water</u>.
But this water is not black.  It's *BRIGHT BLUE*.

Eleven is no longer in the void.  She's now on a --

**EXT. CALIFORNIA BEACH - SUNRISE**

Ocean waves lap against her face.

She catches her breath, pushes to her feet, blinks in the hot
sun.  She looks around, stunned, confused.  *Where is she?*

WE CUT SUPER WIDE:  HUGE EMPTY CALIFORNIA BEACH STRETCHES IN
ALL DIRECTIONS.  LARGE CLIFFS FLANK US ON EITHER SIDE.

A familiar voice echoes across the landscape:

> MIKE
> (heavy reverb)
> El -- are you okay?

**INT. CABIN - MAIN ROOM - DAY**

We're suddenly, jarringly back in the cabin.

Eleven catches her breath in the cabin.

                    ELEVEN
          I'm okay...

                    MIKE
          What's going on?

                    ELEVEN
          I'm on -- a beach.

Shared looks.

                    LUCAS
          ... Okay, maybe I'm dense, but last I
          checked there weren't any beaches in
          Hawkins --

                    MAX
               (ignores this)
          What else do you see?

**EXT. CALIFORNIA BEACH - SUNRISE**

Eleven looks around.  Sees --

                    ELEVEN
          A woman.

A YOUNG WOMAN, maybe late 20s, dirty blonde, beautiful, west
coast hippy aesthetic, standing on the shore.

**INT. CABIN - DAY**

                    ELEVEN
          She's... pretty.
               (beat)
          I think she's... *looking at me.*

**EXT. CALIFORNIA BEACH - SUNRISE**

The Woman starts to clap and smile and cheer.  We think for a
moment that she is clapping at Eleven but then --

WHOOSH!  Water sprays up as a YOUNG BOY sprints past Eleven,
carrying a SURFBOARD, making his way to the woman.

She's cheering for this boy!

**INT. CABIN - DAY**

                    ELEVEN
          There's... a boy.

**EXT. CALIFORNIA BEACH - SUNRISE**

The boy excitedly races up to the woman.  She is clearly his
mother.

                    YOUNG BOY
          Did you see that??

                    YOUNG WOMAN
          Yeah I saw it!!!

                    YOUNG BOY
          That was at least seven feet!!

                    YOUNG WOMAN
          Well whatever it was it almost gave
          me a heart attack --

                    YOUNG BOY
          Ten more minutes -- ?

                    YOUNG WOMAN
          Ten more minutes but any longer than
          that and Dad's gonna be mad --

                    YOUNG BOY
          Okay okay!

The Boy smiles excitedly, then races back into the ocean,
back toward Eleven.  The Young Woman calls out after him --

                    YOUNG WOMAN
          Billy!

The Young Boy turns.  Holy shit.  It's *Billy*.

                    YOUNG WOMAN (CONT'D)
          Watch out for rip currents!

                    YOUNG BILLY
          I know!

Young Billy races past Eleven, jumps onto his board, and
begins to paddle out into the vast ocean.

**INT. CABIN - DAY**

                    ELEVEN
          ... It's *Billy*.

Max suddenly understands.

                    MAX
          It's California.  It's a *memory*.

More shared looks and --

**EXT. CALIFORNIA BEACH - SUNRISE**

Eleven watches Young Billy paddle out into the ocean when --

BOOM!  A DISTANT RUMBLE.  Eleven turns and sees --

A SUPERNATURAL STORM.  IMMENSE DARK CLOUDS SWIRL, RED
LIGHTNING SCARS THE SKY.  VERY MUCH LIKE THE STORM OUTSIDE
THE ARCADE.

**INT. CABIN - DAY**

>                         ELEVEN
>           ... I think I see it.  The Source.

More shared looks from our kids, then --

**EXT. CALIFORNIA BEACH - SUNRISE**

Eleven begins to walk toward the supernatural storm.

Our music rises, THUNDER CRASHES, and --

**EXT. MURRAY'S HOUSE - DAY**

Quiet outside Murray's.  PRELAP THE SOUND OF A PHONE...

**INT. MURRAY'S HOUSE - LIVING ROOM - DAY**

RIIIIIING!  RIIIIIING!  Hopper is pacing, his ear glued to
Murray's phone.  Joyce eyes him while Murray frets.  Alexei,
meanwhile, is peacefully sleeping on the couch.  *Food coma.*

>                         MURRAY
>           Two minutes, Jim!  It's a secure
>           line, but any longer and they could
>           trace you --
>
>                         HOPPER
>           Good!  I *want* them to trace me!

**INT. UNKNOWN SMALL ROOM**

We're suddenly in a windowless space.  There's no sense of
place, but a perfect sense of time:  CLOCKS run around the
wall above wall maps, keeping track of every time zone.

CLOSE ON:  A MAN'S hand reaches down, answers a RINGING
PHONE.

We don't recognize the man -- and his voice is cold,
flat.

                    GOVERNMENT MAN (V.O.)
               (cold, flat)
          Philadelphia Public Library.

                                        INTERCUT WITH:

**INT. MURRAY'S HOUSE - LIVING ROOM - DAY**

Hopper is thrown.

                    HOPPER
               Oh, uh...

Joyce eye-conferences with Hopper. *What's the problem??*

                    HOPPER (CONT'D)
               This is -- Jim Hopper.  Police Chief
               of Hawkins.  Hawkins, Indiana.

No response.

                    HOPPER (CONT'D)
               I, uh, got this number from Sam
               Owens... Doctor Samuel Owens?

                    GOVERNMENT MAN
               What is your identification code?

Hopper winces.  The code.  He forgot about this *Three Days of
the Condor* bullshit!

                    HOPPER
               Oh, ah.  Shit.  The identification
               code...  Ah...

                    JOYCE
               (annoyed whispering)
               You don't know it?

                    MURRAY
               You must be joking.

Hopper digs out his wallet, rummages through it.

                    HOPPER
               Hold on.  I got it here...

He pulls out a tiny slip of paper.

                    MURRAY
               (appalled)
               You wrote it down?  *AND KEPT IT IN
               YOUR WALLET??*

Hopper waves him off. Fuck off!

> HOPPER
> (reading)
> Yeah, OK. It's uh... *Antique Chariot*.

Joyce narrows her eyes. *Antique Chariot?*

> HOPPER (CONT'D)
> Listen -- tell Owens the Ruskies are opening the Gate. He'll know what I'm talking about -- not about the Ruskies but about the Gate. Tell him -- tell him there's an entrance in *Starcourt Mall*. I know how to get in, but I need backup. *A lot of backup*. Have him call me back on this line -- six-one-eight-six-two-five--

Murray mouths a HUGE "NO!," but Hopper flips him the bird, continues --

> HOPPER (CONT'D)
> Eight-three-one-three.

### INT. UNKNOWN SMALL ROOM

The Man absorbs this for a beat. Then, with no emotion...

> GOVERNMENT MAN
> Your message will be relayed.

WHOOM. He hangs up and --

### INT. MURRAY'S HOUSE - LIVING ROOM - DAY

DIAL TONE. Hopper hangs up the phone.

> JOYCE
> What now?

> HOPPER
> We wait.

As Hopper digs out a cigarette, Murray whines --

> MURRAY
> You've compromised me, Jim -- you do realize that, don't you??? I'm going to have to relocate -- !

Joyce tunes out Murray.

                              JOYCE
                    How long do we wait -- ?

                              HOPPER
                    I have no idea --

Hopper lights up his cigarette --

                              JOYCE
                    How can you be so calm -- ?

                              HOPPER
                    I'm not calm --

                              JOYCE
                    Our children are in danger --

                              HOPPER
                    You said they're at the festival --

                              JOYCE
                    Which is *ten miles* from the Gate --

Joyce pushes past Hopper, grabs up the phone --

                              HOPPER
                    What are you doing?  *Joyce?*

Joyce ignores him, dials a number and --

**INT. UNKNOWN SMALL ROOM**

BRRRRRING!  The phone rings again.

The Government Man answers.  His tone just as flat as before.

                         GOVERNMENT MAN
                    Philadelphia Public Library --

                              JOYCE
                    Hi.  This is Antique Chariot's
                    partner --

The Government Man looks confused, thrown off...

**INT. MURRAY'S HOUSE**

Hopper stares at Joyce in disbelief --

                              JOYCE
                    I'm not sure *Antique Chariot* properly
                    conveyed the urgency of our
                    situation --

                    HOPPER
          *What are you doing --   ?*

She holds up a finger, shushing him.

                    JOYCE
          We can't just wait around here for a
          call --

                    GOVERNMENT MAN
          Ma'am, I'm going to need you to stay
          calm --

                    JOYCE
          No -- don't you dare patronize me.

The Government Man looks like he was just SLAPPED.

                    JOYCE (CONT'D)
          I have no idea who you are but you
          seem like a glorified secretary to
          me.  If you don't want to lose your
          job, here's what's going to happen --
          as soon as I hang up, you're going
          get up off your ass, find Owens, and
          tell him what's going on.  We don't
          have time to talk about it and
          neither does he -- he just needs to
          get to Hawkins with his men.  RIGHT
          NOW.  Is that all understood -- ?

                    GOVERNMENT MAN
                 (a little shaken)
          Yes -- yes ma'am --

                    JOYCE
          Thank you and GOOD DAY.

WHAM!  CLICK!  Joyce hangs up the phone.

Hopper can't believe her --

                    HOPPER
          It's been *a minute* Joyce --

                    JOYCE
          *Yeah -- a minute too long.*

Joyce storms over to the couch, shakes the sleeping Alexei.

He blinks awake, groggy, confused --

                    ALEXEI
                (in Russian)
            <What's going on?>

                    JOYCE
        We're leaving, VROOM VROOM.  Back to
        Hawkins.  Come on --

Joyce pulls Alexei off the couch and drags him past a stunned
Hopper and Murray.  They share looks, then follow them, but --

Murray pauses at the door, turns back.  Laying out on the
living room table:

All of Alexei's "Death Star" scribblings.  *Left out.*

Murray doubles back, *snatches them up*, and --

**INT. UNDERGROUND RUSSIAN BASE - DAY - ESTABLISHING**

BOOM!  Boots STOMP close to camera as...

HEAVILY ARMED GUARDS pace the Death Star hallways.

                STEVE (PRE-LAP)
        ... I still don't really feel
        anything do you?

**INT. CREEPY MEDICAL ROOM - DAY**

We're back with Steve and Robin, still in those fucking
medical chairs.  *Waiting.*

                    ROBIN
        No, I still feel... *fine*.  Normal.

                    STEVE
        Same.  I mean -- I actually feel
        kinda... *good*.

                    ROBIN
        Yeah -- same!

                    STEVE
        Ha, what morons!

                    ROBIN
        Yeah, what morons!

                    STEVE
        MORONS!

                    ROBIN/STEVE
          MORONSMORONSMORONSMORONS!

Steve and Robin start laughing hysterically, then...

                    ROBIN
          I think there's something wrong with
          us.

                    STEVE
          Definitely.

WHOOM!  The door suddenly opens again.  They turn as --

Dr. Zharkov and Ozerov walk back into the room.

The Doctor places a MEDICAL BAG down on the table and begins
to calmly remove an ARRAY OF TORTURE DEVICES, placing them on
a tray one by one.  There are SURGICAL TOOLS, PLIERS,
SCISSORS, KNIVES, AND A BONE SAW.  Yes -- a FUCKING BONE SAW.

Steve and Robin, needless to say, are no longer laughing.

                    ROBIN
          Is now the wrong time to say I don't
          like doctors -- ?

                    OZEROV
          Let's try this again, yes?
               (beat)
          Who do you work for?

Steve can't believe this fucking shit --

                    STEVE
          Scoops.  SCOOPS.  AHOY.

                    OZEROV
          And how did you find us?

                    STEVE
          By accident.

Ozerov looks at Zharkov.

                    OZEROV
               (Russian)
          <More lies.>

Dr. Zharkov nods, then turns to the table, considers, then
selects his first instrument of choice: the pliers.

                         STEVE
             Whoa whoa, what are you doing with
             those?

The Doctor crosses to Steve and --

                         STEVE (CONT'D)
             Oh Jesus -- !!!

Clamps the pliers onto one of his fingernails --

                         STEVE (CONT'D)
             WAITWAITWAIT -- !!

Starts to pull *and* --

                         ROBIN
             THE CODE!!!  There was a code -- we
             heard the code -- !!

The Doctor pauses his torture, tension momentarily dropping.

Ozerov moves around to Robin.

                         OZEROV
             Code.  What code?

                         ROBIN
             "The week is long, the silver cat
             feeds, when blue and yellow meet in
             the west blah blah" -- you guys
             broadcast that lame spy shit all over
             town and we snapped it up on Cerebro
             and we cracked it in a day.  A DAY.
             You think you're *so* smart but a bunch
             of kids who scoop *ice cream* for a
             living outsmarted you and now people
             know you're here --

                         OZEROV
             *Who* knows we're here, cyka?

*Oops.*  Robin doesn't answer, fighting back the serum, but --

                         STEVE
             Dustin knows --

                         ROBIN
             Steve -- !

                         STEVE
             Dustin *HENDERSON*.

                         ROBIN
          STEVE!

Ozerov moves to Steve. *This is too damn easy.*

                         OZEROV
          "Dustin Henderson."  Is this your
          small curly hair friend?

                         STEVE
          That's right --

                         OZEROV
          Where is he?

                         STEVE
          LONG GONE, asshole -- LOOOONG GONE.
          I guarantee you by now he's called
          Hopper and Hopper's gonna bring the
          US Cavalry with him and they're gonna
          COME in here with guns a-blazin' and
          YOU'RE *TOAST*.

                         OZEROV
          Is that so?

Ozerov shares an amused smile with the Doctor, when...

WAH WAH WAH!!!!  AN ALARM SUDDENLY BEGINS TO BLARE.

Ozerov tenses just a bit.  Smiling drops.  *Steve can't
possibly be right, can he?*  He hears COMMOTION outside.
SHOUTING.  What the hell?

**INT. UNDERGROUND RUSSIAN BASE - HALLWAY - DAY**

He throws open the door, exits into the hallway, where --

SOLDIERS are racing past, shouting, weapons drawn.  *What the
hell is going on??*  Ozerov strides after his comrades as --

**INT. CREEPY MEDICAL ROOM - DAY**

Steve smirks at the Doctor.

                         STEVE
          Uh oh.

                         DOCTOR ZHARKOV
          You think you're funny, cocky
          American?

                        STEVE
          No.  Like I said.  I just think
          you're toast.

**INT. UNDERGROUND RUSSIAN BASE - HALLWAY - DAY**

Ozerov turns down a hallway, finds...

A GROUP OF SOLDIERS gathered around something, SHOUTING,
panicked.  He pushes his way through them to find --

The floor is covered with SHATTERED PROMETHIUM BOTTLES, that
green liquid spilled everywhere, burning a GIANT SMOKING HOLE
into the floor, Xenomorph-style.  As Ozerov's eyes shoot
wide --

**INT. CREEPY MEDICAL ROOM - DAY**

WHOOM!  THE MEDICAL ROOM DOOR SUDDENLY BURSTS OPEN AND --

                        DUSTIN
          AHHHHHHHHH!!!!

The Doctor looks up in horror to find --

DUSTIN CHARGING INTO THE ROOM, SCREAMING, ERICA RIGHT BEHIND
HIM!!!  HE WIELDS AN ELECTRICAL SHOCK PROD LIKE A SPEAR!

Doctor Zharkov barely has time to react before --

WHAM!!  Dustin THRUSTS the prod into his chest and --

ZZZAP!  IT SENDS A POWERFUL ELECTRICAL CURRENT SHOOTING
THROUGH HIS BODY.  THE DOCTOR DROPS HARD TO THE FLOOR AND --

HE'S OUT.  HIS LAB COAT HISSES WITH FIRE, SMOKING.  *TOAST*.

Steve barely seems to register the violence -- looks at
Dustin.

                        STEVE
          Hey, Henderson, I was *just* talking
          about you!

Robin can barely believe her eyes --

                        ROBIN
          Oh my God oh my God -- !!

Dustin drops the prod, races over to Steve and Robin.

This isn't fun and games to him -- *this is life or death.*

                         DUSTIN
              Get ready to run -- !

As Dustin and Erica quickly work to untie the drugged teens,
ripping off those bindings, the alarm continues to blare:

WAHWAHWAHWAHWWWAH!!!

**EXT. CABIN - NIGHT**

Unnerving quiet.  Night has now fallen outside the cabin.

**INT. CABIN - NIGHT**

The group waits around Eleven, nervous --

                         LUCAS
              How long is this going to take...?

                         MIKE
              I don't know --

                         LUCAS
              I mean, can't you travel as fast as
              you want in your head -- ?

                         MIKE
              I don't know how it works --

                         MAX
              Both of you!  *Quiet.*

Lucas and Mike sit, quieting themselves, as...

We PUSH IN on Eleven.  The sound of the TV static becomes --

The SOUND OF GUSTING WIND and suddenly --

**EXT. BEACH - DAY**

CRACK!  Red lightning forks in the sky.  The storm RAGES.

We're back on the beach, and Eleven is still moving toward
that massive storm cloud.  She's closer now.  Her hair blows
in the wind.

As she walks, she notices that the beach has become much
foggier; it is almost as if she is moving through a cloud.

Something flutters in the air.  She looks up --

It's *SNOW*, falling from the dark storm cloud.  *No.  Not snow.*

SPORES.  Just as she takes this in --

                           392

                         VOICE (O.S.)
                   What the hell is wrong with you??

She returns her attention to the beach.  Up ahead, through a
curtain of fog, BILLY'S DAD has YOUNG BILLY by the arm ---

Young Billy is in a baseball uniform; his dad is clearly the
coach.  His face burns red with anger --

                         NEIL
                   What did we talk about??  Huh?  You
                   gotta slide!!!

                         YOUNG BILLY
                   I -- I know --

                         NEIL
                   You afraid you gonna get hurt??  That
                   it?

                         YOUNG BILLY
                   No --

                         NEIL
                   Then what then?  What?  Did I raise a
                   pussy for a son -- ?!

Young Billy takes the abuse, fighting tears --

There is a GUST OF WIND and Young Billy and Neil blow away --
*becoming spores* --

Eleven hurries past, moving deeper into the storm.  She is
now in what we will call --

**THE MEMORY CLOUD - CONTINUOUS**

The beach is no longer visible, swallowed by fog and spores,
which move like crazy in this ROARING WIND.  (NOTE:  In this
sequence, Eleven is always moving forward, and the storm is
always building in intensity).  Her sense of direction is
already confused -- *lost in a nightmare of dark memories.*

                         VOICE
                   YOU SAW HIM, DIDN'T YOU?!  DIDN'T
                   YOU???

Eleven, startled, turns as she walks, sees Billy's dad
yelling at his mother.

                         BILLY'S MOTHER
                   STAY AWAY FROM ME, AWAY --

Billy's Mother throws a ceramic plate.  It just misses him, smashes an off-screen wall.

                    NEIL
          YOU WHORE -- YOU *BITCH* --

Neil moves in to attack when --

YOUNG BILLY races in, grabs his dad, screaming!

                    YOUNG BILLY
          Stop it, STOP IT!

Neil pushes Young Billy away, then STRIKES the Mother.  On contact --

WHAM-BOOM!  RED LIGHTNING SCARS THE SKY and --

                    YOUNG BILLY (CONT'D)
          MOM!!  MOM!!

Eleven turns, sees Young Billy, just visible through a heavy veil of spores.  It's another day now, and he's on the phone, sobbing --

                    YOUNG BILLY (CONT'D)
          MOM -- PLEASE COME HOME --  NO -- HOW
          LONG -- HOW LONG????

A FRESH CLOUD OF SPORES swallows this memory up, then --

WHOOSH!  YOUNG BILLY suddenly races up from behind Eleven, almost running into her, startling her.  He's chasing another SMALLER KID through this storm.  He slams the kid down onto the ground and starts to punch him over and over and --

                    SMALLER KID
          GET OFF -- GET OFF -- !!!

                    YOUNG BILLY
          Pussy -- PUSSY -- !!!

As Billy continues to punch --

BOOM-CRACK!  More LIGHTNING scars the sky and --

Eleven hurries past, pushing further into the storm.

                    NEIL (O.S.)
          ... This is your new sister --

She turns -- ANOTHER MEMORY:  Billy's dad is introducing Young Billy to a young redheaded girl, 8.

                        NEIL (CONT'D)
          Her name is Maxine --

                        YOUNG MAX
               Max.

Young Billy stares at "Max," clearly not happy about her.

A wave of spores quickly envelops this memory.  The storm
picks up.  Those spores swirl so fast it's almost dizzying,
those red lightning strikes much closer now, scary,
dangerous.  It's almost impossible to see now.

Eleven looks around.  She's lost now.  Lost in this storm.

Wait.  Something ahead.  *TWO BRIGHT LIGHTS*.

She moves toward the lights and --

**EXT. ABANDONED FACTORY - NIGHT**

WHOOSH!  The storm suddenly ends.  It's eerily calm now.

Straight ahead: BILLY'S CAMARO.  Wrecked.  Smashed into a
metal pole.  Music still playing on the radio.  As Eleven
approaches the Camaro, she looks around, sees that the storm
is making a circular wall around her.  She looks up and...

WE CUT TO BIRD'S-EYE TO REVEAL:  SHE'S IN THE *EYE OF THE*
*STORM*.

In the center of this eye... the factory.

As Eleven takes in the factory...

**INT. CABIN - NIGHT**

                        ELEVEN
               I think I found it.  I found... The
               Source.

Everyone shares looks --

                        MAX
            Where -- El?  *Where are you??*

**EXT. ABANDONED FACTORY - NIGHT**

Eleven locates the factory sign.  It reads --

**INT. CABIN - NIGHT**

                      ELEVEN
            ... Brimborn.  Steelworks.

Nancy and Jonathan hurry away.  They race back into the
kitchen area, grab up one of those phone books from earlier,
start flipping through them --

                     JONATHAN
            *Got it* -- 6522 Cherry Oak Drive --

Nancy locks eyes with Jonathan.  Holy shit --

                      NANCY
            That's <u>close</u> --

Jonathan nods.  They've FOUND IT.

Mike turns to Eleven --

                      MIKE
            El, we have it -- get out of there --
            GET OUT -- !

**EXT. ABANDONED FACTORY - NIGHT**

Eleven closes her eyes.  Calming herself.  Then --

WHOOM!  She's suddenly lifted up and flipped and --

**INT. VOID**

WHOOM!  Eleven is suddenly back in the void.  She's RISING
back up off the ground.  *It's HER FALL IN REVERSE.*  As she
rises off the ground, she is once more bombarded with RAPID-
FIRE IMAGES FROM BILLY'S MEMORY.

THE BEACH -- THE BASEBALL GAME -- BILLY'S FATHER ATTACKING
HIS MOTHER -- THE CAR CRASH -- THE MEMORIES RACE PAST US
FASTER AND FASTER AS ELEVEN RISES HIGHER AND HIGHER --

ALMOST TO BILLY NOW -- AND --

WHOOM!  His hand clasps her arm again and --

**INT. CABIN - NIGHT**

WHOOM!  She yanks off her blindfold.  Back in the cabin.

*Fuck that was _intense_.*

Wait.  Something is wrong.

She looks around.  Her friends are gone.

The cabin is empty.  She stands, calls out:

> ELEVEN
> Mike??  Mike -- !!

> VOICE (O.S.)
> He can't hear you.

She turns with a start to find --

BILLY, emerging from the shadows behind her.  His face is
twisted with pulsing veins, his eyes black.

> BILLY
> You shouldn't have looked for me.  I
> see you now.  We *all* see you now.

Off Eleven, terrified, we CUT TO:

**EXT. HEATHER'S HOUSE - NIGHT**

A FAMILIAR RED DOOR opens as...

HEATHER and JANET exit their house.

**EXT. SUBURBAN NEIGHBORHOOD - NIGHT**

Heather and Janet walk down the middle of the street.

Around them, kids play with SPARKLERS, laughing, having fun.

**EXT. SUBURBAN BACKYARD - NIGHT**

BURGERS and HOTDOGS sizzle on an outdoor grill.

A FATHER, 40s, stares at the cooking meat, empty-eyed.  Then,
abruptly, he turns and walks away, passing by --

A SMALL 4th OF JULY PARTY, drinking beer.

> WIFE
> David, where are you going?  David?!

He doesn't answer.  Just keeps walking away.

The meat burns, hissing, spitting, *and* --

**EXT. SUBURBAN HOUSE - NIGHT**

A GROUP OF BOYS plays with fireworks in their backyard.

They start to set one off.  All watching excitedly.  Except
for one -- a YOUNG BOY.  He is walking away.  Eyes empty.

>                    FIREWORKS KID
>          ADAM!!!  You're going to miss it!
>          ADAM!!

He keeps walking away.  The fireworks shoot off behind him --

**INT. CABIN - NIGHT**

Billy steps toward Eleven.  Veins throbbing.  <u>A monster</u>.

>                    BILLY
>          You let us in.

**FLASHBACK TO**

Eleven opening the Gate in season one.

**BACK TO THE CABIN**

>                    BILLY (CONT'D)
>          Now.  You have to let us stay.

Eleven backpedals, scared --

>                    BILLY (CONT'D)
>          Don't you see now?  All this time.
>          We've been building it.
>               (beat)
>          Building it -- just for you.

**FLASHBACK TO**

THE RUSSIAN MACHINE BLASTS TO LIFE -- HITTING THE WALL --
OPENING A CRACK IN THE GATE --

THE FLAYER PARTICLES RISE INSIDE THE FACTORY --

THE RATS EXPLODE -- THIS TIME WE *HOLD LONGER* -- WATCH AS
THEIR FLESH MOVES, FORMING THE FIRST VERSION OF OUR MONSTER --

THE MONSTER SLAMS INTO BILLY'S CAMARO -- CAUSING THE CRASH --

BILLY IS YANKED DOWN INTO THE FACTORY BASEMENT -- A TENTACLE
SNARES HIS FACE --

FLAYED BILLY CHUGS POOL CHEMICALS IN THE POOL STORAGE ROOM --

FLAYED BILLY WATCHES ELEVEN WALK AWAY FROM HEATHER'S HOUSE --

BILLY GRABS HEATHER -- HEATHER FLAYS HER PARENTS --

TOM AND JANET SCREAM IN THE BASEMENT -- AND --

**BACK TO SCENE**

> BILLY (CONT'D)
> All that work.  All that pain.
> (beat)
> All for you.

**EXT. ABANDONED FACTORY - NIGHT**

Heather, Janet, and more Flayed walk toward the factory.

WE CUT HIGH OVERHEAD TO REVEAL: DOZENS MORE FLAYED walking toward the factory from all sides.  *It's just like the rats in the opening episode.*  As they stream into the factory...

**INT. CABIN - NIGHT**

Billy continues to walk toward Eleven.

> BILLY
> Now it's time.  Time to end it.

**INT. ABANDONED FACTORY - BASEMENT - NIGHT**

They walk down the steps into the basement.  Heather is in the lead.  As she nears the monster, her FLESH BEGINS TO *ROT*, SOFTEN, ERODE... MELT.  *Just like the rat.  Just like Bruce and Tom.*  As the flesh on her knees gives way, her melting body folds to the ground --

WHERE IT IS ABSORBED INTO THE BIG MONSTER.

THIS HAPPENS TO JANET.  THEN MRS. DRISCOLL.

THEN ANOTHER FLAYED.  ANOTHER.  ANOTHER.

ONE BY ONE -- THEY ARE SACRIFICING *THEMSELVES.*

WITH EACH ADDED BODY, THE MONSTER GROWS IN SIZE.

THE FLAYED MULTITUDE NOW BECOMING... *ONE.*

**INT. CABIN - NIGHT**

Eleven backpedals from Billy, terrified...

> BILLY
> We're going to end you.  And when
> you're gone, we're going to end all
> of your friends --

                         ELEVEN
          Get away --

                         BILLY
          We're going to end everyone --

                         ELEVEN
          GET AWAY -- !!!

Eleven SCREAMS, thrusts out her hand and --

WHOOM!  Billy *FLIES BACK* at rapid speed *and* --

**INT. CABIN - NIGHT**

WHOOM!  Eleven rips off her blindfold, gasping for air.

                         MIKE
          EL!!!

She's back in the cabin.  The REAL CABIN.

A terrified Mike holds her close --

                         MIKE (CONT'D)
          Are you okay???  Are you okay???

She is breathing hard, crying, both nostrils and ears
spilling blood.

                         MIKE (CONT'D)
          What happened??  What happened??

Off El's terrified look, not sure where to start, SMASH TO --

**INT. ABANDONED FACTORY - NIGHT**

The grate on the factory floor TREMBLES and SHAKES and GROANS
as the monster's growing flesh presses up against it.  This
thing is so large now that it can't fit in the basement --

The pressure becomes too great and --

BOOM!  The grate EXPLODES, metal SHREDS, CEMENT ERUPTS, *and* --

AN ENORMOUS, GNARLED, SLIMY LEG slams down onto the floor --

AND THEN ANOTHER LEG.  AND THEN *ANOTHER*.  And then ANOTHER --

Just as this HEAVING MONSTROSITY BEGINS TO HAUL ITSELF OUT OF
THE BASEMENT, we --

                    <u>END EPISODE</u>

# CHAPTER SEVEN:
## THE BITE

WRITTEN BY **THE DUFFER BROTHERS**

SCREAMING fills the soundscape.  It sounds horrific but --

**EXT. FAIRGROUNDS - NIGHT**

It's just A BUNCH OF HAPPY KIDS screaming their lungs out on
a BIG SWING RIDE, which is spinning through the night sky!

We're at Kline's July 4th Spectacular, now humming with light
and life!  A series of shots show Hawkins citizens having a
blast:

-- AN UNCLE SAM ON STILTS makes his way through the crowd,
excitedly waving an American flag.

-- KIDS play a dart game, popping balloons!

-- A FAMILY eats corn dogs together!

-- KIDS race into a FUNHOUSE!

-- Last but not least, we find THE HAWKINS HIGH SCHOOL
MARCHING BAND, dressed in cheesy patriotic outfits, playing
THE WASHINGTON POST MARCH.  The band finishes the song with a
sort of... pathetic flourish.  As a crowd politely applauds
their efforts --

MAYOR KLINE bounds onto the stage, his bruised face still
caked in makeup.  He leans into his best friend: *the
microphone.*

> MAYOR KLINE
> -- Now doesn't that just lift your
> spirits???  Let's give another big
> hand for the Hawkins High Marching
> Band!!!

The crowd applauds again, louder.  Mayor Kline beams, as if
this applause were actually *for him.*

> MAYOR KLINE (CONT'D)
> I hope you all are having a good time
> tonight?  Are you having a good
> time?!

More APPLAUSE, which carries...

**FIFTY YARDS ACROSS THE FAIRGROUNDS,**

... Where we find KAREN, TED, and HOLLY (holding cotton
candy) climbing into a Ferris wheel chair.  As CARNIE #1
slides a metal bar over their laps, Karen smiles at Holly --

> KAREN
> Uh oh, Dad can't get out now.

402

                    TED
          I don't know why you two enjoy
          torturing me --

                    KAREN
          Because it's *fun* --

                    HOLLY
          Yeah Dad because it's FUN.

CARNIE #2 pulls a lever.  Gears turn, the Ferris wheel jolts
to life and -- WHOOM!  It's suddenly moving, turning!

                    KAREN
          And here we goooo!!

                    TED
          Oh no --

As a petrified Ted watches the ground recede beneath him...

**WE RETURN TO THE PODIUM,**

                    MAYOR KLINE
          -- Okay, enough of me blabbering --
          who here wants to see some fireworks?
               (SOME CHEERING)
          Is that all you got?  WHO HERE WANTS
          TO SEE SOME FIREWORKS??!!

More ENTHUSIASTIC APPLAUSE this time, and THE HIGH SCHOOL
MARCHING BAND now begins to play the SEMPER FIDELIS MARCH.

**ON A FIELD BEHIND THE PODIUM,**

A MAN IN A HARD HAT takes this as his cue.  He lights the
first firework.  FWOOM!  It shoots up into the sky and then --

POP-BOOM!  A pinwheel of colored light erupts in the night
sky.  The crowd OOOHS and AWWWS and   --

**BACK AT THE FERRIS WHEEL**

Karen AWWWS too, smiles at Holly --

                    KAREN
          Wow!!  That was pretty, wasn't it???

                    HOLLY
          Yeah!!!

The carriage now comes to a rocking stop -- they're at the
tippy top of the Ferris wheel!

                    TED
Why are we stopping -- ??

                    KAREN
Because I slipped Jason a five --

                    TED
What -- ?

                    KAREN
Come on -- these are the best seats
in the house!!

                    HOLLY
The best seats in the house!

Ted closes his eyes as BOOM!  More fireworks go off over our
carnival.  It's a beautiful, even epic display --

Holly watches with wide eyes, loving the show, but then...

Beneath dazzling fireworks, she notices something:  THE TREES
ARE MOVING.  This isn't wind.  SOMETHING ALIVE AND UNDENIABLY
MASSIVE is making its way through the forest.

                    HOLLY (CONT'D)
... Mommy, the trees --

                    KAREN
What, baby?

                    HOLLY
The trees *are moving* --

                    KAREN
Why are you looking at the trees,
baby?  Look at the fireworks!  The
fireworks!

POP-BOOM!  Another firework goes off.  Karen applauds.

                    KAREN (CONT'D)
Oooh, that was a big one!!

Holly returns her gaze to the fireworks show.  As another
spectacular firework erupts in the sky, our camera SOARS
THROUGH THE AIR... MOVING THROUGH THE EXPLODING FIREWORKS...
toward those moving trees, which...

... Continue to shudder and *sway*.  Whatever this thing is,
it's moving fast -- AND IT'S FUCKING ENORMOUS!

As some birds scatter into the sky, SMASH TO --

**MAIN TITLES**

**EXT. CABIN - NIGHT**

Fireworks explode in the distance.  We're quite far from the
fair now.  We TILT DOWN to find Hopper's cabin.

> ELEVEN (PRE-LAP)
> He said... he was... building
> something.

**INT. CABIN - NIGHT**

CLOSE ON: ELEVEN.

> ELEVEN
> That it was all... *for me*.

WIDEN NOW TO REVEAL: MIKE, NANCY, JONATHAN, LUCAS, WILL, and
MAX, huddled around her.  A few minutes have passed since she
woke from her encounter with Billy -- and she's clearly still
recovering:  Her small, pale body is draped in a blanket.

> MAX
> ... "Building something" -- is he
> talking about the Flayed? --

> NANCY
> He must be.

> LUCAS
> So he's building an army just like we
> thought --

> MIKE
> Yeah except we were wrong about one
> thing:  He's not building this army
> to *spread* --

> WILL
> (picking up on this)
> He's building it to stop Eleven.

Everyone shares looks at this very unnerving notion --

> MIKE
> ... Last year, El closed the Gate on
> him -- when she did that, I have a
> feeling she pissed him off --

> LUCAS
> Yeah, like -- *royally*.

                         MIKE
          And the Mind Flayer now knows she's
          the only thing that can stop him.
          But if she's out of the way --

                         LUCAS
          Game over.

A beat as this sinks in.  Then --

                         ELEVEN
          He also said... he would kill all of
          you.

                         MAX
          Oh.  Well.  That's nice.

Nancy suddenly stands up -- alerted by something.

She walks away from the group, listens for a beat.

                         NANCY
          You guys hear that?

Everyone listens.

                         JONATHAN
          It's just the fireworks...

Nancy turns back to Eleven, sharply, realizing --

                         NANCY
          Billy -- when he told you all this,
          it was _here_, in _this room?_

FLASHCUT:  *Billy walks toward Eleven in the cabin.*

El nods, scared.  "Yes."  Shared looks.  And then --

Now we hear it too.  Beneath the fireworks: BOOM.  BOOM.
BOOM.  A HEAVY, DEEP SOUND.  UNDENIABLE NOW.  LIKE A _GODDAMN_
_T-REX_.

Will reaches up, touches his neck.  GOOSEBUMPS.

                         WILL
          *He knows we're here.*

**EXT. CABIN - PORCH - NIGHT**

The cabin door flies open as our gang races out.

**EXT. CABIN - DRIVEWAY - NIGHT**

They hurry out onto the gravel driveway, Nancy and Jonathan
in the lead.  They look up the long dirt road, eyes narrowed.

They hear the BOOMING sound.  It seems to be coming from
straight ahead.  But they see nothing but darkness.  *Wait --*

POP-CRACK-POOFF!  A COLORFUL EXPLOSION of fireworks suddenly
erupts, illuminates the sky.  And now we see it:

THE FINAL FORM OF OUR MONSTER.  IT IS HORRIBLE, A THIRTY-
FOOT, SPIDER-ESQUE LOVECRAFTIAN MONSTROSITY COMPOSED ENTIRELY
OF FLESH AND BONE.  WITH EACH HEAVING STEP FORWARD, IT SPRAYS
MUCUS, BLOOD, GORE ONTO THE GROUND.  AND WORST OF ALL...

IT'S STOMPING THIS WAY.  DOWN THE ROAD.  BLOCKING THEIR
ESCAPE.

We push past Nancy, and into a CLOSE-UP of terrified El as--

Our monster unleashes an epic ROAR as fireworks ERUPT behind
it and --

**INT./EXT. LYNX TRUCK - TUNNELS - NIGHT**

FWOOM!!  A LYNX MINI-TRUCK SUDDENLY SOARS OVER CAMERA, ENGINE
ROARING!  It rockets down the tunnel at warp speed!  We're
back underground!  And to our surprise --

DUSTIN is behind the wheel!  He's sweating, laser-focused,
driving like a madman!!!  ERICA sits passenger; STEVE and
ROBIN are in the enclosed cargo area, bouncing around.  They
are pale, sweaty.  The serum hasn't worn off yet...

Steve shouts through the metal partition --

>               STEVE
> Hey slow down up there, what's the
> rush?!

>               ROBIN
> Yeah what is this the Indy five
> hundred -- ??

>               STEVE
> *Three hundred* -- the Indy *three*
> hundred --

>               ROBIN
> It's FIVE HUNDRED --

>               STEVE
> THREE --

407

                          ROBIN
              ONE MILLION --

In the front, Dustin and Erica share horrified looks --

                          ERICA
              What is *wrong* with them?

                          DUSTIN
              <u>I don't know</u> --

Dustin tightens his grip on the steering wheel and --

**INT. UNDERGROUND RUSSIAN BASE - OUTSIDE THE ELEVATOR**

SCREECH!  The truck skids to a stop in front of the elevators
but --

Dustin put on those brakes just a little too late and --

BAM!  The truck collides with some barrels.

**INT. LYNX TRUCK - CONTINUOUS**

Dustin and Erica fly forward, caught by seatbelts, but --

Steve and Robin tumble like laundry in the back, heads
knocking against the walls.

                          DUSTIN
              -- Everyone okay back there??

GROANS in response.

                          DUSTIN (CONT'D)
              They're fine.

Dustin yanks off their seatbelts and --

**INT. UNDERGROUND RUSSIAN BASE - OUTSIDE THE ELEVATOR**

CHOOM!  Erica unlocks the back cargo area --

As Robin and Steve clamber out of the back, dazed and hurting
from the ride, OUR CAMERA SWEEPS OVER to find--

Dustin approaching the elevator doors, his keycard out.

                          DUSTIN
              Here goes nothing --

Dustin swipes the keycard through the control panel.

BEEP!  A light BLINKS GREEN and --

**INT. ELEVATOR SHAFT - NIGHT**

WHOOSH! Cables jerk and swing as the elevator shoots back up the shaft with a ROAR! As it zips past camera, CUT TO --

**INT. ELEVATOR**

The wall RUSHES past us. WIDEN OUT to find...

Steve standing on top of a DELIVERY BOX, waving his arms around as he tries to keep balance in the moving elevator --

                    STEVE
          Whooooaaa --

                    ROBIN
          You look like you're surfing -- !

Dustin and Erica stare at them.

                    ERICA
               (to Dustin)
          They seem *drunk* --

                    DUSTIN
          Why would they be drunk??

Robin pushes Steve and he falls to the ground.

                    ROBIN
               (laughing)
          WIPEOUT!!

Dustin crouches by Steve. Feels his clammy forehead.

                    DUSTIN
          He's burning up --

Dustin peels back Steve's eyelids, Steve slaps him away.

                    STEVE
          Ow!

Dustin looks back at Erica, worried --

                    DUSTIN
          His pupils are super dilated --

                    ERICA
          Maybe they're drugged -- ?

Dustin whips back to Steve, concerned --

                    DUSTIN
          Steve, are you drugged -- ?

                    STEVE
          How many times, Dad -- I don't do
          drugs -- ONLY MARIJUANA --

                    DUSTIN
          Steve this isn't funny.  I need to
          know what they did to you -- are you
          going to die on us or something?

                    ROBIN
          We all die, my strange little child
          friend, it's just a question of WHEN
          and HOW --

Dustin, realizing this is a losing battle, shifts his focus.

                    DUSTIN
          Okay, Steve, listen to me -- they're
          gonna be looking for us up there --
          where did you park your car -- ?

                    STEVE
          Can we make a pit stop at the food
          court first -- ?

                    ROBIN
          OH MY GOD I WANT A HOT DOG ON A
          STICK!

                    DUSTIN
               (ignoring her)
          Steve -- we'll get you both food, as
          much food as you want, but first --
          where's your car -- ?

                    STEVE
          The car's off the board man --

                    DUSTIN
          What -- ?

Steve pulls out both his pockets.  They're empty.

                    STEVE
          They took my keys, like, forever ago.
          Bummer, right?

Dustin shares a look with Erica.  Shit.  And --

                              410

**EXT. STARCOURT MALL - NIGHT**

DING!  The elevator door opens.  Scoops Troop is outside!

Robin and Steve stumble out, suck in the fresh air.

>                    ROBIN
>           Oh my God that tastes so good!  Steve
>           can you taste the air?!!!

>                    STEVE
>           Yes I taste it I taste it  --

Dustin's eyes shoot wide --

>                    DUSTIN
>           *SHIT.*

Up ahead: ARMED LYNX GUARDS.  RACING THEIR WAY.  SHOUTING.

>                    DUSTIN (CONT'D)
>           Come on -- !!!

Dustin grabs Steve, Erica grabs Robin, and suddenly --

The Scoops Troop is back on the run!

>                    STEVE
>           *Why are we running???  WHY ARE WE*
>           *RUNNING -- ????*

As Dustin FLINGS OPEN A DELIVERY DOOR, WE MATCH CUT TO --

**INT. HOPPER'S SHED - NIGHT**

WHOOM!  Nancy THROWING OPEN the door to Hopper's shed.

Her eyes scan the walls, lock onto a DOUBLE-BARRELED SHOTGUN.
She grabs it, starts shoving some shells into her pocket as --

**EXT. HOPPER'S SHED - NIGHT**

Jonathan strides over to a BIG ASS HUNTING AXE.  Its blade
stuck in a tree stump.  He puts a foot down on the tree, then
rips it out of the wood and --

**INT. CABIN - NIGHT**

WHOOM!  The cabin door flies open as our teens enter with
their new weapons.

Our camera swirls and finds our kids, who have smartly begun
to barricade the windows with furniture.

411

Will and Mike shove a bookshelf over a window, Lucas and Max work together to push a mattress over another window, and before long --

We can no longer see outside.  It's *Night of the Living Dead* in here.

                    NANCY
          Hey -- away from the windows -- away
          from the windows -- !

Everyone backs up into the middle of the cabin.

Jonathan raises his axe, Nancy her shotgun, as...

BOOM!  BOOM!  BOOM!  The sound of the monster's footsteps grows louder.  It is drawing closer.  BOOM.  *And closer.* BOOM.  *AND CLOSER.*  BOOM.

The entire cabin begins to shake.  KNICK-KNACKS fall from shelves...  A shadow sweeps across an upper window...  A light sways, begins to flicker.  The tension becomes almost unbearable, but then --

The BOOMING stops.  Silence.  Stillness.

                    MAX
          (low)
          ... Where'd it go...?

                    WILL
          (low)
          It's close...  I can hear it...

And sure enough we can hear it too: THE SOUND OF WET AND HEAVY GUTTURAL BREATHING.  *What the hell is it doing??*

Everyone looks around, uncertain, their eyes slowly moving from one wall to the next.  Nothing... nothing... *nothing* --

BOOM!  A LARGE CLAWED TENTACLE SUDDENLY EXPLODES THROUGH A WALL BEHIND THEM, SHOOTING AT THEM LIKE A NIGHTMARISH MISSILE!  IT SHATTERS FURNITURE IN ITS WAKE AND EVERYONE SCATTERS, SCREAMING, DODGING.  THAT IS, EVERYONE BUT --

JONATHAN.  He charges with his axe, swings, and --

*Connects.*  THUNK-SPLAT!  Black blood SPITS as the sharp axe blade buries into the twisted flesh of the tentacle as --

Jonathan tears the axe out, goes to swing again, but --

HISS!  The tentacle lashes out like a striking snake and --

BAM!  Knocks Jonathan backward, sending his axe --

Scattering into the kitchen.  Jonathan is screwed but then --

BANG!  BANG!  BANG!  Nancy opens fire!  Shotgun shells tear
into its skin.  The tentacle snaps toward her, furious, and --

CLICK!  Nancy is out of ammo.  Shit!  She staggers back
against the wall as the tentacle opens its nasty maw, then
lunges for her in anger, a row of NASTY SHARP TEETH coming
straight for her like daggers, when --

The tentacle suddenly freezes mid-air.  The tentacle twists
and shrieks, then begins to suck back away from Nancy,
further and further, until we reveal --

Eleven, holding out her hand.  She's SNARED this awful thing
with her psychic powers!!!  She flings her arm and twists her
wrist sharply, and --

KA-SPLAT!  One half of the tentacle RIPS OFF, dropping to the
floor like an amputated arm, shrieking in pain and spitting
black blood.  The other severed portion SUCKS back out of the
cabin as --

                    MAX
          -- Holy shi --

BAM!  Another ENORMOUS TENTACLE suddenly punches through a
barricaded window.  Eleven is ready --

She whirls fast and SNARES IT WITH HER POWERS but then --

BAM!  ANOTHER TENTACLE BLASTS THROUGH THE OTHER WALL --

Eleven catches that with her other hand!

WIDEN TO REVEAL:  ELEVEN HAS BOTH ARMS OUTSTRETCHED, HOLDING
BOTH TENTACLES WITH HER POWERS LIKE A BADASS.

She SCREAMS and flings both arms up the same time and --

SPLAT-WHAM!!  Both tentacles RIP apart simultaneously in A
SPRAY OF BLACK BLOOD.  But just as this happens --

BOOM!  THE BIGGEST TENTACLE YET BLOWS THROUGH THE ROOF OF THE
CABIN BEHIND ELEVEN, EXPLODING THROUGH THE RAFTERS, RIPPING
OPEN A GIANT HOLE, SENDING WOOD SHRAPNEL FLYING.

Eleven looks up, sees the tentacle coming for her, but she's
not fast enough this time and --

THWACK!  THE GIANT TENTACLE SNARES HER RIGHT LEG!!

Eleven SCREAMS as its SHARP BONE TEETH CLAMP DOWN ON HER LEG and <u>PULL</u> --

WHAM!  Eleven flips face first onto the ground.  She ricochets off the ground, then --

WHOOSH!  She is pulled backward and sucked up into the air!

> MIKE
> *EL -- !!!*

Mike lunges out and grabs her hand at the last second!!!  But this thing is pulling El with so much force that Mike can't hold her... *his hand slipping from hers...* but then --

Max rushes in, grabs Eleven's other hand, holding her too!

Then Jonathan and Will race in -- joining!!

> MIKE (CONT'D)
> *HOLD ON!!*

But this monster won't let go.  Dragging Eleven toward...

Its DISGUSTING HEAD, which is now visible for the first time through the blown hole in the ceiling.  Its mouth opens wide, revealing a row OF GNARLED RAZOR SHARP BONE TEETH.  IT'S LIKE THE SARLACC PIT IN RETURN OF THE JEDI!

ITS HEAD BENDS TOWARD US, *COMING TO DEVOUR ELEVEN*, WHEN --

BANG!  A shotgun shell suddenly blows through its ugly face. It's --

<u>Nancy</u>, reloaded now, opening fire on this nasty brute.  She fires again -- BANG!  The monster recoils, SHRIEKS, temporarily delayed, as --

Lucas spots the FALLEN AXE, handle jutting out beneath some fallen furniture.  He races over and snatches it up, as --

The others pull Eleven closer to the ground, away from the monster, but that tentacle remains clamped tight onto her leg.  This thing is like a dog with a fucking bone.  Blood is spilling out now from either side of the "clamp."

Eleven SCREAMS in pain.  And --

> LUCAS
> AHHHH!!!!

WHAM!  Lucas charges forward with the axe, leaps onto the coffee table, and swings away at the tentacle.

THWACK-SPLAT! The axe buries itself into the flesh. Sprays black blood! But this fucking thing STILL doesn't let go of Eleven. Lucas yanks the axe back out of the flesh and --

WHAM! Swings again. THWACK! And again. THWACK! And again. THWACK! Hacking at it over and over, tearing into this fucker with everything he's got, black blood spraying back onto his face, until --

SPLAT! The tentacle _finally_ TEARS IN HALF --

As the severed tentacle slurps back up through the roof and back into the mouth of its master --

WHOOM! Eleven drops to the ground. _Finally free._

                    MIKE
          EL -- !!

Mike RIPS the small piece of tentacle off her leg, tosses it. It slithers away like a snake, fleeing from our kids, as...

Eleven climbs back to her feet. Blood streams from her leg, but she fights through the pain, and...

She looks up at this monster that hurt her. And then, in a display of rage that we've rarely seen from her, she thrusts out both hands and SCREAMS AT THE TOP OF HER LUNGS and --

BOOM! A WAVE OF POWERFUL PSYCHIC ENERGY RIPPLES UP THROUGH THE CABIN AND TEARS THROUGH THE ROOF, RIPPING MOST OF THE ROOF APART, AND --

BOOOM!! IT BLOWS A FUCKING HOLE THROUGH THIS LOVECRAFTIAN SPIDER'S UGLY HEAD, LITERALLY SPLITTING ITS HEAD IN HALF!!!

THE MONSTER SCREAMS, IN _TRUE AGONY_ THIS TIME, THEN REELS BACK FROM THE HOLE IN THE CABIN ROOF, _RETREATING FROM VIEW_.

Everyone shares looks. Holy. Shit! Then --

Eleven weakens. Her knees buckle, and she starts to fall but --

Mike catches her in his arms.

                    MIKE (CONT'D)
          El -- _EL!!_

She doesn't look good. Pale, weak, eyes fluttering.

                    NANCY
          GO GO GO GO -- WE _HAVE TO GO_ -- !!!

Jonathan helps Mike with Eleven and --

**EXT. CABIN - DRIVEWAY - NIGHT**

The gang piles into the Wheeler station wagon --

**INT./EXT. STATION WAGON - NIGHT**

A frightened Mike cradles a wounded Eleven in the way back.

> MIKE
> Hold on, *just hold on* -- !!

VROOM!  Nancy turns the key and hammers the accelerator --

As the car rockets away, *escaping*, we TILT UP to find --

The injured monster, FLAILING ABOVE THE CABIN, its fleshy tentacles thrashing wildly in front of a full moon.

Just as its SHRIEK becomes too SHRILL to bear, WE SMASH TO --

**INT. STARCOURT MALL - DELIVERY CORRIDOR - NIGHT**

WHOOSH!  THE LYNX SECURITY sweeping through the back corridors of the mall, searching for the Scoops Troop, who --

**INT. BACK SERVICE CORRIDOR - MOMENTS LATER**

Are further down the corridor.  Dustin and Erica are dragging the drugged Steve and Robin, moving as fast as they can --

> ERICA
> Where are we going???

> DUSTIN
> *Just trust me* --

**INT. STARCOURT MOVIE THEATER - LOBBY**

A door opens as Dustin pokes his head out.

> DUSTIN
> All clear --

He hurries forward, leading the others into the <u>MOVIE THEATER</u>!!  It's like the start of our season -- only now the theater is playing *BACK TO THE FUTURE*!!!  It's opening night!!!

We PRE-LAP the SOUND OF A ROARING ENGINE, then CUT INSIDE as --

**INT. STARCOURT MOVIE THEATER - AUDITORIUM**

*ON SCREEN: THE SPEEDING DELOREAN VANISHES IN A BURST OF BLUE LIGHT!!! AS DOC BROWN HOPS AROUND TO THE TUNE OF SILVESTRI'S ICONIC SCORE, SCREAMING ABOUT "88 MILES PER HOUR" --*

Dustin and the others hurry down the aisle. The place is jam-packed, but thankfully there are a few open seats in the front! Dustin and Erica shove the teens into seats --

>                    ROBIN
>          Oh no no no this is WAY too close --

>                    STEVE
>          Yeah dude these seats BLOW --

>                    DUSTIN
>          Then don't watch the movie --

>                    ROBIN
>          But we want to watch --

>                    DUSTIN
>          Then watch it!!

>                    ANGRY MOVIEGOER #1
>          SHHH!!

>                    DUSTIN
>          Sorry!

Dustin leans in to Steve and Robin, whispers firmly:

>                    DUSTIN (CONT'D)
>          Whatever you do -- don't move. *Got
>          it?*

>                    STEVE
>          Yes, DAD.

Robin giggles at this. Dustin seethes. And --

**MOMENTS LATER**

WHOOM! An exhausted Dustin and Erica drop down into seats on the opposite side of the front row.

>                    DUSTIN
>          Okay it's official, I'm never having
>          kids --

>                    ERICA
>          What are we *doing here*?

                    DUSTIN
               (obviously)
          Laying low, cooling off, like
          Oswald --

                    ERICA
          Oswald was _found_ in the theater and
          _shot to death_ --

                    DUSTIN
          That was _Lincoln._  Guess your
          history's not as good as your math --

                    ERICA
          Oswald was arrested in a theater and
          _shot by Jack Ruby_ --

                    DUSTIN
          Yeah a week later --

                    ERICA
          The point is his plan _didn't work_ --

                    DUSTIN
          Only because it was a set up.

                    ERICA
          Sorry -- ?

                    DUSTIN
          He was just a patsy --

                    ERICA
          I _seriously_ hope you're joking --

                    ANGRY MOVIEGOER #2
          SHHHH!!!

Our kids look back at the irritated moviegoer behind them --

                    DUSTIN/ERICA
          SORRY!

Erica turns back to Dustin, whispers urgently.

                    ERICA
          We need to get OUT of here.

Dustin takes this in.  _Knows she's right._

                    DUSTIN
          Okay... just -- watch Tweedledee and
          Tweedledum, make sure they don't go
          anywhere --

                              418

Dustin climbs up out of his seat --

                    ERICA
          What are you going???

                    DUSTIN
          To get us a ride.

Before Erica can say more, Dustin scurries back up the aisle.

ALAN SILVESTRI'S ICONIC SCORE builds and crashes out and --

**EXT. COUNTRY ROAD**

VROOOM!  The TODDFATHER CONVERTIBLE TEARS down the road --

**INT. CONVERTIBLE**

We're back with our adults.  About damn time!  HOPPER is
behind the wheel, JOYCE passenger, MURRAY and ALEXEI in the
back, going over Alexei's COMPLEX DRAWING of the Russian
base.

                    HOPPER
          -- What's he saying?

                    MURRAY
          ... He's, uh, showing me the location
          of the key, to turn off the machine --

Alexei says something --

                    MURRAY (CONT'D)
          Sorry -- *keys*.  Two keys.

                    HOPPER
          Two-man rule.

                    JOYCE
          Two-man rule -- ?

                    HOPPER
          You've gotta have two men, two keys.
          Like a nuclear launch --

                    MURRAY
              (translating)
          But to, uh, retrieve the keys, there
          is a vault, and to open this vault,
          you must enter, uh... Planck's...
          Constant --

                    HOPPER
          Plank's *what?*

                    MURRAY
Planck's *Constant* --
    (condescending)
It's a very famous number --

                    JOYCE
So we get these keys, then we can
turn off this machine --

                    MURRAY
That's what he says --

                    JOYCE
That's not so bad.  We can do that --

                    HOPPER
"We" can do that?  Joyce -- you do
remember what he said about this base
being impenetrable right -- ?

                    JOYCE
There has to be a way in --

                    HOPPER
Yeah.  Our *military* --

                    JOYCE
Who are coming --

                    HOPPER
No, we don't know that.  You yelled
at them like you were in some parent
teacher conference and then hung up.
Now we don't know what the hell is
going on because we're -- wait, what
are we doing again?  Oh yeah, that's
right, we're going to rescue our kids
from... the big bad Fourth of July
festivities -- !

                    JOYCE
If you don't want to come, turn the
car around -- but drop me off first --

                    HOPPER
Yeah?  You gonna walk to Hawkins -- ?

                    JOYCE
If it gets me away from you, I'll do
just about ANYTHING --

                    MURRAY
Children, children, *CHILDREN*!


                        420

Murray leans his head down into the front seat, right between
Hopper and Joyce.

                    MURRAY (CONT'D)
          This *interminable bickering* was
          amusing at first but it's getting
          very stale and we've still got a long
          drive ahead of us -- so why don't you
          two *cut the horse shit* and get to the
          part where you two admit your sexual
          feelings for one another --

                    HOPPER
          Hey -- !

                    JOYCE
          What is *wrong with you* -- !

                    MURRAY
          Oh, spare me!

Murray leans his bearded face further into the front seat,
swivels to face Joyce, talking fast:

                    MURRAY (CONT'D)
          Yes yes, he's a brute, I know,
          probably reminds you of a bad
          relationship and gosh you'd really
          like a nice man to settle down with --
          but admit it, you're *real curious* to
          know what he's like in the sack --

Before a slack-jawed Joyce can respond --

Murray swivels to Hopper!

                    MURRAY (CONT'D)
          And YOU!  HA!  Well, you're just a
          big man baby who'd rather act tough
          than show his true feelings, because
          the last time you opened your heart
          you got hurt -- *OWIE.*

Murray leans back a bit, once more addressing them both:

                    MURRAY (CONT'D)
          And now, rather than admit these
          feelings, you're dancing around one
          another with this mind-numbing and
          frankly boorish mating ritual.  So
          please, for my sake, either quit your
          bickering, or pull over, tear off
          those clothes, and GET IT OVER WITH
          ALREADY!!!!

Hopper and Joyce stare.  Too stunned to respond.

Murray leans back into his seat.  Proud.

                    ALEXEI
          <What was that?>

                    MURRAY
          <I told them they should have sex.>

                    ALEXEI
               (stunned)
          <They have not had sex?!>

Murray shakes his head and Alexei GUFFAWS as --

Hopper and Joyce remain silent in the front seat  -- stewing,
bright red, wide-eyed, trying to not look at one another,
as --

**EXT. COUNTRY ROAD - NIGHT**

WHOOSH!  The convertible speeds past a sign that reads --

WELCOME TO INDIANA!  And right here we SMASH TO:

**EXT. BIG BUY - NIGHT**

SCREECH!  The Station Wagon swerves into --

Bradley's Big Buy.  This is the grocery store where El stole
the Eggos in season one!  It's closed early because of the
holiday, the parking lot a graveyard.  The car slams to a
stop right by the doors as if this were an emergency room and
then --

**INT. BIG BUY - MOMENTS LATER**

BOOM!  A ROCK flies through the glass window, shattering it!

Our gang hurry through the broken doorway into the store.
Nancy and Jonathan are in the lead, while Mike and Max help
the weak Eleven, still hobbling from her injury.

**INT. BIG BUY - MEDICAL AISLE - NIGHT**

CLOSE ON:  A hand frantically sweeps across a shelf as --

Nancy grabs some RUBBING ALCOHOL, GAUZE, COTTON.

She turns back to the others --

                    NANCY
          Okay, sit her down, sit her down --

Mike and Max help Eleven to the ground.

Nancy crouches beside her --

                    NANCY (CONT'D)
          Let me see --

Mike rolls up El's right pants leg to reveal THE BITE.  And
it's... not good.  SIX DEEP PUNCTURE MARKS IN HER CALF.
LOOKS LIKE A _REALLY_ BAD DOG BITE.  *OOZING BLOOD.*

                    LUCAS
          *Gross.*

Max shoots Lucas a look.  _No._  Nancy dabs a piece of cloth
with alcohol, and goes to clean the wound, but --

Max's hand grabs her wrist, stopping her.

                    MAX
          What are you doing -- ?

                    NANCY
          Cleaning it --

                    MAX
          No -- we need to stop the bleeding
          first, then clean, then disinfect --
          then bandage.
               (everyone looks at Max,
                surprised)
          I skateboard.  *Trust me.*

Max grabs the gauze pads from Nancy and starts to place them
over the wound -- *she's taking over this operation.*

                    MAX (CONT'D)
               (to Mike)
          Hold this -- keep the pressure on it,
          nice and firm, okay?

Mike nods.  Presses down on the bandage.  Max now turns to
the teens --

                    MAX (CONT'D)
          We're going to need some water, soap.

As Jonathan and Nancy nod, head off for the supplies --

Lucas empties out the contents of his backpack.  A bunch of
ridiculous supplies fall out onto the floor --

                    LUCAS
          Does any of this help?

Max stares at the supplies, then --

                         MAX
              No.  Go get me a washcloth and a
              bowl.

                         LUCAS
              A bowl?  Why a bowl -- ?

                         MAX
              *Lucas*.

Lucas salutes, *yes ma'am*, then hurries off with Will, as --

**DOWN ANOTHER AISLE,**

Nancy and Jonathan hunt for water, talking as they move --

                         NANCY
              -- What did that thing look like to
              you?

                         JONATHAN
              ... Like that thing in the hospital,
              only bigger --

                         NANCY
              A *lot* bigger.  Tom and Bruce -- they
              merged, became one, right?  And
              Driscoll said she needed to go back
              to the Source --

Jonathan takes this in -- *holy shit*.

                         JONATHAN
              You think... *Driscoll's* in there -- ?

                         NANCY
              Maybe.  And maybe Heather, Tom, Janet
              too -- God know who else.

Jonathan stares.  This is making him sick.

                         NANCY (CONT'D)
              I don't know how the hell we're going
              to kill it, but if we do --

                         JONATHAN
              We kill all the Flayed --

                         NANCY
              And we end this.  *Maybe*.
                   (beat)
              All I know for sure is:  We need El.

424

Nancy grabs a JUG OF WATER off the shelf, Jonathan grabs
another, and --

**DOWN ANOTHER AISLE - CONTINUOUS**

We now turn our attention to Lucas and Will.  Will is
carrying a washcloth over his shoulder, but they look very
lost as they search for their *bowl*... in the *cereal aisle*.

> LUCAS
> Bowl bowl bowl -- why wouldn't it be
> with the cereal??

> WILL
> (equally confused)
> I don't know.

> LUCAS
> What else do you use a bowl for?

> WILL
> I... don't know.

Suddenly Lucas freezes.  He's spotted something else --
something MUCH more exciting than a bowl...

> LUCAS
> *Oh shit...*

REVERSE TO REVEAL: A MASSIVE JULY 4TH FIREWORKS DISPLAY.

**MOMENTS LATER**

Lucas excitedly heads over to the fireworks display, grabs a
BIG RED ROCKET, and turns back to Will, excited --

> LUCAS
> "Satan's Baby."  You ever shoot one
> of these suckers -- ?

> WILL
> No, is it sweet -- ?

> LUCAS
> That's an *understatement* --

> MAX (O.S.)
> That *doesn't* look like a bowl --

The boys swivel to find Max stomping toward them.  *Caught.*

> LUCAS
> Nah.  It's way *better*.

425

Lucas tosses the rocket to Max, who catches it.

> LUCAS (CONT'D)
> There's a reason that warning label
> says eighteen or older.  This sucker
> is filled with a hundred and fifty
> grams of _black powder_.  AKA
> _gunpowder_.  Strap two of these
> together, it's bigger than an M-80.
> Five of 'em, we've got ourselves a
> stick of dynamite --

> MAX
> You want to kill that thing with
> _fireworks_??

> LUCAS
> You got a better idea?

> MAX
> Uh yeah -- _Eleven_.

> LUCAS
> Against _that_ thing -- she's gonna
> need back-up.

Lucas turns around, starts to grab up some more rockets into
his arms.  Max sighs.  Heads off to find the damn bowl
herself.

**INT. BIG BUY - MEDICAL AISLE**

We DRIFT DOWN the medical aisle, where Mike tends to Eleven.

> MIKE
> Does it _hurt_?

> ELEVEN
> Not... bad.

> MIKE
> I bet it's gonna leave an awesome
> scar.  You'll be even more badass --

> ELEVEN
> Bitchin'.

> MIKE
> Yeah.  _Bitchin'_.

They share smiles.  Then...

> MIKE (CONT'D)
> El...

                    ELEVEN
          Yes?

                    MIKE
          There's something... I've been
          meaning to tell you...

Their eyes lock.  Their breath catches.

                    MIKE (CONT'D)
          It's just... all this... being broken
          up stuff.  It's been hard...

A BURST OF STATIC interrupts --

Mike ignores it.  Tries to focus on the talk.

                    MIKE (CONT'D)
          ... But I'm glad you and Max are
          friends now.  And... I was just
          jealous at first.  And angry.  Which
          is why I said those stupid things.
          It's like -- I only wanted you for
          myself.  And I realize now -- how
          unfair that was.  And selfish.  And --
          I'm sorry.
          But... it's only because I -- I've
          never felt like this about anyone
          before... I mean... they do say it
          makes you crazy --

                    ELEVEN
          What... makes you crazy?

Mike hesitates.

                    MIKE
          You don't know that phrase?  *Blank*
          makes you crazy?

El stares.

                    ELEVEN
          Girlfriends?

                    MIKE
          No, no, not girlfriends --

                    ELEVEN
          Boyfriends?

Mike grows increasingly flustered:

                    MIKE
          No -- it's -- it's.  It's just... I
          think -- no, I know, I know that I --

Another BURST OF THAT STATIC, harder to ignore this time.
Mike turns, annoyed.  Whatever it is, it's coming from
Lucas's supply pile.  Mike's irritation turns to shock
because --

Now he hears a voice too.  A _familiar voice_.

                    DUSTIN (O.S.)
                 (filtered, static-y)
          C -- de red -- do you -- copy -- THIS
          IS A -- CO--- DE R----ED --

Mike and Eleven share stunned looks.  Is _that_...???

Mike crawls over on all fours, grabs out of the pile --
LUCAS'S SUPERCOMM!

                    MIKE
          DUSTIN??

**INT. MOVIE THEATER - PROJECTION BOOTH - NIGHT - INTERCUT**

HOLY HELL -- IT _IS_ DUSTIN!!!  He's in the projection booth
above the theater.

Dustin's eyes shoot wide -- HE REACHED SOMEONE!!

                    DUSTIN
          MIKE -- ???

                    MIKE
          DUSTIN???!

                    DUSTIN
          MIKE!!!

**INT. BIG BUY - MEDICAL AISLE - NIGHT**

Eleven scoots over to Mike, listening wide-eyed now too as --

                    DUSTIN (O.S.)
          OH MY GOD -- OH MY GOD -- listen to
          me, Mike, LISTEN --

**INT. MOVIE THEATER - PROJECTION BOOTH - NIGHT - INTERCUT**

>                     DUSTIN
>           -- I know I've been MIA -- but it's
>           not because I'm mad at you -- I mean,
>           I actually was mad, but also I've
>           been trapped underground in a *secret
>           Russian base.* I know that sounds
>           insane but the Russians have
>           *infiltrated* Hawkins -- the GODDAMN
>           RUSSIANS Mike -- and they have built
>           this giant weapon powered by
>           Promethium --

**BACK IN THE BIG BUY**

But Mike is having trouble hearing Dustin. His voice cutting
in and out, overwhelmed by static --

>                     MIKE
>           Dustin, *slow down*, I can't understand
>           you -- !

>                     DUSTIN (V.O.)
>           They're us--ing -- to -- ope--
>           t--he --
>                (static)
>           -- the G--ate --

>                     MIKE
>           Dustin -- you're cutting out --
>           Dustin -- !

**INT. STARCOURT MOVIE THEATER - PROJECTION BOOTH - NIGHT**

>                     DUSTIN
>           -- And now they're after us but we
>           don't have a way out of here -- so I
>           need you to come get us -- can you
>           get Nancy to drive?? We'll meet you
>           behind the theater --

**INT. BIG BUY - NIGHT**

Mike smacks the side of the supercomm. *What the hell?!*

>                     MIKE
>           DUSTIN??? ARE YOU THERE?? *DUSTIN??*

**INT. STARCOURT MOVIE THEATER - PROJECTION BOOTH - NIGHT**

Dustin isn't hearing anything anymore either --

                    DUSTIN
          Mike, do you copy??   Mike?!   MIKE!

Dustin looks down at his walkie.  A light is BLINKING RED.

Above the light, it reads: LOW BATTERY.

                    DUSTIN (CONT'D)
          Oh come on, NOT NOW NOT NOWWWW!!!

**INT. BIG BUY - MEDICAL AISLE - NIGHT**

                    MIKE
          Dustin, are you there?  DUSTIN???

Nancy and Jonathan walk back in with their water, only to
freeze at the sight of Mike's and El's panicked faces.

*Something's wrong.*

                    NANCY
          ... What is it?

Off Mike, CUT TO --

**INT. STARCOURT MOVIE THEATER - NIGHT**

WHOMP!  A red-faced Dustin racing back into the movie
theater.

He drops down beside Erica, urgent --

                    DUSTIN
          Do you have batteries, double A -- ??

                    ERICA
          *Why* would I have batteries-- ?

                    DUSTIN
          I *always* carry batteries --

                    ERICA
          Then what's the problem -- ??

                    DUSTIN
          I need eight --

                    ERICA
          *EIGHT* -- ?

                    DUSTIN
          It's *fine*, we'll just move to plan
          B --

                         ERICA
          Plan B?   What's *plan B* -- ??

Dustin is about to explain when his eyes go wide --

                         DUSTIN
          Where are they???

Erica looks and our CAMERA WHIPS OVER TO REVEAL --

Robin and Steve's seats are <u>NOW EMPTY</u>.

Off Erica, eyes shooting wide, SMASH TO --

**INT. STARCOURT MALL - OUTSIDE THEATER - UPSTAIRS - NIGHT**

Steve! He's *fine*. At least for now. He's currently
drinking from a water fountain on the second floor of the
mall, slurping that $H_2O$ up like he's been lost in the
desert --

                         STEVE
          *Oh my God oh my God* this is heaven --

                         ROBIN
          So I wasn't super focused in there,
          but like that mom totally wanted to
          bang her kid right -- ??

                         STEVE
          Wait, that hot chick was *Alex P.*
          *Keaton's mom* -- ?

                         ROBIN
          YEAH I'M *PRETTY SURE* --

                         STEVE
          But she's like *the same age* --

                         ROBIN
          HE WENT *BACK IN TIME* --

                         STEVE
          But then why is it called *Back to the*
          *FUTURE* -- ??

                         ROBIN
          Because he needs to get back to the
          future -- but he's back in time so
          the future is actually *the present*
          which is *his time* --

                         STEVE
            WWHAAAAT -- ??

                         ROBIN
            Okay you've had enough, my turn, MY
            TURN --!

Robin elbows Steve out of the way, starts to gulp water.

As a temporarily sated Steve wipes water from his mouth, he
looks up, and... his eyes grow wide.  We think for a second
that he's seen something important, but then we CUT TO --

STEVE'S POV:  He's staring at the glass ceiling above them...
watching as those hexagonal shapes on the ceiling move and
swirl around in a beautiful pattern, *Beautiful Mind-style.*

                         STEVE
            Hey -- Robin, Robin... check out the
            ceiling!

Robin wipes some water from her mouth, steps up to Steve and
looks up at the ceiling.  She sees swirling shapes too.

                         ROBIN
            Oh *wowwww...*

The patterns begin to move in a dizzying speed, whirling
around like the Gravitron, faster and faster and --

Our teen's expressions morph from awe to horror *and* --

**INT. STARCOURT MALL - BATHROOM**

WHOOM!  A green-faced Steve and Robin suddenly explode into a
men's bathroom.  They shove their way into --

**SIDE-BY-SIDE BATHROOM STALLS**

As they bend over toilets and begin to PUKE, WE SMASH TO --

**EXT. FAIRGROUNDS - NIGHT**

WHOOSH!  A carnival ride SWOOPING through the air, children
SQUEALING.  WE'RE BACK AT THE FAIR!!!  WE CRANE DOWN TO --

**THE PARKING LOT AS...**

The convertible pulls into view.  Our adults have arrived!

Hopper parks the convertible, kicks off the engine.  As
Joyce climbs out of the car, Hopper turns back to Murray,
*firm* --

                          HOPPER
          Stay here, go over the plans with
          Smirnoff --


                          MURRAY
          I can help look --


                          HOPPER
          No you'll scare the children --


                          MURRAY
          Jim, if this is about earlier --


                          HOPPER
          Stay put, *Freud*.


Hopper exits the convertible, not in the mood to chat.

Murray watches Hopper and Joyce go, SIGHING like a kid in
timeout, and --


**EXT. FAIRGROUNDS - NIGHT**

Hopper and Joyce wade their way through the crowd.  They scan
for our kids, but there are way too many people here.


                          HOPPER
          ... Say what you will about Larry,
          the man knows how to throw a party.


Joyce doesn't respond, focused on the search --


                          HOPPER (CONT'D)
          Sorry about... him by the way.


                          JOYCE
          Larry -- ?


                          HOPPER
          Murray.  He's a sick man and he
          enjoys getting under people's skin.
          So let's not let it -- *him* -- get
          under our skin, I mean --


                          JOYCE
          I didn't -- I *haven't* --


                          HOPPER
          Yeah okay.  Sure.  You're just...
          quieter than normal, that's all.


                          JOYCE
          I just want to find our kids.

Joyce picks up her pace, moving from Hopper into the crowd. Hopper sighs, pushes after her, hurrying right past --

A PORTA-POTTY just as the door swings open and --

Mayor Kline steps out.  He's rubbing his nose, sniffing. Seems like he's had some *fun* in there.  But then his face goes a shade paler as he spots --

THE BACK OF HOPPER AND JOYCE, threading through the crowd.

We PUSH IN on Kline and then HARD CUT TO --

**EXT. FAIRGROUNDS - ENTRANCE - NIGHT**

FEET FLYING across grass --

Kline sprints through the crowd.  He shoves a TEENAGER out of the way.  The teen flips him off.

> TEENAGER
> Happy fourth *DICK!*

**EXT. FAIRGROUNDS - PARKING LOT - NIGHT**

Kline *hauls ass* to his TACKY CAR, which is parked near the front.  *VIP.*

**INT./EXT. LARRY'S CAR - NIGHT**

Kline leaps into the car, turns on the ignition with shaking hands.  But he doesn't drive away.  *Nope.*  Instead --

He grabs up a MOTOROLA CAR PHONE.  Looks like a fucking brick.

He dials a number.  It RINGS on the other end.  And RINGS.

> MAYOR KLINE
> Come on -- PICK UP PICK UP PICK UP
> PICK UP YOU COMMIE BASTARDS!!!

As the phone continues to ring, SMASH TO --

**EXT. BIG BUY - NIGHT**

Quiet outside the Big Buy.

**INT. BIG BUY - NIGHT**

CLOSE ON: Eggo boxes.  A LOT of Eggo boxes.

We PULL AWAY to reveal we're in the freezer section of the store.  The freezer door is wide open.

434

In fact, as we continue to pull away, we reveal that ALL OF THE FRIDGE DOORS ARE OPEN, sending out a RELAXING HUMMING SOUND to --

Eleven, who sits cross-legged before them.  Her wound is now patched up and she wears an <u>AMERICAN FLAG AS A BLINDFOLD</u>.

The others surround her, leaning against various produce stands, etc.  Waiting quietly.  That is, everyone save for --

Lucas.  He pops open a CAN OF NEW COKE.  PFFF-HISSS!

Max shoots him a look --

> MAX
> (whisper)
> Quiet.

> LUCAS
> (whisper)
> Sorry...

Lucas begins to *quietly* slurp the soda.

> MIKE
> (whisper)
> How do you even drink that -- ?

> LUCAS
> (whisper)
> Because... it's delicious -- ?

> MIKE/MAX/NANCY
> (whisper)
> What?

> LUCAS
> (whisper)
> You all heard me.  It's like
> Carpenter's *The Thing*.  The original
> is a classic, no question about it.
> But the remake...
> (takes a sip)
> Sweeter, bolder, *better* --

> MIKE
> You're *INSANE* --

> LUCAS
> So you prefer the original *Thing*?

> MIKE
> We're not talking about *The Thing*
> we're talking about New Coke --

                         LUCAS
          Same concept dude --

                         MIKE
          It's not the same concept *at all* --

                         LUCAS
          YES IT IS --

                         MIKE
          NO IT'S NOT  --!!

                         LUCAS
          YES *IT IS* -- !

                              ELEVEN
          HEY!

An irritated Eleven yanks down her blindfold.

She shoots daggers at Mike and Lucas.

                    MIKE/LUCAS
          Sorry.

A beat.  Then...

                         MIKE
          Did you... *find him?*

Off Eleven, irritated, SMASH TO --

**EXT. BIG BUY - PARKING LOT**

WHOOSH!  A busted shopping cart wheel TWIRLS across tile as --

Lucas pushes a cart through the front of the store.

                         LUCAS
          -- The movies?!

We WIDEN to reveal that his shopping cart carries about a
HALF DOZEN DOLE BANANA BOXES, each packed with FIREWORK
BOMBS.  Lucas and Max and Will have lassoed those rockets
together with cotton twine from the butcher shop.

                    LUCAS (CONT'D)
          Dustin's so freaked about the Gate he
          decides to go watch a movie, yeah,
          makes *total sense* --

                              MAX
                         (to El)
                    You're POSITIVE he said "Gate," not
                    "great"?

                              WILL
                    Yeah -- like, "This movie I'm
                    watching is great"?

                              ELEVEN
                    It sounded like... *Gate* --

                              MIKE
                    Which would explain how the Mind
                    Flayer's still alive --

                              NANCY
                    We just have to shut it again --

                              WILL
                    And <u>the monster dies</u>.

                              MAX
                    But if not, we always have Lucas's
                    fireworks --

                              LUCAS
                    Keep on mocking my plan, *keep on
                    mocking...*

As Lucas pushes the shopping cart through the broken door...

OUR CAMERA SLOWLY DROPS DOWN TO REVEAL...

SOME BLOOD FROM ELEVEN, on the floor in the medical aisle
next to the boxes of gauze and Neosporin.  There's a bit of a
SICKLY YELLOW COLOR floating about in all that redness...

The yellow begins to bubble. *Hiss*. And --

**INT. STARCOURT MALL - BATHROOM - STALL - NIGHT**

WHOOSH!  NASTY VOMIT SWIRLS DOWN A FLUSHED TOILET AND --

A fatigued Steve drops his head back against the stall wall.

We now cut to Robin in the OTHER STALL, also leaning against
the wall, exhausted, looking up at that ceiling --

                              ROBIN
                    The ceiling stopped spinning for me,
                    is it still spinning for you -- ?

Steve checks the ceiling.

                    STEVE
          Holy shit.  No.  Do you think we
          puked it all out??

                    ROBIN
          I don't know.  Maybe.  Ask me
          something.
               (Russian accent)
          *Interrogate me.*

                    STEVE
          Okay.  Uh... when's the last time
          you...  peed your pants?

                    ROBIN
          Um *actually* earlier TODAY when that
          doctor took out that BONE SAW --

Robin claps a hand over her mouth --

                    STEVE
          OH MY GOD --

                    ROBIN
          It was just a little, just a little!

                    STEVE
          It's still in us!

                    ROBIN
          Shit!  Okay... okay -- my turn --

                    STEVE
          Hit me.

                    ROBIN
          Have you... ever... been in love?

                    STEVE
          Yes.  Nancy Wheeler, first semester,
          senior year --

                    ROBIN
          God, really?  She's *such a priss* --

                    STEVE
          Turns out -- not really.
               (then)
          Have *you* ever been in love?

Robin considers this.

                    ROBIN
          I... don't know, actually --

                    STEVE
          *Boooring --*

                    ROBIN
          Do you still love Nancy?

                    STEVE
          No --

                    ROBIN
          Why not?

                    STEVE
          Because I think I found someone
          better.

Robin's breath catches. *Shit.*

                    STEVE (CONT'D)
          Yeah, it's -- crazy.  It's just --
          Dustin, see, he's always saying I
          need to find my Suzie --

                    ROBIN
          Suzie?  Who's Suzie?

                    STEVE
          Some girlfriend from camp.  But I
          think she might not actually be real.
          Doesn't matter.  The point is, this
          girl, the one I like, it's someone I
          didn't even pay attention to in
          school.  Because I was worried, what,
          Tommy H. would make fun of me?  I
          wouldn't be prom king?  Dustin's
          right -- it's all bullshit.  I
          shoulda talked to this girl 'cause
          this girl is funny, *so funny*, she
          makes me laugh every day, but she
          also -- she makes me *think*.  She's
          super smart.  Way smarter than me.
          She can crack, like, the toughest
          Russian codes.  She's like... *nobody
          I've ever met before.*

This hits Robin like a sledgehammer.  Some awkward silence.

                    STEVE (CONT'D)
          Robin... did you OD in there or...?

                    ROBIN
          ...Nope.  Still alive.

Steve sighs, drops to his hands and knees and crawls
underneath the bathroom stall, making his way into --

**ROBIN'S STALL - CONTINUOUS**

> ROBIN
> What are you doing that floor is
> disgusting --

> STEVE
> I've already got puke and blood on my
> shirt.

Steve leans back against the stall, right next to Robin.

> STEVE (CONT'D)
> So -- what do you think?

> ROBIN
> About -- ?

> STEVE
> *This girl.*

> ROBIN
> I think... she sounds *awesome*.

> STEVE
> What about the guy -- ?

> ROBIN
> I think he's on drugs and he's not
> thinking straight.

> STEVE
> Really?  I think he's thinking more
> clearly than -- like, usual.

> ROBIN
> He's not.  He doesn't even actually
> *know this girl*.  I mean, if he did
> know her -- I mean *really knew her* --
> I'm not sure he'd still even want to
> be friends with her --

Steve is taken aback by this --

> STEVE
> That's not true, *no way* is that
> true --

Robin looks at him, getting emotional --

                    ROBIN
          Steve, *listen to me* -- it's shocked
          me to my core, but... I like you -- I
          actually like you like... *a lot*.
          But... I'm not like your other
          friends, okay?  And I'm *definitely*
          not like Nancy Wheeler --

                    STEVE
          Yeah that's exactly <u>why</u> I like you --

Robin sighs.  She looks away for a beat.  Then, after a deep
breath, she looks back at Steve.

                    ROBIN
          Remember... what I said about Missus
          Click's class -- ?

                    STEVE
          Yeah --

                    ROBIN
          About how I was... obsessed with you,
          and jealous, and all that stuff --

                    STEVE
          Yeah --

                    ROBIN
          It's... not because I had a crush on
          you.  It's because *she* kept staring
          at you --

                    STEVE
          Who kept staring at me -- ?

                    ROBIN
          *Tammy Thompson*.  I wanted her to look
          <u>at me</u> -- but she was obsessed with
          you and your stupid hair and I
          couldn't understand it because you
          were SUCH a douchebag and you would
          always leave all those bagel crumbs
          on your desk and you didn't even like
          her and you asked the dumbest
          questions and it just made me scream
          into my pillow every night --

Steve stares.  Confused...

                    STEVE
          Tammy Thompson's *a girl* --

Robin stares at Steve.

                    ROBIN
          Steve --

                    STEVE
          Yeah?

The stare continues.  And finally -- *the lightbulb.*

                    STEVE (CONT'D)
          *Oh* --

                    ROBIN
          Oh --

                    STEVE
          Holy shit.

                    ROBIN
          *Yeah.  Holy shit.*

Steve drops his head back against the stall.  We can tell his
brain is absorbing this new information -- recalibrating.

Robin lets it sit there for a moment.  Then...

                    ROBIN (CONT'D)
          ... Steve.  Did you... OD or
          something over there?

                    STEVE
          ... Nope.  Just, uh, thinking...

He frowns, seemingly distressed, then turns sharply to Robin.

                    STEVE (CONT'D)
          I mean, Tammy Thompson??  Really?
          She was cute and all, sure, but, like
          -- a total dud.

                    ROBIN
          What -- *no way* --

                    STEVE
          *Yes way.*  She had this dream of being
          a singer -- of like moving to
          Nashville and shit -- so she sang all
          the time -- but she had the WORST
          voice I've ever heard.  It was like --
               (the worst voice ever)
          *"ANd I neEd you nOw toNIGHT -- AnD I
          need YOU more THAN eVer --"*

                    ROBIN
          She did NOT sound like that --

                              442

                    STEVE
          I swear to God, I swear, that's
          actually *spot on* --

                    ROBIN
          You sound like a muppet -- !!

                    STEVE
          Yes that's how she sounded, like a
          muppet giving birth --
                    (worst voice ever, part two)
          "AnD if you ONly hold me tigHT --
          WE'll be hOLDIng on foreVEEEER --"

Robin can't stop laughing, and suddenly our teens are both
laughing, letting out all that tension and emotion and --

BOOM!  The stall door suddenly flies open as --

<u>DUSTIN AND ERICA STORM IN!</u>

Needless to say, they are not amused.

                    DUSTIN
          Okay -- WHAT THE HELL???

Robin and Steve just begin to LAUGH MORE at the sight of
angry Dustin.  Off Dustin, fuming, we make a HARD CUT TO --

**INT. BIG BUY - NIGHT**

CRUNCH!  A FAMILIAR BOOT smashes the glass on the floor.
Then another boot.  CRUNCH.  We WIDEN OUT to reveal that
it's...

<u>BILLY</u>.  Entering the Big Buy.  *Oh SHIT*.  As he steps through
that broken door, the store lights flicker a bit in response
to his presence.

His eyes move across the store like the Terminator.

He locks onto the medical aisle.  He moves toward it and --

**INT. BIG BUY - MEDICAL AISLE - NIGHT**

Billy walks up to the pool of Eleven's blood.

He kneels down, reaches out, presses his hand against it.

As that blood curls around his fingers, CUT TO --

AN EXTREME CLOSE UP ON his eyes.  His pupils dilate rapidly in the flickering light of the store.  *He's tracking Eleven.*

PRELAP:  The sound of a SCREAM as we MATCH CUT TO --

**EXT. FAIRGROUNDS - NIGHT**

AN OVERHEAD SHOT OF A CIRCULAR RIDE SPINNING.

We're back at the fairgrounds!  Loud and fun!!

**EXT. FAIRGROUNDS - PARKING LOT - NIGHT**

It's much quieter in the parking lot, where we find Murray still going over those Death Star plans with Alexei, flipping through papers as they talk (in Russian, of course):

>                    MURRAY
>          <... And why all this -- ?>
>
>                    ALEXEI
>          <If I just turn the keys -- it's like
>          turning off a car -- but then the car
>          still works, does it not?>
>
>                    MURRAY
>          <Yes -->
>
>                    ALEXEI
>          <And do you want the car to still
>          work, or do you want the car to...
>          explode?>
>
>                    MURRAY
>          <I want the car to explode -->
>
>                    ALEXEI
>          <Good.  Then do this.  Just make sure
>          you are nowhere near it when it does.
>          It is not pretty.  Turns people
>          into... *dust*.  And then -->
>
>                    MURRAY
>          <It's over -->
>
>                    ALEXEI
>              (nods)
>          <And I become American citizen -->
>              (motions to fair)
>          <-- and join in the fun, yes?>

Murray smiles at him; he's starting to like this kid.

                    MURRAY
          <Who said you had to be American to
          join the fun?>

**EXT. FAIRGROUNDS - NIGHT**

POV SHOT:  We're now DEEP IN THE FAIR.  Our CAMERA SWINGS
AROUND, taking in all the wonderful sights and sounds as --

Murray leads a wide-eyed Alexei through the fair.  Alexei
is overwhelmed by everything around him.  The crowd, the
lights, the rides, the games, it's almost *too much* to take
in --

                    MURRAY
          <It doesn't get more American than
          *this* my friend -- fatty foods, ugly
          decadence, rigged games -->

Murray steps up to a ticket booth, slaps down some cash.

                    MURRAY (CONT'D)
          Fifteen tickets please --

As Murray waits for his tickets, Alexei surveys the carnival
games around them.  He locks onto THE DART GAME -- KIDS try
to pop balloons.  The prize: A GIANT STUFFED TWEETY BIRD.

His interest is... piqued.

                    ALEXEI
          <They are rigged -- these games?>

                    MURRAY
          <Yes -->

                    ALEXEI
          <They do not look rigged -->

                    MURRAY
          <That's just it, my dear Alexei.
          They have been designed to present
          the illusion of fairness!  But it's
          all a scam -- a trick to put your
          money in the rich man's pocket.
          That, my dear friend, *is America*.>

The Fair Worker hands him the tickets --

                    MURRAY (CONT'D)
          <But hey, *knock yourself out*.>

Murray passes Alexei some tickets, then strides off --

                    ALEXEI
        <Where are you going -- ??>

                    MURRAY
        <To get us the closet thing to food I
        can find -->

Alexei returns his attention to the game.  He takes a deep
breath, then heads for the game, passing right by...

Hopper and Joyce.  They don't see him, because they're too
busy looking for our kids.  Who are... nowhere.  *Wait* --

                    JOYCE
            *Karen* --

Hopper follows her gaze -- spots the Wheelers heading into
the Gravitron!  Shared looks, then they quicken their pace
as --

**INT. GRAVITRON - NIGHT - MOMENTS LATER**

The Wheelers get into position against the wall --

                    JOYCE (O.S.)
            Karen -- !

Karen looks up, sees Hopper and Joyce racing toward them.

                    KAREN
        Joyce -- oh my gosh!  How funny --

                    JOYCE
        Where are the kids --  ?

                    KAREN
        Oh -- I haven't seen them -- I don't
        think they're here yet --

THE GRAVITRON OPERATOR is annoyed at Hopper and Joyce --

                    GRAVITRON OPERATOR
        You two -- up against the wall --
        against the wall -- !

                    HOPPER
            (ignoring this)
        Do you know where they are -- ?

                    KAREN
        Oh gosh -- I can hardly keep track
        these days -- they were at Dustin's,
        then Lucas's, then Max's -- you know
        what it's like... *summer.*

                              TED
                    Knowing them, I'm sure they're
                    getting into some kinda trouble.

Before an appalled Joyce can respond --

Alarms start to BLARE and LIGHTS FLASH!

                         GRAVITRON OPERATOR
                    Last warning you two -- up against
                    the wall -- !!!

                              HOPPER
                    Hey, hold the ride --

                         GRAVITRON OPERATOR
                    On your life, Magnum --

The Operator yanks a lever and the Gravitron begins to spin!
*Are you fucking kidding me??* Hopper and Joyce quickly find a
wall -- which they are promptly sucked up against!

                              KAREN
                    Here we GO!!!!

Holly squeals in delight!  Ted closes his eyes in horror --

                              TED
                    Oh no oh no oh no--

Hopper and Joyce share looks.  They both hate this as much as
Ted does.  As the ride begins to spin faster and faster --

They both reach out... and *HOLD HANDS*!

**EXT. FAIRGROUNDS - NIGHT**

As the Gravitron speeds faster and faster, we PRELAP:

                         *DOC BROWN (PRE-LAP)*
                    *"... Roads... where we're going, we*
                    *don't NEED roads..."*

**INT. STARCOURT MOVIE THEATER**

*ON THE MOVIE SCREEN:  THE DELOREAN LIFTS OFF THE GROUND AND
SPEEDS OFF INTO THE SKY!*

THE AUDIENCE APPLAUDS ENTHUSIASTICALLY AS THE CREDITS BEGIN
TO PLAY, AND --

**INT. STARCOURT MALL - UPSTAIRS**

The excited crowd pours out of the theater and into the (now empty) mall.

**INT. STARCOURT MALL - BATHROOM**

Dustin watches them through a cracked bathroom door.

>                    DUSTIN
>           ... And --

He waits for the perfect moment.  Then --

>                    DUSTIN (CONT'D)
>      *Blend*!

Dustin scurries out of the bathroom.  Steve, Erica, and Robin hurry out right behind him and --

**INT. STARCOURT MALL - NIGHT**

... They merge into the sea of moviegoers, "*blending*."

They walk with the crowd -- and no one seems to notice!

>                    ERICA
>           (amazed)
>      Shit *that worked* --

>                    DUSTIN
>      Of course it worked.  Now we just get
>      on that bus with the rest of the
>      plebes and -- *home sweet home, here
>      we come.*

Steve shares a worried look with Robin.  *Uhhhh...*

>                    STEVE
>      Hey Dustin --

>                    DUSTIN
>      Yeah?

>                    STEVE
>      We... may not want to go to your
>      house.

>                    DUSTIN
>      What?  Why not?

Steve hesitates.  Dustin stares.

                    DUSTIN (CONT'D)
          Why not, Steve???

                    STEVE
          I may have... told them your name.
          Your... full name.

Dustin stares.

                    DUSTIN
          What is wrong with you?

                    STEVE
          I was *drugged* --

                    DUSTIN
          So??

                    STEVE
          *So -- ?*

                    DUSTIN
          SO you *RESIST* -- you tough it out!

                    STEVE
          Easy for you to say -- !

As Dustin and Steve continue to bicker, back to old times...

Robin's eyes narrow.  Up ahead:  TWO LYNX SECURITY GUARDS are
standing by the exit doors, checking moviegoers' shopping
bags as they exit.  Guard #1 smiles at TWO TEEN GIRLS --

                    LYNX GUARD #1
          Sorry for the inconvenience, girls.
          Have a wonderful night.

Robin grabs her friends --

                    ROBIN
          *Guys* --

Everyone follows her gaze -- their faces fall.  *Shit.*

                    DUSTIN
          Abort -- *ABORT* --

They all turn around and start pushing their way *back through
the crowd*, moving this time *against* the sea of people.

                    DUSTIN (CONT'D)
          Excuse us -- excuse us -- sorry --

Lynx Guard #2 sees them.  Starts to follow.


                              449

Steve looks behind, spots their tail --

>                    STEVE
>          This way -- this way -- ! !

Steve pulls them down the escalator -- taking three steps at
a time and --

**EXT. FAIRGROUNDS**

BANG!  A balloon POPS!  APPLAUSE follows.

REVERSE TO REVEAL: Alexei, focused intently, playing the dart
game!  He's got a small audience of impressed children who
are watching him.

>                BALLOON CARNIE
>          That's three!

Alexei barely seems to hear the carnie; he's *focused*.  He
throws the dart.  BANG!  Another balloon POPS.  More APPLAUSE
from the children.  A few more kids now gather around him.
Alexei's drawing quite the crowd!

>            BALLOON CARNIE (CONT'D)
>          ONE MORE FOR THE BIG PRIZE!

Alexei nods.  A little nervous now.  But...

A LITTLE BOY (who we recognize as the "yer dead!!" kid from
season two!) cheers him on --

>                 LITTLE BOY
>          You can do it mister!

Alexei aims.  Takes a breath.  Focusing.  *Throws*.  And --

BANG!  A balloon erupts!  Everyone goes wild and we CUT TO --

**A LITTLE LATER**

Alexei, now *beaming*, carrying his GIANT STUFFED TWEETY BIRD!

Through the dense crowd, he sees Murray, just now walking
away from the corn dog stand with a pair of dogs in hand --

>                   ALEXEI
>          <Murray!!  Look!!!  It's not rigged!
>          It's not rigged!!!>

Murray sees him and that bird, smiles.  WOW!  Alexei smiles
back.  It's a sweet moment.  But then suddenly Alexei's smile
drops.  Between Murray and Alexei, there is a <u>THIRD PARTY</u>:

GRIGORI.  He's moving toward Alexei like a *shark in the water*.

TIME SEEMS TO MOVE SLOW AS MURRAY SEES THE CHANGE IN ALEXEI'S EXPRESSION FROM JOY TO HORROR.  A FLASH OF METAL AS GRIGORI PULLS A GUN FROM HIS COAT, LONG SILENCER ATTACHED.

CLOSE ON:  GRIGORI PULLS THE TRIGGER AND --

BANG!!  Another balloon POPS!  The crowd at the dart stand cheers for the Little Boy, who is now playing!

BACK TO REAL TIME as Alexei looks down, sees stuffing protruding from his new stuffed animal.  He drops the stuffed animal, revealing DARK BLOOD blossoming across his stomach.

Grigori walks past him, not even making eye contact.

> GRIGORI
> <Traitor.>

And then, as quick as he appeared -- he's gone.

Alexei, holding his stomach, takes a few stumbling steps.  The carnival around him becomes a crush of laughing faces and lights, the music distorted, nightmarish.  He starts to fall but --

Murray sweeps in, catches him --

> MURRAY
> Alexei??  Alexei -- ?

But Alexei can't talk -- *can hardly breathe*.  Murray pulls his hands away to discover they're wet, COVERED IN BLOOD.

**MOMENTS LATER**

A frantic Murray helps Alexei to a space between two food stalls, eases him down.  He removes his terrycloth overshirt, presses it over Alexei's wound, desperately trying to stanch the blood.

> MURRAY
> <Keep pressure on it -- I'll get you
> help -- I'll get help!!>

As the color continues to drain from Alexei's face --

Murray sprints back off into the crowd and --

**EXT. FAIRGROUNDS - NIGHT**

Murray scans the fair, frantic, locks onto --

451

<u>Joyce and Hopper</u>.  They are just now stumbling out of the
Gravitron with the Wheelers.  They look a little... *dizzy*.

> MURRAY
> JIM!!!  JIM!!!

Hopper hears his name, looks over to find --

Murray waving at him frantically, hurrying toward him.  He
sees the panic in his eyes -- and the <u>blood on his hands</u>.

And then... Hopper sees something else:

GRIGORI.  Coming for them.  Oh fuck!

> HOPPER
> Joyce, we gotta go -- *<u>we gotta go</u>* --

She looks up -- *<u>sees Grigori</u>*.  Before she can say anything,
Hopper's pulling her away.

The Wheelers watch them go.  A little taken aback.

> KAREN
> They make an odd couple, don't they?

> TED
> Well, you know what they say.
> Someone for everyone.

Off Karen, staring at Ted, CUT TO --

**EXT. FAIRGROUNDS - PARKING LOT - NIGHT**

Mayor Kline is waiting by his car, Grigori's motorcycle now
parked adjacent.  Kline checks his watch, looking
increasingly anxious, as --

**EXT. FAIRGROUNDS - NIGHT**

Hopper and Joyce shove through the crowd and onto --

**ANOTHER THOROUGHFARE,**

Hopper looks around, seems like they've lost Grigori, but --

They spot RUSSIAN GOON #1, who CLOCKS THEM!  *It looks like
Grigori took Larry's advice and brought back-up this time.*

Hop shoves his keys into Joyce's hand --

> HOPPER
> Find Alexei, get to the car, bring it
> around back --

Before Joyce even has a chance to argue, Hopper leaves her, taking a sharp right out of the crowd, making sure Goon #1 sees him.  He shoves through a swing gate and enters...

THE BIG TOP FUNHOUSE!

**INT. FUNHOUSE - NIGHT**

As Hopper moves through a ROTATING BARREL --

**EXT. FAIRGROUNDS - NIGHT**

Goon #1 makes a call on his WALKIE and heads toward the Big Top Funhouse.

**INT. FUNHOUSE - NIGHT**

Hopper sweeps through the first floor of the Funhouse.

There are KIDS in here.  He flashes his badge at the DAD --

>                     HOPPER
>           POLICE -- GET YOUR KIDS, GET THEM OUT
>           OF HERE -- !

The Dad (now freaked) grabs his kids, starts to pull them away toward an EMERGENCY EXIT as Hopper continues forward --

He scrambles up some MOVING METAL STAIRS as --

**BACK OUTSIDE,**

Goon #1 heads through the Funhouse gate.  As he moves through the rotating barrel, he draws a PISTOL WITH A SILENCER --

**INT. FUNHOUSE - NIGHT**

Hopper ascends to the third floor of the Funhouse as --

**INT. FUNHOUSE - NIGHT**

Goon #1 moves through the first floor, then up some steps, tracing Hopper's steps --

**INT. FUNHOUSE - SECOND FLOOR - NIGHT**

Goon #1 moves into --

**A NEW ROOM - CONTINUOUS**

It's filled with COLORFUL PUNCHING BAGS.  He sweeps through the punching bags, gun raised when.  *Wait* -- a noise.

He turns around just in time to see a PUNCHING BAG flying right at him --

IT'S HOPPER!  Heaving with all his might --

WHAM!  The punching bag slams into Goon #1.  *Hard*.  He's knocked backward into a wall, gun skipping loose --

Hopper doesn't wait a beat.  He moves in, begins to pummel the Goon with his fists as --

**EXT. FAIRGROUNDS - NIGHT**

Joyce races through the crowd, searching, frantic, when --

WHAM!  A HAND grabs her.  She whirls, terrified, but --

It's Murray, his eyes wide, and --

**EXT. FAIRGROUNDS - NIGHT**

A shellshocked Murray leads Joyce behind the stall, where --

Alexei is still slumped on the ground.  Now motionless.

> JOYCE
> *-- Oh God --*

Joyce drops down by Alexei.  Shakes him --

> JOYCE (CONT'D)
> -- Alexei??  *Alexei??*

But he's not moving.  He's dead.

Murray chokes back tears.

> MURRAY
> I, I just left him for a minute --
> for a corn dog... a *stupid corn dog.*

As his death hits Joyce like a sledgehammer, CUT TO --

**INT. FUNHOUSE - PUNCHING BAG ROOM - NIGHT**

BAM!  POW!  Hopper and GOON #1 continuing to exchange blows.

They fight across the punching bag room, dodging and ducking between the rows of colorful swinging bags.  The Goon hits Hopper a few times, putting up a a good fight, but then Hopper strikes back, gains the upper hand, and --

KA-WHAM!  KNOCKS THE GOON OUT!

**ACROSS THE FAIR,**

Grigori moves through the crowd.  He loads a fresh mag into
his gun as he heads into the Funhouse, moving through the
rotating barrel as --

**INT. PUNCHING BAG ROOM**

Hopper frantically scans the floor, locates Goon #1's fallen
gun.

He grabs it up, then startles as he hears a RUSSIAN VOICE.  He
swings his gun around, finger on trigger, but --

It's just THE GOON'S WALKIE.  *Jesus.*  Hopper grabs it up as --

**INT./EXT. FUNHOUSE - NIGHT**

Grigori moves through the Funhouse, up the steps to the
second story as --

**EXT. FAIRGROUNDS - PARKING LOT - NIGHT**

Joyce and Murray exit the fair into the parking lot, headed
for the Toddfather, when --

Joyce stops.  She sees Larry waiting by his car -- and right
next to Grigori's motorcycle.  Her face hardens as she makes
a sudden decision, then heads over to him --

>               MURRAY
>     *Where are you going -- ??*

She ignores Murray, continues stomping over to Kline --

>               JOYCE
>     Hi Larry --

He looks up, sees her *flying in*.  His eyes shoot wide --

>               MAYOR KLINE
>     *Joyce --*

He's barely got her name out before --

WHAM-POW!  She SOCKS HIM square in his broken nose.  As Larry
SQUEALS and doubles over, she then gives him a quick kick in
the nutsack for good measure and --

**INT. FUNHOUSE - PUNCHING BAG ROOM - NIGHT**

GRIGORI sweeps into the punching bag room -- sees the fallen
Goon.  *Shit.*  Then he sees --

A funky staircase at the far end of the room.

**A FUNKY STAIRCASE - MOMENTS LATER**

He heads up the steps, through a crooked door, and into...

**INT. FUNHOUSE - BLACK LIGHT ROOM**

... A BLACK LIGHT ROOM.  There are columns, flashing lights, and lots of mirrors, which make the room appear INFINITELY large.  It's disorienting.  Grigori sweeps around, and --

ANOTHER SOUND.  He whirls, _SEES HOPPER!!!_

He OPENS FIRE, and --

BANGBANGBANG!!  _SHOOTS HOPPER THREE TIMES_.  But --

The image cracks.

_It's just a mirror!!_  As the mirror SHATTERS --

Hopper sweeps out from behind a column.  Grigori senses him, turns.  *Too late.*  BANG BANG BANG BANG!  Hopper OPENS FIRE, SHOOTS Grigori four times -- GOT HIM!  Grigori spirals to the floor just as --

Hopper hears RUSSIANS.  This time it's not a walkie.  It's --

**INT. FUNHOUSE - PUNCHING BAG ROOM - NIGHT**

MORE RUSSIAN GOONS, racing through the punching bag room, headed up those funky steps --

**INT. FUNHOUSE - BLACK LIGHT ROOM - NIGHT**

Hopper flees the black light room and bursts out onto --

**EXT. FUNHOUSE - THIRD-FLOOR BALCONY - NIGHT**

His eyes scan for a way out -- lock onto a TWISTY YELLOW METAL SLIDE.

**INT. FUNHOUSE - BLACK LIGHT ROOM - NIGHT**

-- Grigori staggers to his feet, tears off his shirt -- revealing a bulletproof vest.  But one shot got through -- fresh blood streaming down his arm.

>                    RUSSIAN GOON #2
>         <Comrade -- !!>

Grigori turns -- sees the Goons race into the black light room.  Goon #2 then races up to him, concerned, but --

He pushes the Goon away, scowling --

>                    GRIGORI
>         <GET OFF ME!!>

He grabs up his gun and staggers after Hopper as --

**EXT. FUNHOUSE - THIRD-FLOOR BALCONY - NIGHT**

WHOOSH!  Hopper leaps *into* the mouth of the slide --

**INT./EXT. SLIDE - NIGHT**

We're now flying down the slide with Hopper as --

**EXT. FUNHOUSE - BALCONY - NIGHT**

Grigori and his Goons storm out onto the Funhouse balcony. Their eyes scan -- but they can't find Hopper anywhere!

As they search, our camera rapidly CRANES DOWN three stories just in time to find --

**INT./EXT. SLIDE - NIGHT**

WHOOSH! Hopper spitting out of the slide! He scrambles to his feet and --

**EXT. BEHIND THE FUNHOUSE - NIGHT**

-- Races around the back of the Funhouse just as --

SCREEECH! The convertible squeals into view --

Joyce behind the wheel, Murray passenger!! *Perfect timing.* Hopper jumps in the back and Joyce *hammers* the accelerator --

SCREECH! The car speeds away across the dirty road --

**INT./EXT. CONVERTIBLE - NIGHT**

Hopper catches his breath, then --

>                    HOPPER
>          Alexei?? *Where's Alexei?*

An emotional Joyce shakes her head. Just as Hopper takes in this terrible news --

His stolen walkie SQUAWKS. MORE RUSSIAN.

Hopper tosses the walkie to Murray --

>                    HOPPER (CONT'D)
>          <u>Translate</u>.

As Murray listens, his eyes narrow, and WE SMASH TO --

**INT. STARCOURT MALL - FOOD COURT**

The other end of this walkie call. To our surprise, it's not coming from the fairgrounds... it's coming from --

LYNX GUARD #1!!  He is moving through the empty mall, searching for the Scoops Troop!  As he sweeps a flashlight through the Sam Goody windows, our camera swings over to --

LYNX GUARD #2 as he moves into --

**THE FOOD COURT - CONTINUOUS**

He scans the various restaurants, then --

Freezes.  He has spotted something in the reflection of a Great Cookie Company baking rack.  It's an orange T-shirt...

WE NOW DROP DOWN BEHIND THE COUNTER TO REVEAL...

**INT. GREAT COOKIE COMPANY - NIGHT**

The Scoops Troop!  Dustin in that bright shirt.  Their backs are pressed up against the counter and they hold their breath, trying to stay hidden.  But, of course, *too late*...

**INT. STARCOURT MALL - FOOD COURT - NIGHT**

The Guard has seen them.  He signals to his men.

**BEHIND THE COUNTER**

The kids hear voices, footsteps.  They tense.  *Oh shit*...

**BACK OUTSIDE,**

The Guards join up, move toward the kids, when --

WAHHHH.  A LOUD HORN.  The guards spin, startled, aim. It's --

THE FANCY LEBARON DISPLAY CAR!  THE CAR IS... HONKING AND VIBRATING AND FLASHING ITS HEADLIGHTS AND SLOWLY ROTATING COUNTERCLOCKWISE.  BUT -- NO ONE IS IN THE CAR.  IT'S ALMOST AS IF... THE CAR IS ALIVE.

> LYNX GUARD #1
> <... The hell??>

As the Guards stare in confusion, Guard #1 notices something. Something... *above the* car.

We now RAPIDLY CRANE UP AND OVER THE SHAKING CAR TO REVEAL...

ELEVEN STANDING ON THE BALCONY IN FRONT OF JAZZERCISE, ORCHESTRATING THIS CHAOS FROM ABOVE.  HELL.  YES.  SHE NARROWS HER EYES, FOCUSING, AND THEN --

WHOOM!  SHE SUDDENLY THROWS HER HAND FORWARD AND --

FWOOOM!  THE CAR BARREL ROLLS INTO THE GUARDS, SLAMMING THEM
WITH THE FORCE OF A JET-POWERED BATTERING RAM, CRUSHING TWO
LIKE ANTS AND SENDING THE OTHERS FLYING LIKE BOWLING PINS,
THEN --

BAM!  THE CAR CRASHES AGAINST THE NY PIZZA COUNTER.  GLASS
SHATTERS.  THE CAR ROCKS TO A STOP.  AND AT LAST -- SILENCE.

The Scoops Troop rises up from behind the counter.  Their
saucer-wide eyes move from the smashed car to their savior:

Eleven.  As she lowers her hand, the others now step up
behind her into view.  Mike, Nancy, Will, Jonathan, Lucas,
Max!

Our two groups lock eyes.  Finally united!

Lucas narrows his eyes.  Is that --

                    LUCAS
          Erica???

**INT. STARCOURT MALL - OUTSIDE THE GAP ENTRANCE - NIGHT**

The Jancy group flies across the mall into the arms of --

Scoops Troop!  It's absolute end-of-the-Goonies-madness here
as everyone hugs and talks a million miles an hour --

Dustin is near tears as he embraces Eleven --

                    DUSTIN
          Holy SHIT you flung that thing like a
          Micro Machine -- !!

Lucas is more focused on his sister, staring at her like
she's some alien --

                    LUCAS
          What are you doing here???

                    ERICA
               (re: Steve and Robin)
          Ask them it's their fault --

                    STEVE
          True, that's true, totally our
          fault --

                    ROBIN
          I don't understand, what just
          happened to that car -- ???

                    DUSTIN
El has superpowers --

                    ROBIN
I'm *sorry* -- ?

                    STEVE
She flung the car with her mind --

                    ERICA
*That's* El -- ??

                    ROBIN
Who's *El* -- ?!

                    NANCY
I'm sorry *who* are you -- ??

                    ROBIN
Robin -- I, I work with Steve --

                    DUSTIN
She cracked the top secret code --

                    STEVE
Which is how we found the Russians --

                    JONATHAN
Russians?  *What Russians* -- ?

                    STEVE
       (pointing)
RUSSIANS --

                    MAX
Those were Russians -- ??

                    ERICA
Some of them --

                    LUCAS
What ARE YOU TALKING ABOUT -- ?!

                    DUSTIN
Did you guys not get my code
red -- ?!

                    MIKE
We got it OBVIOUSLY we're here aren't
we but I could not understand *half* of
what you said --

                    DUSTIN
*Goddamn low battery* -- !

                              STEVE
                    Dude WHAT did I tell you about
                    wasting that battery -- ?!

                              DUSTIN
                    It all worked out didn't it STEVE --

                              ERICA
                    "Worked out"??  We *ALMOST DIED* --

As the groups continue to bicker, we MOVE PAST THEM, pushing
in on the only one who isn't talking:

Eleven.  She looks paler than usual.  Her eyes glassy.  The
soundscape begins to distort, the voices of her friends
swirling together, becoming a high-end, tinnitus-like sound.

BLOOD BEGINS TO SPILL FROM HER EARS... THEN NOSE... THEN --

HER KNEES BUCKLE AND --

WHOOM!  Eleven collapses to the floor.

Mike is the first to notice --

                              MIKE
                    -- EL??

Mike runs over and drops by her side.

Her breathing is weak, shallow.  She manages a few words --

                              ELEVEN
                    ... Leg -- *my leg* --

As the others race over --

Mike pulls up her pant leg, rips off the bandage to reveal --

THE BITE WOUND.  IT'S A HUNDRED TIMES WORSE THAN BEFORE,
SPREAD ACROSS HER LEG, HORRIBLY SWOLLEN WITH THAT AWFUL
SICKLY YELLOW COLOR, THROBBING WITH STRANGE LIFE.

IT'S LOOKS LIKE THE WORST SPIDER BITE YOU'VE EVER SEEN.

As Eleven's eyes begin to close --

Mike screams --

                              MIKE
                    EL -- EL!!!  EL!!!

Her eyes shut and WE SNAP TO --

**BLACK**

                         END EPISODE


                              463

# CHAPTER EIGHT:
# THE BATTLE OF STARCOURT

WRITTEN BY **THE DUFFER BROTHERS**

**EXT. ROAD - NIGHT**

We FADE UP on an empty country road.  Quiet.  Then --

SCREEEECH!  The TODDFATHER CONVERTIBLE *roars* into view --

**INT./EXT. CONVERTIBLE - NIGHT**

JOYCE is still driving -- her hands clutching tight to the
wheel, the wind rushing through her hair.  A BURST OF STATIC
causes her to briefly glance from the road to --

MURRAY, who is fiddling with the Russian walkie-talkie in the
passenger seat.  Another FLARE OF STATIC and --

                  JOYCE
     *... Still nothing -- ??*

                MURRAY
    Nothing --

HOPPER leans forward from the back seat --

                HOPPER
    *"Food court,"* you're sure they said
    "food court" -- ??

                MURRAY
    I'm *sorry* have my translation skills
    been letting you down??

Murray can tell he's just worried, then, softening --

                MURRAY (CONT'D)
    We don't know it's your kids --

                JOYCE
    Yes we do.

Joyce spins the wheel, taking a hard right turn.  The tires
SQUEAL *and* --

**INT. STARCOURT MALL - ATRIUM - NIGHT**

ELEVEN lets out a PAINED SCREAM.  She's right where we left
her on the floor by the atrium, the OTHERS all around her,
watching, terrified --

And it only gets scarier as Mike sees --

*SOMETHING* MOVE BENEATH HER SKIN.

                MIKE
    -- Something's in there -- !

                    LUCAS
          What -- ???

                    MIKE
          I -- I just saw something move --

Now the others see it -- something moving beneath the skin of
her calf.

                    ERICA
          -- What IS that -- ???

                    DUSTIN
          Oh God oh Jesus --

                    JONATHAN
          Just -- keep talking to her -- keep
          her awake --!!

Jonathan suddenly leaps to his feet and sprints across the
food court.  It's quite the run, but we follow him the entire
way as he leaps over the counter and into --

**TEPANYAKI JAPANESE - CONTINUOUS**

Jonathan searches, panicked, until he finds some FOOD SERVICE
GLOVES.  He slips them on, then grabs --

A BIG SHARP KNIFE.  Oh fuck.  Oh no.  He turns the stovetop
on full blast, then -- FWOOM! -- thrusts the blade in the
fire, rotating it, sterilizing it.  As the blade *glows red* --

**THE FOOD COURT**

The others huddle by Eleven.  Mike squeezes her hand.

                    MIKE
          Just stay with us okay -- ?  Stay
          with us --

She nods, but she's not looking good, fading fast --  her
breathing rapid, her forehead sweating, the color rapidly
leaving her cheeks --

                    ROBIN
          It's not... not too bad -- the goalie
          -- on my old soccer team, Beth
          Wildfire -- this other girl slid into
          her -- and like -- the whole bone
          came out of the skin -- like six
          inches or something it was INSANE --

                    STEVE
          Robin --

                    ROBIN
         Yeah --

                    STEVE
         You're not -- helping --

                    ROBIN
         Sorry --

Jonathan returns now.  Drops by Eleven's side with the knife.

Nancy goes sheet white as she sees him with those gloves,
that hot knife --

                    NANCY
         Do you know what you're doing--?

                    JONATHAN
              (nope)
         Yeah --
              (to Eleven)
         So El this is... probably gonna...
         hurt like hell --

Jonathan hands her a wooden spoon --

                    JONATHAN (CONT'D)
         You can bite down on this, for the
         pain --

Eleven bites down on the wooden handle, then --

*Takes Mike's hand*.

Jonathan holds the knife against her throbbing wound.
Hesitates.  But --

                    MIKE
         *Do it.*

Jonathan -- *in an excruciating to watch moment* -- makes a
slow, precise incision into the inflamed bite.

YELLOW PUS begin to seep out from the incision, bubbling,
hissing with life.  Eleven fights back the pain as --

Jonathan finishes with the incision, drops the knife, then
reaches down with a gloved hand --

                    ERICA
         WHAT -- ?

                    LUCAS
         OH NO NO NO NO NO --

                    NANCY
          JONATHAN --

                    JONATHAN
          STOP TALKING -- !

He goes to dig out whatever that thing is, pushing his hand
into the wound.  But whatever is in there -- it slips away --
escaping somewhere deeper in the skin -- *fleeing* --

                    JONATHAN (CONT'D)
          GODDAMMIITT!!!  GODDAMMIT -- !!

Jonathan pulls out his gloved hand, which is now covered in
nasty yellow goop.  He goes to make another incision, but --

Eleven spits out the spoon, shouts  --

                    ELEVEN
          Stop!  STOP --

Jonathan pulls the knife away, and  --

                    ELEVEN (CONT'D)
          I... can... do it --

Everyone shares uncertain, worried looks but --

Eleven is strong here.

                    ELEVEN (CONT'D)
          I can do it.

Eleven looks down at her wound.  Her look hardens... she
reaches out a hand... toward the wound... narrows her eyes...
and...

SHE BEGINS TO PSYCHICALLY PULL AT THE WOUND. *PSYCHIC
SURGERY*.  THE FLESH BENDS, BLEEDS, CONTORTS, AND SICKLY
YELLOW VENOM OOZES OUT OF HER INFLAMED SKIN, HISSING WITH
POISONOUS LIFE.

                    ROBIN
          Jesus what the fu --

Some turn away, can't watch.  This supernatural surgery is
horrific, disturbing, and painful.  Ultimately -- *too
painful*.

Eleven drops her hand with an exhausted gasp.

She catches her breath, looks at Mike.

                    ELEVEN
          I -- I can... I can feel it --

Mike stays firm, confident.

                    MIKE
          Then you can get it out.

Eleven nods... *Hell yes she can.* She takes a breath, holds
out that hand... and begins to PULL AGAIN. The skin on her
calf throbs, skin moving faster now, as --

Eleven is hit with another wave of EXTREME PAIN. She
squeezes Mike's hand tighter as --

Blood begins to spill from her ears, from her nostrils, more
than is normal, and the soundscape is overtaken by a HORRIBLE
TINNITUS-LIKE SOUND. For a moment, it seems this is only
causing her agony. But then, she lets out a BIG SCREAM --

THE LIGHTS FLICKER -- THE GAP DISPLAY WINDOW SHATTERS BEHIND
HER AND --

A BLOODY FLESHY THING SUCKS OUT OF HER WOUND --

WHOOM! ELEVEN HURLS IT ACROSS THE MALL.

IT'S A PART OF THE MONSTER. A PIECE OF SHARP CLAW, WITH
FLESH HANGING FROM IT. It scatters across the floor.
Lands --

Right by the escalator but --

That flesh is still alive. It starts to crawl away...
*squealing* -- dragging that claw like a tail... when --

BOOM! A boot stomps it, squishing it like a fucking spider.

WIDEN TO REVEAL: <u>HOPPER</u>, with JOYCE and MURRAY close behind!

Our adults stare at the insane scene before them. At --

*Eleven.* Breathing hard on the floor. Exhausted -- but
<u>victorious</u>. As she locks eyes with Hop, we SMASH TO --

                  **MAIN TITLES**

**INT. STARCOURT MALL - UPPER FLOOR - NIGHT**

We PUSH IN on the neon Starcourt sign.

                    MIKE (PRE-LAP)
          The Mind Flayer -- it built this
          monster in Hawkins.
                    (MORE)

                      470

                    MIKE (PRE-LAP) (CONT'D)
          In order to stop El... *to kill
          her*... to pave a way for its entry
          into our world...

We now CRANE past the sign and over the balcony, tilting down
to find...

**INT. STARCOURT MALL - ATRIUM - NIGHT**

Eleven sitting on the center bench in the atrium.  She's
sipping on a soda from Burger King, and she's got a makeshift
icepack on that now swollen, bloody leg, which has now been
elevated.  She's trembling, pale, *incredibly weak*.

Hopper is by her side, while the rest of our gang are talking
by her, sharing information, downloading on the wild events
of this past week...

                    MAX
          And it almost did -- that was just --
          one tiny piece of it --

                    HOPPER
          How big is this thing -- ?

                    JONATHAN
          Big.  *Very big.*

                    LUCAS
          It sort of... destroyed your cabin --

A shocked Hopper takes this in --

                    LUCAS (CONT'D)
          I think it'll be okay but you may,
          like -- need a new roof --

                    STEVE
          So -- just to be clear -- this big
          fleshy spider *thing* that hurt El --
          it's a giant weapon -- ?

                    NANCY
          Yes exactly --

                    STEVE
          But like -- instead of screws and
          metal -- the Mind Flayer made its
          weapon out of... *melted people* --

                    NANCY
          Yes --

                         STEVE
          Yeah okay that's what I thought.
          Just, ya know, *making sure* --

                         JOYCE
          And you're sure it's still alive -- ?

                         MAX
          El beat the shit out of it, but
          yeah -- it's still alive --

                         WILL
          But we close the Gate again --

                         MAX
          We cut the brain off from the body --

                         LUCAS
          And kill it.  *Theoretically.*

Just as Hopper takes this in, a WHISTLE reverberates across
the mall.  Everyone looks up to find --

Murray, hurrying down the escalator.  He waves a set of
familiar PAPERS in the air, and we CUT TO --

**A FEW MOMENTS LATER - FOOD COURT - NIGHT**

An OVERHEAD shot as WHAM!  Murray slams Alexei's HAND-DRAWN
DESIGNS AND MAPS onto a food court table.

He points at a room --

                         MURRAY
          Okay, this is what Alexei called "The
          Hub."  Now this Hub takes us to the
          vault room --

                         HOPPER
          And where's the Gate -- ?

Murray taps another room.

                         MURRAY
          Right here.  I don't know the scale
          on this -- but it seems fairly close
          to the vault, maybe fifty feet or
          so --

                         ERICA
          More like a hundred.

Our adults looks up to find Erica.  She walks over to them.

                              ERICA (CONT'D)
               You just going to waltz in there like
               it's commie Disneyland or something?

                              MURRAY
               I'm sorry -- who are you??

                              ERICA
               Erica Sinclair.  Who are *you*?

                              MURRAY
               Murray... Bauman --

                              ERICA
               Listen, Mister *Bum-man*, I don't want
               to tell you how to do things -- but I
               was down in that shithole for twenty-
               four hours, and with all due
               respect --

Erica swivels to Joyce and Hopper.

                              ERICA (CONT'D)
               You do what this man says, you're all
               <u>gonna die</u>.

Murray scoffs --

                              MURRAY
               I'm sorry, why is this four-year-old
               speaking?

                              ERICA
               I'm ten you bald bastard --

                              LUCAS
                    (appalled)
               *Erica* -- !

                              ERICA
               Just the facts --

                              DUSTIN
               She's right, you're all gonna die --
               but <u>you don't have to</u>.

Dustin moves in.

                              DUSTIN (CONT'D)
               Sorry, excuse me, may I?

Dustin shoves past Murray, grabs his pen, taps the drawing --

                    DUSTIN (CONT'D)
          Yeah, okay, see this room here --

He circles a room with his pen.

                    DUSTIN (CONT'D)
          This is a storage facility.  There's
          a hatch in here that feeds into their
          underground ventilation system.

Dustin draws a line --

                    DUSTIN (CONT'D)
          -- Which will lead you *to the base of*
          *the weapon*.  It's a bit of a maze
          down there -- but between me and
          Erica, we can show you the way --

                    HOPPER
          You can *"show us the way"* -- ?

Dustin looks at Hopper.  Deadly serious.

                    DUSTIN
          Don't worry -- you can do *all* the
          fighting and dangerous hero shit.
          We'll just be your... *navigators*.

Erica sidles by Dustin.  Nods.  Yup.  *Navigators*.

Hopper stares.  We think he's convinced.  Then:

                    HOPPER
          <u>No</u>.

**MOMENTS LATER BY THE LEBARON**

WHOOSH!  Hopper yanks a DEAD LYNX GUARD out from under a
toppled food court table.  As he grabs his SMG, MAGS, a
WALKIE --

A frustrated Dustin and Erica watch from afar.

                    ERICA
          He's gonna die, they're gonna die --

                    LUCAS
          You guys survived.

                    DUSTIN
          *Barely*.  We could have really used
          you guys down there.

                    MIKE
          Yeah well -- we could have used you
          up here too.

                    LUCAS
          Yeah.  We missed you, dude.

                    WILL
          Yeah.  *Big time.*

Dustin is, well... moved by this.

                    DUSTIN
          I... missed you guys too.  *Big time.*

An emotional moment between our old friends is shattered by:

                    ERICA
          Please don't cry nerds --

                    LUCAS
          *Erica* --

                    ERICA
          Keep saying my name, see what
          happens --

                    HOPPER (O.S.)
          Heads up --

Dustin looks up to find Hopper walking toward him fast.

He tosses Dustin a walkie; Dustin catches it.

                    HOPPER (CONT'D)
          You can navigate, but from somewhere
          safe --

                    DUSTIN
          Yeah it's not that simple --

                    ERICA
          That signal won't reach down there --

                    DUSTIN
          Not on *this* -- you'd need something
          with a high enough frequency band to
          relay with the Russians' radio tower.
                    (MORE)

                    DUSTIN (CONT'D)
          But for that to work you'd have to
          find someone who has both been inside
          their comms room _and_ has access to
          their own super-powered hand-crafted
          radio tower, preferably one already
          situated at the highest point in
          Hawkins.  Oh wait.
               (dramatic beat)
          _That's me_.

A cocky Dustin snaps the Russian walkie onto his belt --

                    DUSTIN (CONT'D)
          You want us to navigate?  You've got
          us.  But we're gonna need a head
          start.
               (beat)
          And a car.

Off Hopper --

**EXT. STARCOURT MALL - NIGHT**

WHOOM!  The double doors to the mall open as

--The Scoops Troop bursts out of the mall.

                    STEVE
          Oh man -- now _this_... _this_ is what
          I'm talkin' about...

We REVERSE ANGLE to reveal THE TODDFATHER.  The rest of the
Scoops Troop behind him.  Steve _beams_ like a kid on Christmas
morning --

                    ROBIN
               (not impressed)
          The _TODDFATHER_ -- ?

                    STEVE
          Screw Todd, Steve's her daddy now --

                    ROBIN
          Did you just speak in the third
          person -- ?

                    ERICA
          Did he just call himself Daddy?

Steve ignores his "critics" as he excitedly leaps _over_ the
convertible door and behind the wheel.  As the others climb
in (Dustin and Erica in the back, Robin passenger) --

Steve turns the key, shoots a look back to Dustin --

                    STEVE
          So... where am I going exactly?

                    DUSTIN
          Weathertop --

                    STEVE
          Weather*what* -- ?

                    DUSTIN
          Just... _drive_.

Steve nods, hits the accelerator.  As the convertible speeds
away from the mall --

**INT. STARCOURT MALL - FIRST FLOOR - NIGHT**

KEYS JANGLE as Murray passes Nancy and Jonathan a GIANT RING
OF KEYS to his house, explaining quickly --

                    MURRAY
          Bottom lock, second to top lock,
          third to top, top lock.  When you
          open the door, it'll trigger the
          alarm, the keypad to which is in the
          guest room...  I believe you two will
          remember that room *quite well* --

As our Murray continues to explain his overly complex
security system to our now embarrassed teens, our camera
pulls back to find...

An intense Joyce talking to Will.

                    JOYCE
          ... Listen to me, I need to end this
          -- but I'll be back with you before
          you know it, okay?

                    WILL
               (concerned)
          Mom, I don't know --

                    JOYCE
          You'll be safe there -- I *promise*.
          It's far away from *all* this.  Just
          stay with your brother and do what he
          says, no matter what happens --

                    WILL
          I'm not worried about *me*, Mom.  I'm
          worried about _you_.

Joyce stares.  Role reversal.  She softens.

                    JOYCE
          You don't have to worry about me.
          I'll be okay --  I'll be *okay*...

Joyce pulls him into a fierce hug.  Will winces.

                    WILL
          Okay.  Mom... that's enough.  *Mom*.

But she won't let go.  As she holds him tight, our camera
moves past them to find...

Hopper, who is saying goodbye to a stubborn (but still very
weak) Eleven.

                    ELEVEN
          -- My battery is... low -- but it
          will... recharge.

                    HOPPER
          I know it will, kid, I know --

                    ELEVEN
          *I can fight* --

                    HOPPER
          Yeah.  Better than any of us.  But
          right now, we need you safe... this
          thing is after *you*.  *Not me*.
          Understand?

Eleven hesitates.

                    HOPPER (CONT'D)
          *El?*  Tell me you understand.

She gives a small, reluctant nod, then --

                    MIKE (O.S.)
          We should go.

Hopper turns.  It's Mike and Max, walking over to them.

Hopper nods, starts to help Eleven to her feet, but --

                    MIKE (CONT'D)
          I got her...

Mike wraps his arms around Eleven, supporting her.  Max takes
her from the other side.  As the three friends walk off...

Hopper feels a sudden pang of guilt, then calls out:

                    HOPPER
          ... Hey Mike.

Mike stops and looks back at Hopper.  Hopper really wants to
say something meaningful here, but all that comes out is...

                    HOPPER (CONT'D)
          Be careful.

Mike nods, then continues on his way.  And that's when Hopper
suddenly realizes -- Joyce is standing next to him.

He looks at her.  She looks at him.  And --

                    JOYCE
          *What?*

**INT. STARCOURT MALL - SERVICE CORRIDOR - NIGHT**

Our three adults are now striding down a service corridor --

And Hopper does NOT look happy.

                    HOPPER
          -- Two-man rule -- *TWO* --

                    JOYCE
          Yeah well -- change of plans --

                    HOPPER
          *"Change of plans" -- ?*

                    JOYCE
               (to Murray)
          Please explain to him --

                    MURRAY
          We have two options here Jim -- we
          can turn the machine off, or we can
          explode it --

                    HOPPER
          Says who --

                    MURRAY
          Says the man who *built it* --

                    JOYCE
          We want to explode it --

                    MURRAY
          Or else our heroic efforts will be
          for naught.  This is a three-man
          operation -- *not two* --

                        JOYCE
          *Three*.

As Hop seethes, they push through a service door and --

**EXT. STARCOURT MALL - ENTRANCE - NIGHT**

WHOOM!  The teens and the kids exit the mall.

As Mike and Max help the weakened Eleven, they notice --

                        MAX
          ... El -- you're bleeding --

El reaches up -- wipes some stray blood from her nose.

                        MIKE
                    (concerned)
          ... Are you okay?

Eleven nods.  *But we can tell she's not so sure... something
feels wrong.*  As a worried Mike and Max help her into the
back...

**IN THE FRONT,**

Nancy climbs in behind the wheel.  She slots the keys into
the ignition and turns the ignition and --

EEEE.  The engine grinds but doesn't start.

                        JONATHAN
          What's wrong -- ?

                        NANCY
          I -- don't know --

Nancy turns the key again.  The engine revs a bit, but keeps
making that ODD GRINDING SOUND -- and *still doesn't catch.*

                        NANCY (CONT'D)
          Come on *come on* you can't be
          serious --

                        LUCAS
          Didn't your mom just buy this
          car -- ?

                        NANCY
          Yes -- I'm sure it's fine --

She tries again --


                         480

                         WILL
          Did you leave the lights on -- ?

                         NANCY
          No --

                         LUCAS
          We have gas -- ?

                         NANCY
          Yes -- !!!

She tries again, harder and longer this time, and  --

The car engine begins to SHRIEK!!

                         JONATHAN
          Okay, stop -- STOP -- !

**EXT. STARCOURT MALL - ENTRANCE - NIGHT**

Jonathan leaps out of the car then --

WHOOM!  Pops the hood.  Inspects --

                         JONATHAN
          *The hell -- ?*

Nancy joins him, worried.

                         NANCY
          What -- ?

                         JONATHAN
          The distributor cable -- it's gone.

                         NANCY
          *What -- ?*

Before Jonathan can respond, a GROWL echoes across the
parking lot.  Our teens look up, startled.  It's not a
monster --

IT'S THE CAMARO.  Sitting in the far end of the empty parking
lot, idling creepily, shadowed, *Christine*-style.  *It's BILLY*.

We PUSH TOWARD THE CAMARO as its headlights suddenly kick on
and eerily upbeat music begins to play on the radio.  The
engine revs again -- growling, as if daring them to try
something.

**INT. STATION WAGON - NIGHT**

Our kids watch in the back, unnerved, when --

BAM!  The door suddenly flies open behind them.

It's Nancy --

                    NANCY
          Back in the mall -- !!  BACK IN THE
          MALL -- !!!

As the gang scrambles out of the car, we ABRUPTLY CUT...

**INT. CAMARO - STARCOURT MALL - PARKING LOT - NIGHT**

Inside the Camaro.  Music blasting.  Watching now from a
voyeuristic distance as the teens and kids scurry back into
the mall.  The camera moves up and INTO the rearview mirror
to reveal --

BILLY.  Calmly watching them.  *Eerie.*  As we continue to PUSH
IN on him...

The upbeat music RISES and then RINGS OUT *as* --

**INT. ELEVATOR SHAFT - NIGHT**

WHOOSH!  The elevator ROCKETS down the shaft.

**INT. ELEVATOR - NIGHT**

Our adults are riding the rocky elevator down.

                    HOPPER
          -- And that'll set off the alarm -- ?

                    MURRAY
          According to Alexei.  *May his soul
          rest in peace.*  Which should give you
          two an opening to retrieve the keys
          from the vault --

                    JOYCE
          Then we just follow Alexei's map to
          the observation room, turn the keys,
          and --

                    MURRAY
          *Ka-boom.*  Blow that sucker *sky high* --

                    JOYCE
          Once the Rift is closed, we escape
          back through the vents --

                    MURRAY
          *Right under* their commie noses --

                    JOYCE
          And then -- _home free_.

Murray and Joyce seem very proud of their plan but --

Hopper GRUMBLES -- clearly less certain.

                    JOYCE (CONT'D)
          You know -- just because you didn't
          come up with it doesn't mean it's not
          a good plan --

                    HOPPER
          Never said it wasn't a good plan --

                    JOYCE
          You made a noise --

                    HOPPER
          Again with the noises -- ?

                    MURRAY
          Children, _children_.  The plan is
          good.  A solid B.  Which seems
          laudable, given the situation and
          time constraints.

WHOOM!  The elevator rocks to a stop.

                    MURRAY (CONT'D)
          Dare I say -- if all goes right...
          they'll never even know we were here.

On this optimistic note, the door shoots opens and --

**INT. UNDERGROUND RUSSIAN BASE**

Our adults immediately find themselves face to face with --

FOUR RUSSIAN GUARDS WAITING FOR THE ELEVATOR.  FUCK.

The Guards raise their weapons, SHOUT in Russian, but --

                    MURRAY
          <DON'T SHOOT -- DON'T SHOOT!!!!>

The Guards freeze upon hearing his fluent Russian.

Murray waves Alexei's papers around --

                    MURRAY (CONT'D)
          <Documents, important documents --
          for the Lieutenant-Comrade!!!
                    (MORE)

483

                    MURRAY (CONT'D)
         He called us -- last minute.  Pardon
         our... sloppy appearance.>

                    RUSSIAN GUARD
         <Lieutenant?  What Lieutenant?>

                    MURRAY
         <Lieutenant... Molotov??>

The Russians stare, confused, then --

BANG-BANG-BANG!  Hopper opens fire with his SMG, mowing them
down in a burst of Indiana Jones style PG-13 violence and --

WHOMP!  The Guards crumple to the ground like rag dolls.

                    MURRAY (CONT'D)
         I had that under control.

                    HOPPER
         Sure.

Hopper kneels and... starts _undressing_ one of the guards.

Joyce stares --

                    JOYCE
         _What_ are you doing -- ?

                    HOPPER
         _Improvising._

As Hopper yanks off the Guard's uniform shirt, HARD CUT TO --

**EXT. COUNTRY ROAD - NIGHT**

VROOM!  The Toddfather speeding down a country road --

**INT. CONVERTIBLE - NIGHT**

Steve's big hair blows like crazy in the rushing wind.

Robin sits passenger; Dustin and Erica are in the back.

                    STEVE
         -- How far away is this???

                    DUSTIN
         Relax -- we_'re almost there_ --

                    ROBIN
         -- This Suzie must be pretty special,
         huh??

                    ROBIN (CONT'D)
          I mean -- if you built this thing and
          lugged it all the way to the middle
          of nowhere just to talk to her --

                    DUSTIN
          I mean no one is *scientifically*
          perfect... but Suzie's as close to
          perfect as a human can get.

                    ERICA
          She sounds made-up to me --
               (turns to Steve)
          She sound made-up to you??

Steve hesitates --

                    DUSTIN
          Why are you hesitating, Steve??

                    STEVE
               (unconvincing)
          I'm not, I think she sounds real --
          totally, absolutely real --

Dustin is about to fire back when his eyes shoot wide --

                    DUSTIN
          Left -- turn left --!

Steve looks left.  It's just *farmland*.

                    STEVE
          There's no road dude --

                    DUSTIN
          *LEFT STEVE NOW* -- !!

Steve takes a hard left and suddenly --

**EXT. COUNTRYSIDE - NIGHT**

FWOOM!  The convertible swerves off the road and plows
through a WOODEN FENCE!!  It's now driving through --

**EXT. FIELD - NIGHT**

A tree-lined field!  It's bumpy -- like a wooden roller
coaster.  So bumpy it's hard to talk --

**INT./EXT. CONVERTIBLE - NIGHT**

                    STEVE
          WHERE AM I GOING -- ???

                         DUSTIN
          *UP* --

And sure enough, the Toddfather begins to rise as it travels
up a steep slope.  Steve puts pedal to metal, pushing this
baby for all it's got.

CLOSE ON: the speedometer, trending downward.

                         ROBIN
          WE'RE NOT GONNA MAKE IT --

                         STEVE
          WE'RE GONNA MAKE IT --

But Robin is right.  The car grinds to an anti-climactic
stop.

                         STEVE (CONT'D)
          Come on, COME ON baby -- !!

As Steve hammers the pedals, the front tires spin in place,
kicking dirt -- getting *no traction*.

Robin shoots Steve a look.

                         ROBIN
          I guess the Toddfather has its
          limitations.

Steve stares.  *Shit*.  He shifts the car into park and --

**MOMENTS LATER**

Doors fly open as the gang climbs out of the Toddfather and
begins to quickly scurry up the rest of the way.  OUR CAMERA
SOARS OVER THEM AND TO THE VERY TOP OF THIS HILL TO REVEAL....

CEREBRO.  Still standing, right where we left it, its metal
towers shimmering beautifully in the moonlight.  As our
CAMERA whooshes over its towers:

                         MIKE (PRELAP)
          Cerebro -- do copy?  Cerebro -- do
          you COPY?

**INT. STARCOURT MALL - NIGHT**

Mike is making panicked calls on a WALKIE.

486

                    MIKE
          Cerebro -- I repeat, do you copy?  We
          are trapped in the mall and in need
          of emergency transportation -- I
          repeat...

As Mike continues to relay his message to a currently non-
responsive Cerebro, our CAMERA MOVES PAST HIM, finds --

Lucas, retrieving his WRIST ROCKET from his backpack.  As he
loads it with a ROCK, the camera continues to MOVE and PAN
until we finally find...

Nancy, who is searching one of the DEAD LYNX GUARDS.  She
yanks a HANDGUN out of his holster, checks the mag -- it's
fully loaded.  As she shoves the mag back into the gun --

                    MAX (O.S.)
          You're going to kill him, aren't you?

Nancy looks up, sees a worried Max.  Reassures:

                    NANCY
          This is just... a precaution.  Okay?

                    WILL
          And not just against Billy.  If he
          knows we're here, so does the Mind
          Flayer.

Nancy's eyes go to Mike -- still calling on the walkie.

                    MIKE
          -- I repeat... Cerebro -- do you
          copy?  We are in need of *emergency
          transportation* --

Nancy's gaze then shifts to the crashed LeBaron.

                    NANCY
                (to Jonathan, half-joking)
          No way that will drive, right?

Jonathan shakes his head, but...

                    JONATHAN
          We don't need it to drive -- we just
          need its distributor cable.

The teens share a look.  Then --

**MOMENTS LATER**

More GROANS as the group (including Mike and Lucas) now work together to push the LeBaron.  But this car is, well, _VERY HEAVY_.  Their faces burn red, their muscles strain, and...

WHOOMP!  The LeBaron rocks back against the wall.

> LUCAS
> SHIT!

Everyone doubles over, catches their breath --

> ELEVEN (O.S.)
> Let me try.

The gang turns.  Finds Eleven.  Watching nearby.

> MIKE
> _El --_

> ELEVEN
> I can do it.

**MOMENTS LATER**

Everyone gathers now, watching anxiously behind El as --

She holds out a hand.  She's going to move this LeBaron with her powers.  We PUSH IN ON EL as holds out her right hand... narrowing those eyes... focusing those powers...

Blood begins to drip from her nose... the music builds as...

We PUSH IN on El as she focuses harder... and harder... _and_ --

**INT. UNDERGROUND RUSSIAN BASE - TUNNELS**

VROOM!  A DELIVERY TRUCK _ROARS_ down a tunnel.

**INT. UNDERGROUND RUSSIAN BASE - TUNNELS**

An ARMED GUARD smokes outside some BLAST DOORS.

He hears an approaching ENGINE, looks up to find --

A MINI-TRUCK is pulling up to him.  As it comes to a stop, the armed guard approaches, addresses the driver.

> ARMED GUARD
> <Can I help?>

We now REVERSE to reveal that the driver is MURRAY!  Hopper
sits passenger.  Both men are disguised in RUSSIAN
UNIFORMS!!!

> MURRAY
> <Picking up.>

The Armed Guard scrutinizes these... odd characters.

> ARMED GUARD
> <Do I know you?>

> MURRAY
> <New arrivals.  Landed last night.>

> ARMED GUARD
> <Say goodbye to sunlight.>

> MURRAY
> <Who needs sunlight when we have one
> another Comrade -- ?>

> ARMED GUARD
> <Indeed, Comrade -- !>

> MURRAY
> <... And a bottle of Stolichnaya -->

The Guard BELLOWS at this "hilarious" joke, then smacks a
BUTTON ON THE WALL, and --

**INT. UNDERGROUND RUSSIAN BASE - STORAGE ROOM - NIGHT**

SHOOM!  Metal BLAST DOORS shoot open as --

The truck pulls into the storage room.

**MOMENTS LATER**

CHOOM!  The lock on the back of the truck opens as --

Murray lets Joyce out.  She's been hiding in the back!  She's
also disguised as a male Russian officer -- although her
outfit is wildly oversized.  And she doesn't look happy.

As she hops out the back --

> JOYCE
> (to Murray)
> Why are you talking so much -- ??

> MURRAY
> He was nice --

Murray heads away from the truck.  Joyce climbs out of the
back and nips at his heels, disbelieving --

> JOYCE
> He was *nice* -- ??

> HOPPER
> Maybe we can invite him over after
> all this --

> JOYCE
> I could make a casserole --

> HOPPER
> I'll bring a six pack -- share a
> drink, a few laughs --

Murray ignores them as he heads up the metal steps into --

**THE PROMETHIUM ROOM - CONTINUOUS**

Murray scans the floor, kneels down, grabs a grate, and LIFTS
to reveal THE VENTILATION SYSTEM.  It looks, well... *snug.*

> MURRAY
> Anyone want to trade jobs?

Hopper and Joyce stare, a clear *no thanks*, when --

Murray's walkie CRACKLES TO LIFE.  It's --

> DUSTIN (O.S.)
> BALD EAGLE -- DO YOU COPY?

> INTERCUT WITH:

**EXT. WEATHERTOP - NIGHT**

Dustin and Scoops Troop have made it to Cerebro!!!

> DUSTIN
> BALD EAGLE, I repeat -- this is
> Scoops Troop, do you copy?

**INT. PROMETHIUM ROOM - NIGHT**

Murray raises his walkie, hits talk --

> MURRAY
> Yes I copy --

Steve, Robin, and Erica share looks.  *Holy shit* it *worked!*

490

                    DUSTIN
          *Call sign?*

Murray sighs.

                    MURRAY
               (low)
          Bald Eagle --

                    DUSTIN
          Please repeat?

                    MURRAY
          Bald Eagle, this is *BALD EAGLE* --

**EXT. WEATHERTOP - NIGHT**

Erica gives Dustin a thumbs-up, pleased.  Dustin is too.

                    DUSTIN
          Copy that!  It's good to hear your
          voice Bald Eagle -- what's your
          twenty?

**INT. PROMETHIUM ROOM - NIGHT**

                    MURRAY
          We've reached the vent -- I'll
          contact when I need you.  Until then
          -- *silence.*

                    DUSTIN
          Roger that, Bald Eagle, Scoops Troop,
          going radio silent, ten-ten.  *Over.*

                    MURRAY
          I hate children.

Murray hooks the walkie onto his belt, drops into the shaft.

                    HOPPER
          Good luck.

                    MURRAY
          Remember, if anyone talks to you --

                    JOYCE
          Smile and nod.

Hopper slams the grate over Murray, blocking camera, and --

**INT. STARCOURT MALL - NIGHT**

EEEEE... Metal GROANS as the LeBaron shifts... it's *MOVING*!!!

But then our camera RISES UP over the crumpled hood of the car to reveal that *Eleven isn't moving it*. Instead, it's...

The rest of our gang, only things have changed -- they are now using *TWO BRONZE METAL STANCHIONS* as levers to pry the car off the wall. And it seems to be working!

> JONATHAN
> KEEP GOING -- !!

They let out a collective primal yell, one final push, and --

WHOOM! The LeBaron FINALLY flips right side up with a METALLIC CRUNCH! They did it!

Everyone drops back, exhausted, catching their breath --

Mike shoots Nancy a look --

> MIKE
> Told you -- *physics.*

But there's no time for celebration --

Nancy moves to the hood, tries to open it, but --

> NANCY
> How do we get this open -- ?

> JONATHAN
> There's gotta be a latch --

Jonathan throws open the door, climbs in. As he searches for a latch to pop the hood, checking under the wheel --

An exhausted Max notices something.

> MAX
> What is she doing...?

Mike walks up beside Max, follows her gaze to find --

Eleven. She's in the food court plaza, digging through a trash can. As Mike and Max share looks, *uhhhh*, we move --

**INTO THE PLAZA,**

As Eleven pulls... an EMPTY NEW COKE CAN out of the trash.

She places it on a ledge along the rim of the atrium, then
backs up.  And now we understand -- she's going to try to
crush this thing!  She holds out her hand.  Narrows her
eyes... and...

*WE FLASHBACK TO ELEVEN CRUSHING THE COKE CAN IN SEASON ONE.
THIS IS EASY, EARLY DAYS SHIT.  BUT --*

This New Coke can is not doing *anything* right now...

                    MIKE
          *El --*

Mike and Max approach, worried, but Eleven doesn't even look
at them, doesn't even take her *eyes off that can* --

Our CAMERA PUSHES IN on her as she increases her focus, then
does a matching PUSH IN ON the Coke can.  Closer, _closer_.

Some blood slips from her nose... and...

There is a CREAKING SOUND.  For a moment we think her powers
are working again -- but it doesn't sound like aluminum
crumpling.  It's too sharp, too high-pitched.  It sounds
like... GLASS.  As Max becomes aware of this...

**OVER BY THE LEBARON,**

Jonathan finds the latch below the wheel and --

POP!  The hood flies open.  *Finally.*  As Nancy reaches into
the engine, digging for the cable, we PULL BACK TO FIND...

Will, reaching a hand to the back of his neck.  *Goosebumps.*

**BACK IN THE PLAZA,**

Max follows that GROANING sound, shifting her gaze UP.

THERE IS A DARK SHADOW ON THE SPRAWLING GLASS CEILING
DIRECTLY ABOVE THEM.  THE GLASS BEGINS TO SPIDERWEB.

                    MAX
          *... Mike...*

Mike follows her gaze, his eyes going wide too, as --

**UP ABOVE,**

The glass continues to spiderweb outward --

**OVER BY THE LEBARON,**

WHOOM!  Nancy rips out the DISTRIBUTOR CABLE --

                    NANCY
          *Got it -- !*

**BACK WITH ELEVEN,**

Mike screams --

                    MIKE
          NANCY!!!

She looks at her brother -- then her expression shifts from
relief to fear as she takes in the monster above them.  But
brother and sister are separated by too much distance --

*And that glass is about to break --*

**BACK IN THE ATRIUM**

PUSH IN as Eleven turns, sees it now too.  Just as her face
darkens with fear --

WHAM!  A hand grabs her by the wrist.  It's Mike!  He pulls
her away, Max running too, the trio escaping the atrium
together just as --

**ABOVE THEM**

The ceiling VIOLENTLY SHATTERS, showering glass as --

**IN THE ATRIUM**

THE GIANT MONSTER CRASHES DOWN INTO THE ATRIUM, PLUMMETING
FIFTY FEET INTO THE PLAZA -- KNOCKING THE STARCOURT SIGN ON
ITS WAY DOWN AND --

WHAM!  IT LANDS IN THE ATRIUM, SMASHING THE PLANTER INTO A
THOUSAND PIECES.  THE STARCOURT NEON SIGN SWINGS AND SPARKS
LIKE CRAZY ABOVE AS THE MONSTER RISES UP, REELS BACK ITS
HEAD, AND --

LETS OUT A MONSTROUS, EAR-SHATTERING ROAR -- !

**INT. ELEVATOR SHAFT - NIGHT**

WHOOM!  The freight elevator ZOOMS down the shaft.

**INT. UNDERGROUND RUSSIAN BASE - TUNNELS - NIGHT**

SHOOM!  The elevator door rises to reveal --

GRIGORI AND HIS GOONS.  They've returned "home" from the
fairgrounds.  Their faces abruptly fall as they see --

The now UNDRESSED SOLDIERS that Hop killed.

Other guards are here now --

NERVOUS GUARD
          <We just found them like this -->

Grigori kneels down.  And immediately <u>knows</u>:

                         GRIGORI
          <<u>*The American.*</u>>

Off this, HARD CUT TO:

**INT. UNDERGROUND RUSSIAN BASE - STORAGE ROOM - NIGHT**

Hopper, the "American," pacing in the storage room, nervous.

Joyce, sitting on the steps, watches him.

                         HOPPER
          This is taking too long --

                         JOYCE
          It's fine --

                         HOPPER
          It's not.  It's *not*.

He turns back to Joyce --

                         HOPPER (CONT'D)
          She could've died you know -- she
          almost *did* --

                         JOYCE
          Yeah but she's safe now.  She'll be
          at Murray's soon.  And whatever's
          after her -- it <u>won't find her</u>.  Not
          before we kill it.

Hopper stares at Joyce.  Surprised.

                         HOPPER
          Okay.  That's not how that was
          supposed to go.  You were supposed to
          say, "Yeah -- I told you we needed to
          get back to the kids -- "

                         JOYCE
          Then you'd say something like, "Well,
          it's hard to listen to you when you
          treat everything like it's the end of
          the goddamn world."

They share a smile.  Hopper sits beside Joyce.

                    HOPPER
        You know, despite it all -- I mean --
        the arguing and everything -- I think
        we actually... make a pretty good
        team.

                    JOYCE
        Yeah.  I mean, we made it this far,
        didn't we -- ?

                    HOPPER
        We did.  *We did.*

                    JOYCE
        So... am I hired or what?

Hopper looks at Joyce, surprised.

                    JOYCE (CONT'D)
        Detective Byers does have a ring,
        doesn't it?

                    HOPPER
        Yeah, but, uh, it's hard to serve a
        town you're not living in, Detective.
            (off Joyce)
        I mean, I assume you still... plan on
        moving out of here?

                    JOYCE
        Well... we'll see how it goes...

                    HOPPER
        How... *what* goes?

                    JOYCE
        I was just thinking... if we actually
        do make it out of here -- we deserve
        to celebrate -- right?

                    HOPPER
        Yeah.  I mean yes.  Absolutely.

                    JOYCE
        I hear Enzo's is pretty good.

Hopper stares.  *Is this happening?*

                    JOYCE (CONT'D)
        Maybe Friday.  Eight o'clock?

Hopper tries to stay cool, *stay cool* --

                    HOPPER
          Yeah.  Um -- yeah.  It's just, uh --
          El likes watching *Miami Vice* on
          Friday, which starts at ten, so I
          can't be... out too late --

                    JOYCE
          Should we say seven then -- ?

                    HOPPER
          Seven.  Great.  That -- works.  For
          me.  Meet you there -- ?

                    JOYCE
          How about you pick me up?

                    HOPPER
          Picking you up.  Friday.  Seven.

                    JOYCE
          It's a date.

Hopper blinks.  *Did he hear that right?*

                    HOPPER
          Okay... I just -- want to be super
          clear here so there's no confusion --
          by "date" you mean --

                    JOYCE
          Hop --

                    HOPPER
          Yeah --

                    JOYCE
          Stop talking before I change my mind.

                    HOPPER
          Right.  Yeah.  Okay.

Hopper leans his head against the wall, grinning like a
schoolboy, as --

**INT.  UNDERGROUND RUSSIAN BASE - VENTILATION SHAFT - NIGHT**

CLANG!  Elbows smash against metal as --

A SWEATY and DIRTY and EXHAUSTED Murray wriggles his way
through the tiny ventilation shaft.  *He really did get the
shit end of the stick here.*  He crawls forward into --

**A FOUR-WAY JUNCTION**

He speaks into his radio, through heavy breaths --

>                    MURRAY
>          Scoops Troop -- this is...
>              (ugh)
>          Bald Eagle.  I've reached another
>          junction.

                                        INTERCUT WITH:

**EXT. WEATHERTOP - NIGHT**

Dustin consults with Erica.

>                    DUSTIN
>          This is what -- ?

>                    ERICA
>          The fourth junction --

>                    DUSTIN
>          If memory serves, that was right
>          after the My Little Pony thesis --

>                    ERICA
>          We went left.  So he should go --

>                    DUSTIN/ERICA
>          *Right*.

Dustin calls on the CB, confident --

>                    DUSTIN
>          FLY RIGHT, BALD EAGLE, *FLY RIGHT* --

**INT. VENTILATION SHAFT - JUNCTION - NIGHT**

>                    MURRAY
>          Roger that.  Flying right.
>              (hangs up)
>          *Little shit*.

Murray crawls *right*, continuing onward, as --

**EXT. WEATHERTOP - NIGHT**

>                    ROBIN
>          What's the My Little Pony thesis -- ?

>                    ERICA
>          Don't get him started --

Dustin is about to start anyway when --

                     STEVE (O.S.)
          *Hey guys* --

They look up to find Steve, standing at the edge of the hill,
looking off into the distance. As they walk up to his side,
joining him, we RISE UP AND *PUSH OVER* THEIR BACKS TO REVEAL:

THE MALL. It's far off in the distance, but we can see that
its NEON LIGHTS ARE FLASHING LIKE CRAZY. And not only that:
All of the surrounding lights are flashing too, rippling out
from the mall, like a massive... alarm.

Then -- we hear the ROAR of the monster...

As Scoops Troop shares scared looks --

**MOMENTS LATER**

A panicked Dustin drops down by Cerebro, grabs the CB, and --

                   DUSTIN (O.S.)
          Griswold Family, this is Scoops Troop
          -- do you copy?

**INT. STARCOURT MALL - FOOD COURT - NIGHT**

CLOSE ON: MIKE'S WALKIE. Abandoned on a food court table.

                   DUSTIN (O.S.)
          I repeat, this is Scoops Troop --
          Griswold Family, do you co -- ?

BOOM! A GIANT TENTACLE SUDDENLY SNATCHES THE WALKIE AND --

**BACK ON WEATHERTOP,**

Dustin and the others hear MONSTROUS SHRIEKING SOUNDS coming
out of the speaker as --

**INT. STARCOURT MALL - FOOD COURT - NIGHT**

The monster pulls the walkie up to its mouth, as if examining
it -- then -- FWOOM! Flings it angrily across the mall. As
the walkie ricochets off a neon light and skips across the
ground, all smashed up now, our camera SLIDES BEHIND...

**THE LEBARON,**

To reveal Group ONE (Lucas, Will, Jonathan, Nancy) hiding in
the small space between the busted LeBaron and NY Pizza, as --

**EXT. WEATHERTOP - NIGHT**

The CB radio goes STATIC.  Dead.  Scoops Troop shares
horrified looks as --

**INT. STARCOURT MALL - ATRIUM - NIGHT**

Our MONSTER now marches forward, looking cool but _scary as_
_all hell_ in the flashing neon lights of our mall.  As it
clambers up these steps, making its way out of the atrium, we
DOLLY BEHIND --

**THE NUT SHACK - CONTINUOUS**

To reveal GROUP TWO (Eleven, Max, Mike) hiding, terrified.
Our camera continues to DOLLY, to the other side of the Nut
Shack now, leaving our kids and revealing...

Our monster, now making its way over to that fleshy piece of
it that Eleven removed from her body.  As it bends its head
down, examining it, dripping mucus onto the floor...

**THE NUT SHACK - CONTINUOUS**

We PUSH IN on Eleven, holding her breath, trying her very
best not to scream as --

**BACK OVER IN THE FOOD COURT**

We push in on the cracked walkie.  A very distorted, barely
intelligible voice cuts through the busted speakers --

>                     DUSTIN (OVER WALKIE)
>           -- G -- Wald -- copy -- ?

**EXT. WEATHERTOP - NIGHT**

>                     DUSTIN
>           -- I repeat -- this is Scoops Troop?
>           Do you copy???   DO YOU COPY???

Steve can't take it anymore, starts to head off down the
hill --

>                     ERICA
>           Where are you going -- ??

>                     STEVE
>           To get them the _hell out of there_.
>                (to Dustin over shoulder)
>           Stay here, contact the others --

Steve sprints down the hill toward the waiting Toddfather.

500

                         ROBIN
               *Shit* --

Robin starts to hurry after him when --

                         DUSTIN
               Robin!

She whips back around.  Dustin unhooks the RUSSIAN WALKIE
from his belt.

                         DUSTIN (CONT'D)
               Stay in touch.

He tosses it to Robin.  She snatches it, nods, then continues
down the hill, as --

Dustin turns his focus back to Cerebro:

                         DUSTIN (CONT'D)
                    (urgent)
               Bald Eagle, what's your twenty?

**INT. UNDERGROUND RUSSIAN BASE - VENTILATION SHAFT - NIGHT**

Murray is in another vent now, sweating profusely --

                         MURRAY
               I told *you* *radio silence* --

                         DUSTIN
               Yeah well -- there's a problem --

**INT. UNDERGROUND RUSSIAN BASE - STORAGE ROOM**

Hopper and Joyce hear this.

PUSH IN on Hop as he raises up his walkie, worried --

                         HOPPER
               What kind of problem -- ?

**INT. STARCOURT MALL - NIGHT**

BOOM-SPLAT!  The Monster stomps right past --

Mike and Eleven, who are holding hands, terrified *as* --

The monster now makes its way toward the Great Cookie area of
the food court.  It shoves aside some tables and uncovers --
A DEAD RUSSIAN.  It grabs the dead Russian up with one of its
tentacles as...

**BEHIND THE LEBARON - CONTINUOUS**

Jonathan, Nancy, Will, and Lucas hold their breaths.  Nancy's eyes shift to the LeBaron's cracked rearview mirror.  In the reflection, she can see the monster study the Russian, then toss him aside like litter.  This thing is *very* close to *them* now...

**INT. STARCOURT MALL - NUT SHACK - NIGHT**

Mike peers out from behind the Nut Shack, sees that the monster's back is now turned to them.

He drops back into hiding.  Looks to the escalator.

>                    MIKE
>               (low, urgent)
>      I think we can make it --

Max shakes her head, motions to Eleven --

>                    MAX
>               (low)
>      Not with El's leg --

>                    MIKE
>               (low)
>      We *have to try* --

>                    ELEVEN
>               (low)
>      There's another way --  an exit -- in
>      the Gap --

>                    MIKE
>               (low)
>      You sure -- ?

Eleven nods.  *She's sure.*  Mike considers.  Looks back once more at the monster.  Its back still turned away from them.

Mike looks at Max and Eleven.  *Nods.*  And --

WHOOSH!  They leap to their feet, <u>*bursting out of hiding*</u>. They are briefly, terrifyingly exposed as they scurry to the GAP.  They climb through the shattered display window, climbing over the displays, just about to make it when --

**INT. STARCOURT MALL - THE GAP - CONTINUOUS**

Mike's knee knocks into a DISPLAY RACK!  *Shit.*  It topples to the floor, making a LOUD CLANG!

**INT. STARCOURT MALL - FOOD COURT - NIGHT**

The monster hears it, whirls --

**INT. STARCOURT MALL - THE GAP - NIGHT**

Mike, Max, and El race deeper into the Gap but --

**INT. STARCOURT MALL - ATRIUM - NIGHT**

It's too late.  The monster has heard them!  It stomps toward the Gap, ROARING *and* --

**INT. UNDERGROUND RUSSIAN BASE - MACHINE ROOM - NIGHT**

WHOOM!  Murray knocks out the vent cover, pokes his head like a prairie dog into --

The machine room.  He made it!

He catches his breath, wipes sweat from his brow --

>                    MURRAY
>           (into walkie, proud)
>      Bald Eagle has landed.  Repeat --
>      <u>Bald Eagle has landed</u>.

He climbs out of the vent as --

**EXT. WEATHERTOP - NIGHT**

Dustin and Erica share relieved looks, but --

**INT. UNDERGROUND RUSSIAN BASE - STORAGE ROOM - NIGHT**

Hopper is anything but relieved, pacing in here --

>                    HOPPER
>            (into walkie)
>      How much longer -- ?

**INT. UNDERGROUND RUSSIAN BASE - MACHINE ROOM - NIGHT**

WHAM!  Murray rams a metal container in front of the door, barricading himself in here.  As he catches his breath --

>                    MURRAY
>          (into walkie, annoyed)
>      I DON'T KNOW I'VE NEVER DONE THIS
>      BEFORE --

Murray now grabs Alexei's instructions from his pockets, reads them, then scans the room.  He doesn't find anything that matches up with the drawings Alexei made -- *wait.*

He flips the papers *upside down* and --

                    MURRAY (CONT'D)
          Oh *okay* -- okay okay --

He races over to a large HATCH in the wall, then swings it
open to reveal a mess of WIRES AND FUSES.

                    MURRAY (CONT'D)
                (into walkie)
            Okay -- get ready lovebirds, you're
            almost up to bat --

He starts ripping out wires per Alexei's instructions.  We
CROSSCUT his frantic actions with --

**INT. OBSERVATION ROOM - NIGHT**

... Their repercussions in the observation room, where
PRESSURE GAUGES begin to rise, and LIGHTS begin to flash.

PANICKED SCIENTISTS share frightened looks as --

**INT. RIFT CHAMBER**

Down below, the machine itself begins to *react, sparking a
bit,* its gears churning faster, _something happening._

SCIENTISTS IN HAZMAT SUITS (a few carry MYSTERIOUS METAL
CASES) back away from the misbehaving machine as --

A HAZMAT MAN *slams* a button, sounding an ALARM, and --

**INT. UNDERGROUND RUSSIAN BASE - STORAGE ROOM**

WAH!  WAH!  WAH!  A red alarm begins to flash.  Our camera
swings from the siren to Hopper and Joyce.  *That's their cue.*

They hurry through a door, moving fast, as --

**INT. STARCOURT MALL - FIRST FLOOR - NIGHT**

KA-THWUMP!  Our massive monster bends down by the Gap's
shattered display window and...

**INT. STARCOURT MALL - THE GAP - FIRST FLOOR - NIGHT**

KA-WHUMP!  The monster thrusts one of its enormous appendages
through the broken display window and _INTO_ the Gap.  The
appendage lands in the middle of the kids' section.

Various tentacles peel off from the appendage.

One of the tentacles sees what looks like Eleven -- her
shoulder peeking out from behind a column.

WHOOSH!  It strikes like an angry snake and GRABS --

Eleven!! No, wait -- it's a *MANNEQUIN* WEARING ELEVEN'S DRESS. The jaws clamp around the mannequin's shiny plastic neck, then --

WHOOM! The tentacle yanks the mannequin back toward the Monster's horrible face. The monster studies the mannequin for half a beat, then -- *realizing this isn't her* -- it flings it away. The now slime-covered mannequin lands right by --

The *real* Eleven. She's hiding behind a shoe shelf next to Mike and Max. She stares for a horrified beat at her "killed" doppelgänger, then tightens her grip on Mike's hand as --

**BEHIND THE LEBARON - NIGHT**

Jonathan and the others peer over the top of the LeBaron, see the monster searching the Gap. They drop back down --

> JONATHAN
> (whisper)
> Shit shit shit --

Lucas has an idea. He pulls out... his *WRIST ROCKET*.

**INT. STARCOURT MALL - THE GAP - BEHIND THE COUNTER - NIGHT**

Mike, Max, and Eleven hold their collective breaths while --

Those tentacles *hunt*. Snaking through the store. Pushing through some racks of clothes... about to find them when --

**INT. STARCOURT MALL - FOOD COURT - NIGHT**

Lucas rises up from behind the LeBaron, wrist rocket taut and ready to fire. Holy shit -- is he going to shoot the monster?? *Nope.* He aims away from the monster at --

THE COLORFUL DISPLAY OF BALLOONS which are floating above the now empty LeBaron display area!

**INT. STARCOURT MALL - THE GAP - BEHIND THE COUNTER - NIGHT**

The tentacle swoops around the shelf to find our kids but --

They aren't there. OUR CAMERA SUCKS BACK TO FIND --

They've moved! Hiding behind the front counter now.

But the tentacle continues to hunt for them... it slinks around the counter... *about to find them*... when --

**INT. STARCOURT MALL - FOOD COURT - NIGHT**

FWOOM! Lucas fires. We WHIP PAN with the rock as it SOARS across the length of the mall and --

POP! Two balloons ERUPT. Bullseye! Sounds like a GUNSHOT and --

**OUTSIDE THE GAP**

WHOOM! The monster SNAPS toward the sound, its limb sucking out of the Gap. It lumbers toward the balloons, leaving --

**INT. THE GAP - NIGHT**

Our kids. Holy shit that was close. *Too close.*

> MIKE
> *Let's go -- !*

They hurry on, racing through the dressing room, bursting through the back door, _escaping_ as --

**INT. STARCOURT MALL - NY PIZZA - NIGHT**

Lucas, Will, Jonathan, and Nancy escape into NY Pizza.

Keeping *low and* quiet, they sneak through the kitchen and out a back door which leads them into --

**ANOTHER SERVICE CORRIDOR**

They turn a corner and head into --

**A STAIRWELL**

As they race up to the second floor --

**INT. UNDERGROUND RUSSIAN BASE - HUB - NIGHT**

WAH!! WAH!! WAH!! The alarm sounds through the base as --

SOLDIERS and OTHER PERSONNEL race down those metal steps -- *evacuating.* A PA system drones:

> RUSSIAN PA
> <PROCEED TO EVACUATION RENDEZVOUS,
> TWO, FOUR, FIVE. REPEAT -- PROCEED
> TO EVACUATION RENDEZVOUS TWO, FOUR,
> FIVE -->

**INT. UNDERGROUND RUSSIAN BASE - TUNNELS - NIGHT**

FLEEING SOLDIERS race past a hallway, passing right by --

Hopper and Joyce, hiding in another hallway.

They sweep out and move into --

**THE HUB - MOMENTS LATER**

It's mostly emptied out now.  *So far, so good.*

They race up a flight of stairs, to the second floor --

**INT. UNDERGROUND RUSSIAN BASE - HUB - SECOND FLOOR - NIGHT**

They are almost to the vault room when --

WHOOM!  A door opens and a SOLDIER steps out right in front
of them!  He speaks to them in (unsubtitled) Russian --

> SOLDIER
> <Did Mikhail send for you?>

They share a look with one another, then... SMILE AND NOD.

The soldier nods back, then hurries on his way.  *Phew.*

Hopper walks up to the door, swipes the keycard through a
control panel outside a secure door.  BEEP.  A light blinks
green and they enter --

**INT. UNDERGROUND RUSSIAN BASE - VAULT ROOM - NIGHT**

On the far end of this room: a HIGH-TECH VAULT (*high-tech for
the eighties, that is*).  As they approach --

> HOPPER
> Give me the code --

Joyce consults the papers from Alexei --

> JOYCE
> Six six two six zero eight zero zero
> four --

Hopper punches it into a keypad and --

EEEEEE!!  The vault makes a horrible sound.  A light blinks
RED.  That... *clearly didn't work.*

> HOPPER
> *Again* --

> JOYCE
> Six six two six zero eight zero zero
> four --

EEEE!!  The vault makes the SAME HORRIBLE SOUND.

Hopper grabs up his walkie.

> HOPPER
> MURRAY THIS GODDAMN CODE DOESN'T
> WORK!

INTERCUT WITH:

**INT. UNDERGROUND RUSSIAN BASE - MACHINE ROOM - NIGHT**

Murray pauses from his "sabotage" work:

> MURRAY
> Are you sure??

> HOPPER
> Yes I'm sure --

Murray begins to pace now, pulling at his beard.

> MURRAY
> I suppose it... could be wrong --

> HOPPER
> *How* could it be wrong -- ??

> MURRAY
> The code is a number -- a famous
> number -- Planck's Constant -- I -- I
> thought I knew it --

> HOPPER
> (dawning on him)
> This is *YOUR* handwriting -- ??

As Hop and Murray continue to bicker, CUT TO --

**EXT. WEATHERTOP - NIGHT**

Dustin and Erica, listening.

> DUSTIN
> (mind racing)
> *Planck's Constant...*

> ERICA
> You know it?

> DUSTIN
> Not by heart.  You?

> ERICA
> I am NOT a nerd.  *Nerd.*

Dustin suddenly has a thought -- a *lightbulb moment.*  He blends down, starts to switch the frequency on Cerebro --

> ERICA (CONT'D)
> What are you doing -- ??

Dustin ignores her, keeps searching.  Static FLARES and --

**EXT. STARCOURT MALL - NIGHT**

WHOOM!  The mall doors burst open as Nancy, Jonathan, Lucas, Will burst out of the mall and race to the family wagon.

Jonathan throws open the hood, installs the distributor cable.  Just as he hooks it in --

VROOM!  VROOM!  An engine growls -- it's Billy revving that Camaro.  *Daring them to try to escape.*

Nancy pulls out her gun --

> NANCY
> Get the car started --

As Jonathan and the others leap into the car --

Nancy takes a step toward the Camaro, raises the GUN, as --

**INT./EXT. STATION WAGON - NIGHT**

VROOM!  Keys turn as Jonathan tries to start the car, but... the engine doesn't catch.

> JONATHAN
> No no no no come on come on -- !

**EXT. STARCOURT MALL - PARKING LOT**

A scarily calm Billy watches them from across the parking lot.  He revs the engine, then *shifts into drive* and --

HAMMERS THE ACCELERATOR.

RUBBER BURNS AS THE CAMARO SPEEDS RIGHT FOR THEM!

**INT./EXT. STATION WAGON - OUTSIDE MALL - NIGHT**

*Fuck.*  Nancy opens fire on the oncoming VEHICLE!

BANG BANG BANG!  Bullets pierce the car, punching through the windshield, sparking the hood, but it keeps on plowing toward them like a missile --

>                         LUCAS
>             WE GOTTA GO -- !!!

Jonathan turns the key again, the engine ALMOST catches, but they're almost OUT OF TIME --

**INT./EXT. BILLY'S CAMARO - NIGHT**

Billy speeds up, hitting seventy now -- this is *gonna* hurt --

**INT./EXT. STATION WAGON - NIGHT**

BANG BANG-CLICK.  Nancy runs out of ammo!  *Shit!*  As --

Jonathan turns the key.  It finally starts -- but *too late* --

**EXT. STARCOURT MALL - PARKING LOT - NIGHT**

The Camaro is *about* to hit them -- *kill Nancy* -- when --

A BLURRY YELLOW OBJECT SUDDENLY FLIES FROM OFF-SCREEN AND --

BOOOOOM!  IT COLLIDES WITH BILLY'S CAMARO!!!  IT'S STEVE AND ROBIN IN THE TODDFATHER!!  HELL FUCKING YES!!!!  AS METAL BULLET MEETS METAL BULLET, THERE IS AN EPIC COLLISION AND --

The Camaro goes spinning, crashing to a violent halt --

The Toddfather spins to a stop right by it and --

**INT./EXT. STATION WAGON - NIGHT**

>                         WILL
>             Holy shit --

Nancy can't believe it.  No one can believe it.

**INT. BILLY'S CAMARO - NIGHT**

FWOOM!  The Camaro's engine catches fire as --

Billy lies slumped against the wheel -- bleeding badly -- unmoving.  It seems, at least for now, he's off the board.

**INT./EXT. TODDFATHER - NIGHT**

A dazed Steve looks at a dazed Robin.

>                         STEVE
>             You... *okay?*

                    ROBIN
          Ask me tomorrow.

Robin suddenly hears something, looks up --

                    ROBIN (CONT'D)
          *Oh my God...*

Steve follows her gaze up to find --

THE MONSTER CRAWLING UP OUT OF THE ROOF.  IT ROARS AS --

SCREEE!  The now working station wagon speeds up to them!

                    JONATHAN
          GET IN!!!

Jonathan pops open the "way back."  Robin and Steve leap in.
They've barely settled before Jonathan punches it and --

SCREEEEECH!  As they tear away, our monster ROARS, LUNGES
AFTER THEM, and right here we make a HARD JARRING CUT TO --

**EXT. SUBURBAN HOUSE - SALT LAKE CITY - NIGHT**

CRICKETS.  Tranquility.  We're suddenly and bizarrely outside
a cute suburban house with a perfect manicured lawn.  A LARGE
HAND-BUILT RADIO TOWER sits atop the roof of the house.

Behind the house, a large, beautiful MOUNTAIN RANGE.

CHYRON: SALT LAKE CITY, UTAH.

**INT. SUBURBAN HOUSE - GIRL'S BEDROOM - NIGHT**

The cords of this radio tower sneak through a half-open
bedroom window.  We DRIFT across the bedroom to find...

A girl lying back in bed -- her face mostly hidden behind a
much-read *WIZARD OF EARTHSEA* paperback, when --

                    DUSTIN (O.S.)
               (over radio, low)
          Suzie -- do you copy??

The paperback lowers to reveal: SUZIE!  Whoa.  She's *REAL* --
she's got freckles and glasses and she's everything we could
have hoped for!!  Her eyes narrow as she looks over at --

A HAM RADIO STATION ON HER DESK.  Dustin's voice crackles out
of its speakers, clearer this time, unmistakable:

                    DUSTIN (O.S.) (CONT'D)
          Suzie, *do you copy?*?

                            512

Suzie can hardly believe her ears!!! She leaps out of bed in her nerdy pajamas, races to her desk, snatches up the CB, and --

                    SUZIE
          This is Suzie -- I -- _I COPY_!!!

                                        INTERCUT WITH:

**EXT. WEATHERTOP - NIGHT**

Dustin is so relieved he can barely speak --

                    DUSTIN
          _SUZIE_!!

                    SUZIE
          _DUSTYBUN_???

                    ERICA
              (horrified)
          _Dustybun?_

Dustin waves Erica off -- shut up!!

                    SUZIE
          Where have you been???

                    DUSTIN
          I'm so so sorry -- I've been busy --
          trying to save the world from...
              (screw it)
          Russians and monsters --

Suzie giggles --

                    SUZIE
          Of course you have -- !

                    ERICA
              (to Dustin, angry whisper)
          _Get the goddamn number already_ -- !

                    SUZIE
          Who was that?

                    DUSTIN
          I don't know -- I'm getting some --
              (lying)
          _Interference_, let's shift
          transmission frequency to seventy one
          eight five point three eight --

                    SUZIE
          Copy that, shifting frequency stand
          by --

Suzie and Dustin simultaneously turn their matching Cerebro
dials to this new frequency.  As static FLARES --

**EXT. COUNTRY ROAD - NIGHT**

VROOM!  Tires tear past camera as --

The station wagon speeds down the road.  The monster is
POUNDING behind it like a goddamn T-Rex, *right on its tail!*

**INT./EXT. STATION WAGON - NIGHT**

Steve and Robin watch the pursuing monster out the back
window, terrified, when their walkie crackles to life --

                    SUZIE (O.S.)
          Dustybun, you copy -- ?

                    DUSTIN (O.S.)
          I copy, Suzie, signal is much clearer
          now, thanks --

Robin and Steve share stunned looks.

                    ROBIN/STEVE
          *Suzie* -- ??!!

**INT. UNDERGROUND RUSSIAN BASE - VAULT ROOM - INTERCUT**

Their voices also come out of Hopper's walkie.

                    DUSTIN (O.S.)
          ... Listen, Suzie, this is gonna
          sound super random, but it's *VERY*
          important -- do you know Planck's
          Constant?

                    SUZIE (O.S.)
          Do you know the Earth orbits the sun?

Hopper and Joyce share baffled looks --

**EXT. WEATHERTOP - NIGHT - INTERCUT**

Dustin fills with *huge relief* --

                    DUSTIN
          -- Okay okay I know it starts with
          two sixes, and then -- what's the
          rest again?

                    SUZIE
          Are you messing with me Dustybun -- ?

                    DUSTIN
          No I'm serious -- *deadly serious* --
          like I said, I'm *saving the world* --

                    SUZIE
          Okay let me just be clear on this.  I
          haven't heard from you in a *week* and
          now you want a -- a mathematical
          equation that you SHOULD KNOW -- so
          you can "save the world" -- ???

                    DUSTIN
          Yes --

                    SUZIE
          *Dustybun* -- !

                    DUSTIN
          I'll make it up to you Suziepooh, I --
          I promise --

Erica's eyes shoot wide -- Suziepooh???

                    SUZIE
          You can make it up to me now --

                    DUSTIN
          What -- ?

Suzie smiles, a little mischievous.

                    SUZIE
          I want to <u>hear it</u>.

Dustin's eyes go wide --

                    DUSTIN
          Not right now --

                    SUZIE
          Yes <u>*NOW*</u> Dustybun --

                    DUSTIN
          Suziepooh this is URGENT --

                    SUZIE
          Yes yes you're saving the world I
          heard you the first time.  But --
                    (picks up book)
                    (MORE)

                    SUZIE (CONT'D)
          Ged is also saving Earthsea and he's
          about to confront the Shadow.  So...
          this is Suzie, *signing off* --

She reaches out to switch off her Cerebro but --

                    DUSTIN
          Waitwaitwait, okay, okay, okay!!!

Suzie smiles, pleased --

Dustin looks at Erica, then takes a deep breath... screw it.

He starts to SING!!!  Hesitant at first, low, embarrassed.

                    DUSTIN (CONT'D)
          *"Turn around, Look at what you see--"*

It's the theme song to *The NeverEnding Story*!!!  As Erica
stares at Dustin in growing horror, we make a HARD CUT TO --

**INT./EXT. STATION WAGON - NIGHT**

The "Griswold Family."  Listening too.  Eyes wide.

                    DUSTIN (O.S.)
          *"In her face, The mirror of your
          dreams..."*

**INT. SUZIE'S HOUSE - NIGHT**

Suzie now can't hold back -- she joins in with Dustin,
belting:

                    SUZIE/DUSTIN (O.S.)
          *"MAKE BELIEVE I'M EVERYWHERE, GIVEN
          IN THE LIGHT..."*

**INT. UNDERGROUND RUSSIAN BASE - VAULT ROOM - NIGHT**

Hopper and Joyce stare at their walkie --

                    SUZIE/DUSTIN
          *"WRITTEN ON THE PAGES..."*

**EXT. WEATHERTOP - NIGHT**

Dustin gets more into it now, matching Suzie:

                    SUZIE/DUSTIN
          *"... IS THE ANSWER TO... A
          NEVERENDING STORY!!!  AHHHH!  AHHH
          AHHHH!"*

**INT./EXT. STATION WAGON - NIGHT**

Everyone stares now, horrified as our two nerds harmonize --

> SUZIE/DUSTIN
> *"... REACH THE STARS, FLY A FANTASY,*
> *DREAM A DREAM, AND WHAT YOU SEE WILL*
> *BE..."*

**INT. UNDERGROUND RUSSIAN BASE - MACHINE ROOM**

Murray's eyes go wide, listening too as --

> SUZIE/DUSTIN
> *"RHYMES THAT KEEP THEIR SECRETS, WILL*
> *UNFOLD BEHIND THE CLOUDS..."*

**EXT. WEATHERTOP - NIGHT**

Suzie and Dustin finish their song together --

> DUSTIN/SUZIE
> *"AND THERE UPON A RAINBOW, IS THE*
> *ANSWER TO A NEVER ENDING STORY, AH,*
> *STORY, AHHHHH AHHHAHHA AHAAAH AHHHA!"*

The song finally winds down. Suzie is very emotional now,
filled with TEARS OF HAPPINESS. Then, through her tears:

> SUZIE
> Planck's Constant is six point six
> two six zero seven zero zero four --

**INT. UNDERGROUND RUSSIAN BASE - VAULT ROOM - NIGHT**

Hopper punches the code. The safe blinks green -- opens!!!!

IT WORKED. Holy. Shit. He yanks out a METAL CASE, slams
the vault door closed back onto camera and --

**INT. SUZIE'S HOUSE - NIGHT**

> DUSTIN
> You just saved the world--

> SUZIE
> Gosh I miss you Dustybun --

> DUSTIN
> I miss you *more* Suziepooh --

> SUZIE
> I miss you more multiplied by *all* the
> stars in our galaxy --

WHOOM!  Erica abruptly switches off the radio.

                    ERICA
          Enough.

**EXT. STARCOURT MALL - NIGHT**

WHOOM!  A crumpled car door flies open as --

Billy staggers out of his busted, now *flaming* Camaro.  He's
got a bad cut on his head, dripping black blood, and he's
limping, looking like a *monster from hell.*

A noise off-screen.  He turns, sees --

THE GATE TO THE LOADING DOCK.  *GRINDING OPEN.*

On the other side: Max, Mike, and *Eleven.*

**EXT. STARCOURT MALL - LOADING DOCK - NIGHT**

We PUSH IN on our kids as they see Billy --

He lumbers toward them like Jack Torrance.

                    MAX
          *Shit...*

Max slams the loading gate button, shutting it again and --

**EXT. COUNTRY ROAD - NIGHT**

The monster stops chasing the station wagon and begins to --

*Turn around.*

**INT. STATION WAGON - NIGHT**

A baffled Steve watches this out the back window --

                    STEVE
          It's turning around --

                    NANCY
          What -- ?

                    STEVE
          *It's turning around* -- !

Jonathan looks into the rearview, sure enough, sees --

The monster stomping back toward the mall.

                    LUCAS
          Maybe we wore it out --

                   JONATHAN
          Yeah... I don't think so --

Jonathan spins the wheel hard and --

**EXT. ROAD - NIGHT**

The Station Wagon spins around, tires squealing, as they
start to speed after the monster, *chasing IT now*, as --

**EXT. STARCOURT MALL - LOADING DOCK - NIGHT**

EEEEE.  The loading dock gate is about to close when --

WHAM!  A bloodied hand grabs it at the last second.  <u>BILLY</u>.

He wrenches it open, staggers through, as --

**INT. STARCOURT MALL - SERVICE CORRIDOR - NIGHT**

Mike and Max help Eleven through the maze-like corridors,
searching for another way out of this place --

Eleven is weak, having trouble staying upright as --

**INT. UNDERGROUND RUSSIAN BASE - RIFT CHAMBER - NIGHT**

The machine FLASHES and SPARKS in the Rift room.

A few HAZMAT MEN try to work to repair it while other HAZMAT
MEN rush to the machine room, but the door won't budge --

**INT. UNDERGROUND RUSSIAN BASE - MACHINE ROOM - NIGHT**

The door shudders -- the barricade holding.  *For now.*

We WHIP PAN from the shuddering door to find Murray, yanking
some more levers in the back of the room.  *Sabotage part
three.*

**INT. UNDERGROUND RUSSIAN BASE - OBSERVATION ROOM - NIGHT**

WHOOM!  The observation room door flies open and Hopper and
Joyce burst inside.  Hopper aims his SMG at the scientists --

                   HOPPER
          OUT!!!  EVERYONE OUT!!!

The scientists stare, confused by his English -- so Hopper
provides them a little motivation, firing his SMG into the
air.  BANGBANGBANG!  As the scared scientists finally get the
message, fleeing for the door --

Joyce looks out toward the RIFT, which is growing -- *opening.*

Hopper joins her, takes in the horrific sight of this thing.

                    HOPPER (CONT'D)
          ... You ready to end this?

Joyce nods. *Hell yes she is.* She slams the silver case onto
the counter, unsnaps the locks, opens it. Inside --

TWO SILVER KEYS. *Just like the opening of our season.* And --

**INT. STARCOURT MALL - SERVICE CORRIDOR - NIGHT**

WHOOM! Max, Mike, and Eleven turn a corner, find --

A FREIGHT ELEVATOR. An escape -- thank God!!

They race up to it, SMASH the call button, when --

The lights in the hallway begin to flicker. They turn --

It's Billy. Rounding the corner. *He's found them.*

He begins to stagger toward them, but --

Max steps forward, brave.

                         MAX
          Billy -- you -- you *don't have to do
          this* --

Billy keeps walking, breathing fast, quickening his pace.

                    MAX (CONT'D)
          Billy -- your name is Billy -- *Billy
          Hargrove* --

But Billy keeps coming toward them  --

                    MAX (CONT'D)
          You live on 4819 Cherry Lane --

Almost on them now --

                    MAX (CONT'D)
          I'm Max -- your --

*WHAM!* Billy grabs Max, slams her against a wall. As her
frail body slumps to the floor --

                         MIKE
          NO -- !

Mike attacks, but Billy strikes him hard across the face.
Fast, brutal. As Mike goes down hard too, right by Max --

Eleven SCREAMS, staggers forward, thrusts a hand out, but --

It does _nothing_. Billy grabs her hand, twists it --

Eleven SCREAMS IN PAIN then --

WHOOM! Billy slams her head back against the freight
elevator doors -- her head strikes the metal and she drops,
_limp_.

Billy now reaches down, seizes her body, and --

Starts to carry her back down the corridor as --

**INT. UNDERGROUND RUSSIAN BASE - OBSERVATION ROOM - NIGHT**

Hopper and Joyce are now at opposite key terminals.

>                    HOPPER
>                (into walkie)
>        Murray -- you all set down there?

**INT. UNDERGROUND RUSSIAN BASE - MACHINE ROOM - NIGHT**

Murray flips one last lever --

>                    MURRAY
>                (into walkie)
>        All set --

His eyes snap to the door. Still shuddering, starting to
open. _That barricade won't hold much longer._

>                MURRAY (CONT'D)
>        -- But I've got some company which
>        I'd love you to _obliterate_.

**INT. UNDERGROUND RUSSIAN BASE - OBSERVATION ROOM - NIGHT**

>                    HOPPER
>                (into walkie)
>        Will do. Hold tight.

Hopper places down the walkie, inserts his key in one slot.

Joyce inserts her other key into the other slot.

A charged look between them.

>                HOPPER (CONT'D)
>        On three.

>                    JOYCE
>        On three.

>                    HOPPER
>        One... Two --

BAM!  Hopper is suddenly and very violently thrown forward, so hard his head CRACKS the glass.  As Hopper drops to the ground, dazed, his SMG scattering, we reveal --

GRIGORI.  You have *got* to be kidding!

Joyce scrambles for the dropped SMG but--

WHAM!  Grigori grabs her too -- throws her into a console, hard.  As her body slumps to the ground --

Grigori raises up a walkie --

> GRIGORI
> <The Americans -- I've found them -->

Before Grigori can get out more, an enraged Hopper -- now bleeding badly -- charges him from behind, screaming, and tackles him hard into a computer console but --

Grigori rebounds quick and before we know it fists are flying as these two mortal enemies --

BEGIN TO FIGHT.

**INT. STARCOURT MALL - SERVICE CORRIDOR - NIGHT**

CLOSE ON: Eleven's now bloodied face as Billy carries her through the sputtering, dark corridors, slung over his shoulder.  He throws open a door and --

**INT. SCOOPS AHOY! - NIGHT**

... Carries her through Scoops.  Our once happy ice cream shop is now rendered ominous, scary in the strobing lights.

WHOOM!  Billy rips open the security gate and --

**INT. STARCOURT MALL - NIGHT**

... Carries the limp Eleven out to the precipice of the sunken atrium.  He lays her down like a sacrificial offering.

Eleven's eyes blink, consciousness returning as...

Billy kneels by her, just like with Heather, and whispers:

> BILLY
> Don't be afraid.  Try and stay very
> still.  *It will be over soon.*

And that's when El hears it.  A NOISE.  She looks up. Sees...

THE MONSTER.  Crawling back down into the mall atrium.

Off Eleven, horror growing, SMASH TO --

**INT. UNDERGROUND RUSSIAN BASE - OBSERVATION ROOM - NIGHT**

WHAM-BAM!  Bare knuckles slamming flesh!  We're back with
Hopper and Grigori, who continue to duke it out.  Grigori
grabs Hopper, throws him through a door and out onto --

**INT. RIFT CHAMBER - BALCONY - NIGHT**

The walkway above the weapon, which is sparking like crazy.

Hopper is barely on his feet before Grigori is on him again,
and now these two men are exchanging blows on this balcony,
with sparks *flying* and gears *churning* behind them as --

**INT. STARCOURT MALL - NIGHT**

Billy stands, takes a step back away from Eleven as --

The giant monster fully drops into the atrium.  It's time.
Its mouth PEELS OPEN revealing those rows of razor sharp
teeth.  Eleven braces herself as it bends to devour her
when --

BANG-POP!  A BRIGHT RED EXPLOSION suddenly ERUPTS right by
the monster's head.  *Wait*.  That wasn't an explosion.  It
was --

FIREWORKS!!  The monster looks up, enraged, finds --

Lucas and Will on the balcony in front of him!  They're back
-- and they've got a banana box worth of firework bombs.
Will passes a lit bomb to Lucas --

                    LUCAS
          FLAY THIS YOU UGLY PIECE OF SHIT!!!

Lucas tosses it.  BOOM!  It hits the monster right in the
head, a bullseye!  Another burst of smoke and light erupts
and --

The monster staggers back, dazed, when --

BOOM!  Another FIREWORK BOMB hits the monster, this time from
the balcony near the escalator!  It's Jonathan and Nancy!
Then --

BOOM!  ANOTHER FIREWORK BOMB, this time from Steve and Robin,
who are on the balcony over by Waldenbooks!

Our teens and kids are all working together, attacking from all directions, each with their own banana box! The Monster SHRIEKS IN PAIN as a barrage of fireworks erupt around it in an INSANE DISPLAY OF COLOR AND LIGHT AND SMOKE and --

INT. UNDERGROUND RUSSIAN BASE - RIFT CHAMBER - NIGHT

WHOOM! Grigori lands a punch, then a kick, sending --

Hopper tumbling down a flight of stairs and onto --

A lower platform. Hopper is now right by the machine, which continues to spark and rumble as --

INT. STARCOURT MALL - NIGHT

BOOM-CRASH! Another firework erupts! The Monster REELS --

Billy, of course, feels the _same pain_. _HIVE MIND_. He drops down by Eleven. He grits his teeth, biting back a scream as black veins ripple up and down his body.

Eleven climbs to her hands and knees, scrambles away, trying to escape, but --

WHOOM! Billy grabs her, drags her back, and PINS HER TO THE GROUND AS --

INT. UNDERGROUND RUSSIAN BASE - OBSERVATION ROOM - NIGHT

WHAM! A hand slams onto a desk as --

A dazed Joyce climbs back onto her feet. Bleeding badly. But she finds enough energy to stumble up to the observation window. Through it, she can see Hopper and Grigori fighting.

INT. RIFT CHAMBER - LOWER BALCONY

Hopper takes another punch to the jaw. POW! He falls back against a railing, right by some churning gears, almost chewed alive, as --

INT. STARCOURT MALL - SERVICE CORRIDOR - NIGHT

Max regains consciousness... she crawls over to Mike, who is still on the ground, not moving --

                    MAX
          ... Mike -- can you hear me???
          MIKE???

As Mike begins to blink, _waking_ --

**INT. STARCOURT MALL - NIGHT**

Our Monster SHRIEKS and lashes at our heroes with its tentacles as it's struck by another firework, but --

**ON THE BALCONY**

Lucas and Will are at the bottom of their banana boxes.

> WILL
> WE'RE ALMOST OUT -- !!!

**ON THE OTHER SIDE OF THE BALCONY**

So are Robin and Steve.  Only a few more bombs remain.

Steve screams into his walkie --

> STEVE
> DUSTIN -- WE'RE OUT OF TIME!!

**EXT. WEATHERTOP - NIGHT**

Dustin hears this, relays --

> DUSTIN
> *HURRY!!!  CLOSE IT NOW -- !*

**INT. UNDERGROUND RUSSIAN BASE - OBSERVATION ROOM - NIGHT**

-- Joyce hears this warning on her walkie.  *Fuck.*  Her eyes move from Hopper and Grigori out on that bridge to --

The two keys.  *Can't turn both on her own.*  Then -- *an idea.*

She removes her oversized Russian belt, lassos the buckle around the first key, then drags the belt out and tries to reach the second key with her hand.  But she still can't reach it!  It's too far.  As she stretches for it, desperate --

**INT. STARCOURT MALL - SERVICE CORRIDOR - NIGHT**

Max helps Mike to his feet --

> MAX
> You okay?

Mike nods.  But --

> MIKE
> El -- *where's El??*

**INT. STARCOURT MALL - NIGHT**

Billy continues to hold Eleven down.  To our surprise, Eleven
stops struggling.  And, instead -- *speaks*:

> ELEVEN
> ... Seven feet...

Billy looks at her.

> ELEVEN (CONT'D)
> You told her... the *wave was seven
> feet*...

*FLASHBACK:  AN OCEAN WAVE CRASHES --*

*FLASHBACK:  BILLY'S MOM WATCHES FROM THE SHORE, SMILING.*

> ELEVEN (CONT'D)
> You... ran to her.  Onto the...
> beach.

We move in on Billy as this memory begins to take hold...

*FLASHBACK: BILLY RACING TO HIS MOM -- HIS FEET SPLASHING
THROUGH THE SHALLOW WATER -- A BIG SMILE ON HIS FACE --*

> ELEVEN (CONT'D)
> She wore a big hat... for the sun...
> with a black... ribbon...

*FLASHBACK: ABSTRACT IMAGES OF MOTHER'S HAT --*

> ELEVEN (CONT'D)
> A long dress... with a red and
> blue... flower...

*FLASHBACK: ABSTRACT IMAGES OF MOTHER'S SHOES --*

> ELEVEN (CONT'D)
> Yellow sandals... covered in...
> sand...

The Mind Flayer in Billy tries to fight it off, fight off
this happy memory, an internal battle...

> ELEVEN (CONT'D)
> She was pretty... so *pretty*... And
> you...

*FLASHBACK:  YOUNG BILLY RACES BACK OUT INTO THE OCEAN.*

> ELEVEN (CONT'D)
> You were... *happy*...

*FLASHBACK: YOUNG BILLY SMILES -- THE LAST MOMENTS OF HIS INNOCENCE --*

                    ELEVEN (CONT'D)
          I could tell... she... loved you...

The memory begins to *reach Billy* -- it's working!!

**INT. UNDERGROUND RUSSIAN BASE - OBSERVATION ROOM - NIGHT**

Joyce continues to stretch for the key as --

**INT. RIFT CHAMBER - NIGHT**

WHAM!  Grigori slams Hopper against a railing.  It seems like all is lost but then --

WHAM!  Hopper headbutts Grigori, stunning him.

The dazed Grigori is now standing right in front of those churning gears.

                    HOPPER
          I'LL SEE YOU IN *HELL* --- !!

Hopper kicks Grigori with all he's got left, knocking Grigori back into the spinning gears of the machine.  As Grigori is *sucked back* into the gears --

BLOOD splatters *Raiders of the Lost Ark*-style *and* --

KA-BOOM!  A portion of the machine erupts!  Metal shrapnel flies and an unstable electric current shoots out across the room -- a few feet from zapping Hopper like a lightning bolt.

Hopper staggers away from it.  WIDEN TO REVEAL:  This energy bolt has created a deadly barrier, *trapping him out here on this bridge as* --

**ON THE BALCONY**

Lucas tosses another firework and --

                    WILL
          *WE'RE OUT!!!*

Lucas looks at the others -- they're all out too!  Fuck!

The monster -- no longer distracted -- now turns its attention back to Eleven --

TIME SLOWS DOWN AND EMOTIONAL, CLIMACTIC MUSIC BEGINS AS --

**INT. SCOOPS AHOY! - NIGHT**

Mike and Max, dazed from Billy's attack, stagger out into
Scoops, just in time to see the monster push its head through
a cloud of colorful firework smoke.  Its head peels back open
-- it flashes its teeth.  We think it's all over now.

And that's when it happens:

BILLY STEPS IN FRONT OF ELEVEN.  PROTECTING HER.  A HUMAN
SHIELD!!

The monster pauses, thrown off.  One thing is now clear:  If
the monster wants El, it's going to have to *get through Billy
first* --

**INT. UNDERGROUND RUSSIAN BASE - OBSERVATION ROOM - NIGHT**

Joyce stretches for the key, straining, as --

**INT. STARCOURT MALL - NIGHT**

 The monster fires out a tentacle at Billy.  But --

Billy is fast and strong and grabs it -- holding it back, but
then -- THWACK!  Another tentacle attacks him from the side,
burying its teeth deep into his ribs -- then another tentacle
attacks him from the other side -- then another -- another --

The monster is puncturing his body from all angles.

Billy screams in pain as --

**INT. SCOOPS AHOY! - NIGHT**

Max watches in shock as this monster kills her brother --

> MAX
> BILLY -- !!!

**EXT. WEATHERTOP - NIGHT**

Dustin screams into the CB --

> DUSTIN
> *CLOSE IT -- NOW!!!  CLOSE IT!!!*

**INT. UNDERGROUND RUSSIAN BASE - OBSERVATION ROOM - NIGHT**

Joyce finally reaches the key -- _got it_!  She looks out the window once more, sees Hopper trapped behind that wall of electricity.  He can't get back to her.  Their eyes lock.  A thousand words with one look.  He gives the smallest of nods.

**INT. STARCOURT MALL - NIGHT**

The monster _punctures_ Billy's chest with the middle tentacle -- he _drops_ --

Max screams -- El looks at the giant monster in terror --

**INT. UNDERGROUND RUSSIAN BASE - OBSERVATION ROOM - NIGHT**

Joyce turns the keys.  And --

**BLACK**

A beat.  A breath.  Then --

**INT. RIFT CHAMBER - NIGHT**

BOOOM!  The laser beam retracts and --

KABOOOOOOOM!  The machine ERUPTS, sending a tidal wave of electricity across the room --

The Hazmat Scientists are lifted into the air, then _EVAPORATED, TURNING INTO ASH AS_ --

**INT. OBSERVATION ROOM - NIGHT**

A blinding green-white light fills the observation room --

Joyce shields her eyes as --

**INT. RIFT CHAMBER - NIGHT**

The Rift begins to close --

**INT. STARCOURT MALL - FOOD COURT/ATRIUM - NIGHT**

The Monster staggers back from Eleven, reeling in pain, SHRIEKING, as --

**INT. RIFT CHAMBER - NIGHT**

The Rift closes the rest of the way and --

**INT. STARCOURT MALL - NIGHT**

The monster CRASHES to the ground with an earth-shattering THUD!

**INT. OBSERVATION ROOM - NIGHT**

The strong white-green light begins to dim.  Joyce can now see again, out into the room.  The Rift is gone.  But...

So is HOPPER.  All that's left: a flurry of smoke and ash.

**INT. STARCOURT MALL - ATRIUM - CONTINUOUS**

Mike pulls Eleven into a tearful embrace while --

Max drops by Billy.

>                     MAX
>           Billy????  Billy???

He looks at her once last time.  Then his eyes go still.

The black veins begin to recede from his body.

Max shakes him --

>                     MAX (CONT'D)
>           Billy???

But he's not moving anymore.  Not breathing.

*Billy is dead*.

As tears stream down Max's cheek --

**INT. RIFT CHAMBER - NIGHT**

Joyce stumbles down into the Rift room.  She looks around for Hopper, frantic.  But there is no sign of him anywhere. Then, out of the smoke, a hand grabs her from behind --

She whirls.  It's Murray.

>                     MURRAY
>           Jim?  *Where's Jim???*

As Murray takes in her pained look, he suddenly understands.

But there's no time to ask more questions:

WHOOM!  RUSSIAN SOLDIERS burst into the observation room above.  Shouting.  Murray drags a devastated Joyce back toward the machine room and --

WE PRELAP A STRANGE SOUND: WHOOSH, WHOOSH, WHOOSH...

**EXT. WEATHERTOP - NIGHT**

Dustin and Erica look up, drawn by the sound.

Their eyes shoot wide...

>                    DUSTIN
>          *Holy mother of God...*

It's a SWARM OF HELICOPTERS. As they SOAR over Weathertop, we reveal there are U.S. FLAGS on the tails.

It's the U.S. MILITARY! Our music now SWELLS to even bigger heights, overtaking nearly all sound as WE NOW MOVE INTO A MONTAGE:

**EXT. STARCOURT MALL - PARKING LOT - NIGHT**

The lead chopper lands in front of the mall entrance.

The door to the chopper opens and SAM OWENS steps outside, followed by a cadre of soldiers, all armed to the teeth.

As more choppers begin to land behind them --

**INT. UNDERGROUND RUSSIAN BASE - STORAGE ROOM - NIGHT**

Joyce helps Murray out of the ventilation system when --

BOOM! The sound of a door flying open. They turn, see --

AMERICAN SOLDIERS charging toward them, rifles raised.

Murray and Joyce shoot up their hands --

>                    MURRAY
>          Don't shoot -- American -- we're
>          Americans -- AMERICANS -- !!!

**INT. UNDERGROUND RUSSIAN BASE - TUNNELS - CONTINUOUS**

WHOOSH! Another SQUAD OF SOLDIERS sweep through the hub, clearing the various rooms. The place is deserted.

The Russians are gone.

**INT. UNDERGROUND RUSSIAN BASE - RIFT CHAMBER - NIGHT**

Owens moves into the Rift room. Sparks, fire all around him.

He walks up to the edge, looks out the cliff wall, at that now closed Rift, the edges still glowing a bit, as...

**EXT. STARCOURT MALL - LOADING DOCK - PARKING LOT - NIGHT**

The loading dock gate opens to reveal...

The soldiers helping the battered Joyce and Murray.

Joyce freezes as she looks up and sees the entire gang sitting on the back of two military med trucks. Our couples are all together: Lucas and Max, Mike and Eleven, Nancy and Jonathan. An emotional Will leaps off the truck and races into the arms of his mother. As she holds her youngest son, pressing his head to her chest, tearful --

Joyce sees Eleven walking around, looking for Hopper.

Eleven takes in Joyce's look. And it hits her...

Hopper isn't here.

On this heartbreaking realization, FADE TO --

**BLACK**

We hold on black for a long beat, then... CHEESY MUSIC begins to play as a *1980S "HARD COPY" STYLE NEWS PROMO begins!*

**EXT. DOWNTOWN HAWKINS - DAY**

*We show terribly directed VHS shoots of our town.*

> REPORTER (V.O.)
> *Welcome to Hawkins, Indiana. A
> wonderful place to grow up... to
> raise your family... to walk your
> dog --*

*VHS footage of SMILING CITIZENS -- and a DOG???*

> REPORTER (V.O.)
> *But then, two months ago, on July
> fourth... everything changed.*

*Our cheesy music takes a dark turn and we HARD CUT TO --*

**EXT. STARCOURT MALL - NIGHT**

*Shaky VHS footage of Starcourt Mall on fire.*

> REPORTER (V.O.)
> *A terrible tragedy struck this small
> town --*

*Dramatic NEWSPAPER HEADLINES rush past camera. We highlight some bold, scary words, which have been cheesily inverted:*

THIRTY DEAD.  TRAGEDY.  ARSON.  NEGLIGENCE.  CITIZENS DEMAND
JUSTICE!  MAYOR UNDER FIRE!  We then SMASH TO --

A MAP OF INDIANA.  As we ZOOM IN on Hawkins.  Crudely
animated blood begins to drip out of the dot that marks it...

>          REPORTER (V.O.)
>     But this was not this small town's
>     first brush with tragedy --

We CUT TO A PHOTO OF BARBARA HOLLAND, ZOOMING in on those big
glasses...  More headlines.  BARBARA HOLLAND -- MISSING --
FOUND DEAD --

>          REPORTER (V.O.)
>     Mysterious deaths, government cover-
>     ups, a bizarre chemical leak --

A STILL PHOTO OF BOB NEWBY.  ZOOMING in on that smile...

**EXT. HAWKINS LAB - DAY**

We now ZOOM IN on Hawkins Lab, the music ominous --

>          REPORTER (V.O.)
>     Is it all linked?  All a vast
>     conspiracy?  The fault of a
>     disgraced, corrupt mayor?

**EXT. COURTHOUSE - DAY**

MAYOR KLINE is led out of a courthouse in handcuffs, hounded
by REPORTERS --

>          REPORTER (V.O.)
>     Or is something <u>more</u> going on in the
>     Heartland?  Can a <u>town itself be</u>
>     <u>cursed</u>?

**EXT. ROAD - NIGHT**

We ZOOM IN on the Welcome to Hawkins sign -- only "awkins"
has been crossed out with red spray paint, replaced with
"ELL."

It now reads:  "Welcome to HELL."

**INT. SUBURBAN HOUSE - DAY**

>          REPORTER (V.O.)
>     <u>Some</u> believe a rise in Satanism is to
>     blame.

We ZOOM IN on a shot of a D&D MANUAL and GAME BOARD.

                      REPORTER (V.O.)
             To find out, tune in tonight at
             8 PM... for HORROR IN THE HEARTLAND,
             on CUTTING EDGE!

As a metallic "CUTTING EDGE" title flies onto screen.  An
animated knife slices the title in half, and right here we
CUT TO --

**EXT. HAWKINS - ESTABLISHING - DAY**

VROOM!  A BMW *slicing* past camera, kicking up some fall
leaves.  Summer is over.

**EXT. STRIP MALL - DAY**

The BMW turns into a small strip mall.  And --

Steve and Robin climb out -- in regular clothes for the first
time ALL SEASON!  As they walk, Robin looks over a résumé --

                      ROBIN
             Did you really put your mom as a
             reference -- ?

                      STEVE
             Why not?  She's like -- *super*
             *respected.*

Robin rolls her eyes, passes the résumé back to Steve.  As
they head into FAMILY VIDEO together, we PRELAP A VOICE:

                      OLD MAN (PRE-LAP)
             *What* is your favorite color?

                      GALAHAD (PRE-LAP)
             Blue... no, yellow --

**INT. FAMILY VIDEO - LATER**

*MONTY PYTHON AND THE HOLY GRAIL* is playing on a small TV.
As Galahad is sucked into that crevice, we PULL OUT to find:

Robin and Steve waiting behind the counter while a MANAGER
studies their résumés, his sneakers kicked up on the counter,
his face is hidden behind their résumés.

                      MANAGER
             MMM hmmm mmm hmmm.

                      ROBIN
             Just to be clear... we weren't fired
             -- the mall burned down and, like,
             killed a bunch of people.

The manager finally lowers the résumés.  Holy shit.  It's --

KEITH!  Formerly of the Palace Arcade.

                    KEITH
          Thanks for sharing.  Didn't know.

He tosses their résumés, points at Robin.

                    KEITH (CONT'D)
               (abruptly shifting)
          Three favorite movies.  Go.

                    ROBIN
          *The Apartment, The Hidden*
          *Fortress, Children of Paradise.*

Keith's impressed.  He turns to Steve, who's already
sweating.

                    KEITH
          You.  *Go* --

                    STEVE
          Favorite movies?

                    KEITH
          Did I stutter?

                    STEVE
          Uhhh.  *Animal House.*  For sure.

Steve looks around the store for more ideas --

                    KEITH
          Eyes on me, Harrington.

Steve snaps back to Keith.

                    STEVE
          *Star Wars* -- ?

                    KEITH
          *A New Hope* -- ?

                    STEVE
          What -- ?

                    KEITH
          WHICH Star Wars?

                    STEVE
          The one with... the teddy bears.

Keith looks horrified.  Steve snaps his fingers --

> STEVE (CONT'D)
> Oh, OH, *and* that one that just came
> out -- the one with the DeLorean and
> Alex P. Keaton trying to bang his
> mom.  That's top three for me.  For
> sure.  Yeah -- classics --

Keith holds up a hand, he's heard enough.  He nods to Robin.

> KEITH
> You start Monday.
> (to Steve)
> You start... *never*.

Steve deflates.  FUCK.  But Robin isn't giving up yet --

> ROBIN
> (to Steve)
> Can you just -- give us a minute?

> STEVE
> Why -- ?

> ROBIN
> Steve --

> STEVE
> Yep --

As Steve walks away, Robin leans over the counter, close to
Keith.  She keeps her voice down.

> ROBIN
> Keith.  Listen.  I know his taste is
> a little... pedestrian.  But the
> dingus has... *other qualities* --

> KEITH
> He's a douchebag of the *highest order*
> *Robin* --

> ROBIN
> Yeah.  Okay.  He was a prick to us
> in high school, I'll grant you that.
> But...

Robin leans closer, whispers:

> ROBIN (CONT'D)
> He remains a TOTAL chick *magnet*.

                    KEITH
          Yeah, okay, and this is relevant to
          me how -- ?

                    ROBIN
          Ummm... Earth to Keith.  The ladies
          come in *just* to see him.  In droves.
          *DROVES*.  We sold so much ice cream
          they had to call in an extra shipment
          from Michigan -- from goddamn
          Michigan, Keith!  And these ladies --
          they're hot Keith... SO smoking hot.
          But there are just... too many.  Too
          many for just Steve.  He needs...
          *assistance*.

Keith turns bright red.  But, then, skeptical --

                    KEITH
          What's in this for you?
               (disgusted by the mere thought)
          You got a *thing* for him or something?

Robin looks over at Steve, who has just knocked over a large
Elvira cardboard stand-up.  He scrambles to right Elvira,
taking down a shelf of movies in the process.  *What a dingus.*

                    ROBIN
          No.

Robin turns back to Keith.

                    ROBIN (CONT'D)
          We're just... *friends*.

Off Keith, surprised, we CRASH TO:

**EXT. BYERS HOUSE - DAY**

The door to the Byers house swings open and --

Jonathan and Nancy burst out, carrying out a BED FRAME --

                    JONATHAN
          Slow down, slow down -- !

                    NANCY
          Sorry -- you still got it?

                    JONATHAN
          Yeah --

                              537

CUT WIDE TO REVEAL:  Jonathan and Nancy carry the bed frame down the porch steps and toward... A MOVING TRUCK parked in the driveway.  *Whoa.*  Our camera now CRANES DOWN to reveal --

A FOR SALE SIGN stuck in the ground.  Now marked as -- SOLD!

Holy shit -- the Byers are moving!!

> MAX/LUCAS (PRELAP)
> (singing)
> *"Turn around, Look at what you see,*
> *In her face, The mirror of your*
> *dreams -- "*

**INT. BYERS HOUSE - LIVING ROOM - DAY**

Max and Lucas are singing Dustin's love song as they pack some moving boxes.

> LUCAS/MAX
> *"And what you see will be, Rhymes*
> *that keep their secrets, Will unfold*
> *behind the clouds -- "*

Max shoots a look to Dustin.

> MAX
> Did we get that verse right, *unfold*
> *behind the clouds* -- ?

> DUSTIN
> Yes, but you're butchering it so
> *please stop* --

> LUCAS
> Then why don't you join in Dustybun?

> MAX
> Yeah Dustybun why don't you join us?

> DUSTIN
> You guys are so funny you should go
> on Carson --

> MAX
> Can't I just hear your rendition -- ?

> DUSTIN
> No --

> MAX
> Pleeease just *one verse* -- ?

                    DUSTIN
          No, no, you may not, it is reserved
          for Suzie's ears and Suzie's ears
          ALONE --

As Max and Lucas roll their eyes, Will walks in from the
hallway carrying a stack of D&D books.  He drops them into a
box marked DONATIONS.

                    MIKE
          Whoa dude that's the donation box --

                    WILL
          I know.  I'll just use yours when I
          come back.  I mean -- if we still
          want to play.

                    MIKE
          Yeah but -- what if you want to join
          another party?

Will shakes his head, smiles.

                    WILL
          *Not possible.*

The two old friends share a smile, as...

**INT. BYERS HOUSE - JONATHAN'S ROOM - DAY**

Jonathan steps back into him room.  Looks around.

REVERSE TO REVEAL: An empty room.

                    NANCY
          Is that... everything?

                    JONATHAN
          I think... *maybe.*

He checks his closet -- sure enough, it's empty, the shelves
wiped clean.  As he takes this in, a little shell-shocked...

                    JONATHAN (CONT'D)
          Seventeen years of my life... packed
          up in a day...

Nancy walks up behind him, wraps her arms tightly around him.

                    NANCY
          What if I just -- don't let you
          go...?

Jonathan turns to face her.

                    JONATHAN
          I think the new owners might kick us
          out --

                    NANCY
                (half-joking)
          You can stay in our basement --

                    JONATHAN
          Your dad would love that --

                    NANCY
          We could hide you in a tent.  Like
          El.

Jonathan smiles a bit at this.  Nancy does too.  But then her
smile fades... She knows this is just a dream.  Her eyes fill
with tears.

                    JONATHAN
          ... Hey...

He takes her hand...

                    JONATHAN (CONT'D)
          *It's gonna be okay...*

Nancy nods.  *Yeah.*  They're both fighting tears now.  He
turns her hand over to reveal that scar on her hand.  Traces
it a bit with his finger.

                    JONATHAN (CONT'D)
          As a wise man once said, we've got
          "shared trauma..."

Nancy smiles faintly through her tears.

                    NANCY
          So what's a little more, right?

                    JONATHAN
          *What's a little more...*

He lifts her hand, kisses her scar.  As they hold each other
in this now empty bedroom, we SLOWLY PULL AWAY, and...

**INT. BYERS HOUSE - WILL'S ROOM - DAY**

WHUMP.  A shirt lands into another moving box as --

Eleven packs up her clothes, which have been hanging in
Will's closet.  She goes to retrieve another shirt when --

She eyes a TOY DRAGON on the top shelf.  She tries to grab
it.  Can't.  It's too high -- out of reach.  But *there is
another way.*  She holds a hand out, concentrating hard...

We PUSH IN on the dragon... waiting for it to move...
hoping... but...

Nothing happens.  Her powers *are still gone*.

>                    MIKE (O.S.)
>           ... They'll come back.

Eleven turns to find Mike.  Stepping into the room.

>                    MIKE (CONT'D)
>           I know they will.

Eleven takes this in, not as confident.  Mike reaches up,
stands on his tiptoes, grabs the dragon, hands it to El --

>                    ELEVEN
>           Thanks.


>                    MIKE
>           You packed your walkie, right?

>                    ELEVEN
>           Yes --


>                    MIKE
>           Because you know I'm going to steal
>           Cerebro from Dustin and call you so
>           much you're gonna to have to turn it
>           off, right -- ?

Eleven blushes at this, feeling a little better now.

>                    ELEVEN
>           Did you -- talk to your mom?  About
>           Thanksgiving?

>                    MIKE
>           Yep.  Got the okay -- I'll be there.
>           And then Christmas, I was thinking
>           maybe you could come here -- you and
>           Will.  It could be before or after
>           Christmas or whatever Missus Byers
>           wants -- but I was thinking Christmas
>           day could be super fun because we'll
>           have like cool new presents to play
>           with -- sorry I realize that just
>           made me sound like a seven-year-old --

                    ELEVEN
          No.  I like presents, too.

                       MIKE
          Yeah.  Okay.  Cool.

                    ELEVEN
          *Cool.*

Eleven smiles, turns to go with the dragon when --

She stops, turns back.

                 ELEVEN (CONT'D)
          Mike?

                       MIKE
          Yeah...

                    ELEVEN
          That day at the cabin, you were
          talking to Max, and I -- I heard.

                       MIKE
          Sorry I -- I don't think I follow --

                    ELEVEN
          What you said.  How you... feel.

Mike blushes --

                       MIKE
          Oh that -- that was just -- you know
          -- heat of the moment stuff -- we
          were arguing -- I don't even really
          remember -- it's just -- you know --
          wait -- what did I even say exactly?

                    ELEVEN
          Mike.

She steps toward him.  Then --

                 ELEVEN (CONT'D)
          I love you... too.

Eleven leans in and --

KISSES HIM!  A big sweet smooch!  Before a stunned Mike can
respond, she swivels around and strides out of the room.

Off Mike, slack-jawed, we CUT TO:

                        542

**INT. BYERS HOUSE - JOYCE'S ROOM - DAY**

A BOX labeled "HOPPER." We RISE UP to find --

Joyce packing the box. She's keeping Hopper's stuff -- still somehow *hopeful*. But as she packs up one of his shirts, she hears a CRINKLE. She reaches into the shirt pocket, pulls out...

A FOLDED PIECE OF PAPER. She unfolds it, sees it's covered in writing. At the top of the paper is written "HEART TO HEART."

She smiles to herself, remembering their talk, when --

> ELEVEN
> Donation box?

Joyce turns, sees Eleven in the doorway, holding up that dragon --

> JOYCE
> Um -- yeah -- sure.

Eleven notices the letter --

> ELEVEN
> What -- is that?

> JOYCE
> Oh, it's just --
> (laughs a bit)
> The speech Hopper wrote you guys.
> You and Mike.

Eleven stares at her.

> ELEVEN
> Speech?

> JOYCE
> Yeah -- the heart to heart.

Another blank look from El. And suddenly it hits Joyce --

> JOYCE (CONT'D)
> He never talked to you... did he?

Eleven shakes her head. Joyce can't help but shake her head. *Of course he didn't.*

> ELEVEN
> Can I... read?

**INT. BYERS HOUSE - WILL'S ROOM - A LITTLE LATER - DAY**

Eleven lies on the floor in Will's room.  As she begins to
read the note, we hear Hopper...

> HOPPER (PRE-LAP)
> ... I know this is a difficult
> conversation... but I care about you
> both, very much...

**INT. CABIN - NIGHT (FLASHBACK)**

We're now BACK IN TIME with Hopper as he practices his speech
in the cabin, pacing about, anxious.

> HOPPER
> ... And I know you care about each
> other very much.  And that's why it's
> important that we set these
> boundaries moving forward.  So we can
> build an environment where we all
> feel comfortable, trusted, and open
> to... sharing our feelings.
> Feelings, feelings...

Hopper suddenly stops pacing.  Screw it.  He grabs a pen,
pulls out a chair, sits at the kitchen table.  A deep breath.
Then...

Begins to write.  An addendum.  As he writes, using his own
words this time, his voiceover takes over, carrying us
through our FINAL MONTAGE:

> HOPPER (V.O.)
> Feelings.  Jesus.
> (small laugh)
> The truth is... for so long, I'd
> forgotten what those even were.  I'd
> been stuck in one place.  In a...
> cave you might say.  A deep dark
> cave.

**EXT. BYERS HOUSE - DAY**

We're now outside the Byers house as everyone says their
goodbye to the Byers.  Lots of hugging, lots of tears.

> HOPPER (V.O.)
> And then -- I left some Eggos out in
> the woods and you came into my life
> and -- and for the first time in a
> long time, I started to feel things
> again.  I started to feel...  Happy.

**A LITTLE LATER**

Mike fights back his tears as he watches the moving truck
drive away from the house.  It's towing Joyce's car; Joyce
drives, El rides passenger.  Jonathan follows behind in his
own car, with Will as his passenger.  *The Byers boys
together.*

Lucas and Dustin put their arms around Mike -- comforting
their friend.

> HOPPER (V.O.)
> But lately... I guess I've been
> feeling... distant from you.  Like
> you're... you're pulling away from me
> or something.

**INT. CABIN**

We drift through Hopper's battered cabin.  Shafts of sunlight
pierce through the gaping holes as we drift across the dusty
fridge and TV...

> HOPPER (V.O.)
> I miss playing board games every
> night.  Making Triple Decker Eggo
> Spectaculars at sunrise.  Watching
> westerns together till we doze off...

**INT. MOVING TRUCK - DAY**

We take in Eleven and Joyce, both in their own worlds, full
of emotion, as they drive out of Hawkins, wind blowing
through open windows...

> HOPPER (V.O.)
> But I know you're getting older...
> growing -- *changing*.

**EXT. BYERS HOUSE - DAY**

Our gang of kids hop on their bikes.  Mike takes one last
look at the house, then bikes off.  The others follow,
leaving behind the Byers house forever...

> HOPPER (V.O.)
> And I guess -- if I'm being really
> honest -- that's what scares me.  I
> don't want things to change.

**INT. JONATHAN'S CAR - DAY**

Will fights back tears as he watches Hawkins pass by out the
window.

                    HOPPER (V.O.)
          So I think maybe that's why I came in
          here -- to try to maybe... stop that
          change.

**INT. WHEELER HOUSE - DAY**

Mike returns home.  He sees his MOM, cooking dinner.

He hugs her.  She holds him.

                    HOPPER (V.O.)
          To turn back the clock  -- to make
          things go back to how they were...

**INT. MOVING TRUCK**

Eleven looks out the window at the passing landscape.
*Thinking of Hop.*

                    HOPPER (V.O.)
          But I know that's naive.  It's
          just... not how life works.  It's
          moving, always moving, whether you
          like it or not.  Full steam ahead.
          And yeah...

**INT. MAX'S HOUSE - BILLY'S ROOM - DAY**

Max sits alone in Billy's room.  His stuff is still here.

                    HOPPER (V.O.)
          Sometimes that's painful.  Sometimes
          it's sad.

**INT. SINCLAIR HOUSE - ERICA'S ROOM - DAY**

Dustin and Lucas present Erica with a box labeled DONATIONS.

                    HOPPER (V.O.)
              And sometimes...

**INT. SINCLAIR HOUSE - ERICA'S ROOM - DAY**

Erica drops the box on the floor... curious.  She opens it to
find... Will's D&D manuals.

                    HOPPER (V.O.)
          It's surprising.  *Happy.*

**INT./EXT. MOVING TRUCK - COUNTRY ROAD - DAY**

The moving truck drives past a sign that reads: "NOW LEAVING
HAWKINS."

Eleven looks out the window at the passing scenery.

> HOPPER (V.O.)
> So you know what?  Keep on growing
> up, kid.  Don't let me stop you.
> Make mistakes.  Learn from 'em.  And
> when life hurts you, because it will,
> remember the hurt -- the hurt is
> good.  It means you're out of that
> cave.

## INT. CABIN - NIGHT (FLASHBACK)

*We're back with Hopper, huddled over his desk as he finishes writing the letter --*

> *HOPPER (V.O.)*
> *But please, if you don't mind, for
> the sake of your poor old dad --*

## INT. BYERS HOUSE - WILL'S ROOM - DAY (FLASHBACK)

*We're back in time as Eleven -- still sprawled out on Will's floor -- finishes reading the letter.*

> *HOPPER (V.O.)*
> <u>*Keep the door open three inches.*</u>

*Eleven smiles through tears.  Wipes away a tear.  And --*

## EXT. BYERS HOUSE - DAY (FLASHBACK)

*Jonathan, Nancy, and Will carry out the final boxes.*

*They load them into the now full moving van, then --*

*Jonathan pulls the truck door down.  All finished.*

## INT. BYERS HOUSE - LIVING ROOM - DAY (FLASHBACK)

*Joyce is the last one in the house.*

*She pauses by the front door, turns, and takes one last look around... at this now empty house... with all its memories -- good, bad, and everything in between.  This is now <u>the past</u>.*

*She leaves, shutting the door behind her.*

*We hold on the empty house for a time.*

*Then we slowly...*

**FADE OUT.**

We think credits are surely going to begin now.  But then we
hear the sound of GUSTING WIND.  Some white particles blow
across the dark frame and suddenly we find ourselves
moving...

**EXT. RUSSIAN LAB - NIGHT**

Through the dark night sky.  As more and more white particles
sweep across frame, we realize it is *snow* and we're in the
midst of a heavy winter storm.  Out of this storm emerges...

The Russian Lab from our opening scene.

CHYRON:  KAMCHATKA, RUSSIA

**INT. RUSSIAN PRISON - NIGHT**

CLOSE ON: BOOTS STRIKING CONCRETE AS --

TWO RUSSIAN PRISON GUARDS move fast down a corridor, passing
a row of prison cells.  GUARD #1 approaches a cell door,
pulls out his keys to unlock it but --

WHAM!  GUARD #2 grabs his arm, stopping him --

                   RUSSIAN PRISON GUARD #2
          <Not the American.>

The first guard nods, then moves to an adjacent cell, unlocks
it.  Inside --

A SKINNY RUSSIAN PRISONER.  As soon as he sees the two
guards, he backs away, scared.

                    RUSSIAN PRISONER
        <No -- please, no, no, no -->

The Guards grab him and yank him out --

               RUSSIAN PRISONER (CONT'D)
        <NO NO NO NO -- !!!!>

**INT. PRISON - CORRIDOR - MOMENTS LATER - NIGHT**

The Guards drag the prisoner kicking and screaming down the
corridor --

                    RUSSIAN PRISONER
        <LET ME GO!  LET ME GO!!!>

**INT. PRISON - STAIRWELL - MOMENTS LATER - NIGHT**

-- And down some cold, dark, steep steps, leading him into
the subterranean depths of this awful place --

> RUSSIAN PRISONER
> <Please -- I am innocent -- I am
> *INNOCENT* -- !!!>

**INT. PRISON - DARK CELL - NIGHT**

WHOOM!  A heavy metal door flies open as --

The guards toss the man onto a damp concrete floor, then --

WHAM!  They shut him inside.

We hear BOLTS LOCKING and FOOTSTEPS WALKING AWAY.  The
terrified prisoner leaps up and pounds on the door, begging
to be let out, tears streaming down his eyes.

                    RUSSIAN PRISONER
          <LET ME OUT!!!  LET ME OUT!!!  YOU
          CAN'T LEAVE ME HERE!!!  PLEASE!
          PLEASE!!!!>

Then, hearing a GUTTURAL SOUND, he pauses... and turns.

His eyes grow wide.

A HULKING SHAPE slinks forward out of the shadows from the
back of this dripping wet prison.  As the shape moves
forward, we see it's a creature on all fours.  It looks like
an oversized DEMODOG, slimy muscles rippling across its legs
and heaving, arched back.

As the prisoner weeps in terror, the monster's knees bend and
then, with the horrible sound of cracking bones and tearing
flesh, it lifts, STANDING, taking the nightmarish form of --

A DEMOGORGON.

The Demogorgon lunges forward, straight at this horrified
prisoner, *straight at us* -- opening its horrible mouth,
exposing rows and rows of teeth -- and right here we --

                    END SEASON